Colonial Discourse and Gender in U.S. Criminal Courts

Routledge Advances in Criminology

1 **Family Life and Youth Offending**
Home is Where the Hurt is
Raymond Arthur

2 **China's Death Penalty**
History, Law, and Contemporary Practices
Hong Lu and Terance D. Miethe

3 **The Politics of Antisocial Behaviour**
Amoral Panics
Stuart Waiton

4 **Hooked**
Drug War Films in Britain, Canada, and the United States
Susan C. Boyd

5 **The Violence of Incarceration**
Edited by Phil Scraton and Jude McCulloch

6 **Violence, Prejudice and Sexuality**
Stephen Tomsen

7 **Biology and Criminology**
The Biosocial Synthesis
Anthony Walsh

8 **Global Gambling**
Cultural Perspectives on Gambling Organizations
Edited by Sytze F. Kingma

9 **Social Class and Crime**
A Biosocial Approach
Anthony Walsh

10 **Security and Everyday Life**
Edited by Vida Bajc and Willem de Lint

11 **Women and Heroin Addiction in China's Changing Society**
Huan Gao

12 **Colonial Discourse and Gender in U.S. Criminal Courts**
Cultural Defenses and Prosecutions
Caroline Braunmühl

Colonial Discourse and Gender in U.S. Criminal Courts

Cultural Defenses and Prosecutions

Caroline Braunmühl

Routledge
Taylor & Francis Group
NEW YORK LONDON

First published 2012
by Routledge
711 Third Avenue, New York, NY 10017

Simultaneously published in the UK
by Routledge
2 Park Square, Milton Park, Abingdon, Oxon OX14 4RN

Routledge is an imprint of the Taylor & Francis Group, an informa business

Library of Congress Cataloging-in-Publication Data

Braunmühl, Caroline.
Colonial discourse and gender in U.S. criminal courts : cultural defenses and prosecutions / by Caroline Braunmühl. — 1st ed.
p. cm. — (Routledge advances in criminology ; 12)
Includes bibliographical references and index.
1. Sex discrimination in criminal justice administration—United States. 2. Minorities—Legal status, laws, etc.—United States. 3. United States—Politics and government. 4. Colonies—Law and legislation. I. Title.
HV9950.B73 2012
347.73008—dc23
2011039708

ISBN13: 978-0-415-89925-3 (hbk)
ISBN13: 978-0-203-12375-1 (ebk)

Typeset in Sabon
by IBT Global.

Printed and bound in the United States of America on acid-free paper by IBT Global.

For Dirk von Braunmühl
my brother, whom I would have chosen among thousands

and in the name of solidarity among the many who struggle,
in one way or another, for radical social transformation.

Contents

List of Tables ix
Acknowledgments xi

PART I
Introduction 1

PART II
Theoretical Perspective 7

PART III
The Corpus of Cases 23

PART IV
Ethnicizing Prosecutions and Defenses: 'Culture' and 'Gender' in Trial Parties' Argumentative Strategies and in the Debate About 'the Cultural Defense' 37

1 Biases and Blindspots in the Debate 39

2 Cultural Profiling: The *Patriarchal Other*—First Case Study 50

3 'Cultural Defense' I: The *Oppressed Third World Woman*—Second Case Study 74

4 'Cultural Defense' II: The *Patriarchal Other*—Third Case Study 104

5 Conclusion: Cultural Information or Gendered Colonial Discourse? 120

PART V
Resistance/Instabilities: The Spectrum of Discursive Politics in Trials Involving 'Cultural Evidence' and the Involuntary Subversion of Hegemonic Discourse 131

6 Contesting 'Cultural Evidence': Adversarial Opposition or Mutual Collusion? 133

7 Witnesses and Hegemonic Consensus 161

8 Beyond Mere 'Resistance': The Spectrum of Instabilities Fracturing Hegemonic Trial Discourse and What Difference They Make 181

PART VI
Conclusion: Practical/Theoretical Implications 197

Appendix: Overview of the Cases (with Commentary) 209

Cases, Constitutional Amendments, Rules of Evidence, and Statutes Cited 225

Abbreviations 229

Notes 231

Glossary of Legal Terms 259

References 263

Index 275

Tables

III.1 The Corpus of Cases: Formal Characteristics 30
III.2 The Corpus of Cases: Substantive Characteristics 32

Acknowledgments

My first debt goes to the organizations that have generously funded my research—the *Deutsche Forschungsgemeinschaft* / German Research Foundation (*DFG*), covering the period of 2000 to 2003, and the German *Programm zur Förderung der Chancengleichheit für Frauen in Forschung und Lehre*, whose funding has covered two periods between 2004 and 2006. Next, I wish to thank two successive "generations" of supervisors and examiners of the PhD thesis upon which this work is based: Professor Dr. Klaus F. Geiger, who has provided wonderful supervision and support for the project from its inception, Professor Dr. Andreas Gestrich and his colleagues and former students at Trier University; Professor Dr. Susanne Krasmann, Professor Dr. Stephan Moebius, Professor Dr. Paula-Irene Villa, Professor Dr. Urs Stäheli, Professor Dr. Antje Wiener, and Prof. Dr. Christine Landfried—who have made it possible for me to earn the PhD degree after I had abandoned the project temporarily. I thank scholar of law Professor Kenneth B. Nunn for commenting upon a legal interpretation I offer in this book—a comment I have taken to heart even as I maintain a different opinion from his. I also thank my editor at Routledge, Max Novick, for believing in this book as well as for valuable advice and support. I am grateful to Carey Nershi of IBT Global and to all other persons who have contributed to the production of this book, even as I do not know their names. Further, I want to express my gratitude to the following persons for support and sustenance of intellectual as well as emotional kinds: Peter Grönert; my extended family, including Patrick, Hilde, and Carlchristian von Braunmühl as well as Aja Klemm; Steffi Benner, Pavel B. Jiracek, Manuela Pelz, Franzis Daniela Groß, Petra Gütgemann, Thomas Scholz, Norman Heinrich, Marion Lawendel, and Marie-Theres Federhofer, along with countless others who have accompanied and inspired me from more afar. Dorsie Black has accommodated me repeatedly during my research stays in the U.S—and in more ways than "just" literally: thank you! Last but not least, although I cannot name them all individually, I want to thank in anonymous form the numerous attorneys (at both prosecutors' and defense attorneys' offices), as well as one judge, one former defendant, and his mother, for kindly providing me with many of the materials—transcripts and appellate briefs—upon which this study is based.

Quotations from the following publication are reproduced in this book with the permission of its author, Leti Volpp, and of Harvard University / Law School:

Leti Volpp. 1994. "(Mis)Identifying culture: Asian women and the 'cultural defense'." *Harvard Women's Law Journal* 17: 57–101.

Quotations from the following publication are reproduced in this book with the permission of its author, Leti Volpp, and of the Columbia Law Review Association, Inc.:

Leti Volpp. 1996. "Talking 'culture': gender, race, nation, and the politics of multiculturalism." *Columbia Law Review* 96: 1573–1617.

Part I

Introduction

[E]ducation for social change is not so much about new information as it is about disrupting the hegemonic ways of seeing through which subjects make themselves dominant.

Razack (1998, 10)

This study offers a close reading of several U.S. criminal trials in which 'cultural evidence' was presented—or, put differently: discourses of cultural difference. The debate about what has come to be termed 'the cultural defense'—conducted for the most part in law reviews—has focused on the question of whether or not that defense should be permitted in one form or other. In contrast, I am here concerned with how such 'evidence' is actually put to work at trial. In doing so, I include what has been systematically overlooked in the debate, and is in fact obscured by the very term 'cultural defense' around which it has taken shape: 'cultural evidence' presented by the state to prove a criminal defendant guilty as charged.

My starting point is the widely shared observation that presenting 'cultural evidence' at trial lends itself to reinforcing stereotypes about minorities (e.g., Volpp 1994; Maguigan 1995; Boulette Taylor 1998, 467–468; Suri 2000; Phillips 2007, Ch. 3; Renteln and Foblets 2009, 336; see also Maeda 2000)—an observation all the more salient where such 'evidence' is used *against* a defendant by the prosecution, rather than on behalf of her. A closer look at a number of such trials confirms the concern about the possibility of stereotyping to a depressing extent, as we shall see. I have sampled for the purposes of this study appeals cases in which gender figured as part of, and in connection with, 'cultural evidence' either presented at trial, or which was offered but not admitted by the trial judge.[1] Nearly half of the 'cultural' prosecution and defense strategies surveyed revolve around gendered subordination in so-called other cultures, and I have chosen to focus my study upon these particular strategies. All of them coalesce around the same rhetorical figure: whatever the specifics of the 'evidence' presented and the culture concerned, its representation is framed by a construction of patriarchal relations in 'non-Western' countries or their diasporic offshoots in the U.S. as Other to a supposedly more, or even entirely, gender-egalitarian West. This is the central notion around which colonial and gendered stereotyping take place in the cases involving 'cultural evidence' which I have examined. The fact that this motif is so prevalent among cases in which cultural differences are negotiated in connection with gender attests to its hegemonic status.

Critical voices in the debate about the 'cultural defense' have noted the colonial (Volpp 1994, 1996; Koptiuch 1996; Razack 1998; Lawrence 2001; McKinley 2009; Deckha 2009, 267) and unfeminist (Maguigan 1995) character of the figure of a gender-egalitarian West constructed in opposition to a patriarchal 'rest' (Hall 1992) of the world—upon which I will elaborate in Part IV—and have pointed out its instantiation in a number of high-profile 'cultural defense' strategies. While the risk of stereotyping has been identified, what follows is the first book-length study of how the different agents at trial interact in the construction of 'cultural evidence'.[2] Some critics have appealed to the workings of the adversary system to contest and rebut stereotyped 'cultural evidence'—that is, to a responsibility by the opposing party to question such stereotypes and to offer 'experts' of its own to counter them. Thus, Maguigan asserts (citing the U.S. Supreme Court in the second of the following quotes):

> In cases in which appropriate evidentiary rulings require the admission of cultural evidence, the burden falls on prosecutors to expose any flaws in the use of the material. Prosecutors must be held to a standard of performance in which they rebut cultural stereotypes *with accurate information and reasoned argument* (1995, 90, my emphasis).

> The Supreme Court has noted that fact-finders are able to sort through the thickets of expert evidence: ' . . . Vigorous cross-examination, presentation of contrary evidence, and careful instruction on the burden of proof are the traditional and appropriate means of attacking shaky but admissible evidence.' The Supreme Court's optimism about 'the capabilities of the jury, and of the adversary system generally' applies equally to the ability of prosecutors and jurors to view defense cultural evidence with skepticism (1995, 96–97).[3]

Volpp concurs:

> While considering cultural evidence when culture is contested, and not a static essence, is admittedly a daunting task, trials are designed to sort through the thickets of competing expert evidence, as Holly Maguigan points out (1996, 1592–1593).

> Maguigan and I ask that prosecutors and community groups challenge evidence as irrelevant when it is based on stereotypes *with little basis in reality*, provide testimony to demonstrate how particular cultural notions

> are contested within communities, and present evidence that is based on *accurate descriptions* of the pressures that individuals face, both within their communities and without (ibid., 1612–1613, my emphasis; see also Sacks 1996, 548; Boulette Taylor 1998, 459–460; Suri 2000, 137; Levine 2003, 78–79; Friedman Ramirez 2009, 210, 211).

But as I will be showing, the figure of the Patriarchal Other vs. a 'modern', gender-egalitarian West emerges largely uncontested from the discourses of the various contributors to trial discourse. On the contrary, while in some trials there is lively contest over the 'cultural evidence' presented—by way of cross-examination, the presentation of counter-experts, or both—we shall see that both parties to a trial tend to share in common certain colonial and gendered assumptions, as a result of which the opposing positions jointly stabilize, between them, the figure of the patriarchal 'rest' of the world and its co-construction, of a West more 'advanced' in matters of gender. Far from truly deconstructing each other, as one theorist of the adversary trial would have it (R.P. Burns 1999, 58, 60–61, 68, 132; see also S.L. Burns 2008, 108), the two sides of the adversary system coalesce around a shared hegemonic common sense. And, as I will be showing, this is true not only for the trial attorneys but for the witnesses too: while there is much antagonism between attorneys and witnesses (opposing as well as, sometimes, witnesses the attorney has called herself), and while criticisms are offered, few of these question certain basic assumptions of colonial and patriarchal discourse. This is the case with both lay and expert witnesses, and with both witnesses accepted by the trial judge as experts in 'cultural evidence' on grounds of academic specialization, and of being 'native' to the culture at issue. Hegemonic discourse, I conclude, is constitutive not merely of the reasoning and strategic approach of the legal personnel, but also of other academic, professional and everyday worlds, as demonstrated by witnesses' testimony.

Thus this study cautions against placing faith in a reason imagined to be autonomous of the discourses it is expected (by some contributors to the debate at issue) to criticize—and therefore, against a notion of the adversary system as being defined by a prediscursive and truly critical sort of reasoning. Likewise, this study cautions against a notion of 'cultural evidence' as *information* potentially unmediated by discourses—and therefore, against a notion of stereotypes as distorted information which could potentially be corrected in virtue of being rendered innocent of normative overtones, for instance, by offering better-qualified expert witnesses to counter the 'cultural evidence' presented by the other side. That is to say, I want to introduce to the debate about the 'cultural defense' a *discourse-theoretical approach*.[4] I shall argue throughout that approaching cultural differences as a matter, purely, of discourses occurring in the courtroom, rather than of facts about Other cultures potentially unmediated by their being *represented* in a hegemonic U.S. setting, is the method most likely to succeed in avoiding the pitfall of ontologizing Eurocentric, colonial, and patriarchal norms and assumptions as the truth about another culture. As I will argue, ontologizing such norms and assumptions is the single most problematic practice in trials where 'cultural evidence' is offered; the most fundamental step whereby hegemonic discourse is naturalized as something other than a discourse—namely, a matter of facts and disinterested reasoning. This practice circumscribes nearly all contributions to the debate about the 'cultural defense', as we shall see—including the most critical and valuable among them. (Contributions to which my argument is otherwise strongly indebted.) In this way as well as a number of others, which remain to be detailed, the debate has reproduced certain features of the construction of gendered 'cultural evidence' in criminal defense and prosecution strategies themselves, and has thereby itself helped to buttress hegemonic discourse. The approach to 'cultural evidence' which I am proposing is consciously Eurocentric: It attempts to make a 'virtue' of the empirical ignorance that hampers nearly everyone dealing with multiple cultural differences (i.e., with more than the up to two or three cultural strands into which some of us are socialized), including in the criminal courts. It does so by strictly treating what occurs in the courtroom as discursive *constructions* rather than unmediated facts, while attending to the normative features of those constructions, and to their naturalization as inherent properties rather than constructs. Specifically to those features of discourse that buttress vs. undercut notions of white/Euro-American or male supremacy. This forms an attempt to decenter the latter, along with Eurocentrism, *from within*—as an alternative to the empiricist and proto-colonialist approach of seeking to know 'the real other' as if we could ever be sure that 'information' about that 'other' is unbiased in Euro-, andro-, heterocentric as well as racialized and gendered terms (compare Spivak 1988a).

The empirical rewards of the alternative approach exemplified by this work are far from a mere conclusion that trials involving a 'cultural defense' or culture-based prosecution are settings in which colonial and patriarchal discourses are reproduced without any disruption. On the contrary, this study places an additional focus upon the moments of *instability* that register in the course of their reproduction. No contribution has as yet attended to what may be destabilizing to the stereotyping with which such trials are rife.[5] This is due in large part to the fact that the debate about the 'cultural defense' has been conducted mainly by legal scholars and much less so by scholars in the social sciences or humanities. Whereas the former have attended primarily to the question of whether or in what form a 'cultural defense' should be permitted, the latter would be interested in examining the actual dynamics in terms of which the relevant trials are conducted. It is my hope that the present study will generate interest, not exclusively among those already concerned with the 'cultural defense', but also among scholars in the social sciences and humanities at large. Specifically, I want to set an example of how (micro-)sociology may benefit from opening up to insights generated by poststructuralism. Just as students of the 'cultural defense' have relied upon the notions of an autonomous reason and of 'culture' as a matter of 'facts' about 'the Other', so too do we continue to encounter a construction of human subjects as autonomous, rational agents in control of the choices they make in the mainstream social sciences. This voluntarisitic, rationalist bias has been particularly evident in microsociological studies of the (criminal) trial, from Atkinson and Drew (1979) through to Matoesian (1993; 2001; 2005; 2008) and the more recent *law in action* literature (e.g., Lynch and Bogen 1996; Travers and Manzo 1997; S.L. Burns 2004; Scheffer 2006, 2007; Travers 2008, 400–402)—all of which examine the operation of law in practice.

In contrast, poststructuralism posits a human subject that is *constituted* by historically specific discourses, and whose 'choices' and reasoning are dependent upon such discourses, rather than being autonomous and universal in character. As Derrida has written, "[i]n this typology, the category of intention will not disappear; it will have its place, but from this place it will no longer be able to govern the entire scene and the entire system of utterances" (1982, 326). The fact that fundamental criticism of colonial and patriarchal discourse is so rare in the cases I have examined—despite the adversarial arrangement of the U.S. trial, and despite the testimony of witnesses with very different experiential, academic and professional sources of knowledge about the 'cultures' they testify about—is very much in line with the tenet that historically contingent discourses enable and constrain what we are able to think and perceive. The utter uniformity of what comes to be said by multiple speakers about 'culture' and 'gender' in the trials with which my study engages is in line with the notion of *hegemonic* (e.g., colonial and patriarchal) discourses constitutive of our 'common sense' and our framing of 'facts'. It is due to this uniformity that my study of events within the trials under scrutiny that are analyzable as subverting colonial and/or patriarchal discourse encompass occurrences that may have come about *unintentionally*. Thus this work carves out a space for the nonrational in human conduct and in institutional structures such as the adversary criminal trial—attending to the limits and even to the subversion of agents' intent. If the criminal trial is a setting in which a fundamental critique of the hegemonic consensus in matters of cultural and sexual difference is pursued very rarely, it does leave room for the generation of counter-hegemonic discursive *effects*, not all of which can be traced to an "intending subject of resistance" (Moore-Gilbert 1997, 88, who attributes that formulation to Gayatri C. Spivak).

In Part II of this work, I set out the theoretical premises guiding my approach to the trials under study. In Part III, I detail the composition of the corpus of cases I have constructed, which consists in the trial transcripts, in appellate briefs, and/or the appellate opinions through which I identified the cases concerned. Here I will account for the chosen focus of this study, which is upon a small number of the trial transcripts. The bulk of the study consists in its empirical part as well as in an integrated discussion of its relevance to the debate about the 'cultural defense'. In Part IV, I give an overview (using three case studies, which make up Chapters 2 through 4) of the construction of 'cultural evidence' in criminal prosecution and defense strategies. Here I include an account of the debate itself, and outline my critique of the shape it has taken (Chapters 1 and 5). Part V turns to the question of whether and how colonialist and patriarchal constructions of 'cultural evidence' are resisted or otherwise subverted within the trial process. Firstly, it analyzes the roles played in the constitution of such 'evidence' by the two principal axes of interaction structuring the U.S. criminal trial: that of trial strategy and counter-strategy, i.e. between the opposing attorneys (Chapter 6), and that confronting attorney and witness, both within the same party to the trial and across the competing camps (Chapter 7). Secondly, in the final empirical chapter (8) I illustrate the role of the unintentional in the subversion of hegemonic trial discourse, and round off the picture by offering an overall assessment of the difference made by the *combined* destabilizing effects I attribute to various events occurring contingently within the trial process, whether intentionally or otherwise. I consider this question explicitly against the backdrop of participants' practices of papering over such effects, either by ignoring them or by engaging in activities restabilizing to hegemonic discourse—concretizing my assessment through a final, exemplary case study. In the concluding Part of this work (VI), I expound on the relevance that I think attaches to this study for social inquiry. I also offer some considerations as to the political implications of this work, which I ground within reflections in social theory. However, I do not provide any suggestions as to what consequences ought to result from my findings in terms of policy. Unlike with most of the literature concerning the 'cultural defense', policy questions are unaffected by what this work has to offer. It cuts one level deeper than that, namely, to our fundamental *understanding* of what occurs in the setting under study, and of what hampers social change at a more basic level than that of any apparent quick-fix solutions: the discourses that both enable and limit our imagination.

A note about my procedure in writing this text: in its empirical part, my discussion ranges close to the material examined. Sometimes it would have seemed distracting to me to integrate broader issues into my step-by-step analysis of the relevant trial transcripts. I return to the overall argument, and address larger questions raised by the empirical inquiry, mostly at the beginning and in the concluding sections of the chapters concerned. So, if you find yourself having objections in mind that are not addressed at any given point in the text, please bear with me until the conclusion to the relevant part.

Finally, in a number of instances I shall address the same extracts from the trial transcripts under study repeatedly, so as to illuminate them from several different angles as provided by the various dimensions of this study.

Part II
Theoretical Perspective

> *All my books . . . are little tool-boxes . . . if people want to open them, to use this sentence or that idea as a screwdriver or spanner to short-circuit, discredit or smash systems of power . . . so much the better*
>
> Foucault, cited in Mills (2004, 15)

This work does not operate in terms of a closed theoretical apparatus. Rather, my analysis proceeds in the terms of a set of loosely interconnected theoretical concepts which have been constitutive of my intellectual formation, and which I reconstruct in this Part. It is a set of concepts current in the field of Cultural Studies, especially in the sociologically inflected strand of British Cultural Studies (Turner 2003) that is perhaps most centrally associated with Stuart Hall (Morley and Chen 1996; Gilroy, Grossberg, and McRobbie 2000). As sketched in the epigraph in regard to Foucault, I borrow from a number of theorists particular terms that they have utilized—without thereby meaning to take on board other aspects of their theories—whilst substituting my own specific understanding of those terms for theirs. The concepts that frame the analysis which follows find mutual coherence in the twin perspectives of discourse-theoretical epistemology and postcolonial feminism (with each of which Cultural Studies is closely aligned). The structure of this Part is as follows: First I elaborate upon my understanding of patriarchal, racist, and colonial discourse from a postcolonial-feminist perspective. Next, I expound upon discourse theory as the epistemological position adopted in this work, distinguish it from the epistemological position of (popular) empiricism, and outline some fundamentals of the politics of discourse analysis resulting from the former position. Finally, I elucidate the theoretical terms most central to my study of the corpus of court cases to be introduced in the following Part (III).

COLONIAL/RACIST/PATRIARCHAL DISCOURSE

My approach to colonial, racist, and patriarchal discourse is framed by the perspective of postcolonial feminism (Mohanty 1994, 2003; Spivak

1986, 1988a, 1988b; Lewis and Mills 2003). This is a hybrid of feminist and postcolonial critique, whose central premise is the *intersectionality* of relations of domination defined by sexual difference and by racial/cultural difference, respectively: that is, the premise that these categories must be analyzed and thought of as mutually implicating, rather than as autonomous from each other (Crenshaw 1991; Volpp 1994; 1996; 2001). My particular orientation as regards the political intersection between gendered/racialized/colonial discourses is to attempt to construct feminism, antiracism, and postcolonial critique as mutually compatible in terms of the interests that they articulate, rather than as existing in mutual antagonism or competition (compare Ware 1992). This implies a conception of political interests as something constructed within discourses, rather than as being prediscursive in status—an issue to which I return below.

Postcolonial critique and the associated critique of racism broach the power relations implicated in, and indeed actively established by, discursive dichotomies such as First World/Third World, North/South, East/West, or white/Other (Said 1978; Spivak 1990; Moore-Gilbert 1997; Gilroy 2004; Loomba, Kaul, and Burton 2005b). Feminism is analogously concerned with the (power-implicative) distinctions between male/female and heterosexual/Other. The particular "brand" of postcolonial feminism that I orient to is shaped by certain aspects of Butler's writings (1993; 1999). Following Butler, I adopt the position that sexual difference is exclusively discursive in character, rather than having a prediscursive ontological (e.g., biological) status. There is nothing 'natural' in heterosexuality according to Butler (1999, 9–11). Instead, she maintains that compulsory heterosexuality (ibid., xxx) is a matter of socially imposed norms that enforce a strict distinction between male and female sexes: not being clearly identifiable as either one or the other (and as heterosexual) is to be stigmatized and socially excluded (or 'abject', as Butler frames it) to the point of being unintelligible (ibid., 22–24; 1993, 1–3). Butler thus highlights the normative-prescriptive and exclusionary character of the concept of sexual difference (and associated concepts), and hence, the fact that it is implicitly hierarchical—contrary to the fact that, hegemonically, sexual difference is treated as a neutral descriptor of a natural given (ibid.; 1999, 22–24, 9–11). She recognizes not only the exclusionary effect of 'sexual difference' vis-à-vis those not readily categorizable in the terms of the 'heterosexual matrix' (ibid., 194n6), but also the fact that that matrix privileges the masculine over the feminine (ibid., 14–18, 23; 2004, 8–9). For my purposes, it is not necessary to delve any further into Butlerian theory here. Suffice it to state that my understanding of patriarchy is informed by that theory in that I conceive of sexual difference as a discourse that, in being historically arranged in a way that privileges the 'male' and devalues the 'female', advances unegalitarian social relations between men and women—at the same time that it *produces* them as sexed subjects, in the first place.[1]

My understanding of racial difference is analogous: I see no prediscursive, biological, or other basis to racial distinctions among human beings. That is, I conceive of racial difference as, likewise, a purely discursive effect that serves to establish and sustain relations of domination among those thus distinguished. These relations of domination I identify by the term *white supremacy* (hooks [sic] 1995)—with which I use 'racism' synonymously. Just as *patriarchy* in my usage designates an asymmetrical social relationship effected by a discourse, so do these two terms.

Colonial discourse is closely associated with racist discourse, as alluded above. It is a way of framing the social in terms of racial and/or cultural difference which emerged in the context of European colonialism. In a way that is, again, analogous to the discourse of sexual difference as analyzed by Butler, colonial discourse is historically defined by an opposition between 'the West' and the 'rest' of the world (Hall 1992) that is both binary and hierarchical, privileging the first term as superior and the norm. Colonial discourse historically has been strongly inflected by a racializing discourse of biological difference: 'Western' and 'white' are closely associated, though not *invariably* coterminous in recent times.[2] I conceive of colonial discourse as a way of framing *cultural difference*. Cultural difference to my mind differs from sexual and racial difference in that, I would argue, it does not exist *exclusively* in virtue of discourses that would bring about such difference performatively: Eurocentrism, for instance, is a way of privileging European cultural particularities that may not be globalized to the extent of being universal, i.e., of having erased all discourses that differ from a Eurocentric way of constructing the world (see Gates 1991, 464–466). There is thus a reality to cultural difference that is not exhausted by the existence of discourses that declare 'cultural differences' to exist (thereby bringing them into the world). Rather than being brought about exclusively by such a (second-order) discourse, 'cultural difference' exists partially in virtue—and should be conceptualized in terms—of a divergence between (first-order) discourses, or ways of constructing the social. In not being accountable for in terms of a mere performative effect, cultural difference is more like class difference than like sexual or racial difference. But, as with class difference, we have no discursively unmediated access to cultural difference: there are alternative possibilities of framing such difference, and there is no way of constructing it that is 'the one correct' way of doing so—as I insist throughout this work. Colonial discourse (and, similarly, racist discourse) is one way amongst others of *framing* cultural difference. My central premise in critiquing that discourse is to abstain from contrasting it with some supposedly more accurate construction of cultural difference. Instead—as with patriarchal and racist discourse—I attempt to follow suit to Butler's politics of exposing and critiquing the normative, hierarchizing character of that discourse. Which character belies these discourses' pretensions merely to offer a neutral description of an inherent, prediscursive state of affairs.

EPISTEMOLOGY

Discourse Constitutes Its Objects

With the last statement, I have implicitly begun to address the epistemological position of discourse theory, and the politics that result from that stance. I now want to do so more explicitly. Discourse theory maintains that our thinking and perception are rendered possible, while also being circumscribed and positively shaped, by *discourses*. Thus Foucault writes: "The fundamental codes of a culture—those governing its language, its schemas of perception, its exchanges, its techniques, its values, the hierarchy of its practices—establish for every man [sic], from the very first, the empirical orders with which he will be dealing and within which he will be at home" (2002, xxii). He also terms discourses "practices that systematically form the objects of which they speak" (1972, 49). I take this to mean that perception and thought are not so much subjective in an idiosyncratic sense as they are *systematically organized* in ways that are at once cognitive and social—social in the sense of being (a) shared by collectivities at a given historical moment, and (b) of *ordering* the social in ways that implicate power and norms. Discourses are thus constitutive of the social, and of the 'objects' in terms of which we are able to conceive of the social—objects such as cultural, racial, and sexual difference.

Here there is a need to distinguish, as I did above, between objects that are purely performative effects (as I have argued of sexual and racial difference), and objects whose existence is not exhausted by the latter being *declared*—and thereby, brought about—in virtue of a second-order discourse (as I have argued of cultural and class difference). I also distinguish between objects that exist exclusively in virtue of being *discursive* entities (as I have maintained of sexual, racial, and cultural difference), and objects whose existence is not exclusively discursive in character (as I would say of class difference). When I write of 'the ontological' in this work, I am referring to social reality as it is constituted both by discourses and in ways that are not exhausted by the discursive, such as in economic inequalities or in acts of physical violence. The ontological is what our discourses refer to and to which we cannot have unmediated access, at the same time that we reconstitute it in specific ways in the act of discursively constructing (by 'referring' to) it. It is inescapable that, in constructing the social, we position it in essentializing terms as having an ontology independent of our discourses—and an ontology that we posit to be accessible to us in unmediated fashion. Yet, this is but what may be termed a "necessary theoretical fiction" (Spivak 1990, 136; see also ibid., 148).[3] That is how I understand Spivak's statement that "one cannot not be an essentialist" (ibid., 45). She expands:

> Since one cannot not be an essentialist, why not look at the ways in which one is essentialist, carve out a representative essentialist position,

> and then do politics according to the old rules whilst remembering the dangers in this? That's the thing that deconstruction gives us; an awareness that *what we are obliged to do, and must do scrupulously, in the long run is not OK* (ibid., my emphasis).
>
> Derrida said, at a certain point—I don't think this is in print—'Deconstruction is not an exposure of error, it is a vigilance about the fact that we are always obliged to produce truth'. You know, this is the thing that is striking about it. It's not some kind of a negative metaphysical caper because there's nothing positive in the world; it's an examination, over and over again, of the fact that *we are obliged to produce truths, positive things* . . . (ibid., 46, my emphasis; see also ibid., 104)

It is in virtue of this position that discourse theory differs from the critique of ideology (Barrett 1991) in my understanding: While either approach involves making truth claims (as any discourse is compelled to do), discourse theory, unlike ideology critique, marks the discursive character of that gesture at the metalevel.

Discourse-theoretical epistemology is distinct from empiricist epistemology. I cannot here do justice to empiricism as a philosophical position. What is more relevant for the purposes of this study is what may be termed a 'popular empiricism', or common-sense empiricism. By this I am designating the view that our sensual perceptions are unmediated—i.e., that we are able to perceive the world 'directly', without the intervention of categories of either a conceptual or normative character. Secondly, I am thereby designating the idea that our thoughts and the categories constitutive of them derive from sensual experience, rather than vice-versa. From the point of view of popular empiricism, cultural, racial, and sexual differences would be prediscursive givens, the latter two of which are plainly accessible to sight—i.e., they would not be viewed as being (partial) effects of discourses, as I have stated that I conceive of them. From the perspective of discourse theory, this is to essentialize what is (at least partially) a product of our discursive constructions of the world. I also refer to this process as naturalization or ontologization—meaning that what I take to be a discursively mediated social construction is being represented as prediscursive, and as being accessible to us without the mediation of discourses. Discourse theory, and especially its feminist and postcolonial variants, is at heart a project of de-essentializing 'the order of things'. Foucault writes:

> we must not imagine that the world turns towards us a legible face which we would have only to decipher; the world is not the accomplice of our knowledge; there is no prediscursive providence which disposes the world in our favour [sic]. We must conceive of discourse as a violence which we do to things, or in any case as a practice which we impose on them (1984, 127).

> What, in short, we wish to do is to dispense with 'things'. . . . To substitute for the enigmatic treasure of 'things' anterior to discourse, the regular formation of objects that emerge only in discourse (1972, 47).

It is in the sense of such a de-essentializing project that I understand Spivak's (little-explained) pronouncement that "positivist empiricism"—which "define[s] its own arena as 'concrete experience,' 'what actually happens'"—forms "the justifying foundation of advanced capitalist neocolonialism" (1988a, 275): Namely, in the sense that (neo-)colonial discourse (and, I would add, patriarchal and racist discourse) are politically aligned with empiricism to the extent that they declare cultural/sexual/racial difference to be prediscursive and self-evident in character. A central aspect of those discourses' effects of power, inasmuch as that declaration masks their socially constructed, alterable character, and naturalizes the hierarchies that they establish (Butler 1999, 9–11, 22–33). To quote Spivak again: "That ideology is strongest which operates as nature" (1990, 140).

It follows from the discourse-theoretical epistemological position that analysis cannot rest content with distinguishing true from false representations: if there is no one privileged, 'truest' way of rendering reality (the ontological), then the critique of discourses' connections with power and social inequality cannot be limited to denouncing misrepresentations of reality. Rather, what parades as '*the truth*' is inherently political. Foucault puts it thus:

> . . . truth isn't outside power, or lacking in power . . . Truth is a thing of this world: it is produced only by virtue of multiple forms of constraint. And it induces regular effects of power. Each society has its regime of truth, its 'general politics' of truth: that is, the types of discourse which it accepts and makes function as true; the mechanisms and instances which enable one to distinguish true and false statements, the means by which each is sanctioned; the techniques and procedures accorded value in the acquisition of truth; the status of those who are charged with saying what counts as true (1980a, 131).
>
> There is a battle 'for truth', or at least 'around truth'—it being understood once again that by truth I do not mean 'the ensemble of truths which are to be discovered and accepted', but rather 'the ensemble of rules according to which the true and the false are separated and specific effects of power attached to the true', it being understood also that it's not a matter of a battle 'on behalf' of the truth, but of a battle about the status of truth and the economic and political role it plays (ibid., 132).

In line with my earlier outline of discourse-theoretical epistemology, Foucault is here suggesting that 'truth' is a *construction* (governed by historically specific rules), and in virtue of this is political through and through. I understand his statement in the first of the above two quotes—the one that truth "is produced only by virtue of multiple forms of constraint"—as saying that each rendering of truth excludes other possible ways of constructing the latter (compare Mills 2004, 11). Thinking of discourses of cultural, racial, and sexual difference, we may add to this power-implicative fact the tenet that—as Butler suggests of the discourse of sexual difference specifically (1993, 1–2; 1999, 22–24; see above)—constructions of the social are *invariably* normative in character, rather than potentially merely descriptive. It is in line with this tenet that (as stated earlier) the analysis conducted in the empirical part of this work attends to effects of power produced in virtue of the normative, hierarchizing character of colonial, racist, and patriarchal discourses, and to their naturalization in virtue of empiricist epistemology—as against contrasting the representations entailed in them with a supposedly more accurate rendering of 'reality'. I hope to show, in particular, that what I term a "consciously Eurocentric" approach to discourses of cultural difference—one that refuses to contrast a colonialist construction of such difference to a supposedly more correct rendering of 'the other'—can go a long way towards undermining the power effects of colonial discourse: both in virtue of exposing those effects, and of attending to what subverts that discourse in the process of its citation. This approach avoids colonizing others on the grounds of claiming a privileged access to 'the truth of their culture'. (An argument I will develop in more detail in the Part IV.) Which is a risk that—while pertinent, in my view, to whoever engages in such a practice—is politically especially problematic when its subject is 'white', as I am.

The analytic politics I have outlined constitute a second dimension that distinguishes discourse theory from ideology critique in my view: I would identify the latter with an approach of focusing upon representations of social reality in terms of distorting vs. correct (and hence, politically innocent) *empirical information*—as against the discursive approach of analyzing the politics of truth (Barrett 1991, 139–140) entailed in the *frameworks* through which we cannot but represent 'facts' pertaining to the social. Whereas the first endeavor buttresses the empiricist notion of a conceptually and normatively unmediated access to social reality, the project of discourse theory is to undermine precisely that notion.

It is because, from a discourse-theoretical perspective, there can be no such thing as unmediated 'cultural evidence' or 'cultural information', then (as it is called in the courts and in the literature regarding a 'cultural defense'), that I invariably place these terms in quotes. I also do so with the term 'cultural defense' in order to accentuate the point that, if 'discourse' is coterminous with 'culture' (see above), then there is no legal defense that would *not* be 'cultural' (compare Demian 2008). (I will offer further comments on why 'cultural defense' is a misnomer at the beginning of Chapter 1.) I follow the same "policy" in regard to the term 'expert(s)'—whose constructions of 'truth' need to be treated with especial circumspection due to the connotation of political neutrality that attaches to their position as speakers (see Foucault 1980b, 83–85 regarding the status of 'science'). For the same reason, I frequently place in quotes the term 'lay', especially when referring to 'lay' testimony about 'culture' given or offered by a person from the relevant background, but who was not judicially qualified as an 'expert': just as 'expert' is a term of epistemic and social valuation, so the term 'lay testimony' tends to devalue the relevant testimony in my judgment. Finally, depending on context, I often place in quotes (gendered) racializing/ethnicizing categories such as 'white' or 'Chinese woman' so as to mark their status of discursive constructs.

Discourse Constitutes the Subject

A second characteristic of discourse theory—at least in its poststructuralist form—is that discourses are viewed as being constitutive, not merely of the objects of which they speak, but of its speakers as well, i.e., of the human subject (Macdonell 1986). Thus I noted above that thought and perception are conceived of here as being both enabled and constrained by historically specific and shifting discourses (Foucault 1972; 2002). But, more fundamentally, poststructuralist discourse theory postulates that there is no such thing as *human nature*; that our constitution as subjects is entirely an effect of discourses[4]—albeit an unpredictable, rather than fully determined, effect (Butler 1999, 182; 1997b, 15–18; 1993, 95). Thus, Foucault remarks that "discourse is not the majestically unfolding manifestation of a thinking, knowing, speaking subject, but, on the contrary, a totality, in which the dispersion of the subject and his discontinuity with himself may be determined" (1972, 55). An implication of this is that there is no such thing as (full-fledged) *autonomy*: given that we cannot make fully transparent to ourselves the discourses constitutive of us,[5] and that our choices and ideas are dependent upon such discourses, so can those choices and ideas never be fully transparent to us. In that sense, we lack a self-determination and a self-transparency that would make us autonomous or founding subjects—that is, subjects who are truly foundational *of* the discourses that they put to work, rather than vice-versa.

As with empiricist epistemology, the notion of the autonomous, founding subject is historically closely associated with racist/colonial, patriarchal, and other exclusionary discourses. This is the case in that the fiction of an autonomous subject historically has been taken to characterize primarily middle-class white men, to whom their various Others—women/people of color/'white trash' (Wray and Newitz 1997)—have been opposed in devaluing terms as lacking autonomy due to either biological inferiority or cultural/psychological immaturity. Hierarchical oppositions such as that between autonomy and dependency, or mind and body, which idealize the first while inferiorizing the second term, have thus underpinned these exclusionary discourses, and have been central targets of feminist and postcolonial critique (e.g., Benjamin 1988; Butler 1997b, Introduction and

195–198; 1999, 17; Bhabha 1994; Gilroy 1993; see also Hall 1996, 5). It is due to this implication, of the "Enlightenment" notion of a subject defined in terms of autonomy and (hence, necessarily) of a self-transparent reason, in racialized/colonialist and gendered Othering—an implication upon the nature of which I will expand in the Conclusion to this book (Part VI)—that the latter sets out to accentuate the *limits* of our intentional command over the discursive practices we engage in, and over their social/signifying effects: whether in the form of our involuntary participation in the reinscription of hegemonic discourses or of its inadvertent subversion. This focus is meant to counterbalance the traditional bias of microsociology towards analyzing discursive and other practices as being (strategically) rational; a bias that serves to reinscribe the notion of a self-determined, self-possessed subject associated with mastery over himself *as well as* his "Others". That bias is very apparent in the sociological literature about trials, as mentioned in the Introduction (Part I), and as will be discussed further in my Conclusion (Part VI).

A further implication of discourse theory's conception of the subject is that power—rather than being analyzed as something possessed and wielded by some people over others (as is quite common in other forms of feminist and antiracist critique)—is analyzed as, chiefly, an effect of *discourses*. While discourses such as racism empower some over others, they *produce*, e.g., *both* 'whites' and 'blacks' as subjects positioned asymmetrically vis-à-vis one another. Foucault writes:

> We should try to grasp subjection in its material instance as a constitution of subjects. . . . [P]ower is not to be taken to be a phenomenon of one individual's consolidated and homogeneous domination over others, or that of one group or class over others. What, by contrast, should always be kept in mind is that power . . . is not that which makes the difference between those who exclusively possess and retain it, and those who do not have it and submit to it. Power must be analysed [sic] as something which circulates, or rather as something which only functions in the form of a chain. It is never localized here or there, never in anybody's hands, never appropriated as a commodity or piece of wealth. Power is employed and exercised through a net-like organisation [sic]. And not only do individuals circulate between its threads; they are always in the position of simultaneously undergoing and exercising this power. They are not only its inert or consenting target; they are always also the elements of its articulation. In other words, individuals are the vehicles of power, not its point of application. . . . The individual, that is, is not the vis-à-vis of power; it is, I believe, one of its prime effects. The individual is an effect of power (1980b, 97–98).

In line with this view, my emphasis in analyzing racist, colonial, and patriarchal discourses (as well as their destabilization) is, not primarily on who it is that reproduces or destabilizes these discourses (e.g., 'white' or 'black' subject; 'man' or 'woman'), with a view to how they (dis-)empower themselves/others in doing so. Instead, I place more emphasis on the overall power effects of these discourses' reproduction (e.g., white supremacy/male supremacy) or subversion, as such: effects that are occasioned whoever it is that is instrumental to citing the relevant discourse (and is reconstituted in its terms in the process).

CENTRAL CONCEPTS

Discourse/Discursive Frame

With the above remarks about my overall theoretical perspective and analytic politics in place, let me expound on my use of a few specific terms central to the analysis which follows. To begin with, the term *discourse*. I use it in two senses, the difference between which will be apparent in context. I call 'discourse', both the conceptual resources which verbal practices (as well as other signifying practices) draw upon—i.e., by which they are enabled and constrained—, and those practices themselves. Any signifying practice is thus a discourse or discursive practice. The conceptual resources drawn upon by such practices encompass (most centrally for our purposes) colonial, racist, and gendered/patriarchal discourses. Earlier I have characterized their *modus operandi* in terms of their respective establishment of a discursive object (cultural/racial/sexual difference) in binary, hierarchizing, and essentializing terms. More generally, by 'conceptual resources' I am referring to what is conceptually presupposed by, or implied in, a given instance of practiced discourse. Here I include specific connotations of given terms as I associate them, on the premise that such associations draw upon a socially shared common sense (which, as I explain below, is constituted by the overall reservoir of discourses available at a given time to the subjects constituted in terms of them).

As an alternative to 'discourses', I also occasionally use the term *discursive frame*. I do so as a way of referencing conceptual resources that are more specific and partial than could be said of an entire discourse, such as patriarchal discourse. Whereas 'patriarchal discourse' in my usage is what establishes humanity in terms of two sexes, overall, there are specific discursive frames (e.g., patriarchal) that, for instance, relate to 'motherhood', in particular. In the case of colonial discourse, I consider the notion that patriarchy is (more) particular to non-Western 'cultures' one such specific discursive frame for constructing—for instance—'evidence' received in a criminal trial. I have chosen the term 'discursive frame' inspired in part by how Wetherell and Potter have characterized what they call "interpretative repertoires" (1992, 90), which term they use as an alternative to 'discourses'. They define interpretative repertoires as "broadly discernible clusters of terms, descriptions and figures of speech often assembled around metaphors or vivid images" (ibid.).

Common Sense—Hegemony—Counter-Discourse—Constitutive Outside

Common sense in my usage is the overall universe of discourses (and discursive frames) available to those constituted in their terms at a given time. I use this term so as to accentuate the tenet that what common sense is usually taken to consist in—experience and our capacity for reasoning—is organized by historically specific and shifting discourses. Common sense encompasses competing discourses. Those discourses which are most dominant, i.e., which have taken the strongest hold within the constituency of subjects among whom they circulate, I call *hegemonic*—a term associated chiefly with Gramsci today (Laclau and Mouffe 1985), but which I use in the much simpler sense just designated. Hegemonic discourses tend not to be recognizable to us *as* discourses. Instead, they tend to be naturalized, coming across as the way things *are*, or as *the* self-evident way of reasoning (compare Fairclough 1989, Ch. 4). I distinguish the hegemonic from common sense because hegemonic discourses are not (equally) self-evident to *all* of the subjects to whom they are accessible at a given time. This is because hegemonic discourses (e.g., patriarchal discourse) sometimes compete with *counter-discourses* (e.g., feminist discourse) which both oppose them and are entangled with them to varying degrees. (For instance, feminist discourse is entangled with, or indebted to, patriarchal discourse in that it cannot but operate in terms of sexual difference—a term which, I have argued, is definitive of patriarchal discourse. Still, feminist discourse reframes sexual difference in terms that attack the patriarchal hierarchization of the male over the female and, oftentimes, the naturalization of 'sexual difference'.) Only to the extent that a discourse—or certain aspects of a discourse (e.g., the concept of sexual difference)—are *fully* hegemonized will they be definitive of common sense as a whole. (For instance, we are unable to conceive of a human being without a sex [Butler 1999, 22, 44]. This means that sexual difference is hegemonic to the extent of circumscribing common sense as a whole, in the sense that it circumscribes everyone's imagination.) In contrast, it makes sense to speak of *hegemonic* common sense when addressing an issue with respect to which competing discourses are available, such that the hegemonic option—while it may be 'self-evident' to many—needn't be to everyone.[6]

The notion that counter-discourses can be shaped by, i.e., that they may mirror to a large extent, those (hegemonic) discourses which they oppose is central to this work. For, as stated in the Introduction (Part I), few of the participants to the trials to be examined question the basic assumptions of colonial, racist, and patriarchal discourse which I have outlined above. This is the case even with contributions that offer up partial resistance to, or that criticize, other participants' deployment of those discourses. So strategies of resistance are not necessarily autonomous from what they oppose. As Foucault states, "resistance is never in a position of exteriority in relation to power" (1990, 95). This relationship of antagonistic indebtedness[7] of counter-discourses to hegemonic discourses indexes discourses' constitutive power—that is, the fact that they shape the way we are able to think, to perceive, and to strategize.

My analysis of the *debate* as to 'the cultural defense' is similarly shaped by a methodological principle that has been demonstrated *in actu* by Butler; perhaps most clearly in her essay, *Is Kinship Always Already Heterosexual?* (2004, Ch. 5). While, here, she analyzes a different public debate, her procedure in doing so is to look for common premises shared—and treated as self-evident or 'natural'—by most, if not all positions that structure the debate as a discursive field. By the same token, her reading of the structural relationship between the contributions making up that field attends to what this underlying hegemonic consensus, jointly presupposed by those contributions, excludes from the purview of what counts as an intelligible discursive possibility for framing 'the issue' for debate. As Butler elaborates:

> [P]olitics, as it is constituted through [the, C.B.] discourse of intelligibility, demands that we *take a stand, for or against* gay marriage; but critical reflection . . . demands that we ask why and how this has become the question, the question that defines what will and will not qualify as meaningful political discourse here. . . . Thus, to become political, to act and speak in ways that are recognizably political, is to rely on a foreclosure of the very political field that is not subject to political scrutiny. Without the critical perspective, politics relies fundamentally on an unknowingness—and depoliticization—of the very relations of force by which its own field of operation is instituted (ibid., 107, my emphasis).

In the context of gay marriage, an example of what is foreclosed by posing 'the issue' as a matter of either advocating or opposing that option would be forms of living that transgress the institutions of marriage and monogamy as such, whether heterosexual, homosexual, or otherwise. What transgresses these institutions thus forms a *constitutive outside* (1993, 8, 22; 2003, 131) to what is delimited as the field of possible positions on the subject; an outside rendered invisible—a conceptual impossibility—by how the terms of what is 'up for debate' are framed. Critical reflection, from this perspective, thus consists in tracing the foreclosures one commits in structuring the field of available discursive options in specific ways (as any discursive frame inevitably does)—often by the very manner in which 'the central question' is posed. Butler calls for a double-edged approach which involves *both* staking political claims—thereby operating in the socio-discursive terrain as currently structured—*and* critically examining the (hegemonic) foreclosures one colludes in making in the process (2004, 108–109). Against a possible rejection of such an approach as impractical, she cautions:

> We may think that double-edged thinking will lead us only to political paralysis but consider the more serious consequences that follow from taking a single stand in such debates. *If we engage the terms that these debates supply, then we ratify the frame at the moment in which we take our stand.* This signals a certain paralysis in the face of exercising power to change the terms by which such topics are rendered thinkable (ibid., 129, my emphasis).

With this book, I hope to contribute to changing the terms by which so-called 'cultural evidence' is rendered thinkable; to shift them in a more critical, reflexive direction. Guided by the methodological principle just outlined, I will be analyzing certain parallels in the discursive parameters that define—on the one hand—the main opposing positions within the debate as to 'the cultural defense' and—on the other—the discursive practices of the competing parties, and of mutually (seemingly) antagonistic individual speakers, within the criminal trials at issue in this debate. In particular, I will attend to various dimensions of a hegemonic common sense that welds together the opposing positions at issue, while pinpointing certain constitutive exclusions upon which that common sense relies, and which it renders invisible. Excluded possibilities which I want to introduce into the debate as a hitherto-foreclosed *alternative* way of discursively framing 'the problem' at hand.[8]

Interpellation—Performativity as Citationality—Struggle for Hegemony—Chains of Equivalence—Articulation

Discourse constitutes the subject in virtue of *interpellation* (Althusser 1971, 160, 162). Of this Althusserian concept (which, contrary to its deployment in the present work, he uses in the context of 'ideology'), I wish to borrow the following dimensions of meaning: The subject is constituted in the terms of a given discourse in virtue of a misrecognition whereby she feels that she re-cognizes herself as having always-already been the kind of subject constructed by the discourse, and as freely choosing that discourse as her perspective, when in fact it is the discourse that has produced her in the first place (ibid., 162–170). That is, whereas the subject thinks herself foundational of the discourse practiced by her, and identifies herself as *essentially* the kind of subject established by that discourse (i.e., as merely being 'mirrored' by it [ibid., 168]), in reality she is an *effect* of the sense of being 'hailed' by it (ibid., 162–163; Heath 1981, 101–102, cited in Hall 1996, 7). This understanding of interpellation roughly accords with Mills' rendering of the term to the effect that "individuals are called upon by texts to recognize themselves as particular types of individuals (for example, as consumers, as workers, as parents and so on)" (2004, 146). But it adds to this version of the concept the fact that interpellation entails a misrecognition, as Althusser insists (1971, 170)—i.e., that the subject mistakes herself for the origin of her discourses and other practices when she is but their effect.

This notion of a misrecognition approximates the concept of interpellation to the Butlerian one of *performativity*. According to the latter concept, discourses exist only in their *citation*, that is, in virtue of constantly being repeated. It is in virtue of compulsively citing certain hegemonic discourses that the subject comes into being—i.e., that she is constituted in the terms of the relevant discourses (1993, 12–16). But we are compelled to assume ourselves as the authors of our acts; the very grammar of the language in terms of which we must think entails that assumption (ibid., 12; 1999, 27–28). Yet it is a false assumption, as Butler, too, argues (ibid.; 2004, 150; 1997b). I will occasionally invoke her notion of the performative instead of the term interpellation, namely in contexts where I wish to accentuate the productive character of discursive practices—that is, the fact that they bring about what they proclaim to exist independently of themselves. This is in distinction from the Althusserian emphasis upon the subject's sense of *recognizing* herself, and the world, in a given discourse as in a mirror—that is, upon how discourse produces a 'sense of reality'.

Dominant and contestatory discourses compete with each other for hegemony at a level involving the psychic: it is at the level of unconscious identification and fantasy that the subject is constituted in terms of one discourse or another (Hall 1995; Mercer 1994, esp. 280; Bhabha 1995, 7–16; see also Hall 1996). That is, being interpellated by a discourse involves an affective investment in the way it pictures the world, in the collective 'self' as part of which the discourse constitutes the subject in question, and in the 'others' in distinction from whom that 'self' is constituted (Hall 1995; 1996). The *struggle for hegemony* involves attempting to capture the imagination of those whose 'consent'—or whose sense of 're-cognition'—one wishes to win. To posit this is to maintain that 'interests' are themselves a matter for discursive construction (compare Hall 1995, 66–67). Rather than trying to enlighten subjects about their 'true interests'—understood as existing prediscursively—struggle for hegemony involves constructing the relevant discourses in ways that make them appealing to those one wishes to win over. This pertains, too, to the relationship between different discourses: Laclau and Mouffe have formulated the notion of *chains of equivalence* as a way of framing the task of building political alliances among (potentially) progressive movements such as feminism and antiracism (1985, 182–185).[9] According to them, discourses do not necessarily have in-built and (absolutely) fixed political trajectories—or essences—and hence, they have no intrinsic, fixed relationships with each other. Rather, elements from particular discourses may be *articulated* to each other in ways that reframe their political trajectory (ibid., 168–171). Thus, for instance, while humanist discourse historically was articulated (e.g.,) to colonial discourse in such a way as to justify imperialism, according to Laclau and Mouffe, rather than being discarded for that, it can and needs to be articulated upon discourses such as antiracism and feminism instead (ibid., 116–117; see also ibid., 155–156, 159–160, 176 for an equivalent argument regarding democratic discourse). 'To articulate' here means, roughly, to connect together in a way that will inflect each of the elements to the connection (compare ibid., 105; see also Slack 1996). In similar fashion, I hold that it is central to a feminist and antiracist politics to frame these in such a way as to provide for an alliance between the two movements, rather than for competition or other forms of antagonism.[10] It is in this spirit that the present work proceeds.

Preferred Meaning

The notion of a '*preferred meaning*' has been formulated by Hall (1980) in the theoretical context of semiotics. I "import" it into the context of this (non-semiotic) study for the limited purpose of designating the following idea: The same text entails different possibilities for being read. Such readings have much to do with the discourses from within which texts are being received. This implies the position that a reading need not be oriented by authorial intention, i.e., by how the speaker/writer/institution *intended* their text to be understood (ibid., 135; see also Hall, Connell, and Curti 1981, 99–100). However, Hall puts forward the notion that there *are "dominant or preferred meanings"* (1980, 134, original emphasis) 'encoded' in texts. (He states this in the context of television communications that encode historical events into messages which will in turn be decoded by their recipients:)

> Any society/culture tends, with varying degrees of closure, to impose its classifications of the social and cultural and political world. These constitute a *dominant cultural order*, though it is neither univocal nor uncontested. This question of the 'structure of discourses in dominance' is a crucial point. The different areas of social life appear to be mapped out into discursive domains, hierarchically organized into *dominant or preferred meanings*. . . . We say *dominant*, not 'determined', because it is always possible to order, classify, assign and decode an event within more than one 'mapping'. But we say 'dominant' because there exists a pattern of 'preferred readings'; and these both have the institutional/political/ideological order imprinted in them and have themselves become institutionalized (ibid., 134, original emphasis).

The process of producing "*dominant meanings*" (ibid., original emphasis), Hall adds,

> consists of the 'work' required to enforce, win plausibility for and command as legitimate a *decoding* of the event within the limit of

> dominant definitions in which it has been connotatively signified (ibid., 135, original emphasis).

The 'preferred meaning', I take it, accords with the *hegemonic* version of a given text (whether visual or verbal). In line with that notion, this work shows that, while participants to criminal trials tend strongly towards packaging their statements or questions in terms of hegemonic discourses, the so-called 'cultural evidence' they are thus constituting can also be received from within—*re*framed by—an alternative, counter-hegemonic perspective. Chapter 8 exemplifies the possibility of reading the trial transcripts concerned for features and events subversive of their dominant meaning—which meaning is apparent throughout the empirical part of this book—through the alternative discursive lens provided by postcolonial-feminist discourse theory, as outlined above.

It is now time to turn to the corpus of cases to be considered in this study.

Part III
The Corpus of Cases

COMPOSING THE CORPUS

This Part is framed narratively, so as to track the process whereby I composed the eventual corpus of trials and other court hearings considered in this work, as I narrowed down to its eventual substantive focus (summarized in the Introduction [I] and developed further in the empirical Parts of this work (IV and V). This means that you will need to bear with me for information about the ultimate shape and size of that corpus, which I shall offer only eventually (see also Tables III.1 and III.2).

The corpus of cases upon which I have ultimately based this study forms a portion of a larger corpus of criminal cases which I had sampled initially, when I had a much vaguer idea of my research questions. My initial interest was a very open one relating to how, overall, 'race'/'culture' and 'gender' intersect in the negotiation of guilt/innocence in U.S. criminal courts. Consequently, I searched a commercial legal database for appellate opinions whose texts gave an indication that 'race' and/or 'culture' was explicitly addressed in court hearings at trial level in connection with (rather than independently of) gender. I selected opinions that indicated a use, at trial level, of verbal cues such as "Indian male" or "white women". I looked for cases involving both discourses of race and of culture because racist and colonial discourses are closely intertwined, and 'culture' today is often invoked as a cover or euphemism for notions that remain racialized. By this I mean that distinctions of culture often run along lines of skin color, namely, dividing the 'West' against the 'rest' of the world. Within the national boundaries of the U.S., distinctions of culture likewise oftentimes run along lines that differentiate Euro-American culture from all others. As we shall see, this tendency is very marked in the trials I have composed into a corpus (both the extended initial and the smaller final one).

My search for cases covered the years 1965 through 2000 (the year during which the search was conducted)—albeit with a heavy bias in favor of cases decided at appellate level since 1970, a time span to which I had initially limited my queries. Eventually I chose 1965 as a somewhat arbitrary cut-off point for my search because it is in this year that the Voting

Rights Act was passed—one possible date that may be used to demarcate the beginning of the post-civil rights era.[1] My interest in the discursive role of race in U.S. criminal trials concerned its use after formal racial equality had been introduced throughout the United States—i.e., the time since the U.S. has projected an image of itself of which equality before the law is constitutive (Omi and Winant 1994).[2] For, it was the tension between any continued differentiating roles played in court by 'race'/'culture', and their intersections with 'gender', one the one hand, and formal equality before the law, on the other, that I was concerned with. My search for cases covered the whole of the United States, at both the state and the federal levels. I included both levels without distinction because—as with other legal or formal distinctions that will be addressed in this Part—these would appear not to impinge upon my research interest. Similarly, I have included in the original, larger corpus court-martial cases in addition to other criminal ones, as I assumed that the discourses of interest to me would play out in similar ways in either category of criminal court case.

I searched for *appellate opinions* because this is the only way known to me of systematically identifying court cases according to specified keywords: The entire U.S. legal system is based upon the case law composed of the various hierarchical levels of (published) appellate opinions (U.S. Supreme Court, U.S. Courts of Appeal and District Courts, State Supreme Courts and Courts of Appeal). An additional, tremendous advantage in focusing on cases that went on appeal is financial in nature: only with such cases have trial transcripts already been prepared and are thus at least comparatively affordable.[3] On the other hand, my focus on appeals cases has resulted in a heavy bias, among the cases selected for this study, in favor of crimes that yielded a high sentence (because convictions resulting in such sentences are appealed more often, given the common duration of an appeal, namely, several years), along with a nearly absolute bias in favor of convictions: with but one exception, all of the cases in the corpus I composed initially resulted in a conviction rather than a full acquittal.[4] There is also a close-to-total bias in the corpus in favor of trials, as against other court hearings—possibly because, again, guilty pleas tend to result in lower sentences than convictions by trial, and hence, will not be appealed as often. Thus only four cases in the initial, larger-sized corpus of cases resulted in a guilty plea rather than actually going to trial (with the court hearings making these cases relevant to the present study having been pretrial or sentencing hearings).

My search for appellate opinions covered trials and other court hearings in which the categories 'culture/race' and 'gender' discursively intersected in various forms—not just of 'cultural evidence' that was admitted, but also of such 'evidence' that was proffered (by either the attorney or a prospective expert witness) yet not admitted. I also included instances in which questions on the subject matter had been put to a witness by an attorney without having first been judicially qualified as 'evidence', as well as cases of racialized/culture-related remarks made in an attorney's opening statement or closing argument. I thus treated as irrelevant the legal terms on grounds of which the discourse in question was treated as problematic on appeal. These included, but were not limited to, complaints of improper argument or improper questioning, and of improperly excluded or admitted evidence. The cases I identified encompassed both instances where the defense had engaged in the relevant, racialized/ethnicizing and gendered discourse, and ones in which the prosecution had done so.

I took care to phrase search queries in terms neutral as to the particular ethnic/racial categories concerned (e.g., using "cultu!" but not "Mexic!"; "race" but not "black"). I did so because my interest related to discourses of *difference*, as such, and in *how* the lines of distinction would be drawn—rather than in the representation of any particular categories of 'ethnicity' or 'race'. This is important because, as mentioned earlier, in most instances those discourses of difference encountered within the material I retrieved actually do make distinctions along lines of skin color or First vs. Third World, even when skin color is not mentioned. This indicates that (gendered) discourses of '*culture*' in that material tend to be *racialized*—i.e., marked by categories of 'race' without necessarily acknowledging that this is the case. Overwhelmingly, references to 'culture' within the legal opinions retrieved through my database search relate to people of color rather than so-called white people. This practice constitutes the hegemonic culture—namely, Euro-American or (at a global level) Western culture—as culturally unmarked or universal. It is also in line with the fact that, hegemonically, 'race' is taken to refer to people other than 'whites', elevating 'whiteness' to the status of the *racially* unmarked; the norm. Beside references to (most usually) people of color, my searches yielded frequent results relating to 'gang culture' or 'drug culture'. I excluded these cases because my research interest related to constructions of race/ethnicity rather than subculture. While constructions of the latter may well be racialized, too, if so they seem to pose a special case that I have felt to be beyond the scope of this work to pursue. I also resolved to exclude cases addressing child sexual abuse as these seem to me to pose similarly special issues in regards to gender, to such an extent that it is questionable whether the discourses of childhood concerned are actually gendered in the first place.

My initial search resulted in a corpus of 113 cases overall. I certainly could have enlarged this figure had I continued searching; however, I stopped the search when I felt that the size of the sample was beginning to turn unmanageable. Even apart from this measure, the initial corpus size is not devoid of arbitrariness, as in a few cases the answer to the question of whether the categories race/culture and gender had been treated in conjunction with or independently of one another at trial level was subject to my judgment. (I have tended to draw the line "conservatively", excluding all cases in which these categories do not clearly intersect. In the eventual, smaller-sized corpus, to which I shall turn later on, 'culture' and 'gender' intersect explicitly throughout in that all cases concerned address gendered domination in the context of cultural differences.) From the said pool of citations, I obtained transcript and/or brief materials in all those cases where the appellate opinion does not give a sufficient indication of all that what was said at trial level in connection with those categories. (I did so by contacting the relevant trial and/or appellate court or, sometimes, the defense attorney's or prosecutor's office involved.) This pertained to 77 cases overall (13 of which I excluded from the initial, larger-size corpus based on my inspection of the materials).

My next step after reviewing the transcripts and briefs I had ordered was to map the cases by the subject areas, or themes, in terms of which 'race'/'culture' and 'gender' had intersected at the trial-level hearing(s). Beside a proportion of cases that I left unclassified as they did not appear to form into any thematic cluster (a little under a fifth of the original corpus), the trials seemed to me to condense around four (partially overlapping) subject areas, which I proceeded to identify in terms of discursive figures familiar from colonial, racist, and gendered discourses: (a) patriarchal relations in so-called 'other cultures'; (b) 'miscegenation'[5]; (c) race/culture, femininity, and sexuality; and (d) race/culture, masculinity, and delinquency. Cases falling in any of these subject areas tended to instantiate or to address, in different variations—hegemonic or (partially) contestatory—, certain stereotypes in which race/ethnicity and gender intersect in historically well-established forms. I will here limit my account to that discursive figure which, for reasons to which I shall turn shortly, I have made the focus of this study: Throughout the initial corpus of cases, wherever male domination or gendered inequality is addressed in the context of cultural differences, this occurs in such a form that such inequality is pictured as being more pronounced in 'the Other culture' (which in but one or two cases is non-Western or a culture 'of color'[6]), if not as entirely absent from Euro-American culture. As I will explain in more detail in the next Part (IV, Chapter 1), this places the representation in question in firm continuity with gendered colonial discourse, in the context of which it has been given a name by Spivak—who describes it in terms of a motif of "[w]hite men saving brown women from brown men" (1988a, 297).

Only a minority of the cases making up the initial corpus entail 'cultural evidence' which was either admitted or ruled inadmissible by the trial judge. Nearly half of these (fourteen out of thirty) fall in the thematic group upon which I have eventually come to focus this study—namely, cases addressing male domination as a matter of cultural differences. Apart from cases involving 'cultural evidence', I found that a large majority of trials contain only a few lines, paragraphs or pages of transcript bearing on subjects related to 'race'/'culture' and 'gender'. In contrast, those trials involving 'cultural evidence' (either admitted or heard by the trial judge but eventually ruled inadmissible) developed the relevant subject over tens or even hundreds of pages. Qualitatively, too, these cases seemed to offer up much more material for analysis. In particular, it struck me that, whereas references or allusions to 'race'—most of which occur in the form of attorneys' questions or arguments, and which are often complained of as improper already at trial—are relatively overt appeals to 'prejudice', talk of 'cultural difference' is much more readily received in terms of an unmediated, merely descriptive reference to reality: the putative reality of 'Others'. Especially when such talk receives judicial sanction as official '*evidence*'. Moreover, as mentioned above, the lines of demarcation usually drawn in cases involving 'cultural evidence'—along boundaries corresponding to the distinction 'Western'/'white' vs. Other, even if that distinction is not verbally made—indicates that 'cultural difference' in the courts tends to become an issue in the context of colonial discourse, which divides the world into 'the West' vs. 'the rest', and that that discourse in the form encountered here is racialized, in that cultural distinctions conform with unmentioned racial ones. I came to feel that colonial discourses that present themselves as neutral, descriptive 'evidence' relating to culture are politically and intellectually much more challenging than the occasional direct reference to race (given that the latter constitutes a fairly obvious appeal to 'prejudice'). All the more so considering that that empiricist conception of 'cultural evidence' is reproduced in the bulk of the literature regarding what has come reductively to be called 'the cultural defense'.

As I immersed myself in the debate concerning that 'defense' (which debate I discuss in the next Part [IV, Chapters 1 and 5)], I also found that it has focused very predominantly upon cases that could be addressed in terms of male domination in 'Other cultures'—i.e., in terms of what has emerged as one of the predominant themes in the initial corpus of cases itself. That is, the discursive figure that positions patriarchy as somehow (more) peculiarly non-Western, while it is the most prominent figure among those cases in the corpus that involve 'cultural evidence' (whether offered by the defense or the prosecution), is actually singularly prominent in the said debate, to the extent that that debate addresses matters of gender. What I find particularly troublesome is that, in this discursive figure, feminist rhetoric is appropriated to ends that are at once imperialist and patriarchal (complicit with Euro-American patriarchy insofar as its persistence is being disavowed or minimized)—as I will argue in the next Part of this work (IV). Moreover, the fact that that figure features so prominently in the debate about the admissibility of 'cultural evidence' in criminal cases (not to mention its role in more large-scale discursive events, such as its service to legitimizing the U.S. invasion of Afghanistan in 2001) indicates that this appropriation of feminist rhetoric continues to play a central political role in (racialized) colonial discourse (compare Dustin and Phillips 2008; Phillips and Saharso 2008; Razack 2008). (As Razack states, "it is virtually impossible to name and confront the violence that Muslim women [like all groups of women] experience at the hands of their men and families without providing ideological fuel to the 'war on terror'" [ibid., 107].) The appropriation of feminist rhetoric makes it possible to "sell" what is effectively an unegalitarian discourse as precisely the opposite, namely, as being egalitarian in intention and effect. It is for the reasons recounted in the last two paragraphs that I have resolved to focus the present study upon those cases in which the figure of what I will call 'the Patriarchal Other' is instantiated. The present work is conceived, then, as a critical intervention into the debate as to a 'cultural defense'.

I have chosen to include in the ultimate, reduced corpus of cases *all* those that instantiate the figure of the Patriarchal Other. Beside the trials in which 'cultural evidence' relating to that figure was presented (nine in number), this encompasses five cases in which such 'evidence' was proffered but ruled inadmissible, as well as seven cases in which it assumed the form of what on appeal was, in some instances, alleged to be improper argument or improper questioning. In one further case, a co-defendant brought up the subject at sentencing, while in another, the prosecutor explained a peremptory challenge he exercised against a potential juror in terms of the theme in question. Finally, there is one case in which that theme was raised by the judge both orally and in his published opinion.

I have included in the final, reduced corpus only those cases in which gender relations in some 'Other culture' were actually coded, within the trial discourse itself, as asymmetrical, i.e. as a matter of male dominance or women's subordination. By contrast, I have excluded from it cases where gender relations in 'Other cultures' would only be coded as a matter of inequality/domination by a feminist perspective brought to the text *from without*. This is because I consider that it is only in the first form that the discursive figure in question displays the features I have attributed to it above, namely, an appropriation of feminist rhetoric to effects that are both colonialist and support a dissimulation of patriarchy in the West (including the hegemonic, 'white' U.S.).

The result of this selection is a corpus of twenty-four cases overall. These span the years 1979 through 1998; as I had mentioned, they are drawn from a search that covered all U.S. courts during the years 1965 through 2000—with a bias towards cases decided on appeal after 1969. Tables III.1 and III.2 give an overview of the cases concerned in terms of the characteristics I consider most important for the purposes of this study.

THE FOCUS OF THIS STUDY

Of the twenty-four cases making up the corpus upon which this study is based, the latter focuses upon two central case studies, and treats five cases overall. As I had mentioned, and as will be shown in the empirical Parts of this work (IV and V), the figure of the Patriarchal Other is constructed in a highly uniform fashion across the corpus: In every trial, within the overall case corpus which I had composed initially, in which gendered domination or inequality is addressed as such, it is addressed as being more pronounced, or even as existing solely, in the relevant 'Other culture'. (The few exceptions to this that there are on the part of individual speakers are treated in the Appendix as well as in Part V.) This is so whatever the particular 'ethnicity' concerned—of which many are encompassed in the reduced corpus (see Table III.2), but all except one or two of which are 'Third World' (see n. 6, this Chapter) (in most instances, concerning first-generation migrants to the U.S.). Due to this uniformity, it is sufficient for this work to focus upon a small number of trials in-depth, as a basis both for demonstrating that uniformity (Parts IV and V), and for studying events and features that undermine the colonial and gendered discourses intersecting in the discursive figure of the Patriarchal Other (Part V).

I have chosen the cases focused upon in the empirical Parts of this work for qualitative reasons. The two main case studies are among the longest, most voluminous trials in the corpus. On the one hand, they are highly particular (and quite different from each other) in terms of their evidentiary constellation; yet, they thereby demonstrate all the better the shared features of the discursive figure with which this work is concerned. Thus, one trial exemplifies a prosecution based upon ethnicity; the other, a 'cultural defense'; one features a male defendant, the other, a female one; one trial exemplifies the use of 'culture' to stigmatize the defendant; the other, a deployment of 'culture' that tries to render her sympathetic; one, an attempt to prove that a given form of conduct occurred; the other, an explanation of a conduct that was undisputed as such. Finally, in one case, the 'cultural evidence' was introduced through academic 'experts'; in the other, through persons "merely" 'native' to the culture concerned, rather than with any formal education regarding the subject. We shall see that the difference made by these contrasting features is ultimately very limited; that they add up to mere variants of what I shall argue is a single discursive figure.

Beside the two main case studies just addressed, three additional trials are featured in the empirical portion of this work. In Part IV, which analyzes the construction of 'cultural evidence' in the trial strategies surveyed, I focus upon the said principal case studies as well as upon a smaller, comparative one that complements these. It does so principally in that, whereas the two main case studies instantiate the figure of the Patriarchal Other in a tone that condemns the Other culture (in one trial, in a form that condemns a 'patriarchal' Other male; in the other, in that of seeking to render sympathetic a defendant constructed as Oppressed Third World Woman), in the third case, the Other's sexism is legitimized rather than overtly stigmatized—albeit to an ultimately very similar effect, as I will argue. (Additional reasons for choosing this third case will emerge in the course of Part IV.) In Part V, concerned with the question of how and to what extent hegemonic constructions of 'cultural evidence' are either resisted or otherwise destabilized in the course of its collaborative constitution by participants to criminal court hearings, I refer to four cases overall: Chapters 6 and

Table III.1 The Corpus of Cases: Formal Characteristics

Case name (trial level)	*Year of court hearing*	*Type of court hearing*	*State (trial court)*	*Convicted of (inter alia)*
[Cao] vs. State	1986	trial	Alabama (Montgomery Cir. Ct.)	capital murder
[Chemmanoor] vs. State	1993	trial	Texas (Denton Cty. 16th Dist. Ct.)	murder
[Chung] vs. State	1991	trial	Georgia (Cobb Cty. Super. Ct.)	felony murder
[Le] vs. State	1997	trial	Georgia (Bibb Cty. Super. Ct.)	aggravated assault
People vs. [Gonzalez]	1993	trial (sentencing stage)	Illinois (Lake Cty. Cir. Ct.)	1st-degree murder
People vs. [Lopez] &[Singh]	1993	trial	California (Sta. Clara Cty. Super. Ct.)	1st-degree murder
People vs. [Merlino]	1979	trial	California (Sta. Clara Cty. Super. Ct.)	2nd-degree murder
People vs. [Shen]	1991	trial	California (Riverside Cty. Super. Ct.)	2nd-degree murder
People vs. [Xiong]	1983	trial	New York (Monroe Cty. Supr. Ct.)	2nd-degree murder
[Singh] vs. Cambra: see *People vs. [Lopez] & [Singh]*				
State vs. [Arrisgado]	1993	trial	Hawaii (1st Cir. Ct., Honolulu Cty.)	1st-degree murder
State vs. [Galicia]	1992	trial	Wisconsin (Milwaukee Cty. Cir. Ct.)	1st-degree intentional homicide while armed
State vs. [Her]	1990	trial	Minnesota (Ramsey Cty. Dist. Ct.)	3rd-degree rape
State vs. [Ku]	1995	trial	Ohio (Franklin Cty. Ct. of Common Pleas)	assault
State vs. [Kubicek]	1992	trial	Missouri (St. Louis Cty. Cir. Ct.)	conspiracy to commit murder in the 1st degree

State vs. [Lee]	1998	trial	Minnesota (Dakota Cty. Dist. Ct.)	1st-degree criminal sexual conduct
State vs. [Saidani]	1992 or 1993	trial	Ohio (Hamilton Cty. Ct. of Common Pleas)	felonious assault
State vs. [Seyoum]	1993	trial	New Hampshire (Grafton Cty. Super. Ct.)	1st-degree murder
State vs. [Smith]	1994	pretrial/trial	Wisconsin (Milwaukee Cty. Cir. Ct.)	1st-degree murder
State vs. [Vue]	1990	trial	Minnesota (Ramsey Cty. Dist. Ct.)	1st-degree criminal sexual conduct
U.S. vs. [García] et al.	1989	sentencing hearing/ guilty plea	New York (U.S. Dist. Ct.)	money laundering
U.S. vs. [Ibrahim] et al.	1993	trial	Illinois (U.S. Dist. Ct.)	acquitted (bankruptcy fraud)
U.S. vs. [Okute] & [Onyekachi]	1994	pretrial hearing relating to the 'cultural' expert testimony	New Jersey (U.S. Dist Ct.)	conspiracy to distribute heroin
U.S. vs. [Perea]	1992	sentencing hearing/ guilty plea	New York (U.S. Dist. Ct.)	knowing and intentional possession of cocaine with intent to distribute
U.S. vs. [Ramírez-Arellano]	1988	sentencing hearing/ guilty plea	Missouri (U.S. Dist. Ct.)	distribution of cocaine

Note: See the section listing "Cases, Constitutional Amendments, Rules of Evidence, and Statutes" for citations to the reported appellate opinions on the cases making up the corpus described in Tables III.1 and III.2. See the Appendix for brief accounts of, and commentaries upon, these cases.

Table III.2 The Corpus of Cases: Substantive Characteristics

Case name (trial level)	*'Culture' introduced by*	*'Culture' introduced in form of*	*Ethnicizing category in terms of which gender relations addressed*	*Ethnicizing/gendering categorization applied (primarily) to*
[Cao] vs. State	defense	expert testimony, admitted	Vietnamese	male defendant
[Chemmanoor] vs. State	state	expert testimony, admitted; questioning of 'lay' witnesses	Indian	male defendant
[Chung] vs. State	defense	expert testimony, not admitted	Chinese/Taiwanese	male defendant
[Le] vs. State	defense	expert testimony, not admitted; attorney's opening statement and closing argument	Vietnamese	woman defendant/male victim
People vs. [Gonzalez]	defense	expert testimony, admitted	Mexican/Mexican American	male defendant
People vs. [Lopez] & [Singh]	state	expert and 'lay' testimony, admitted	Sikh	male defendant
People vs. [Merlino]	state	questioning of witness; closing argument	Italian	male defendant
People vs. [Shen]	defense	expert testimony, admitted	Chinese	woman defendant
People vs. [Xiong]	defense	'lay' testimony (expert testimony ruled inadmissible)	Laotian	male defendant/woman victim
[Singh] vs. Cambra: see *People vs. [Lopez] & [Singh]*				
State vs. [Arrisgado]	defense	expert testimony, admitted	Filipino	male defendant/woman victim
State vs. [Galicia]	state	questioning of witness	'machismo' [not specified further at trial, but specified as 'Hispanic' in appellate brief]	male defendant

State vs. [Her]	defense; state	expert testimony, admitted	Hmong	alleged women victims
State vs. [Ku]	state	questioning of witnesses; opening statement	Korean	male defendant/woman victim
State vs. [Kubicek]	state	jury selection: peremptory strike	Middle Eastern/Indian	woman prosecutor/male prospective juror
State vs. [Lee]	state	expert and 'lay' testimony, admitted	Hmong	male defendant/woman victim
State vs. [Saidani]	state	questioning of witness; closing argument	Muslim/Moroccan	male defense witness/male defendant
State vs. [Seyoum]	defense	closing argument	Ethiopian	woman victim
State vs. [Smith]	defense	written pretrial motion to admit expert testimony, denied	African American	male defendant
State vs. [Vue]	state	questioning of witness; closing argument	Hmong	alleged woman victim/male defendant
U.S. vs. [García] et al.	defense	co-defendant's statement	Colombian	self (male co-defendant)/ woman defendant
U.S. vs. [Ibrahim] et al.	defense	expert and 'lay' testimony, admitted	Arabic/Jordanian	woman defendant
U.S. vs. [Okute] & [Onyekachi]	defense	expert testimony, not admitted	Nigerian/Igbo	woman defendant
U.S. vs. [Perea]	judge	judge's oral statement and published opinion	Colombian	woman defendant
U.S. vs. [Ramírez-Arellano]	defense	argument to judge	cultural difference [Puerto Rican]	woman defendant

Note: In all cases in which expert testimony on 'culture' was admitted, the closing argument of the party concerned also addressed that subject. For the sake of brevity, I do not specifically mention this in Table III.2.

I specify the form in which 'culture' was introduced into a court case as 'questioning' of a witness when merely a few questions were asked of a given witness, and as '(lay) testimony' when a substantial portion of testimony related to the subject.

See the section listing "Cases, Constitutional Amendments, Rules of Evidence, and Statutes" for citations to the reported appellate opinions on the cases making up the corpus described in Tables III.1 and III.2. See the Appendix for brief accounts of, and commentaries upon, these cases.

7, which scrutinize the strategies of resistance pursued by opposing attorneys and by witnesses, respectively, each address the two main case studies alongside a supplementary one that instantiates an unusually effective move of resistance on the part of an attorney, in one case, and a witness, in the other. Finally, in Chapter 8—which concludes this second empirical Part by re-examining the colonial and patriarchal discourses circulating in the trials with a view to their instabilities and the political difference these make—I consider only the two main case studies, with a focus upon one of them. This makes sense in that my purpose here is less to provide an overview of the corpus's discursive features or *Gestalt*, as a whole. Instead, here I see it as my task to convey an impression of the cumulative impact of numerous, heterogeneous fractures to hegemonic discourse materializing *in a single given trial*, so as to place in perspective the stability and power of the discourses concerned.

My strategy of representing the corpus, as just detailed, has the great advantage of acquainting you (relatively) closely with two of the trials, each of which will be illuminated from a number of different angles. Given the immense amount of evidentiary particulars entailed even in those two cases (not to mention in the corpus as a whole)—which I need to recount in significant detail in order for you to appreciate how the gendered discourses of 'culture' operate in constituting 'the evidence'—any more inclusive strategy of selecting case studies would have seemed unmanageable to me. However, in the Appendix, I offer brief accounts of all of the twenty-four cases that form the basis of this study.

A note about my "policy" concerning proper names: There is an inevitable tension between the priorities of protecting the privacy of the human beings involved in the criminal cases at issue, on the one hand, and of being transparent with respect to what cases I study, on the other. I have tried to do some justice to each goal by pursuing a mixed strategy. As regards those cases that form part of the original, larger corpus, but not of the eventual, smaller one upon which this study is based, I list the true case names—which contain the names of the defendants concerned—in the table of cases (see the section entitled "Cases, Constitutional Amendments, Rules of Evidence, and Statutes Cited"). The reasoning behind this is that the mere mention of a case name barely affects the privacy of the subjects involved any further, considering that appellate opinions have already been reported in all of these cases (which often use the full names of persons and places mentioned). Likewise, when addressing cases outside my corpus which have figured in the public discussion about 'the cultural defense', I use the real case names/defendants' names for the sake of identifiability. In contrast, for the twenty-four cases of which the ultimate corpus is formed, and of which I offer accounts in the Appendix, I have altered personal names—and therefore also, the case names which identify the defendant—in order to protect the privacy of the people concerned (including in the table of cases, and in Tables III.1 and III.2).[7] This includes cases which have figured in the discussion as to 'the cultural defense'. In addition, for the five cases discussed in the main body of this work, I have anonymized U.S. place names except for the state, county and court names specified in Table III.1—which I do provide for the sake of transparency. Readers who want to consult the appellate opinions in question, or to order court documents, can identify the relevant real names in the opinions concerned, for which I do provide the proper publication details (see the section entitled "Cases, Constitutional Amendments, Rules of Evidence, and Statutes Cited" as well as the Appendix). A second reason why I treat the persons involved in the twenty-four cases studied for the purposes of this work anonymously—which includes defendants/(alleged) victims, lay and expert witnesses, as well as attorneys, judges, and other court personnel—is that, as explained in Part II, my conception of power is such that I want to take the focus off questions of personal blame. My criticism of colonial, racist, and patriarchal discourses is intended less as an indictment of 'guilty individuals'—which I hold to be unproductive politically (Butler 1997a; 1997b)—and more as an attack against the power relations established by unegalitarian discourses, as such. That is, I am trying to target these discourses as *social* phenomena.

We are set now to venture into the empirical part of this work.

Part IV

Ethnicizing Prosecutions and Defenses

'Culture' and 'Gender' in Trial Parties' Argumentative Strategies and in the Debate About 'the Cultural Defense'

> *[A] more detailed accounting of some of the cases involving cultural evidence belies a pattern of either cultural insensitivity* [sic] *or a gender bias.*
>
> Hoeffel (2006, 327)

1 Biases and Blindspots in the Debate

As stated in the Introduction to this work, the debate about the 'cultural defense' has focused on the question of whether or not such a defense should be permitted, and if so, in what form (e.g., Friedman Ramirez 2009; Morgan and Parker 2009). That is, it has been framed in terms of "whether to permit criminal defendants to introduce cultural evidence" (Maguigan 1995, 36). This focus has systematically shielded from view the fact that 'cultural evidence' has been used by prosecutors as a strategy of proving criminal defendants guilty.[1] Indeed, the very term coined as the object of the debate—"cultural defense" (e.g., Anonymous 1986; Renteln 2004; Foblets and Renteln 2009[2]) (or, sometimes, "culture defense" [Torry 2000; Reddy 2002])—obscures that fact.

Some of those contributors to the debate who have opposed a 'cultural defense', or have proposed that it be restricted in some form (e.g., to sentencing rather than a trial's guilt phase [Hallevy 2009]), have pictured it as advantaging minority defendants over majority ones (Goldstein 1994, 161; Cardillo 1997, 95; Coleman 2001, 997; 1996, 1096; Morgan and Parker 2009, 206). Allowing immigrant or minority defendants to invoke culture in their defense, the assertion goes, provides them with an argument not available to accused persons from the 'mainstream':

> [T]o the extent that cultural evidence is used to determine the outcome of criminal cases and to excuse some perpetrators of crimes, it results in disparate treatment of immigrants and other members of American society (Coleman 1996, 1096).

This claim has long been answered, e.g., by Maguigan—who points out that, on the contrary, to bar 'evidence' about marginalized cultures from the courtroom would be to discriminate against minority defendants (1995, 53; see also, inter alia, Boulette Taylor 1998, 469; Suri 2000, 109; Lee 2003, 109, 124; Song 2007, 88–89, 100–101; Phillips 2007, 82–83). For, the available criminal defenses in fact constitute cultural defenses for members of the majority. (As pointed out in Part II, this is the reason why I invariably place the term 'cultural defense' in quotes.) An assumption to the contrary would imply that hegemonic culture is, in fact, no culture. In order to even make equal use of existing criminal defenses (as against benefiting from 'culture' as a separate, formal defense)—to which state of mind is central—minority defendants need to be able to present 'evidence' relating to their social and psychological context, which in the case of majority defendants tends to be known and taken for granted due to its hegemonic standing. For that very reason, 'evidence' relating to cultural difference is already—albeit irregularly—admitted in criminal cases as legally *relevant* 'evidence' (Hoeffel 2006; Friedman Ramirez 2009, 207; Maguigan 1995, esp. 56–59).

The fact that prosecutions based upon a defendant's (or an alleged victim's) culture have occurred reinforces this point. For, considering this, it is absurd to even debate whether defendants should be able to do the same: if it is permissible, on grounds of relevance, to be found guilty based upon one's cultural identity—arguably an infringement of the constitutional right to equal protection of the laws[3]—, it would amount all the more to discrimination if minority defendants were to be barred from making reference to their cultural identity—likewise, on grounds of relevance—as part of their legal defense. That culture-based criminal prosecutions have been systematically ignored within the debate about a 'cultural defense' is surely significant. For, it effectively amounts to an anti-immigrant or anti-minority bias insofar as it forms the prerequisite to constructing that defense as a privilege enjoyed by immigrant or minority defendants. See, for instance, the following statement, which comments upon a rape case that involved a 'cultural defense':

> The Moua case and others pose an ethical and social question as to whether foreign newcomers should be held responsible for crimes under United States law. Lack of cultural conformity and ignorance of United States law by such people pose serious threats to the court systems and communities in which they settle. . . . As previously noted, the courts' refusal to accept the 'cultural defense' will pressure foreign newcomers to conform to the American identity (Sams 1986, 345, 350; similarly: Hallevy 2010).

An anti-minority bias has been especially evident in some 'feminist' contributions to the debate—most prominently, Coleman (1996) and Okin (1999, esp. 22–23). Some such contributors have focused primarily upon cases in which 'evidence' as to non-hegemonic cultures was admitted as part of the defense in prosecutions dealing with male violence against women (Rimonte 1991; Spatz 1991, 626; Gallin 1994, 725, 741–744). Nearly all of them have argued that a 'cultural defense' will serve to legitimize women's subordination in non-Western minority groups. While this concern is legitimate as such, it has been framed in terms of a claim—asserted (Coleman 1996; Young 1992; Gallin 1994; Okin 1999, 16–17) or implied (Rimonte 1991;

Goldstein 1994, 162–163; Cardillo 1997; Mendelsohn 2004, 1022–1023; see also Levine 2003, 75)—that such cultures are more patriarchal than hegemonic Western culture. The prominence of that claim in the debate about the 'cultural defense' replicates its centrality to criminal trials negotiating 'cultural evidence' themselves, which we will witness throughout this work. This claim is contentious to say the least. A number of commentators have taken issue with it (Volpp 1994, 1996, 2000, 2001; Koptiuch 1996; Razack 1998; Lawrence 2001; Boulette Taylor 1998, 466–467; Deckha 2009). As they have pointed out, the widespread construction of the West as being more 'advanced' than other cultures in matters of gender equality, or even as entirely gender-egalitarian,[4] serves to distract from persisting patriarchal norms and practices in hegemonic U.S. culture and politics, which subordinate women from both the dominant and marginalized cultures (Song 2007, 102; Volpp 1996, 1604–1605; 2000, 115–116). In my view, this places that construction in fundamental tension with feminism—even though avowed feminists have been instrumental to reproducing it. In doing so, they have lent a hand to colonial discourse (Volpp 1996; Koptiuch 1996; Razack 1998, 2008). For, the claim that the West is less patriarchal, or even entirely post-patriarchal, resonates strongly with an historically established motif that serves to underwrite a hierarchy according to which the West is culturally or racially superior to the rest of the world. Spivak has labeled that motif in the context of the British Empire as follows: "White men saving brown women from brown men" (1988a, 297; compare Koptiuch 1996, 216, 230–231). A label that foregrounds the imperialist agenda entailed in this representation, justifying as it did a colonial intervention masquerading as 'the civilizing mission'. (Just as that representation was called upon to justify, in more recent times, the U.S. 'intervention' in Afghanistan [compare Volpp 2006, 1634–1635].) As a shorthand, I will refer to that representation—which will be at the center of this work—as the figure of the Patriarchal Other, or of Patriarchal Other Culture(s).

As a subvariant of that figure, I shall also be invoking the figure of the Oppressed Third World Woman. In doing so, I have in mind Mohanty's (originally 1986) article on "the production of the 'Third World Woman' as a singular monolithic subject" in certain feminist texts (1994, 196; see also Koptiuch 1996, 226–227). Mohanty characterizes "the image of an 'average third-world woman'" (1994, 199) in the texts she scrutinizes in the following terms:

> This average third-world woman leads an essentially truncated life based on her feminine gender (read: sexually constrained) and being 'third world' (read: ignorant, poor, uneducated, tradition-bound, religious, domesticated, family-oriented, victimized, etc.). This, I suggest, is in contrast to the (implicit) self-representation of western women as educated, modern, as having control over their own bodies and sexualities, and the 'freedom' to make their own decisions (1994, 199–200).

By invoking a figure of Oppressed Third World Woman I am also referencing Razack's construction of such a figure—essentially, of the 'brown woman' to be saved from brown men by white men in Spivak's coinage (see above)—in the context of claims for asylum in Canada premised upon gender-based persecution:

> I suggest that the binary of the civilized West/the uncivilized East characterizes most feminist and legal discourse about gender persecution. . . . I suggest that women's claims are most likely to succeed when they present themselves as victims of dysfunctional, exceptionally patriarchal cultures and states. The successful asylum seeker must cast herself as a cultural Other, that is, as someone fleeing from a more primitive culture. That is to say, it is through various orientalist [sic] and imperialist lenses that women's gender-based persecution becomes visible in the West. Without the imperial or colonial component, claims of gender persecution are less likely to succeed and asylum is denied (1998, 92–93).

As in Mohanty's text, an opposition between (more) self-determined Western/white women and the lack of agency ascribed to women of color or 'Third World' women is constitutive of the figure of the Oppressed Third World Woman as understood in this work—similarly to what Razack observes regarding:

> how women's human rights advocates have taken up the issue of FGM[5] [, namely, that] what most feminist positions share on this issue is a failure to engage Third World women as subjects. Western feminists have imagined Exotic Other Females [sic] in need of their benevolent protection (ibid., 97).

> [R]acist constructs operate on the logic that women of the Third World are to be pitied, and pity is unlikely to emerge when the women in question demonstrate that they are also strong individuals who can make decisions to flee and survive (ibid., 113).

The notion of certain social arrangements being '*more* patriarchal' than others presupposes a purely quantitative concept of cultural difference (namely, as a matter of degrees) that will inescapably use ethnocentric criteria for constructing the scale on which those degrees will be measured. In my view, this makes it a flawed instrument for an analysis of patriarchal social relations. It also makes it a notion prone to hierarchizing (essentialized) 'cultures' within a framework indebted to colonialist dichotomies such as that between the archaic and the modern, the barbaric and the civilized, and despotism and democracy (compare Volpp 1996, 1588–1589). Historically as well as in the present, it has in fact been central to buttressing those dichotomies, as I have already alluded. Witness the response by

Elizabeth Holtzman, then District Attorney of Brooklyn, to a 1988 trial in which a defendant successfully asserted a 'cultural defense' to killing his wife—as well as the entire sample of quotes below:

> There should be one standard of justice—not one that depends on the cultural background of a defendant. *There may be barbaric customs in various parts of the world*—that cannot excuse criminal conduct here. Anyone who comes to this country must be prepared to live by and obey our [sic] laws (cited in Koptiuch 1996, 216, my emphasis; see also Young 1992; Okin 1999, esp. 17).

> Many of the women murdered by their families in the name of family honor are murdered in advanced western societies that have open-gate policies and are absorbing immigrant populations (Hallevy 2010, 440).

> [A] recognition of the cultural defense would demonstrate that the United States tacitly consents to the violence toward women that is practiced throughout the world. Other countries condone violence toward their women. For example, Islamic countries treat the murder of a wife less seriously than the murder of a stranger. In India, many young wives are killed because of small dowries. These women are not protected in America if a cultural defense can exculpate their husbands (Goldstein 1994, 162–163, footnotes omitted).

> Immigrants living in America must abide by American law. We cannot risk lessening the sanctity of life in this country or the victimization of women and children because of spurious arguments about cultural traditions that do not apply in America (Morgan and Parker 2009, 208).

For, as the editor of the recent symposium issue of *Judicature* on "The Unique Challenges of Cross-Cultural Justice" (2009) expounds in summarizing the contribution by the co-authors last cited above:

> Morgan and Parker raise a number of objections to the cultural defense (both principled and practical), arguing basically that allowing immigrant defendants to assert cultural defenses violates principles of equal protection, and that formally recognizing the defense would endanger U.S. society by, inter alia, putting the country's women and children at the risk of practices such as honor killing, female genital mutilation, and sex slavery (Ridgway 2009, 191).

As Volpp comments upon this line of argument:

> The presumption that the United States and its fictive unified culture is per se more progressive and more protective of women and

> children than the culture of Asian and African immigrants is the most rehearsed United States cultural nationalism: 'West is best' (Volpp 1996, 1604–1605).

Instead of the colonialist opposition between a patriarchal 'East' (or South) and a (more) gender-egalitarian 'West', I consider more productive a conception of patriarchal practices as differing from each other *qualitatively* (i.e., in kind) across social and cultural contexts (compare Volpp 2001, 1217; Song 2007, 4; Honig 1999, 38).[6] I do so even as I realize that the relativist implication of that conception may be politically disenabling in certain instances. In such instances, I would indeed make use of a quantitative comparison between differing degrees of patriarchal subordination in *specific practices* (compare Song 2007; Phillips 2007), in the spirit of strategic essentialism (Spivak 1988c, 205–207). Doing so differs from classifying 'cultures', conceived of as integrated wholes, in terms of their gendered character, given that practice's complicity with colonialist/racist hierarchical scales ranking 'races' and 'cultures' in terms of their respectively imputed worth (e.g., Okin 1999, 19–21).

To return to the instantiation of the motif of Patriarchal Others in the debate about the 'cultural defense': As has widely been pointed out, to oppose such a defense on the grounds that it would give leeway to other cultures' patriarchal practices is to be forgetful (to put it benignly) of the deeply patriarchal character of the U.S. legal system and hegemonic common sense at large (Phillips 2007, 97). Chiu (1994) was the first to state that 'cultural defenses' seem to be successful specifically when the supposedly culturally 'different' norms invoked resonate with norms of the dominant culture—especially with gendered norms, often of a patriarchal character. She argues that the results of some of the most prominent 'cultural defense' cases indicate that hegemonic judicial audiences recognize the cultural affinities in those cases, rather than what is truly unfamiliar to them in 'the evidence'. She views this as a position that blends assimilationism and exclusion—as two historically established hegemonic positions vis-à-vis Asian Americans, who are often at the center of a 'cultural defense'—in such a way that difference is reduced to sameness. The central axis around which familiarity is constructed, Chiu maintains, is "the dominant culture's perception of gender roles" (1994, 1119). The outcomes of some of the 'cultural defense' cases that have been most prominent in the debate are explained by U.S. patriarchal ideology, according to her: in the 'cultural defense', "[t]he judicial process becomes an opportunity for white society to reify sexism and to reinforce and reconstruct the subordination of women through another culture" (ibid., 1120).

Many others have since repeated Chiu's argument in different guises (Sing 1999; Lee 2003, Ch. 4; 2007; Phillips 2007, Ch. 3; Song 2007, Ch. 4; Hoeffel 2006, 315–320; Levine 2003, 80–82; Torry 1999, 138). For instance, it has been pointed out that certain 'cultural defense' cases that achieved high profile in the media because male defendants got away with little punishment for raping or killing a woman were fully consonant with a sexist bias in the criminal defenses that they actually used—such as the defense of 'adequate provocation' (in which the victim tends to be blamed for 'provoking' the aggressor) and the 'mistake of fact' defense to rape (in which the defendant alleges that he mistook the victim's behavior for consent) (Lee 2003, 112–120; Song 2007, Ch. 4).

Chiu's insight is central to a deconstruction of what passes for 'cultural evidence'. For, it establishes that 'information' offered about patriarchal '*Other*' cultures is tailored to *U.S.* sensibilities, including a patriarchal normative economy. Chiu illustrates her point by arguing that the outcomes of a number of high-profile cultural-defense cases are based on an appreciation of *factual* cultural similarities, rather than on differences. For instance, she asserts with reference to one highly problematic 'cultural defense' to a rape case involving a Hmong defendant and putative victim that "Hmong and American sexual concepts are the same" (ibid., 1116; see also Phillips 2007, Ch. 3; Song 2007, Ch. 4). I consider more productive developing her insight in such a way as to regard the 'cultural evidence' offered in U.S. courts strictly as a *U.S. discourse* about sexual and cultural difference. Whatever 'information' about other social worlds enters that discourse will do so in a form mediated by concepts hegemonic in 'America'. Specifically, 'evidence' offered at trial forms part of *strategies* of argument that are tailored, by definition, to a U.S. audience. Once we accept this as a given, it becomes impossible to attribute the patriarchal patterns discernible in such trial strategies to 'the other culture', whether exclusively or primarily. Instead, it must then be recognized that only to the extent that U.S. audiences can be expected to be receptive to a sexist logic of argument will 'cultural evidence' appealing to such logic be deployed.

It is in order to clarify this point that, in the present Part, I want to examine in detail the strategies of argument used in some such trials. Where the 'cultural defense debate' has focused upon a limited number of high-profile cases primarily in terms of their *outcomes*—with a bias towards cases that resulted in a very light sentence[7]—, it is when we look at how such cases are *argued* that it becomes most apparent that gendered 'cultural evidence' is deployed as part of a shared discourse that entails little variation across the most diverse evidentiary constellations: a discourse that endlessly reiterates the myth of a (more) gender-egalitarian, implicitly superior West. (Contrary to Hoeffel's claim, cited in the epigraph above, that "a more detailed accounting of some of the cases involving cultural evidence belies a pattern of either cultural insensitivity [sic] or a gender bias" [2006, 327]. A claim I shall return to in Chapter 6.)

In contrast, the example of Chiu is just one case in point illustrating the tendency, throughout the literature about the 'cultural defense', to construct 'cultural evidence' as a matter of plain facts; of accurate vs. incorrect information (e.g., Van Broeck 2001; Torry 1999, 2000; Magnarella

1991; Winkelman 1996; Wong 1999; Foblets and Renteln 2009; *Judicature* 2009).[8] For instance, Suri states that "admitting 'evidence of' culture . . . enables the attorneys to show *who the defendant actually is*" (2000, 136, my emphasis; see also ibid., 120; Wong 1999, 396; Frischknecht 2009, 259–262, and Hoeffel 2006, as discussed in Chapter 6). Similarly, Friedman Ramirez writes: "Absent cultural evidence, it may be simply impossible for a judge and jury to grasp *what actually happened* in a particular case" (2009, 207, my emphasis). A statement which invokes notions of evidentiary 'discovery' and legal 'factfinding' that distract from the discursively constitutive character of those endeavors. It calls to mind Spivak's claim, cited earlier, to the effect that "positivist empiricism"—which "define[s] its own arena as 'concrete experience,' '*what actually happens*'"—forms "the justifying foundation of . . . neocolonialism" (1988a, 275, my emphasis; compare Part II). Which claim I hope to substantiate in the present Part.

For further illustrations of the empiricist treatment of 'cultural evidence' as a mere matter of correct vs. false information, we may turn to the appeal, made by critics of stereotyped 'evidence' of this sort, to the workings of the adversary system as a remedy. Thus Renteln argues that:

> [I]t is certainly important that the cultural defense not be implemented in such a way as to disseminate *false stereotypes*. This depends on judges requiring that evidence meet high standards. The stereotype objection [to the cultural defense, C.B.] is not one of principle but, rather, one of practice. If the defense could be invoked carefully, then this problem might be avoided or at least minimized (2004, 198, my emphasis; see also Frischknecht 2009, 259–262).

Similarly, Maguigan has called upon prosecutors to rebut stereotyped 'cultural evidence' by effective cross-examination and by calling well-qualified 'cultural experts' in turn (1995, 96–97; see also Sacks 1996, 548; Kim 1997, 125; Boulette Taylor 1998, 459–460; Suri 2000, 137; Levine 2003, 78–79).

> In cases in which appropriate evidentiary rulings require the admission of cultural evidence, the burden falls on prosecutors to expose any flaws in the use of the material. Prosecutors must be held to a standard of performance in which they *rebut cultural stereotypes with accurate information and reasoned argument* (Maguigan 1995, 90, my emphasis).

Volpp agrees, stating that:

> Information about a defendant's culture should never be reduced to stereotypes about a community, but should concretely address the individual's location in her community, diaspora, and history. Maguigan and I ask that prosecutors and community groups challenge evidence as irrelevant when it is based on *stereotypes with little basis in reality*,

> provide testimony to demonstrate how particular cultural notions are contested within communities, and present evidence that is based on *accurate descriptions* of the pressures that individuals face, both within their communities and without (1996, 1612–1613, my emphasis).

> What is at issue in cases involving cultural evidence is the weight it is given, the responsibility of prosecutors to introduce additional evidence regarding culture *so that perceptions of culture are not distorted*, judicial training on cultural issues, and the question of qualifications of expert witnesses who testify about cultural practices (Volpp 2000, 105n93, my emphasis).

In addition, Song has argued that putting on several experts will tend to diversify the perspectives from within a given culture, thus reducing the risk of having that culture reified by its more patriarchal adherents (2007, 107):

> [S]tate legislatures might devise an evidence rule that instructed prosecutors to include a range of perspectives from within affected communities about the practice in question. Courts might also seek the aid of academics or professionals with knowledge of the groups in question. It is dangerous to rely upon any one expert (. . .), but devising a code of ethics for expert witnesses and establishing a community of peer review and accountability on such matters could help counter distortions or abuse of cultural evidence (2007, 107).

The call for experts (see also Donovan and Garth 2007, 138; Renteln 2009, 81–82; Frischknecht 2009, 259–262; Winkelman 1996, 159) would appear to imply a notion of stereotypes as a distortion of cultural 'information' that could, in principle, be rendered in the one correct way—rather than in terms of a normatively inflected discourse that *invariably* mediates the information relayed, including information that is not demonstrably incorrect (as I have proposed in Part II). To problematize only a distortion or overgeneralization of facts[9] is to reproduce the empiricist idea that facts pertaining to the social could in principle be rendered neutrally, without either a normative inflection or a mediating perspective that excludes alternative ways of framing 'the facts'. As pointed out in Part II, neither type of mediation can be avoided according to discourse theory. While, on the other hand, we cannot steer entirely clear of essentializing our constructions of the real (i.e., of disavowing, at least implicitly, its constructedness, and the mediated character of our cognitive access to it), the poststructuralist perspective cautions that—to paraphrase Spivak—essentialism "in the long run is not OK" (1990, 45; see Part II). That is, essentialism is both theoretically untenable and politically harmful. Therefore, in what follows, I want to make the case for considering the 'evidence' of cultural difference relayed in U.S. courtrooms as *constructions* mediated by discursive frames "domestic" to the U.S. I propose to consider the figure of the Patriarchal Other as one such mediating frame, which—given its uniform reproduction within those trials in my case corpus in which gendered subordination is negotiated—evidently enjoys hegemonic status. I thereby want to move the debate beyond the idea that an empirically correct rendering of 'facts' about Othered cultures would do away with the problem of 'stereotyping' or, put more aptly: with hierarchizing discourses that are devaluing to human subjects.

I shall present three case studies in this Part. As explained in the previous Part, I have altered the defendants', victims' and witnesses' names to protect their privacy as well as to take the focus off individualized questions of blame for the constructions at issue. Those familiar with the trials in focus, two of which are often mentioned in the literature, will recognize them regardless. The first case study—of the trial *People vs. Lopez and Singh*—is an example of the constellation whereby the prosecution, rather than the defense, relies upon 'cultural evidence' as a way of proving the defendant guilty.[10] (The unsuccessful appeal by one of the defendants was based in part on the complaint that the judicial admission of such 'evidence' had denied him due process.[11]) This case study is meant to fill the void left by the systematic oversight of culturally based prosecutions in the debate about a 'cultural defense'. In the 1993 trial, the State of California attempted to infer the most likely past conduct of one of the defendants from his ethnicity and gender, and tried to incite xenophobic resentment against him. This prosecution thus instantiates a prototype of a racialized bias which is, albeit, also entailed in 'cultural *defenses*'—including those in which a male minority defendant tries to benefit from patriarchal discourses. Representing such defendants as patriarchs within a framework that renders patriarchy as 'foreign' to U.S. shores forms but the other side of the coin of the racist stigmatization entailed in some prosecution strategies, such as that against Singh—since even a representation of this kind which *legitimizes* the defendant's actions stigmatizes him as a sexist *Other.* (A stigmatization which, as stated above, is colluded in by those contributors to the debate who have reproduced the representation of the defendants concerned as being culturally Other in virtue of their patriarchal stance.) This similarity will be apparent from the third case study, *State vs. Cao*, who was tried in Alabama in 1986—a relatively classic instance of a *sexist* 'cultural defense', except that the woman blamed for the male defendant's violence here was not herself the crime victim; instead, the couple's children had been killed.[12]

I will contrast this briefer, comparative case study with the 1990 California trial *People vs. Shen*, involving a 'cultural defense' on behalf of a *woman* defendant charged with killing her child.[13] Here, too, colonialist Othering was highly salient—this time, in the shape of the figure of the Oppressed Third World Woman constructed in opposition to the agency attributed to 'American women'. (All three accused—first-generation migrants in each case—were constructed as differing culturally from Western society.) The main point of my comparison between these two cases is, however, to show that 'cultural evidence' is not framed in patriarchal terms merely in trials where a male defendant seeks to benefit from 'cultural evidence'. On the contrary, I will argue that in *People vs. Anne Shen*, the 'cultural evidence' presented assumed relevance to the trial at least in part in virtue of a patriarchal normative economy '*native*' to the U.S. This is the case even though the 'cultural evidence' involved was not obviously untrue—rather, its representation by a whole battery of 'experts' was shaped by a patriarchal *normative frame*, which also directed the very selection of cultural 'facts'. Moreover, the qualifications and the diverse perspectives provided by the 'experts'—several of whom were themselves first-generation immigrants from the region in question—failed to undo the uniform figure of a (more) gender-egalitarian, implicitly superior West in terms of which all of them related 'the facts'. The overdetermination of the 'evidence' as to culture by U.S. patriarchal discourse will become even more apparent through the comparison with the trial of *State vs. Cao*, the case involving a *male* killer of his offspring—in which seemingly similar 'cultural evidence' was articulated in normatively very different, gendered terms that, likewise, catered to U.S. patriarchal discourse. Taken together, the three case studies (presented in Chapters 2 through 4) demonstrate that colonial discourse and patriarchal discourse—like all discourses of the social—operate in terms of the normative inflection (and a corresponding selection and rendering) of 'facts', even where there is no indication that their representation is empirically distorting. They will thus provide firm grounds for my argument against treating 'cultural evidence' as just that: evidence, or potentially unmediated information. An argument I shall return to at a more theoretical level in Chapter 5, which concludes the present Part (IV).

2 Cultural Profiling

The *Patriarchal Other*— First Case Study

In *People vs. Lopez and Singh*, two defendants were tried jointly for the murder of Sardeep Johl.[1] Defendant Malkit Singh, who will be in focus here, was accused of having hired Samuel Lopez, the other defendant, to kill Johl. The defendants disputed all involvement in that deed. 'Culture' was invoked by the prosecution to prove that Singh had acted as charged. That is, unlike in those 'cultural defense' cases most discussed in the literature, 'culture' was here used, not merely to *explain* a behavior that went undisputed (i.e. with reference to state of mind), but in fact to prove that the defendant had engaged in the criminalized conduct, in the first place. This resulted in a construction of culture in the most essentialist and determinist form, as a means of imputing 'predictive' value to defendant Singh's ethnicity. The jury followed the prosecution's request and convicted the defendant of first-degree murder with an attendant special circumstance.[2] On appeal the conviction was affirmed up to the level of the U.S. Supreme Court, which denied the defendant's petition for a writ of *certiorari*.[3] The appellate defense maintained that the prosecution's discourse had denied the defendant his constitutional right to due process.[4] Thus the state's highly racialized discourse was given the implicit sanction of the highest U.S. court.

Singh was identified at trial as a Sikh—a religious and cultural affiliation associated with the Punjab state in India. He was a first-generation migrant to California. The state's theory of the case was as follows: Sardeep Johl, the murder victim, had divorced Malkit Singh's sister years before he was killed. According to the prosecution, women divorced against their will in Sikh culture are considered "damaged goods" difficult to remarry, and a financial "burden on the family".[5] This will cause a loss of face to the entire family.[6] The extended family of the woman will pressurize the husband to maintain the marriage—violently, should other means fail.[7] That was what had allegedly occurred in this case. According to the prosecution, it had occurred in this instance years after the divorce took place because, just before the murder, Johl had made a trip to India and was suspected by his ex-wife's family to have been looking for a new wife there—something allegedly felt to be an additional insult.[8] Malkit Singh was argued to have been at the head of the family conspiracy against the victim, and to have arranged the murder for hire, based upon individualized evidence as well as the 'cultural evidence' that he was the divorced woman's brother—presumably, the oldest brother.[9] The 'cultural evidence' further established that the Sikh family is male-dominated, and that decisions and actions on behalf of the family tend to be taken by elder males.[10] The state made much of the fact that this 'evidence' as to 'Sikh culture in general' was consistent with the individualized evidence in the case.

As far as defendant Singh was concerned, this evidence consisted mainly in the following: When questioned by the police, the defendant had at first denied having recently been in contact with his later co-defendant—a demonstrable lie.[11] There was evidence that members of the Singh family had tried to convince Sardeep Johl not to divorce,[12] and had tried to pressurize him back into the relationship: various arguable threats had been uttered against both Johl and his then girlfriend by different members of the extended family.[13] One witness testified that, shortly before Johl was murdered, Malkit Singh had uttered a death threat against him.[14] Moreover, the prosecution offered into evidence phone records according to which phone calls (repeated and of short duration) had been placed from Singh's home and place of work to members of his family, the victim, and to the second defendant (as well as to one of his alleged accomplices, who was not a defendant in this trial[15]) shortly before and after the murder, but not immediately preceding or following it.[16] In addition, one call had been placed from the victim's apartment (who at the time had been at the airport returning from India) to the home of defendant Singh shortly before the murder—even though Johl had not been in sociable contact with Singh at the time.[17] The state emphasized the consistency between the phone records and what its 'cultural theory' stated about the role of (elder) male family members. Finally, an informant to police who had shared a cell with Singh in jail testified that the latter had confessed to him having planned and paid for the murder.[18]

As we shall see, the motif of the Patriarchal Other Culture in this trial formed but one element of an overarching theme familiar from colonial discourse: the 'evidence' was being framed by an opposition between 'American' individual liberty and the supposedly illiberal, oppressive, and coercive character of Sikh culture. Thus the extended family as a whole (rather than merely the men dominating it) was constructed as a major agent oppressive of individual liberty, based upon its role in arranging marriages and in policing their maintenance. Western marriage was implicitly rendered as being devoid of coercive or "unfree" aspects in contrast with arranged marriage. Moreover, the prosecution constructed Sikh culture as being prone to violence in general.[19] As further elements contributing to the overarching opposition between 'American' liberalism and 'Sikh' illiberalism—identities that were constructed as mutually exclusive, such that Sikh Americans were being excluded from the definition of 'the American'—the motif of Patriarchal Other Cultures was invoked in part in the context of the Sikh notion of divorced women being considered damaged goods and a burden to their family of birth, as well as in support of the notion that males tend to dominate the activity of extended families directed at preventing a divorce or restoring a marriage.[20] Thus Sikh society was characterized overall as a patriarchal society. There was no explicit assertion that American society is not patriarchal. But as we shall see, the prosecution suggested that the invoked characteristics of Sikh society are distinctive to it. Once this idea had been questioned by the defense (including in regards to male domination in the Sikh social formation), the state sought to establish that at least women's subordination is much less pronounced in 'American' than in Sikh culture. That is, the implicit suggestion that 'America' is not patriarchal was replaced by the equally familiar, quantifying construction of its being *less* patriarchal (or, more 'modern') than its Sikh Other. A construction which (as argued in the preceding chapter) is, likewise, suited to hierarchizing the West over and above the 'rest'.

The fact that the figure of the Patriarchal Other was not as central to that hierarchy in this trial as in most others in my corpus is easily explained by the circumstance that the victim in this instance was male rather than female. Rather than a victim/defendant constellation cross-cutting sexual difference, the constellation here is male/male, with women central to the "plot" actually figuring on the side of the alleged perpetrators rather than on the victim's (chiefly, the defendant's sister). It thus would have been inconvenient to stress victimhood on the part of Othered women. Since the male victim was also a Sikh, it would have been equally inapposite to overemphasize the supposed patriarchal character of Sikh men, lest sympathy might be swayed away from the victim. (The prosecution did its best to distance Sardeep Johl from Sikh culture by constructing him as an educated man eager to assimilate to the U.S. culture that afforded him the right to liberate himself of his arranged marriage—over and against Sikhs such as the defendant who remained tradition-minded.[21]) Rather than to place gender center-stage, it made strategic sense for the state to foreground the overall coercive, oppressive character imputed to Sikh culture, and thus, its depriving the victim of his liberty as an individual.

Unlike in the 'cultural defense' cases discussed in the literature concerned with that subject, in which academic scholars deliver the 'cultural evidence' as expert witnesses, in *People vs. Lopez and Singh* that 'evidence' came in through a number of individuals constructed as experts on the basis of being Sikhs. (All of them testified for the prosecution; some under subpoena.[22]) Four of these witnesses were personally involved in the case: the victim's brother, mother and father as well as an acquaintance of both the victim and his ex-wife (defendant Singh's sister). They were questioned about Sikh culture without having been qualified as expert witnesses by the trial judge. The prosecution's main witness as to Sikh culture, however, was so qualified[23]—based upon his being a Sikh as well as on the fact that he was a police officer with experience in criminal cases. He had been interviewed prior to trial by both the prosecution and the defense,[24] but appears otherwise to have been uninvolved in the case. As we shall see, it is of significance that his knowledge of Sikh culture was constructed as such based upon his "identity", rather than on academic expertise. For, this will turn out to have been no less problematic a construction than the rendering of *academic* knowledge as objectively valid (contra Volpp [1994], as will be discussed in Chapter 3; see also D'hondt 2010, 72–73, 89–91) which occurs in many other cases (compare Chapter 3 for the second case study in this Part): The prosecution's way of validating the testimony of its 'cultural expert' as reliable reinforced (and in turn relied upon) an utter homogenization of Sikh culture, and an erasure of all subjectivity of perspective, interpretation, and judgment, from Sikhs' relationship to 'their culture'. With these preliminary remarks in place, let me embark upon the case study proper.

ESTABLISHING SIKH DIFFERENCE

The interplay between the 'cultural evidence' and the evidence implicating defendant Singh personally in the murder was highly suggestive. Arguably, the latter evidence would have been a sufficient basis for convicting Singh. But what made the prosecution's case look so water-tight was the match between the two types of 'evidence'. For instance, the records of telephone conversations linking Singh to the victim, the second defendant, and members of his extended family assumed the status of incriminating 'evidence' in good part because it seemed consistent with the motive supplied by the 'cultural evidence', as well as with the alleged predictability of men's role in family activities pertaining to the saving, or restoration, of a marriage. The interplay between the 'evidence' as to Sikh culture 'in general' and the evidence linking Malkit Singh directly to the murder relied upon an utter homogenization of Sikh culture, and a racialized mode of cultural determinism according to which a given Sikh person's conduct in a given situation is, in fact, "predictable"[25]—at least if he may be taken for a "traditional" Sikh[26]. Such a determinism would be unthinkable in application to 'Euro-American culture' (Volpp 2000, 96, 113). Moreover, the state constructed violence as being rooted in what it cast as a self-identical, invariant Sikh "value system", such that a violent character was imputed to Sikh culture as such, establishing Sikhs as 'predictably violent' in specific situations. This prosecution strategy effectively amounted to criminalizing Sikh culture as such. It is for this reason that that strategy may be termed 'cultural profiling', in analogy to racial profiling whereby skin color serves as a proxy for criminality (Meeks 2000).

In the following account of the state's procedure of proof, I will first focus upon how establishing Sikh culture in the terms of a criminal profile depended upon rendering it as highly specific and as maximally integrated, rather than as existing as a heterogeneous set of individualizable norms, beliefs, and practices that come in variations depending on who one talks to.[27] For, the more integrated and uniform the Sikh "value system",[28] as the prosecutor called it, the more "predictable"[29] the conduct of individual Sikh persons. Highlighting the specificity of Sikh culture also entailed setting it apart as much as possible from 'American' culture (read: Euro-America), i.e., on maximizing cultural difference. Following my account of these basic parameters of cultural essentialism in the prosecution strategy, I will focus upon how the state naturalized that essentialism through an empiricist epistemology. I will then turn to how cultural difference was constructed in terms of the hierarchical dichotomy of Sikh illiberalism vs. U.S. liberalism, and will indicate, finally, how the motif of the Patriarchal Other Culture figured as part of that dichotomy.

The extracts which follow show in what terms the prosecution established a self-identical essence for Sikh culture. The first two quotes are taken from the state's opening statement; the latter from the direct examinations of two of the state's 'cultural' witnesses:

> He [Sardeep Johl] was a Sikh by religion and by upbringing and I believe the evidence will disclose to you that the Sikh culture is a subgroup of the greater Indian culture. And the Sikhs represent a fairly small minority of the population, but they do very definitely have a very definite culture and value system.[30]

> You will hear through the testimony in this case that as a result, perhaps, of part of this peculiar value system that is unique to the Sikh culture, that not only is divorcing or casting away your spouse in fact a dangerous thing to do, but one could exacerbate that position and perhaps up the potential for drastic consequences by seeking a new spouse. It's bad enough to cast off your wife. To go out and remarry is twice the insult.[31]

Q As I understand it then there are very specific cultural traits of the Sikh people?
A Yes.
Q And those traits have come with the Sikh people that are in the United States now from Punjabi [sic] essentially in fact?
A Yes.[32]

Q There's been some testimony in this area, but let me ask you, in your opinion does the values of the Sikh community here in the United States, do they accurately reflect the values that you had learned as a Sikh growing up in India?
A I don't know about in India, you know, I just learn about what is going on in here [sic].[33]

The phrasing, "accurately reflect", is used in court to identify physical evidence that a given witness has perceived previously. That is, it suggests an absolute identity of a given physical object with itself. Thus the state not only pictured Sikh culture in terms of a uniform 'value system', but also had it that the Sikh diaspora in California exhibits no variation whatever on Sikh culture in India. In answer to the defense's insistence that many U.S. Sikhs may be 'Americanized'[34]—a strategy I will discuss extensively in Chapter 6—, the prosecution insisted that its theory of Sikh difference applied at least to 'traditional' Sikhs, in terms of which it identified Malkit Singh. (It did so in part on the grounds that Singh wore a turban[35]—something constructed by the state, in cooperation with its cultural expert witness, as a reliable sign of a "traditional" orientation in a Sikh man[36].) Here is an extract from the closing argument:

> I presume you have no questions left that being a member of the Sikh culture is different from being a member of the general population of the United States there are just certain values that are adhered to. / Did—did Mr. [Singh] fall into that, that group of Sikhs that continued to adhere to those conservative Sikh believes [sic]? Well, in his interview with the police, among other things, Mr. [Singh] said I have three sisters and I have a wife. I work two jobs, because I have to take care of the family. By clearly taking care of the extended family which includes not only your wife and sisters, especially an unmarried sister, Mr. [Singh] recognized. [sic] He—he also said we marry in our customs. It's in the culture. It's against our religion to marry outside. It doesn't sound too—too Gosh darn Americanized to me.[37]

The state thus set up an opposition between Sikh and American cultures, marking the former as Other to the U.S. So it was on the basis of a colonialist and culturally essentialist discourse that the prosecution construed Sikhs' behavior as maximally predictable in certain situations:

Q (by Mr. [counsel for the prosecution]) In terms of the scope of behavior that the spurned wife's family *might be expected* to engage in, you've indicated at a minimum, as I understand it, that going and talking with the husband would be included. Would you expect also that a husband continuing to insist upon divorce *would be expected* on many occasions to be the subject of violent revenge or retribution?

A Yes.[38]

But the state went further than this. Rather than merely predicting individual behavior from generalizations about Sikh culture, the state also pursued the inverse path—that of inferring culture from some Sikh individuals' conduct—only to infer, in turn, that Malkit Singh and his extended family, allegedly being traditional Sikhs, may have acted accordingly. This made the prosecution's 'cultural theory' circular. The state developed this approach as follows: Since Sardeep Johl had been killed years after having divorced, it sought to establish that efforts at reconciliation continue beyond divorce, or alternatively, that the ex-wife's extended family will also attempt to prevent the husband from remarrying. (The victim had been suspected by Singh's family of trying to find a new wife during the trip to India which he made just before he was murdered. He returned unmarried, however.) But the 'cultural expert', Joga Kaur, held that it is uncommon for either of this to occur—even though efforts at reconciliation continuing beyond a divorce have been known to happen, he testified.[39] Kaur was then asked by the state:

Q (by Mr. [counsel for the prosecution]) I sure apologize for asking long convoluted questions, but I'll probably continue doing it.
We were talking about how common or uncommon it is in the Sikh culture, based on your experience, for a family to make some effort to try to prevent the remarriage of a divorced Sikh male.
Do you remember that general area?
A Yes.
Q Do you have an opinion or do you have knowledge of *the* Sikh cultures [sic] and traditions *which* would explain such activity taken by a wife's family in those—on those occasions when such action is taken?
A Well, I think it's not common for the family members, again, to try and reconcile the marriage for—could be a lot of reasons, could be one of the biggest things is to keep faith within the community.
Could be, you know, a lot of other things over there that we don't see could be behind closed doors whether it's financial and other—
Q Well, let me ask you this, you indicated that one possible area of concern or one possible area of analysis would be financial. Explain the ability [sic] of the term financial to this particular question?[40]

The witness explained that, in arranged marriages, the prospective spouse's earning power is a central factor. The state then pursued this "area of analysis"[41] as follows:

Q Is it your testimony then that in the arranged marriage that the goals of the parties arranging the marriage are not necessarily just to achieve a love interest between a husband and wife?
A Not usually.
Q It goes to other things such as how much money the prospective new addition to the family might be able to bring in?
A Sure.
Q Okay. Is that a factor that plays then in [sic] the decision of a family to attempt to achieve a reconciliation where a marriage has gone awry?
A It's a possibility.

Q And when you say "a possibility", is that something that you've seen personally over the course of your years, not only of practicing Sikh faith, but also enforcing the law in [county X]?
A Yes.
Q As I understand it then the families having made a good bargain and brought a good money earner to the family feels [sic] some stake in having that person remain a part of their—
A Yes.
Q —family member's [sic] life?
A Yes.[42]

Obviously, one would be hard-pressed to find to be culturally unique having a financial stake in maintaining or seeking to restore a marriage—much as the part played by the extended family might be construed as being culturally specific. Even so, as the second-last quote above shows, the prosecution tried to "culturalize" whatever reasons the witness invoked for the allegedly rare effort on the part of a Sikh family to prevent a remarriage or restore the prior marriage. (For, as we can see in that quote, the witness basically speculated as to different possible reasons—from financial ones through to that of wanting to "keep faith within the community"[43].) Why was it important to the state to impute cultural motives to such conduct, even though the witness had described it as uncommon? In my assessment, this was in order to render more compelling the idea that the Singh family had in fact acted in accordance with the alleged cultural pattern, of exercising violence against a female family member's ex-husband should he remarry, or (alternatively) should he refuse to take back his former wife. This indeed amounted to circular reasoning. As Phillips has written of 'cultural defense' cases: "the individual is read off the culture, and the culture off the individual in turn" (2003, 13).

'EVIDENCING' CULTURE

The prosecution's procedure of proof was premised upon unexamined assumptions about 'culture' which I have demonstrated above—namely, essentialist assumptions about its being a self-identical, integrated 'system' absolutely different from other cultures. These assumptions were never exposed as assumptions. Instead, the prosecution treated 'culture' as a purely empirical matter. Its empiricist approach to 'culture' was being utterly naturalized as the self-evident way of dealing with that subject. (As we shall see, the defense and the trial judge had their own share in that naturalization.) That is, the 'evidence' elicited about Sikh culture was being treated by the state as a matter, purely, of 'facts'—as is common to the treatment of 'evidence' in the courtroom generally. Thus, in responding to the defense's argument that the logic of proof relied upon by the prosecution was racialized, the state asserted on rebuttal with reference to Sikhs:

> But Mr. [counsel for defendant] and Ms. [counsel for co-defendant] present to you the fact that these folks are nonviolent. That's just balderdash. And I ask you to believe me not because I'm the D.A., because I'm telling you, but because it's what came from the stand. It's the facts of the case.[44]

> I don't make up the facts, ladies and gentlemen, I just present them as they are gathered by the police.[45]

One source of authorizing those 'facts' as objective was the appeal to *scientific* objectivity entailed in such expressions as "predictable" and "quantifiable":

Q In general, are there certain members of the family, whether it's a bride's family or a groom's family for that matter—are there certain members of the family that you would expect to be more actively a participant in family matters such as attempting to reconcile marriage partners?
A It's—usually the parents or the close relatives, brother, sister, et cetera.
Q In determining which family members would be, within the Sikh community, would be most dominant in family matters such as the reconciliation of a marriage gone bad. Is [sic] there any gender which *predictably* is more looked upon as the responsible family member?
A Would be the male.[46]

A Well, I think it's different the fact that once it's divorce you go on your merry way, if you want to call it, whereas because of the East Indian tradition and staying within the community it's usually taken a little bit more seriously than, let's say, here in America.
Q When you say a little bit more seriously you mean a very small amount of difference, or is there an appreciable *quantifiable* difference in the level of violence that you expect in a Sikh marriage; is there an issue as opposed to a non-Sikh marriage?[47]

Note how, contrary to the state's pseudo-scientific rhetoric, some of its questions actually try to influence the testimony. Thus in the first of the above two quotes, the witness's answer to the first question is neutral as to gender. This militates against any notion of predictable gender roles, but which yet is put forth in the subsequent question.

However, the primary means of validating as objective the 'cultural testimony' for the prosecution was not its appeal to science. Rather, the prosecution primarily appealed to the *experience* of its 'culture witnesses' based upon their being Sikhs. This matched absolutely its notion of Sikhs' predictable behavior. For, it was based upon the same construction of Sikh culture as absolutely uniform, and of its subjects, as lacking heterogeneous perspectives, interpretations, and judgments as to Sikh norms and practices. Spivak has described the elimination of effects of subjectivity from the ethnological notion of the 'Native Informant' as follows:

> One hears, for example, that some of the theoretical stuff that's produced, let's say, in France, is naturally accessible to people from Africa, from India, from these so-called natural places. If one looks at the history of post-Enlightenment theory, the major problem has been the problem of autobiography: how subjective structures can, in fact, give objective truth. During these same centuries, the Native Informant, who was found in these other places, his stuff was unquestioningly treated as the objective evidence for the founding of so-called sciences like ethnography, ethno-linguistics, comparative religion, and so on. So that, once again, the theoretical problems only relate to the person who knows. The person who *knows* has all of the problems of selfhood. The person who is *known*, somehow seems not to have a problematic self. These days, it is the same kind of agenda that is at work. Only the dominant self can be problematic; the self of the Other is authentic without a problem (Spivak 1990, 66, original emphasis).

In fact, the prosecution treated its Sikh witnesses as interchangeable *exemplars* of 'their culture', rather than as subjects of it. Witness the following extract from Joga Kaur's direct examination:

Q Can you explain to the jury in your own terms perhaps generally the basic tenets of the Sikh faith, what the Sikh religion is comprised of?

A Basically to my—the way I interpret it is just—

[Counsel for defendant]: Well, I object. I don't think it's proper that we get your interpretation. If he's an expert in—as to what the traditions are he can give an objective dissertation, but he's—

The court: That's sufficient. I think that the objection is properly sustained, that it should be generally accepted beliefs within the religion.

Q (By [counsel for the prosecution] Sorry for using imprecise terminology. The Sikh values and beliefs that you and your family have followed and been raised in, based on your own personal knowledge are those the values and beliefs in cultural traditions that are common to the Sikh people *in general*?

A Yes.

Q In other words, the Sikh faith that you have been raised in and thus have personal knowledge of is that *the same* as the Sikh values and opinions in the Punjabi [sic]?

A Yes.

Q And as those values and traditions have been *transplanted* to the Sikh population in California you have continued to be conversant with those values and beliefs, because they are your own?

A Yes.

Q With that understanding then, and also if my question at any point seems to be asking for either *speculation* on your part or a personal belief that is at odds with the commonly accepted values within the Sikh population here in the United States, I would ask you at this point to be advised that my questions are intended to elicit information about the Sikh traditions and values here in California *in general* as you know them to be.

With that understanding then can you give a brief introduction to the jury as to the general tenets of the Sikh culture and faith?

[Counsel for defendant]: Well, I object, has he qualified him as an expert?

[Counsel for the prosecution]: I think that—okay. Yes, I will. I will ask the court to accept Lieutenant [Kaur] as an expert in the values and traditions of the Sikh people.[48]

The contentious assumption here is that it is, indeed, possible to make such generalizations about Sikh culture without speculating—or to characterize Sikh culture without interpreting it. If one assumes that 'Sikh culture' is not, in fact, as uniform as Singh's prosecution had it, and that its appropriations by different subjects will be at variance from each other, then it should be clear that different Sikhs' testimony will indeed produce different versions of 'Sikh culture': that experience of Sikh culture is neither uniform nor discursively unmediated. The prosecution's dichotomization between 'personal beliefs' and 'commonly accepted values' served to eliminate such heterogeneity from its notion of culture. This was, however, a notion that—while it *framed* all of the 'evidence' elicited about Sikh culture from the relevant prosecution witnesses—itself was barely examined. To just what extent 'culture' was treated as a purely empirical matter—and hence, a matter on which individual experience has absolute authority as an objective, reliable source of knowledge—is apparent from the following two quotes, which are also taken from Joga Kaur's testimony on direct examination:

Q In your experience within the Sikh community—well, how can I phrase this?

Assume for the time being that a male child is born within the Sikh community. Thereafter can you tell the ladies and gentlemen of the jury what feelings are engendered in a Sikh father? Obviously, I'm including it as a base. Every father we presume loves his children, as we presume every mother does as well.

Beyond that as a—as a matter of fact, matter of culture, can you tell the jury whether there are any special feelings that you would become familiar with concerning a father's relationship with a male child?

[Counsel for defendant]: Well, I'm going to object. I think this goes too far. This is asking him to mind read to [sic] what the culture might think in a particular situation. He—he's already testified that variables have changed, this has really gone too far, judge.

The court: Perhaps you could rephrase the question as it relates solely to the Sikh religion.

[Counsel for state]: I will, your Honor.

The court: All right.

Q (By [counsel for state]: The last question, Lieutenant [Kaur], whether there are certain feelings commonly recognized within the Sikh community by you, which pertain to the arrival of the male child, feelings common to Sikh fathers with respect to their sons, *and I'm not asking you to speculate as to any particular individual feelings*, what I'm asking you for [sic] cultural relationships with the father's relationship to the son?

A It's usually stronger than if it was a daughter.

Q And in your experience, from both being raised within the Sikh community as well as being a law enforcement officer encountered with the—with a large Sikh population, can you tell the ladies and gentlemen of the jury whether there is any *predictable* or common value in terms of a Sikh father wanting to personally maintain the presence of the son and instill in him personal values of the Sikh culture?

A If I'm reading your question, it usually as I stated, it tends to be stronger that the father usually wants to keep the child with him regardless of what the consequences or what happens, okay, during a marriage. They're usually a lot stronger towards the son than it is towards the daughter, not that it's not there either, okay.

Q Okay. I want to make sure that my question is clear to you so that the answer can be equally clear, *is this a matter of culture*?

A Yes.

Q —something you've *seen culture-wise*?

A Yes, it is.[49]

Q And with that proviso now with your knowledge and personal experience within the Sikh community—

A Yes.

Q —you've indicated that efforts to seek a reconciliation of the two parties even after a divorce has become final are not—that's not something that's unknown in your experience?

A Yes, Sir.

Q Because there are, as I understand it then, some families, some Sikh families who *for whatever reason* will continue to attempt to achieve a reconciliation of the husband and wife even after the law says they're legally no longer married?

A Yes.

Q And I think then the question that I was attempting to rephrase to you after the objection ruling, is whether the *reasons in your experience* behind a family's continuing to seek a reconciliation of the husband and wife even after a divorce are based on cultural values of the Sikh people?

A Yes.

[Counsel for defendant]: I object. I think this is beyond expertise, *the fact that he may know someone within that culture who acted in a particular way and then to speculate based on the broader traits as being the motivating force* is beyond what you can do as an expert in this area.

The court: Well, that's proper cross-examination, Mr. [counsel for defendant], but repeat the question as within the framework that I've requested, Mr. [counsel for the prosecution].[50]

At the end of the first extract, the prosecutor asks the witness whether he has *seen* that it is "a matter of culture" rather than of "particular individual feelings" if a Sikh father feels more strongly about a son than a daughter, and will attempt to keep the child with him. In other words, the matter is put as if it were a question of observation analogous to an eyewitness's perceptions. That this question is a question of *conceptualizing* culture, individual feelings, and their relationship to each other, as I would maintain, drops entirely from the picture. The tenet of a primacy of experience as a source of knowledge—the theoretical position of empiricism—is thus used as the grounds of authorizing the witness's generalizations as to the feelings of any given Sikh father about his children, and as to his "predictable" conduct in the event of a divorce. Incidentally, the testimony established that Sardeep Johl had not initially tried to obtain custody of his son.[51] In fact, there was a legal dispute between the ex-couple as to how much child support Johl was to pay to his ex-wife.[52] It was only years after the divorce, shortly before he was murdered, that he had made plans with his lawyer to press for custody.[53] Thus the testimony as to Sikh culture 'in general' was here used as a *stand-in* for individualized evidence, which failed to fit the putative cultural pattern. (This evidence was brought in to allege an additional motive for the Singh family to have the victim assassinated—even though the ex-wife's attorney disputed having had any knowledge that Johl planned to seek custody.[54])

In the second extract, the prosecutor similarly asks whether "whatever reason" that may prompt "some Sikh families" to "continue to attempt to achieve a reconciliation" even after a divorce is "based on cultural values of the Sikh people" *in the witness's experience*. Again, I would hold that it is a matter of classification, i.e. a conceptual matter, whether reasons motivating a given conduct (especially if unspecified) are constructed as a matter of culture. Indeed it is, again, a question of conceptualizing *culture* that will determine the answer. The prosecutor's question might, for instance, be viewed as tautological if *all* human conduct is taken to be enabled and constrained by cultural norms: the answer would then have to be "yes" in all conceivable cases. The state's conceptualization of culture as forming a polar opposite of individual, apparently "un-cultural" conduct or feelings (as in the previous quote) is being naturalized as inhering in 'facts' subject to the witness's experience. Again, the validating question at the beginning of the second extract appeals to "personal experience" as if 'culture' were a matter for eyewitness testimony.

The judge's objection ruling at the end of the second quote above appears to miss the point of the objection. Arguably, the latter contests the arbitrary character of the witness's response to the question of whether or not the reasons for the conduct in question are cultural. Arbitrary because the answer cannot, as I have argued, be based upon experience in a theoretically unmediated sense. This may be taken to be what the defense attorney is referring to when he alleges that the witness is being encouraged to speculate (i.e., to make interpretations rather than observations). To be sure, the defense attorney's objection is itself circumscribed by an empiricist framework that distinguishes between 'speculation/interpretation' and 'observation', as if the latter were possible, in principle, in a discursively unmediated form. (See also the defense attorney's construction of science as *more* objective or less mediated than personal experience, in the phrase "objective dissertation" in the third-last of the quotes above—to which I will return in the chapter about strategies of contesting 'cultural evidence' in court [Chapter 6].) Still, the trial judge, in overruling the objection, refers to the questioning framework he had requested earlier, namely, that the testimony be limited to matters of the witness's personal experience.[55] He thus reinstantiates the very assumption that the objection seems to me to be contesting: that the question of whether whatever reasons some Sikh families' continuing to seek a reconciliation after a divorce may be based on would be premised upon "cultural values of the Sikh people" is a matter of personal experience, rather than discourse or 'speculation'. In the first extract above, the judge similarly fails to answer to the point of the objection when he asks the prosecutor to "rephrase the question as it relates solely to the Sikh religion". The judge thus contributed substantially to the empiricism in terms of which the 'cultural evidence' in *People vs. Lopez and Singh* was framed. Given the arbitrary character of the witness's responses—both due to the suppression of the testimony's and the examination's discursive character, and to the speculative character of the generalizations entailed in the testimony—it can safely be stated that what came to figure as 'cultural evidence' in this case was highly contingent. Contingent as much upon the prosecution's rather leading style of questioning, and on the particularities of the witness's relationship to, and experiences of, 'Sikh culture', as on judicial rulings, such as those quoted above, which authorized the arbitrary results of this procedure as empirically valid, officially acceptable 'evidence' (see also Ch. 8, n. 26).

'ILLIBERALISM' AS OTHER

I will now turn to the colonialist dichotomies in terms of which 'Sikh difference' was framed, and as part of which the motif of 'Patriarchal Others' figured in the prosecution's case. We have already witnessed some instances of those dichotomies above, but here they will be in focus. I begin by assembling some of the relevant general statements about 'Sikh culture', and will then turn to specific features in terms of which its construction was supported by the state. The following extracts from the prosecution's closing argument as well as the rebuttal illustrate the normative overtones in terms of which it framed 'the evidence':

> Mr. [Singh], what about the laws in the United States? What about the laws that say when a couple are no longer compatible that it's quite simply legal and proper to accept and [sic] divorce, and that once the courts have sanctioned that divorce both parties are back to the status quo and they're both single. What a Westernization. They're living by the rules of the United States. / What you don't understand, what Mr. [Singh] did understand and wanted [Sardeep] to understand, was the laws in the United States is not what we're talking about. We're playing this game by Sikh rules and by those rules I go to your parents to get them to make you come back to [Jaswinder].[56]

> I ask you to return verdicts of guilty not because it's a punitive way to get back at the defendants. It is in fact nothing more than an indispensable civic duty that is owed to the community. To ensure that by forcing on a criminal law so that we can remain essentially a civilized society based on the law that's discussed and to return just verdicts for guilty as charged. Thank you.[57]

The second extract contains the final words of the rebuttal—i.e., the last that the state said to the jury. The association of *U.S. law* (in opposition to 'Sikh rules') with the "civilized" in these quotes to my mind does assume an ethnicizing connotation; that is, one that excludes Sikhs from "civilization". The state's rhetoric of resentment climaxed in the following statement on rebuttal:

> You don't want to know the culture involved. That by itself has been known in some instances to lead to death.[58]

While this is arguably the most overtly Othering, stigmatizing, even criminalizing statement in the trial transcript, it is important to stress that the prosecution's overt rhetorical moves of this kind merely spelled out more explicitly what would have been entailed in its procedure of proof anyhow, even in the absence of such moves. For, the very attempt to establish a 'predictability' to the conduct of Sikh persons, combined with the alleged violence that formed the substance of the conduct at issue, already entailed such Othering and criminalization.

In opposition to the violence, coerciveness, and conservatism imputed to Sikh culture, the state associated Westernization—and hence, the West/'America'—with modernity and progress:

> Q I understand your testimony to be that the newer generation of Sikhs here in the United States have tended to become more *modernized or westernized* to a greater or lesser degree; is that correct?
>
> A Yes.[59]
>
> Q In respect to one of the questions asked by Ms. [counsel for the co-defendant] you've indicated that members of the Sikh community here in the United States have *progressed somewhat towards Westernization*, I guess, would be the appropriate term, do not feel compelled to wear the traditional garb, the traditional beard, okay, et cetera, but seem to have assimilated to one degree or another into Western societies; is that correct?
>
> A Yes.
>
> Q Did I understand you correctly however that those—those members of the Sikh community who continue to wear the turban and honor the other manifestations of the traditional Sikh culture, in your opinion fall within the more *conservative* or tradition-following members of the community?[60]

Here are the normatively loaded dichotomies of conservatism vs. (an implied) liberalism, and of backward traditionalism vs. progressiveness, that are so characteristic of colonial discourse. The association of the 'American' with "freedom" is also present in the following statement from the rebuttal:

> The relationship, that divorce, is becoming less uncommon than it is in the old country, however, whereas to split up, especially where the husband says I want *freedom*, I am taking the opportunity to leave, and the wife doesn't want that, where she continues to uphold her end of this very traditional end of this marriage contract then you can expect violence. That is an insult, it's an insult to the family, it's a problem to the family, and that's exactly what we have in this situation.[61]

The construction of the U.S. as liberal and protective of individual rights was especially salient in the state's rendering of social norms against 'intermarriage' as peculiarly un-American—an utter irony considering the history of 'anti-miscegenation' laws in the U.S., and their connection to the racism reproduced in the prosecution strategy:[62]

Q I guess, what I'm saying is obviously there's no—there's no law forbidding a marriage of a woman of Sikh extraction to any other human being that she might encounter in the United States, correct?
A Yes.
Q Can you tell the ladies and gentlemen of the jury, however, whether or not there are cultural pressures upon a Sikh woman from her family members to remain within the Sikh culture and marry a man who is of the Sikh persuasion himself?
A It's the old tradition, again, going back to the old tradition that it's always—you try to stay within the Sikh religion. Whereas the new generation, I guess if you want to call them that, growing up here in America are more Americanized to the point of where they still try to stay within the East Indian division, but still have a tendency to go outside of the Sikh religion.
Q Okay. Would I be correct in assuming that perhaps the affect [sic] of Americanization or culturalization within the United States might have more profound affects [sic] on persons of the Sikh community who are the product of families that have been here longer?
A Yes.
Q In other words, second or third generation—
A Yes.
Q —something like that?[63]

> And finally, on another occasion he [Malkit Singh] said that the reason for talking to [Sardeep] and his parents is that no one would marry his sister. What do you mean no one would marry your sister? If she's—this is the United States, if she's single she's fair game. She could go out and marry anyone who takes a fancy to her. Isn't that how our society works? Quite clearly he says no one will marry my sister, and that's a big serious problem. Yes, it is. If you are adhering to strict Sikh traditions.[64]

Several other details highlighted by the state contributed to its colonialist construction of Sikh vs. American culture. One was arranged marriage. Here is an excerpt from the state's opening statement:

> You'll hear that within the Sikh culture that Mr. [Johl] was raised within perhaps the norm for marriage is arranged marriages in which the parents of the prospective bride and groom get together in advance and essentially arrange a contract of marriage. The two participants then frequently never have seen one another even until the time of the actual marriage ceremony. / You will find that quite unlike the culture in the United States, in which I presume all of us were raised, that the contract of marriage, once entered into, has significant emotional, legal, cultural, perhaps far beyond that [sic], that we're familiar with. It

> is in fact by the majority of the Sikh culture deemed to be an institution that remains intact for life and it carries with it very serious economic as well as social implications for the two participants.[65]

These statements about "Sikh" marriage are constructed in opposition to 'our' culture—an 'us' which constructs the jury in culturally homogeneous terms, and from which Sikhs are being excluded. Yet the latter part of the extract, regarding emotional, legal, cultural, social, and economic implications of the institution of marriage would be fairly uncontroversial in application to hegemonic U.S. culture. But what the prosecution seems to be implying here is that marriage is somehow handled (more) lightly in the latter culture. The terms "contract" and "institution" seem to me to invoke a notion of marriage in the U.S. as something other than that—perhaps as a matter primarily of heterosexual romance and a nuclear family built upon it. Certainly, though, a heaviness seems to be implied in the above description of marriage among Sikhs—something associable, again, with unfreedom. This holds even more for the state's construction of divorce in Sikh culture, as is clear from the following statement from the state' s opening (reproduced from above):

> You will hear through the testimony in this case that as a result, perhaps, of part of this peculiar value system that is unique to the Sikh culture, that not only is divorcing or casting away your spouse in fact a dangerous thing to do, but one could exacerbate that position and perhaps up the potential for drastic consequences by seeking a new spouse. It's bad enough to cast off your wife. To go out and remarry is twice the insult.[66]

The extended family was constructed by the state as a major coercive agent, given its role in both arranging and policing marriages:

> And for a substantial period of time, in fact a number of years following the separation and divorce I believe, the evidence will show to you that a conspiracy arose and was carried out over a substantial period of time, the goal of which conspiracy was to pressure or force Mr. [Johl] to give up his right to become and remain a single man and in fact come back to the woman [Jaswinder], to in fact reconcile at whatever cost.[67]

> Mr. [Singh]'s statements in fact described how that effort was a family wide [sic] joint effort, that the whole family was pointed in that direction to keep the pressure on [Sardeep Johl] to in fact make him come back and make good on that arranged marriage contract regardless what [sic] the laws allowed [Sardeep Johl] to do as the [sic] member of the society here in the United States.[68]

Finally, the subject of violence itself contributed heavily to establishing Sikh culture as oppressive and coercive. The prosecution did not limit itself to the particular alleged pattern of violence attendant upon divorce, but set up Sikh culture in general as especially violent as a matter of culture:

Q By virtue of your own roots within the Sikh community as well as your law enforcement experience in [county X], are you familiar with violence, the potential for violence, generally within the Sikh community based upon cultural values?
A Yes.[69]

PATRIARCHY AS OTHER

In *People vs. Lopez and Singh*, patriarchy was not explicitly constructed as being absent from hegemonic U.S. culture. Rather, it was thematized by the prosecution only with respect to Sikh culture—which arguably suggested that it is specific to the latter:

Q Is the Sikh culture a male or female dominated [sic] society, a matriarchal or patriarchal society?
A It's male dominated [sic].[70]

But when, on cross-examination, the cultural specificity of male domination was questioned—for instance, the male domination of the family—, the prosecution responded as follows:

Q (by [counsel for the prosecution]) Do you find any difference in the degree of dominance of the senior male member of the family in the Sikh culture as opposed to generally in American culture?
A Well, again, it's unwritten rule [sic] that it's more in the Sikh religion than it is in the American culture.
Q Okay.
A The father or the elder member of the family is usually, you know, or the—or the final say so [sic], I guess, in a decision making.[71]

That is, the prosecution resorted to constructing a quantitative difference between different degrees of families' male domination. A construction which, in Chapter 1, I have identified as a variation on the colonialist opposition between a gender-egalitarian West and a patriarchal 'rest' which is hardly less problematic.

Among the specific elements contributing to the construction of Sikh culture as peculiarly patriarchal was the moment of a Sikh father's stronger feelings towards a son as compared to a daughter, which I have already documented. Another was the notion of a divorced woman being a financial "burden on her family":

Q (by Mr. [counsel for the prosecution]) Let me ask you this, Lieutenant [Kaur], have you had an opportunity to, in your life, to—actually it's situations here, of situations in which there's a breakup of the marriage and the Sikh woman, the support of the Sikh woman became an issue?
A Yes.
Q And based on that experience, your own personal observations and experience, can you tell the ladies and gentlemen of the jury whether it's common in such a situation for the woman then to become the subject of support of her family; *in other words, burden on the family*?
A Yes, Sir, it has.[72]

A more central element to the construction of Sikh culture as (more) patriarchal was the notion that a divorced Sikh woman is considered "damaged goods". This element was given a distinct rhetorical inflection by the prosecutor. The first of the following quotes is taken from the direct examination of the victim's father; the second one, from the state's opening statement:

Q Can you tell me whether, unlike perhaps the situation here in the United States, a woman once married in the Sikh community who then was divorced and left by her husband, would such a woman be considered in some fashion damaged goods?
A Well, if husband and wife cannot put up together then divorces are becoming common now.
Q Okay. You might have heard that somewhere else. My question really is, within the Sikh culture and tradition, is it when a woman has been married and thereafter left by her spouse, is it common for her to be looked upon as in some fashion damaged goods or an unmarketable commodity?
A Yes.[73]

> Mr. [counsel for defendant] says, you know, life for [Jaswinder] was not going to be bad because of the divorce, she's not a tarnished woman, she lives in the community, she does live in the community. All this about a divorce being so onerous for herself, ladies and gentlemen, the D.A. made it up. Well, in the interviews with Mr. [Singh] he says my sister cannot remarry. She must marry a Sikh, because she has to marry in the culture. Sikh men won't marry, they'll go to India and get a new wife now, *meaning unused*.[74]

My sense of these extracts is that they contribute to the overall construction of Sikh society as oppressive. When the defense questioned (in its cross-examination of the expert witness Joga Kaur) whether the notion of dumped women being 'damaged goods' was inapplicable to U.S. society, the prosecution's procedure on redirect examination assumed a tone of moral indignation—as if it were indeed offensive to make that suggestion:

Q As I understand in answer to some of the questions on cross-examination, you indicated that, oh, let's see, a female family member being divorced then being considered damaged goods.
Some Americans feel the same way about their children; is that what you're testifying?
A Yes.
Q Well, do you see a difference, a very clear difference in degree as to those feelings?
A Well, I see the difference of the fact that it's—again, it's an unwritten rule over here that in the East Indian community the female is looked down upon after a divorce. Regardless of what her rank, what her financial capacity is, she's looked down upon.
Q By the community?
A By the community within that—within where she resides.
Q Okay. And in India, in the Punjabi or Punjab area of India, among the Sikh community is the looking down upon a woman who has been divorced by the community even more marked?
A It's more there than it is here, yes.
Q And would you be willing to admit that in the Sikh culture in general that it's a much stronger feeling than in the non-Sikh culture in the United States?
A Yes.[75]

This tone of moral indignation shows that the state's construction of Sikh culture as patriarchal formed one element of its stigmatizing construction as illiberal in general, and that this was a normatively loaded construction. It was loaded in a way that appropriated feminist rhetoric to the effect that gendered inequality is *oppressive*—which, in suggesting that U.S. society is at least less oppressive in this regard, was to make that rhetoric serviceable to a colonial discourse of Western superiority.

But perhaps the most central element in the prosecution's invocation of a patriarchal Sikh culture was its attempt to construct as predictable Sikh (elder) males' conduct as part of a family 'conspiracy'. We have already encountered the following quote in a different context:

Q In general, are there certain members of the family, whether it's a bride's family or a groom's family for that matter—are there certain members of the family that you would expect to be more actively a participant in family matters such as attempting to reconcile marriage partners?
A It's—usually the parents or the close relatives, brother, sister, et cetera.

Q In determining which family members would be, within the Sikh community, would be most dominant in family matters such as the reconciliation of a marriage gone bad. Is there any gender which predictably is more looked upon as the responsible family member?
A Would be the male.[76]

But the prosecution also applied its notion of a predictable gendered division of roles to the carrying out of any violent measures decided upon within the family:

Q (By [counsel for the state]) Assume hypothetically that a Sikh woman has been married and born children to her, and that the husband then seeks divorce, obtains divorce. Assume further that the Sikh seek [sic] woman opposed the breakup of the marital relationship and actively sought to have the relationship continue. And assume further then that some violence was done to the husband who caused the breakup of the relationship *as a result of the breakup of the relationship*. Do you have an opinion as to whether it would be *common or uncommon for such violence to be done by the male members of the estranged wife's family*?
[Counsel for defendant]: Objection, asked and answered at least two—at least twice.
[Counsel for state]: I don't think so.
The court: I'm not sure. I'm going to overrule the objection of [sic] the form of the question.
If you understand it, Lieutenant, you may answer.
The witness: It's not common.
Q (By [counsel for state]) Pardon me?
A It's not uncommon for the family members of the female side to take some type of action.
Q I asked this clarifying question only because in your preceding answer you said it's not common and you said it's not uncommon, not uncommon sounds like a double negative it's—I suppose I can ask it this way.
Is it common?
A It's common.[77]

Here, 'cultural profiling' comes particularly close to racial profiling in that it is applied to males—i.e., in that gender forms part of the "criminal profile" (Gaynes 1993): In effect, ethnicity and gender (along with age) combine as a major basis of implicating the defendant in a crime. The profile established here consists, precisely, in the figure of a violent Patriarchal Other—albeit in an unusual variant in this case, for the violence is more commonly constructed as being directed at women. But for this difference, *People vs. Lopez and Singh* illustrates in hypostatized form what is, however, likewise at stake in 'cultural defense' cases: the stigmatizing, even criminalizing effect of picturing men as patriarchal and violent based upon 'their culture'. This effect, which has been ignored by 'feminist' critics of sexist 'cultural defenses', such as Coleman (1996) and Okin (1999), is all the more pronounced in trials such as the one examined here, in which 'culture' and 'gender' are deployed as a means of implicating a defendant in a crime. That, in a case such as this, the trial rhetoric is seemingly critical of patriarchal social relations, rather than sexist, takes away nothing from its colonialist character. In dissimulating the patriarchal character of U.S. society, such rhetoric is also contrary to the goals of feminism, rather than supportive of it. Commentators such as Coleman and Okin have replicated this anti-feminist effect in making arguments that mimic a rhetoric such as that used by Singh's prosecutor (compare Chapter 1). The selective focus of the debate about the 'cultural defense' upon culture-based (ethnicizing) defenses, which has systematically shielded from view the occurrence of culture-based prosecutions, has contributed further to shielding from view the racialized character of the discourse of Patriarchal Other Cultures. Framing the debate in terms of the question of "whether to permit criminal defendants to introduce cultural evidence" (Maguigan 1995, 36) has made it possible to picture the matter as privileging minority defendants over and above others, read: so-called 'whites'.

In the above account, I have emphasized the role of empiricism in naturalizing the normative, devaluing character of the prosecution's discourse as an inferiority inhering in Sikh culture—not just in virtue of that discourse's overtly rhetorical aspect but also of its seemingly more value-neutral function of 'predicting' Sikhs' conduct. The latter aspect of the prosecution's discourse is, likewise, hierarchizing in that the determinism entailed in it reduces Sikhs to something less than human subjects, in a way that would be unthinkable in application to so-called 'whites' collectively. In *People vs. Lopez and Singh*, it is obvious enough that the value-laden character of the prosecution strategy is racist no matter whether the theory of the individual case is correct or not—and even assuming that its notion of Sikhs' predictability were true. This is due to the systematic difference that the state's procedure of proof makes between Sikhs and 'non-Sikhs', and to the hierarchizing character of that difference. While it is tempting to insist that it is empirically false to treat human conduct as predictable in the manner that Singh's prosecution did for Sikhs specifically, ascertaining the "ideologically" problematic character of its discourse, as I have done above, is not dependent upon that step. On the contrary, *People vs. Lopez and Singh* is a case illustrative of the service that treating culture as a matter of potentially unmediated 'facts' does to imperialist and racist discourse in virtue of ontologizing the inferiorizing and exclusionary Otherness that they produce, as if it inhered in the 'culture' so constructed (compare Part II). I thus consider it politically more wise not to take sides as to the question of whether the representations of 'culture' at trial are true or not (see also Chapter 5). In my next case study, of the trial *People vs. Anne Shen*—the subject of the following chapter—, it will be all the more apparent that the possible truth of the 'cultural evidence' presented did nothing to undermine the colonial and patriarchal effects of the discursive frame in terms of which it was rendered. On the contrary, here too, empiricism functioned such as to reify those effects as a matter of objective 'evidence'—this time, in the guise of science rather than primarily of personal experience. The following chapter therefore will provide further grounds to the case for a discourse-theoretical approach to 'cultural information' in criminal courts which I am trying to make in the present Part.

3 'Cultural Defense' I

The *Oppressed Third World Woman*—Second Case Study

As is common in 'cultural defenses', culture in *People vs. Shen* was invoked so as to explain a conduct that was undisputed as such: Shen admitted to having killed her eight-year-old son.[1] What was contested at trial was her mental state at the time of the crime: the defense maintained that she had killed him in 'the heat of passion', which would have formed grounds for a verdict of manslaughter, while the prosecution insisted that the act had been committed 'with malice aforethought', meaning a verdict of second-degree murder.[2] The jury followed the prosecution's argument in Anne Shen's first trial, on which this case study is based.[3]

Significantly, 'culture' as presented at trial was arguably irrelevant, partially if not entirely, to the said legal question—at least in terms of how that question was framed by the jury instructions in the first trial. My assessment here is contrary to the appellate opinion in this case: on appeal it was held that at the defendant's retrial, which was ordered on other grounds, the trial court could not refuse (as had the trial judge during Shen's first trial) to instruct the jury that Shen's cultural background may be considered by it in assessing the question of her state of mind.[4] 'Evidence' as to her cultural background had been offered in the first trial in support of the defense's theory that she had committed the killing as part of a failed suicide attempt, and out of a benevolent motivation.[5] The prosecution, by contrast, maintained that the suicide attempt had been faked, and that Shen had killed her son so as to get revenge against his father.[6] (Both theories of the case were heavily gendered and steeped in patriarchal norms, as we shall see in this chapter and in Chapter 6, respectively.) The Court of Appeal of California held that Shen's contested motivation was legally relevant (see also Ch. 4, n. 13). It did so on the grounds of case law regarding heat of passion—a finding of which legally negates malice aforethought and, therefore, reduces second-degree murder to manslaughter[7]—according to which:

> the fundamental of the inquiry is whether or not the defendant's reason was, at the time of his act, so disturbed or obscured by some passion not necessarily fear *and never, of course, the passion of revenge* to such

> an extent as would render ordinary men of average disposition liable to act rashly or without due deliberation and reflection, and from this passion rather than from judgment.[8]

Contrary to that position, one instruction received by the jury in the first trial reads:

> Neither fear, *revenge*, nor the emotion induced by and accompanying or following an intent to commit a felony, nor any or all of these emotional states, in and of themselves, constitute the heat of passion referred to in the law of manslaughter. *Any or all of such emotions may be involved in a heat of passion* that causes judgment to give way to impulse and rashness. Also one or more of them may exist in the mind of a person who acts deliberately and from choice, whether such choice is reasonable or unreasonable.[9]

That is, revenge as a motive—according to how the jury was instructed to reach a verdict, whether or not that instruction formed proper law—would not have negated the defense's position that the killing was committed in the heat of passion. (Indeed, the prosecution made just that argument in its closing statement—despite its own vigorous contestation of the defendant's motivation at trial.[10]) In my view, the only possible conclusion is that Shen's motive in committing the killing was irrelevant to the legal question of her state of mind at the time of the crime as that question was defined at trial—much as her alleged motive formed a core issue of the 'evidence' offered by both the defense and the prosecution. Since, as we shall see, the defense's 'cultural evidence' pertained very largely to her *motive* in killing her son,[11] I agree with the prosecution's position (as articulated in its closing argument) that that 'evidence' had no bearing upon her state of mind in legal terms as defined at trial—at least to the extent that it pertained to the moral quality of her motive in committing the killing, rather than to the legally mandated questions.[12] This would mean that the 'cultural evidence' was relevant in great part to the construction of Anne Shen as a moral subject rather than legally—a construction that could easily affect the verdict, which jurors need not ordinarily account for in public. Namely, the 'cultural evidence' lacked legal relevance to the precise extent that the defense deployed it as a means of *distancing Shen from the notion of a 'bad mother'* by constructing her motive as having been benevolent towards her son, as we shall see—when, legally speaking, it could easily have conceded revenge as one possible motive fully consistent with the manslaughter verdict it was requesting from the jury. But this possibility would have required the defense to draw upon *feminist* discourse in "rehabilitating" its client in a more unapologetic manner critical of patriarchal discourse. Instead, as I shall demonstrate in this chapter, the defense allowed itself to be placed on the defensive vis-à-vis that discourse; specifically, the norm of maternal devotion and self-sacrifice, which placed the accused under threat of being condemned by the jury as the ultimate traitor to that norm. That possibility—of jury nullification—is one which attorneys always need to reckon with, *whether or not* 'the evidence' admitted can be construed as being legally relevant: The struggle to win the consent of the jury takes place in part on the terrain of discursive struggles for hegemony; it is a struggle to capture jurors' imagination, to interpellate them in terms of one discourse rather than another (compare Part II)—as a means to the end of achieving a favorable verdict.

But whether or not one agrees with the above analysis, according to which the 'cultural evidence' as to motive admitted in this trial was irrelevant in terms of the version of the law treated as valid by those involved; namely, in that—according to that version—the moral quality of Shen's motive did not "[have] any tendency to make the existence of any fact that is of consequence to the determination of the action more probable or less probable than it would be without the evidence" (to quote the definition of "relevant evidence" provided by Federal Rule of Evidence 401 [Fed. Rules Evid. 401]) (compare n. 12, this Ch.): Even if one reaches the contrary conclusion that the 'cultural evidence' as to motive *was* defined as being legally relevant by the jury instructions provided at trial, it still remains the case that the jury's task would have been difficult, if not impossible, to disentangle from gendered discourse. For, each party to the trial based its interpretation of the motive for the homicide in a construction of Shen's moral/psychological *character*, overall—a notion of 'character' that cannot but be highly gender-connoted in a case of a woman accused of having killed her own child: Whether the jury chose to believe that the defendant had acted out of benevolence or on a motive of revenge was in significant part a question of whether those concerned would find her more credibly represented in terms of the notion of a 'good mother' (defense) or that of a 'bad' one (prosecution). That is to say, the 'common sense' that jurors needed to draw upon in answering the central questions to be posed according to the instructions they received is an inherently gendered one—all the more so in a case as drenched in a specifically gendered normative significance as this one. But even generally speaking, none of us can be certain that our determination of credibility, and of the likelihood with which a given subject would feel and act in one way or another, is not impinged upon by gendered distinctions between different 'types' of human subject ('men' vs. 'women'; 'types of woman', etc.)—distinctions which, as argued in Part II, are charged with unegalitarian, patriarchal norms. In the case at hand, the most salient norm would be the one that continues to define women more essentially in terms of motherhood than it does men in terms of fatherhood, and to hold female parents to the relevant moral expectations more strictly. In this chapter and in the following one, I shall demonstrate just how heavily the defense's argumentative strategy, and its construction of Anne Shen as a subject, was implicated in patriarchal discourse (see also Chapter 6 on the prosecution's counter-strategy). As we shall see, it is against the backdrop of this fact that the 'cultural evidence' as constituted, and contested, in the trial at hand, assumed *discursive* relevance—whether or not it was also legally relevant. In what follows, I shall analyze the discursive function of the gendered 'cultural evidence' presented by the defense.

Let me now summarize this 'evidence'. 'Culture' played into the defense's theory of the case in three overall respects. Firstly, it was argued that in killing her son and allegedly attempting suicide, Shen had acted in accordance with a practice known in Eastern Asia, of parent-child suicide. This practice was allegedly mandated in the event of a mother's suicide, especially if the child might be neglected in the future when left behind.[13] The defendant had allegedly believed that, upon death, she and her son would enter another world together, in which she had faith on religious grounds.[14]

This theory of the killing was placed under strain, however, in virtue of the fact that Shen had barely fulfilled the role of a mother during the boy's lifetime, as the prosecution pointed out. Instead, she had left Ed seventy days after his birth to grow up with his father in California, while she had returned to live in Macau—her place of residence before she had come to stay with the father, Larry, and had fallen pregnant as well as given birth.[15] She had maintained contact with Larry, but had not sent any cards or gifts to Ed during most of the period of separation.[16] She had seen her son again only twice: once when he was taken to visit Anne by Larry in 1988, one year before his death, and once in the U.S. on the occasion when Shen had killed him.[17] This was the case even though Shen had visited the United States on another occasion, without going to see the boy.[18]

'Chinese culture' was invoked, too, to explain this evidentiary situation. This was where the notion of Oppressed Third World Women came in, in the shape of the stereotype of submissive Chinese women. I will argue later on how it was that this 'evidence' was, in fact, stereotyped. For there was no lack of an individualization of the person Anne Shen: her biography was detailed extensively from the defense's perspective. Shen's first husband-to-be had died before the marriage.[19] Her first actual marriage had resulted in a divorce.[20] This had caused her humiliation because being divorced amounts to a stigma in Chinese culture, the defense maintained.[21] After Shen had met Larry, who was married to an allegedly infertile woman, he eventually invited her to the U.S. on the promise of divorcing his wife and marrying Anne.[22] But he failed, for ten years to come, to make good on that promise. Instead, he kept Shen as a lover in a separate apartment without his wife's knowledge.[23] At trial, Larry Shen maintained that he had merely wished to obtain a child from Anne due to his wife's infertility.[24] According to the defense, the defendant returned to live in Macau without her son because illegitimacy forms an unbearable stigma to mother and child in Chinese culture.[25] So either staying unmarried in the U.S. as a mother to Ed, or taking him to Macau would have meant a loss of face to them both. (The defendant did not even tell her own daughter, a child from her first marriage, of Ed's existence.[26]) Shen testified that she had believed that her son would be fine growing up with Larry and his wife.[27] She maintained no contact with Ed, the defense held, because she thought this might upset his normal life with what she understood were his legal parents.[28]

During her second visit to the United States following her original separation from Ed, however, she visited Larry and Ed both because she missed the latter, and because his grandmother (Larry's mother) was ill and expected to die.[29] Anne Shen testified that, on the occasion of that visit, the grandmother had told her that Larry was treating Ed badly and that Anne had better take care of the boy herself.[30] Shen also testified to having once seen Larry slap Ed.[31] During this visit to the United States, Larry finally married Anne.[32] (He had divorced nine years earlier but had not let her know.[33]) She was aware that this could have been due to the fact that she had pretended to him to be rich.[34] (She had done so at an earlier point in order to get Larry to bring Ed to Macau to see her, as she was missing him badly.[35]) When she asked Larry about this, he responded that she had no right to speak until she produced the money.[36] Distraught at having been used by her husband, Shen decided to return to Macau.[37] However, on the night of the killing—according to her testimony—Ed told her that his Dad had a girlfriend, who owned the house in which they were staying, and that he was treating Ed badly.[38] According to the defense, it was disappointment and worry at her son's treatment by his father that caused her to kill him and to try to take her own life.[39] According to the prosecution, it was jealousy and the desire to get back at Larry Shen that had motivated the act.[40] As stated above (see also n. 12, this Ch.), this dispute was irrelevant to the legal finding as to whether the crime was committed in the heat of passion (negating malice aforethought and, therefore, a verdict of murder). For, considering CALJIC 8.44 received by the jury during the defendant's first trial together with 'the evidence' presented there, both a motive of revenge, and one of benevolence (or some mix of the two), were compatible with a finding of *either* heat of passion *or* malice aforethought.

'Culture' figured in a few other respects in the defense's 'evidence' in ways pertinent to the motif of Patriarchal Other Cultures. The fact that Anne Shen had not ever asked Larry to make good on his promise of marriage, but instead had merely waited for years for this to occur, was explained in terms of her socialized subservience qua traditional Chinese woman.[41] So was the fact that she obeyed Larry's command, shortly before the killing, not to speak until she had produced the money she had pretended to him to possess.[42] The defense also held that Shen, qua traditional Chinese woman, had had no experience in challenging a man's will, and therefore would not even have thought of pressing for custody—which in China had traditionally remained with the man in the event of a divorce. Lastly, the suicide attempt itself was explained in terms of cultural identity: the defense argued that, traditionally, suicide had been the only way out of an intolerable situation for many Chinese women.[43]

There was, finally, a third 'cultural' factor to Shen's defense: the latter held that Chinese mothers maintain closer physical contact with their children than Western mothers, and feel so closely connected to them that they assume that they know what their children are thinking.[44] The relevance of this moment of the 'cultural evidence' was not explained, but may be interpreted to have been intended to suggest that the defendant had thought that she knew that Ed wanted to die with her.[45] But, arguably, this piece of 'evidence' also served as an essentialist stand-in, at the level of 'culture in general', for the lack of evidence as to Shen's bond with her son individually. It served, in other words, to suggest that Anne Shen was a devoted mother in virtue of being a Chinese woman.

Before further analyzing the discursive function of the above aspects of Shen's 'cultural defense', and documenting its form, let me summarize how the relevant 'evidence' was brought in. At this level, *People vs. Shen* complements the trial in the case *People vs. Lopez and Singh*, discussed above. Whereas in the latter trial, the witnesses as to 'culture' were treated as being qualified primarily on the grounds of sharing the relevant cultural identity, in Shen's trial, four expert witnesses were offered on grounds of their academic expertise. Two of them were also held to share culturally similar roots to the defendant's. One was a psychiatrist with publication experience in transcultural psychiatry; he was a Taiwanese migrant to the U.S.[46] One was a clinical psychologist with a specialty in "ethnic minority mental health issues"; he was a first-generation Chinese American man originally from Hong Kong.[47] These two witnesses had interviewed the defendant; one of them had also conducted psychological tests upon her.[48] A third 'expert' was a U.S. clinical psychologist with expertise in cross-cultural psychology, who had reviewed materials relating to Anne Shen and, like the first two experts, had written a report for the defense.[49] The final expert witness as to 'culture' was a U.S. anthropologist with extensive research experience in Hong Kong and mainland China (where the defendant had grown up[50]), albeit in matters not related to gender.[51] He merely testified in relation to Chinese culture in general, without specific reference to the defendant. The racial classification of the expert witnesses is unknown to me. At least the first three of these 'experts' were paid by the defense;[52] apparently none testified under subpoena.

As I have alluded, in my assessment the 'cultural evidence' offered in *People vs. Shen* was articulated in such a way as to satisfy a patriarchal norm salient, not (merely) in distant China, but in the U.S. courtroom that was the setting of the invocation of that 'evidence'. Shen, qua killer of her own child, was at risk of being judged as a quintessential traitor to the norm of motherly duty—a gendered assessment that could easily have influenced the verdict, for which jurors need not ordinarily account except amongst themselves. In order to appreciate this discursive function of the 'cultural evidence', it is essential not to naturalize the notions of a good (devoted) vs. bad (neglectful) mother, which is underpinned by the patriarchal norm according to which a mother's first duty is to her child. It is essential to do so neither in the context of Chinese nor of American culture. That is, it is important not to reify the 'cultural evidence' as a matter of 'facts' about 'another culture', *or* about the person Anne Shen: "Shen" should be approached as a discursive construction within a defense strategy—or, to appropriate Spivak's words: as "an inaccessible blankness circumscribed by an interpretable text" (1986, 264). For, as soon as we consider the 'evidence' presented as a matter of mere facts, we cannot appreciate its rhetorical functionality within discourses such as that of patriarchy. In this regard I differ from Volpp's (1994; 1996) approach to the case, and to similar cases such as that of Susan Smith (see below). Volpp treats these cases in terms of facts that actually motivated these defendants' conduct, rather than as discursive constructions. As I will argue later on, Volpp's assessment of these cases risks reifying patriarchal norms underpinning the construction of the 'cultural evidence'. In what follows, I will look, instead, at what makes the 'evidence' presented about 'China'—which is necessarily selected from a pool of possible 'information', and is arranged in one discursive form to the exclusion of other possible ones—*appealing* from the point of view of a U.S. normative economy.

From this perspective, the claim that Shen had killed her son with a benevolent motivation was directed at distancing her 'character' as much as possible from the notion of the 'bad mother' and to approximate it as closely as possible to that of the 'good mother' instead. The second main strand of the 'cultural evidence'—that pertaining to her subordination in Chinese culture—was oriented to the same goal. For, it was meant to excuse the fact that Anne Shen had not fulfilled the maternal role during her son's lifetime. With the help of the stereotype of the subservient Chinese woman who had ever suffered from the separation from her son, but had felt powerless to end it, the defendant could be pictured as a devoted mother at least 'on the inside'. From this perspective, what motivated the defense's resort to the notion of the Oppressed Third World Woman was a patriarchal norm salient in the courtroom itself—i.e., in hegemonic U.S. culture. In tension with this fact, patriarchy in this trial, too, was constructed largely as being particular to the Other culture, rather than as pertaining in specific forms in the West as well. That is, what I am arguing was a patriarchal mode of construction of Anne Shen by the defense (including, in part, by herself) was disavowed as such—even as that disavowal was, at the same time, being subverted by the said tension. It was primarily the disavowal of the patriarchal character of U.S. society that rendered the defendant's representation stereotyped, inserting it into the colonialist dichotomy between an egalitarian West and a despotic East. That is, the stereotyped character of this 'cultural defense' derived, not necessarily from a misrepresentation of 'facts' about 'China' or Macau (I have not tried to verify these independently), but from the hierarchizing co-construction of an implicitly superior West that went with their representation. This relational character of constructions of an 'other' becomes invisible once we focus upon the correctness vs. distortion of the 'facts' presented about his/her reality.

In what follows, I will first focus upon the appeal to the patriarchal norm of motherly duty entailed in the case made by the defense, in the shape of its construction of Shen's motivation for the killing as benevolent towards her son. I will then briefly discuss that strand of the 'evidence' concerned with Chinese women as mothers, which appealed to the same norm as prevalent in the U.S. Next, I turn to the defendant's construction as subservient based upon her cultural identity, and to the notion of the Patriarchal Other in terms of which it was rendered. Thereafter, I will argue that the defense's representation of Anne Shen highlighted benevolence and subservience over and above certain moments in her biography as constructed at trial that may be interpreted in terms of resistance and self-affirmative behavior. I take this as an additional indicator that the defense took shape under a gendered normative pressure that militated against (or at least rendered more difficult) offering such an interpretation of her behavior—which would have been more consonant with a feminist perspective upon the defendant. Finally, I elucidate some of the means by which the defense attorney and his 'cultural' expert witnesses validated the knowledge promulgated by them as authoritative. This occurred by way of appeal to their academic expertise about 'Chinese culture' in a way that may be characterized as empiricist, in that the discursive, perspectival, and normative character of such expertise was largely rendered invisible.

RECODING THE KILLING

In the U.S., killing another person is coded as an act of aggression. For a mother to kill her child is potentially considered the ultimate treason to the norm of motherly duty, that is, to the norm that a mother should place her child's interests over and above her own. (I will be discussing other possible interpretations of maternal infanticide in Chapter 4.) One defense expert actually invoked that punitive stance towards 'infanticidal' mothers in describing how Anne Shen was treated in jail by fellow inmates:

Q Yes. And with respect to the time when she was first taken to [town X] General Hospital the day after [Ed] died and the time you saw her in October, had she attempted suicide again?

A Yes.

Q Where?

A In the jail. She was beaten up, quote—I heard that from the ward attendant that some of the prisoner [sic] jump [sic] on her to beat her up. So for her own safety, she was isolated to seclusion room.

Q Yes.

A And if I may, one information in my own personal experience, I had the privilege to defend another Japanese woman by the name of Kimura who drowned herself with her two children, attempting group suicide. Same thing with [Anne]'s case. And at that time when Mrs. Kimura was put into the jail in Los Angeles, some of the prisoners say, "I don't feel guilty to kill seven people or my cousin, but I would never kill my daughter."

That was absolutely terrible and the most serious thing in their mentality.

So *this kind of woman* is considered to be—I mean *the woman who kill own children* [sic] *would be considered to be the most sinful person even by the standard of the prisoner.*

So both of them were jumped up by these people, and I could understand the situation.[53]

The 'cultural evidence' helped recode the killing committed by Anne Shen as the opposite of a "bad mother's" act. It helped reframe it as the act of a benevolent, devoted mother, rather than that of "the most sinful person". Thus, two defense 'experts' described her motivation as follows:

Q Well, I'm interested in knowing, Doctor: What was the significance of the depression in [Anne]'s thought processes in the decision to strangle [Ed]?

A It was very—in my expertise as a transcultural psychiatry, in my familiarity, with my familiarity with the Chinese cultural translate [sic] and from the information interview I obtained from [Anne], she thought she was doing that out from the mother's love, mother's responsibility to bring a child together with her when she realized that there was no hope for her or a way for her to survive in this country or on this earth.

Q Well, are you telling us that the death of [Ed] was her act of love?

A Yes. It's a mother's altruism. This may be very difficult for the Westerner to understand because I have dealt with many other so-called children who are sent to me from the children bureau [sic]. Children can be easily taken away from the mother in our agencies' mind [sic]. Social worker, when they dicovered [sic] child abuse case or whatever case, children can be easily taken away from the parents.

But in the Asian culture when the mother commits suicide and leave [sic] the children alone, usually they'll be considered to be a totally irresponsible behavior, and the mother will usually worry what would happen if she died, "Who is going to take care of the children? Anybody can supply the real love that mother could provide," so and so.[54]

A . . .

And then in terms of what are some of the alternatives then for her. In—perhaps in this country, even with a traditional woman may, may see other options [sic]. But in her culture, in her own mind, there are no other options but to, for her at that time, but to kill herself and take the son along with her, so that they could sort of step over to the next world *where she could devote herself, all of herself to the caring of the son*, caring of [Ed].

Q Was that the motive for killing him?
A Motive, if you will, yes.
Q What was her purpose?
A Her purpose is to, is that she, is, in many ways is, is a benevolent one. It's a positive one where she believed—and this, this sounds sort of implausible to some, some of us whose, who are raised in another culture. That what she believed was that she was not exactly killing him but, through death, both of them would be reunited in the next world where she could provide the kind of caring that [Ed] did not get in this world.[55]

Much as these 'experts' invoke the cultural difference of Shen's act, the difference alleged is designed to appeal, precisely, to the U.S. norm of the devoted mother—in accordance with the argument by Chiu (1994) and others, discussed in Chapter 1, that 'cultural defenses' are successful specifically when the supposedly culturally 'different' norms invoked resonate with gendered norms of the dominant culture. One of the defense witnesses just quoted went so far as to construct the suicide attempt itself as having occurred for Ed's sake—that is, as a mother's ultimate self-sacrifice:

Q I see. Well, what was [Anne] telling you about her thoughts of the other world at that time?
A She told me wondering that is a heaven, paradise. She thought *the only way* to find out a way out is to bring this [Ed] [sic] to go together so the mother and son can finally live together in the other heaven, other world if that cannot be done on this realistic earth.[56]

A . . . She would feel that she couldn't really do the duty to the son, so *the only way to fulfill her duty* when she realized her son was neglected and not to be cared by anybody in the future, she thought the way to go is to the heaven.[57]

One might wonder how it is that patriarchy could have been represented as essentially Other to U.S. society by the defense given its own strong appeal to a patriarchal norm domestic to that society. The answer is that maternal duty, and Shen's alleged desire to fulfill it, were not coded as being related to patriarchy. Rather than in terms of a cultural norm, the defense seemed to treat that duty in universalist, even naturalizing terms—as an "objective" duty and a natural desire in a mother. Thus:

Q Well, let's back up, then, Doctor, to the night that [Ed] died.
Based upon the information you have accumulated in this case from your history, from [Anne], from the data that was provided to

you in the police reports, emergency room records, paramedic records, [town X] General Hospital psychiatric records, could you tell us what her mental status was at the time of [Ed]'s death?

A She was very sad, very depressed, and very disappointed, very worrying about what is going to happen to [Ed]. And she felt very hopeless despair—that would be probably the best term to describe the mental status at that time—with a lot of guilt feeling, too, not being able to care for the son *as a mother is supposed to be* [sic].[58]

Q . . .

Well, was it her belief that her act with [Ed] was killing him?

A Certainly it would involve death. But then it was not killing him in the sense of of try to maliciously, viciously try to exterminate another person. But it is, it is more, on [sic] more benevolent, more positive way so that she could provide the care through going with [Ed] sort of to the next world *where there's nobody else that she has to attend to.*[59]

Whereas the first of these two extracts appears to treat it as an objective, inherent duty for a mother to care for her offspring, the second constructs 'attending to her son' as an all-encompassing desire in the defendant, whose fulfillment on earth may actually have been constrained by the patriarchal character of the "*other*" culture: her exploitation by her husband, Larry (which the defense attorney culturalized as 'Chinese'[60]), and her absence from her son's life in the past due to the stigma against 'illegitimacy'. In other words, the defense strategy legitimized and reified the opposition between 'good' and 'bad' mother, and the underlying norm of maternal duty, in a fashion that was indeed *defensive*, rather than marking it in critical terms as a *patriarchal* norm.

A perspective upon *People vs. Shen*, or other similar cases, which treats her act in empiricist terms of cultural or biographical 'facts', and/or which slides outside the discursive perspective by taking her (self-)construction at trial for an authentic representation of her experience, risks replicating this reification of the patriarchal norm in question. There is a risk for this to occur especially in cases where one might sympathize with the defendant from a feminist perspective. Here I want to engage critically with Volpp's comments upon cases of mother-child suicide generally, and upon *People vs. Shen*[61] in particular. Volpp has pointed to mother-child suicide cases as prime examples of instances in which the introduction of 'cultural evidence' might be advocated in accordance with the value of anti-subordination (1994, 59–60, 84–91, 97–99; Volpp, n.d.). Volpp formulates that principle as "a commitment towards ending all forms of subordination [which] should inform the decision of whether or not to support the informal use of cultural information on behalf of a defendant in a given case" (1994, 59, see also 97–99). Specifically, she has pointed to Anne Shen's case as an instance in which 'cultural evidence' was legitimately admitted, despite the risk of essentialist stereotyping (ibid., 84–91, 97–99).

Volpp advocates "a sympathetic understanding of women defendants who might be considered in a political or social sense to be victims", and criticizes Coleman (1996) for "[vilifying] women who try to commit parent-child suicide . . . as being 'remarkably similar' to Susan Smith" (1996, 1585)—a white woman "who did not actually try to kill herself, and who, after killing her children, alleged that her children had been kidnapped by an African American man" (ibid., 1583). Volpp here evaluates the actual act of (attempted) parent-child suicide, rather than its construction in discursive strategies, in moral terms, and imputes a morally higher quality to it than to an act of killing one's children without attempting suicide. In my view, this risks buying into the patriarchal discourse of good vs. bad mothers. A feminist stance, I feel, would need to question this moral distinction, and would need to affirm any self-interested or even aggressive aspects to a given woman's conduct, rather than taking at face value an interpretation of it that constructs it as altruistic or benevolent in intention—possibly against the backdrop of a patriarchal norm such as that of maternal self-sacrifice. One should guard, that is, against idealizing Shen's conduct in terms that are in line with that norm.

This is possible, however, only on condition that one considers her representation at trial in terms of a discursive strategy, rather than of facts about her life as such: if the defense's construction of her intention in killing her son is taken for granted as a fact—that is, as 'evidence' about a 'different' cultural and psychological reality—, then one loses sight of its serviceability to the U.S. patriarchal notion of a 'good mother'. Thus, Volpp cites from the trial testimony (as cited in the appellate opinion in Shen's case [1994, 88–89nn139–40]), including some of the extracts catering to the notion of the 'good mother' which I have quoted above, without in any way commenting upon the patriarchal character of that notion (1994, 88–90). Instead, she lauds the 'cultural evidence' presented on Shen's behalf, in contrast with that offered in another case (of a man who had killed his wife)—which she criticizes as colonialist on grounds of its being empirically inaccurate:

> [The defense expert]'s bizarre portrayal of divorce and adultery in China in fact had little basis in reality. . . . Pasternak's description of 'Chinese society' thus was neither substantiated by fact nor supported by his own testimony. The description was in fact his own *American* fantasy (1994, 70, original emphasis).

In contrast:

> Compared to Dong Lu Chen's case, [Anne Shen]'s case presents a more compelling reason to admit cultural information and a more *accurate*

and individualized portrayal of cultural factors influencing the defendant's behavior (1994, 84, my emphasis).

While Volpp acknowledges that stereotyping played into Shen's case (ibid., 90), she concludes that "[Anne Shen] was not presented as alien and other" (ibid.). Sacks goes even further, stating that "*People vs.* [*Shen*] provides a good example of appropriate treatment of cultural information" (1996, 548–549; see also Deckha 2004, 40–42). In contrast, I would insist that Shen was indeed Othered within her legal defense—not merely in a colonialist form (as remains to be shown), but also in virtue of her rendering in terms of a patriarchal norm, which established a gendered pressure not to highlight any self-interested and insubordinate aspects of her conduct. Perceiving this aspect of her Othering presupposes approaching her representation at trial as a construction to be examined, not for its putative empirical accuracy, but for its normative character. I will return at a later stage to this discussion about Volpp's contribution, in order to pinpoint its wider implications. Here I want to continue discussing the details of Shen's 'cultural defense'.

A CHINESE MOTHER IS A LOVING MOTHER

The 'evidence' relating to the mother-child bond in China included the following:

Q All right. I'd like you to tell us, please, about the subject of relationship [sic] between mother and child in the traditional Chinese setting.

A Chinese babies and small children are treated with a lot of care and affection and experience much greater frequency and intensity of personal conflict [sic], contact, especially by touch with their mothers, than is true of their counterparts in the West. For a mother, infant time is very strong, and some observers say that it leads on the part of both the mother and the child to a feeling of virtual fusion, that "I can feel what my child feels," or "I can feel what my mother feels."[62]

A . . .

By and large, what it comes down to is that Chinese mothers hold and touch their infants more and talk less with them than do Western mothers.[63]

These assertions were obviously generalizing as to 'Chinese' and 'Western' culture. But whatever the empirical foundation for that generalization, and whatever its applicability to Anne Shen, this 'evidence' was clearly serviceable to the *Western* expectation of motherly devotion to their children: Its introduction was oriented to approximating Shen to the *Western* ideal of the devoted mother, based upon her putative 'difference'. That the norm of the devoted mother was the domestic discourse framing the 'evidence' as to 'Chinese difference' became nearly explicit when, on cross-examination of the 'expert' quoted above, the prosecution expressed what appears to have been indignation at the suggestion that the mother-child bond is closer in 'China' than in 'the West':

Q Doctor, let me ask you a couple of quick questions on the mother/child bond in Chinese culture.

You testified, I think, this morning and perhaps again this afternoon, basically in your opinion, that there's a closer bond between mother and child in China than there is in the United States. Is that—

. . .

Q *You mean to tell me* that Chinese mothers modernly spend more physical contact with their babies than Swedish mothers or American mothers?

A I would say that this is the case. But the difference is not all too known. All *good mothers* fondle their children and handle them and stroke and caress them, kiss them, and so on and so forth. All I'm saying is that Chinese mothers quantitatively do that more than comparable Western mothers. That is a fair conclusion from the existing but admittedly limited imperial [sic![64]] research.[65]

The latter question appears to treat the suggestion that the mother-child bond may be less intense in the West as an insult—thereby exposing that women are being required, in Euro-America, to be maximally devoted to their children. This requirement was here, again, cited in an affirmative form, rather than being marked as a patriarchal norm.

THE *OPPRESSED THIRD WORLD WOMAN*

Q Explain by reference to [Anne's] cultural background why she would not be assertive to the father of her son with respect to maintaining her relationship with her son.

A Chinese women are not encouraged and, as a rule, have little practice in being assertive with men and especially so with their husbands.

So, again, the cultural virtue is to win over the man's good will by being patient, uncomplaining, longsuffering and by abiding by the wives' [sic] traditional role which then, in the best scenario, would be recognized and rewarded by the husband.[66]

This quote perhaps best clarifies the function of the notion of Oppressed Third World Women within Anne Shen's defense: it was serviceable to approximating her as closely as possible to the notion of a 'good mother' who was merely prevented by external pressures—namely, her gendered oppression and socialized subservience—from fulfilling that role during her son's lifetime. This helped excuse (at a moral rather than legal level) her absence from her son's life and, in virtue of this, served to render more credible the idea that she had killed Ed out of a benevolent or even altruistic motivation.

It is not my intention to dispute the expert testimony about Chinese women's social position. To the extent that it is very generalizing (at least with regard to 'traditional Chinese women') and in line with stereotypes of submissive Asian women (Chiu 1994, 1086–1088), this is not the only problem with it. Irrespective of its truth status, what makes that 'evidence' colonialist is the hierarchical matrix within which it is co-constructed with a notion of the West that renders the latter as (more) advanced in matters of gender equality. That distinction at trial was constructed either in the version in which Western patriarchy is arguably conceded as such, but is constructed as being less pronounced than in the Other culture (see the previous chapters) or—for the most part—as a binary opposition, of an (absolute) presence vs. absence of women's subordination. In the second of the following quotes, which illustrate the latter variant, the defense attorney contrasts a "typical American woman's" likely reaction to the situation the defendant was facing with the latter's response of attempted parent-child suicide:

Q Well, is there any explanation as to why *this Chinese woman* would permit or tolerate the man to direct what's to happen with her life?

A I don't want to be too typical [sic], but it is true that many anthropologists would agree that Chinese woman's role is quite different from the Western woman's role.

Their [sic] role of the Asian women is characterized as a passive, submissive role rather than assertive kind of dominant role you might see in this country.[67]

Q In contrast, a *typical American woman* from American culture who felt her man had done her wrong, felt her life was hopeless, how would you expect that typical American woman to react when the walls came crumbling down?

A I think the typical reaction would be anger, consciously expressed and personally accepted against the husband who had rejected and disappointed her in taking recourse to the opportunities open to her in the legal system and elsewhere in order to assure the best possible deal for her financially and in terms of custody in that situation.

Q Why weren't these choices available to [Anne]?

A Because [Anne] was just not aware on the basis of cultural experiences and background that she could prevail against a man and especially in a country where the legal and political and social rules were obscured to her.

> [Larry], as I understand, is a U.S. citizen. She is just a temporary visitor in this country. She, I understand, speaks very little English. She just would not know where to turn or what to do in order to do it.
>
> Plus culturally, there is deep-seated expectation [sic] that if it's a woman against a man, the woman loses, the man wins, the man prevails.[68]

In the first extract, note that the defense attorney's question constructs subservience as an exotic phenomenon in a woman that must be related to Shen's classification as 'Chinese'. So the question, and not merely the answer, constructs 'American women' as being assertive towards men in binary opposition to 'Chinese women'. Note also the utterly homogenizing implication of that binary frame in regard to both categories, which is premised in part upon situating "Asian women" outside "this country", i.e., as foreign (Volpp 1994, 66, 61–62).

The second quote is perhaps even starker in setting up a homogenizing stereotype, not merely of Chinese women, but of "a typical American woman from American culture". The very notion that there is a single 'type' of American woman, and of American culture, implies that the prototype is imagined as 'white' and Euro-American—identities that are thus privileged as the unmarked norm. The idea that the "typical American woman" would resort to the court system and fend for the best possible financial deal also seems to me to entail a heavy class bias. For, doing so may not be a self-evident option to all women in the U.S., especially given the costs of hiring an attorney. Like Anne Shen, many immigrant women may also find the legal system inaccessible to them for cultural and linguistic reasons—quite apart from the fact that resorting to divorce might endanger one's legal status (Balram 2005), or expose one's illegal status in the U.S. The very act of positing a "typical American woman" is thus premised upon excluding from the category "American" all those who fail to fit the given description (including the defendant). Apart from questions of empirical accuracy, however, the colonialist character of the opposition between 'American women' and women like Anne Shen rests primarily upon the hierarchical form of that opposition: while it constructs Shen as lacking in agency, the former are characterized as being more self-determined, if not more rational.[69] This is even more evident in the following quote by the same 'expert':

Q Can you explain why, with reference to [Anne]'s cultural background, why suicide would be deemed to be an appropriate solution to an intolerable problem?

A Yes. In [Anne]'s case, her cherished hopes that by waiting long enough, by not pushing, by being patient, hardworking and thrifty, that she would bring her husband around to recognize her as a virtuous woman, deserving of the status of a wife and mother, when these hopes were dashed, then she had nothing else to turn to.

> In Chinese culture, as I have already mentioned, there are no strong prohibitions against suicide. Suicide is regarded as neither sinful nor shameful. And so she just had no experience, no training to channel her frustrations, either outward by aggressing against her husband verbally or otherwise, or *constructively, by envisaging some sort of another solution, about leaving [Larry] without fight to get the custody of [Ed]*. That was just outside the cultural reality that she knew it [sic].
>
> So she had run out of possible courses of action and solution. And yet the example of suicide was culturally very prominent, especially for wronged and disappointed woman [sic], for woman [sic] who had been provoked into her own death. And so that is what she turned to.[70]

Whether or not the 'information' given about the 'other culture' is accurate, that 'information' in the above quotes comes as part of a co-construction that is hierarchizing in character, privileging the 'West' over and above 'the rest' within the terms of an Enlightenment discourse whose normative parameters are defined by the notions of progress, equality, and self-determination, amongst others. In these quotes, Western women are situated outside patriarchy and, as such, as more 'advanced' in terms of autonomous agency.

Chinese women's subordination was constructed at trial in terms of a number of specific elements, which here I want to enumerate. They both contributed to "explaining" the defendant's absence from her son's life, and served to appeal to the stereotype of Asian women which pictures these as subservient to the point of self-effacement—a stereotype that constructs 'Asian women' in terms of the Western patriarchal ideal, as Chiu has observed (1994, 1086–1088). Both functions of this aspect of the 'cultural evidence' were inextricable from each other: it was in virtue of appealing to an existing stereotype that this 'evidence' achieved credibility, and possibly raised sympathy, from a hegemonic point of view.

One element of the relevant testimony was the notion that being an unwed mother carries a stigma in 'Chinese culture'. For instance:

> Q I see. Well, on that subject, sir [sic], are there any cultural taboos or prohibitions against unwed mothers?
>
> A There is. It is very shameful. One loses a tremendous amount of face being an unwedded mother.[71]

Secondly, we have already witnessed one instance of the testimony according to which it would have felt inappropriate to Anne Shen to ask Larry to make good on his promise to marry her. Here her own testimony contributed to constructing her as subservient qua 'Chinese woman':

> Q When you became pregnant, did you ask him [Larry] any questions about when you would be married?

A No.
Q Why not?
A Because he already mentioned everything before I came in 1979. I was embarrassed to bring it up again.
Q Why were you embarrassed to bring it up again?
A Because I'm a Chinese woman.
Q What does that mean?
A Things like that should be brought up first by the male.[72]

I have also already quoted one extract positing that, qua Chinese woman, it was inconceivable to Anne Shen to fend for the custody of her son. A particularly stark statement as to her subordination in this regard is the following, taken from the cross-examination of one of the defense 'experts':

Q Did defendant [Shen] feel guilty about leaving [Ed] behind for seven years?
A Guilty, I think, is not the word, because she felt that she had no choice in the matter, that if, if the man wants his child, especially his son, then that's what he gets. That was her perception. And she felt it was no more realistic to oppose it than to sort of oppose the forces of nature, that that's how the world operated.[73]

The same 'expert' explained that, in waiting for Larry Shen to make good on his promise of marriage, the defendant had followed a cultural role model:

Q Can you explain by reference to Mrs. [Shen]'s cultural heritage why she would wait from 1981 until 1989 to pursue a relationship with her son?
A Having lived throughout her life in China, she would have plenty of examples and models of other women before her having done just that. That the man leaves China to earn money, and the culturally prescribed duty for the woman is to wait patiently, uncomplainingly, passively, until such time as her husband or her man may return.[74]

He also asserted the following:

Q Can you explain why, with reference to Chinese, [Anne]'s Chinese cultural background, why she would remain silent in response to her husband's comment not to speak unless she paid money if she ultimately did not speak [sic]?
A As I understand it, her husband virtually commanded her not to speak. And as a traditional Chinese woman, she has lifelong experience and training of obeying men's commands. If he told her not to speak, then her automatic response was to do just that.[75]

Finally, as we saw further above in this section, even suicide was constructed by the defense as a course of action somehow characteristic of Chinese women.

In the above examples, Anne Shen is indeed constructed as being subservient to the point of self-effacement (specifically, in the form of her alleged suicide attempt)—and, as such, as absolutely Other to 'American/Western women' who, as we have seen, are rendered as assertive, even dominant, within the defense strategy. Much as Shen's construction as an absolute victim is evocative of sympathy, in my view it dehumanizes her in virtue of depriving her of agency. This occurs, not through the 'cultural information' provided about her in isolation, but in virtue of the normative character of the opposition set up between 'the West' and 'the rest'. To just what extent the defense hypostatized the defendant's (and 'traditional' Chinese women's) subservience is evident in the following quotes—the first, from her direct examination; the second, the defense attorney's comment upon that sequence made during his closing argument. In the first extract he makes reference to the position Shen was found in, with her wrist slashed:

Q Why did you put a wastebasket under your bleeding hand?
A I did not want the floor to be dirty.[76]

> Why did she put her arm over the edge to collect the blood? So as not to cause a problem for anyone else, *totally subservient woman*.[77]

THE THREAT OF TRANSGRESSION

I have already stated what function was served by constructing the defendant in terms of the notion of the Oppressed Third World Woman. In fact, the strategic need to establish her as maximally altruistic in character (so as to render credible her alleged motive for killing her son, despite her 'failure' to fill the role slot of a mother to him during his lifetime) produced an incentive for the defense to also hypostatize her gendered subordination and socialized subservience: the more oppressed and the more 'lacking' in the ability to assert herself, the more readily excusable her absence from Ed's life. But some of the 'evidence' relating to Shen's biography as rendered at trial actually could be interpreted as posing a threat to her assessment as being a "totally subservient woman" (see the last quote above): that is, it could be interpreted, precisely, as 'evidence' of assertiveness and a stance transgressive of patriarchal norms on the defendant's part. After all, she had engaged in sex outside marriage (something constructed by one 'expert' as a sexual transgression not just in 'American' but in 'Chinese culture' too[78]). She testified that she had wanted to fall pregnant and had not used any birth control.[79] So she had transgressed, too, against the prohibition against sexual *reproduction* outside marriage despite the heavy social sanctions against doing so. (While she had admittedly done so in the expectation that Larry would eventually marry her, she had yet taken the risk that he might not.) Finally, her leaving Ed with his father could be read as a refusal to be punished for the said transgressions in virtue of suffering the stigma imposed as a social sanction against them. This would, simultaneously, amount to a refusal to fulfill the norm of motherly duty (if there is such a norm within Shen's social context) under particularly oppressive conditions. Certainly, Shen's conduct constituted a transgression from the point of view of *Western* patriarchal norms.

Arguably, the defense's hypostatization of her subservience served to compensate for these transgressive indications of agency and self-assertion—as well as for the very definite agency entailed in her having killed her son. So did the defense's rather excessive emphasis upon her benevolent feelings and altruistic motives vis-à-vis Ed, which tended to distract from any self-interested aspects of her behavior. In my view, it is essential to a feminist perspective upon this case not to idealize the defendant in line with patriarchal norms of femininity, as I have argued earlier. Likewise, to fear that highlighting any self-interested aspects of her conduct would be to construct her as 'egoistic' and 'a bad mother' would be to naturalize the patriarchal norm concerned. It is important, rather, to affirm those features of her conduct that may be interpreted as being transgressive of patriarchal social orders—as an indication of the latter's failure entirely to shape the world in their own terms. The defense, however, tended to highlight altruistic over and above self-interested inclinations on the defendant's part. Thus, much as her patriarchal oppression was cited as an excuse for her absence from her son's life, and for her having seen no other option but to resort to the failed suicide attempt in which she allegedly wanted to take Ed "along", at times it could seem that even her interest in avoiding a situation intolerable to herself by these means was deemed by some of the 'experts' an insufficient excuse, which was backgrounded in favor of her alleged concern for her son. One example consists in those instances of the expert testimony, quoted further above in this chapter, where even the alleged suicide attempt itself was cast as having occurred in order for Anne Shen to take better care of Ed in the other world. In the same vein, one of the 'experts' said:

A . . . And in some sense the kind of alternatives that she, if you would perhaps, you know, it's not as rational as an alternative that the only way she saw out [sic] was perhaps—you know, maybe that's the best word is the way she saw how to get out of that situation was quite culturally determined.

Q What do you mean by that: her way out of the situation? What are you referring to?

A I was, I was thinking—I was, I was trying to explain is that her, she believe [sic] at that time that she had been lied to by, by, by [Larry].

> *But more importantly* that [sic] she believed that that evening what she found out was that [Larry] was not taking care of [Ed] as a father would be expected to do, did not provide the paternal love that was, that she all along thought [Ed] was receiving. And that was very distressful for her.[80]

The statement that Shen believed she had been lied to by Larry would appear to refer to Ed's revelation, on the night of his death, that Larry had a girlfriend, with whom he was spending that very evening.[81] Shen's imaginable jealousy, disappointment, and anger at Larry for betraying her (which were being highlighted by the prosecution) are backgrounded in the above quote in favor of her concern for Ed's treatment by his father, in regards to her motivation for the homicide and alleged attempted suicide. Similarly, in the following extract, Shen's plan to return to Macau is constructed, not as an abandonment of Ed, but as a *sacrifice* she wanted to make for him. The extract refers to the conversation during which Anne had asked Larry Shen whether he had married her only for her money, to which he had responded that she had no right to speak until she produced the money:

Q Did she make any decisions about her life as a result of the, that experience of marriage conversation with [Larry] in the car, visit to the lawyer?

A She had a lot of mixed feeling that time. Naturally, she like to stay with [Ed], but if she's staying in the United States, she thought [Larry] would ask her the money. And if she didn't give her [sic] [sic] the money, which she did not have the money, she couldn't talk, no right to speak up or communicate with [Larry].

So this is not the kind of situation she likes to spend the rest of her life [sic]. If she brings a son to Macau, probably she would meet objection of [Larry]. Besides, in Macau she did not tell anybody in her own social circle that she had such an illegitimate child.

So in both way [sic], either to stay here or to go back to Macau, would be a kind of, very difficult situation, and she was really caught up in that kind of dilemma what to do at that time.

However, for the sake of her children, she decide, inclined to go back to Macau.

Q Without [Ed] or with [Ed]?

A Without [Ed]. *That would be a lot of sacrifice on her*, giving up her own so-called son, which made her more guilty because she was already quite guilty that she was not capable or able to take care of her own son as a mother over the last eight years.[82]

In a way similar to the previous extract, Shen's self-interested motive for wanting to return to Macau is mentioned, only to be backgrounded in favor of her concern for 'her children's sake'.[83] In this way, what could have been interpreted as resistant moments in the defendant's actions and intentions was being flattened out by the notions of the servile Chinese woman and altruistically inclined mother, as a means of satisfying the demand placed *in the U.S.* upon women to treat their children's interests as more important than their own.

The treatment of the subject of anger on the part of the defense provides further support for my proposition that the defense's construction of 'Chinese patriarchy' was serviceable to a disavowed U.S. patriarchal normative economy. As I have argued, whether or not anger figured among the defendant's feelings during the moments preceding the killing, and whether or not the latter was motivated by a desire to take revenge against Larry, was irrelevant to the legal finding of whether the killing was committed "in the heat of passion", and therefore, to the legal aspects of the jury's verdict (as requested by the defense vs. the prosecution). Yet these questions were covered repeatedly within the (re-)direct and especially the cross-examinations of defense witnesses. At various points, defense witnesses proved evasive on the subject, or even disavowed any anger in the defendant. For instance, one 'expert', who had conducted psychological tests upon the defendant, only conceded that they indicated anger on her part when confronted with individual test questions by the prosecutor. The first of the following two extracts is from the witness's direct examination; the second, from his cross-examination:

Q Dr. [X], was there anything in the examination of [Anne] from a psychological point of view to suggest that she was killing [Ed] out of revenge against, out of a sense of revenge against [Larry]?
A From the psychological testing?
Q Yes.
A The psychological testing probably would not show, would not be relevant to that. But it had a lot—To that specific question—
Q Yes.
A To a lot, you know, on more general question [sic] of whether she is an angry, hostile, impulsive person, the testing are [sic] not consistent with it.
Q What does that mean: "They're not consistent with it"?
A The testing data are not consistent with that [sic] she's an angry, hostile, aggressive person.[84]

Q All right. With reference to the SCL 90 portion of the test, particularly the answers to questions No. 24, 67, and 81—that is temper outbursts that you could not control, which is 24; 67, have an urgence [sic] to break or smash things; and 81, shouting or throwing things—Doctor, wouldn't you say that those responses indicate anger and hostility?
. . .
A Yeah. That would, that would in some ways, yes, someone who would, who has problems with temper, with, would be a possibility of that.

What she, what she said to me was that was how she was feeling inside. And during that week there was no temper outburst from what I could gather. But that's how she felt.

Q At the time of the test?

A The one-week period that this test was measuring.

Q All right. And No. 67, Doctor?

A Again, you know, that was how she felt rather than something she does; that is, angry, aggressive, and impulsive.
And 81 is the last one?

Q Yes, sir [sic]. 81. Shouting or throwing things.

A She—in that one, she was saying that sometimes she felt like screaming and shouting. She specifically also said there that throwing was not part of it. But, you know, this asked for two things, and she didn't know how to answer that one. But she said the shouting was a part. At times she felt like screaming because she just could not feel that, she could not put everything, controlled [sic] inside.[85]

Given the second passage—which itself seems somewhat biased, in that the witness insists that anger was 'merely' an inner state, rather than one Shen was prone to act on—, his response in the first of the above extracts does seem evasive, in that it disavows the defendant's anger as indicated by the test results. Such instances of an evasiveness on the subject of anger on the part of witnesses for the defense again contribute to an image of Anne Shen as less than a full agent; an image which was being stabilized in virtue of constructing her as a traditional, subservient Chinese woman. In fact, that identity was invoked directly as grounds for the suggestion that she either would not have felt anger towards Larry, or that she would not have acted outwardly on that anger. The first alternative applies to the following quote, of the same 'expert' I have last cited:

Q Doctor, in this case, is it true that the defendant here had every reason to be angry with her husband?

And I cite you these examples that we've heard in this case.

For example, she had an illegitimate child. She was ashamed of that and wouldn't tell anyone except, I think, from the evidence, anyway, just one person in China. She wasn't married to [Larry] when she had the child. And he had another wife who he was married to. She left, leaving her son [Ed] behind in the United States. Larry didn't send her any money—at least apparently as much money as she had hoped for.

According to your client [sic], when [Larry] did visit her twice in Hong Kong or Macau, on one occasion he asked for money. And when she came to the United States finally in '89, he made her sleep alone.

And those instances we have heard about, would you agree that those would cause your client to be angry at [Larry Shen]?

A Remember that this is, *[Anne] is a very traditional Chinese woman.*

Q But—
A The issue—
Q Let's back up a sec. Okay?
A Yeah.
Q Answer my question first, if you can.
A *I was going to answer that in the sense that, you know, anger may be there, but it may more be hurt that is more dominant than anger.*[86]

The prosecution here clearly relates Shen's anger, not to Larry's treatment of Ed, but to her own sense of having been abused and rejected by Larry. Such anger would not merely constitute a sense of agency on the defendant's part, but would amount to a moment of self-assertion—contrary to the notion of the 'traditional Chinese woman' circulated by the defense. That notion here is actively deployed to ward off the transgressive impression of such self-assertion by the defendant—transgressive, that is, to a Eurocentric patriarchal sensibility. A similar purpose was served by the defense's introduction, through one of its 'experts', of two 1958 studies of suicide and suicide attempts among 'Chinese' in Hong Kong.[87] As the 'expert' elaborated, according to these studies the highest risk of suicide at that time (the study was not being historicized by him) existed for women, especially younger women, who had been provoked by a social superior—most commonly, their father or husband:[88]

Q Well, what is the role in the Chinese culture of suicide for a woman? What is the significance of that?
A . . .
Specifically in regard to Dr. Yab's research findings, suicide is turned to when a person is aroused to extreme anger yet has a lifetime of training against expressing anger directly or of, through some sort of harmful or hurtful acts, and then the person turns against herself and ends up by destroying herself or attempting to do that.[89]

It was thus suggested that, to the extent that a Chinese woman might in fact harbor anger, she would turn it against herself in a suicidal rage, rather than against another person. On cross-examination, the same witness conceded that "there's no question that she [Anne Shen] was enraged against [Larry]".[90] On redirect, he was asked by the defense attorney:

Q Is it culturally consistent for [Anne Shen] not to have acted on her anger?
A Yes. Chinese women traditionally have been provided with very few direct outlets for their anger. They're supposed to be meek and subordinate and compliant and unassertive.
Q Well, in this situation, would you comment upon the District Attorney's inference that [Anne] utilized [Ed] as an instrument of her anger toward [Larry]?[91]

The defendant's identity of 'Chinese woman' was thus invoked as a safeguard against the inference that she had *killed Ed* out of anger and a desire for revenge against Larry. Much as such a motive would be morally problematic, it would yet constitute another instance of agency and self-assertion on Shen's part. It was in part a patriarchal sensibility hegemonic in the U.S. that rendered the possibility of such a motive threatening to the defense, particularly given that the defendant was a woman accused of having killed her own child. (It may have been threatening, too, in the case of a male defendant accused of killing his child, but the threat was potentially augmented by Shen's being a woman/mother. I shall return to this point in the subsequent, comparative case study of *State vs. Cao*[92]—a *man* accused of having killed his children [see Chapter 4].)

VALIDATING 'THE EVIDENCE'

Despite the utterly normative character of the discourses instantiated in Anne Shen's defense, the 'evidence' presented was rendered by it as objective and purely empirical knowledge in a way that both naturalized the hierarchies entailed in it, and repressed the categorization work that went into the essentialist classifications involved. Besides the testimony already quoted, consider the following extract of expert testimony:

Q I'd like to ask you some questions, if you don't mind, Doctor, about the subject of the *Chinese culture*.
A Yes.
Q I'd like to focus your attention, then, on that culture, perhaps *contrasted with* what might be referred to as *our American culture*.[93]

This dichotomous 'us/them' framework underpinned the entire 'evidence', of course. As in *People vs. Lopez and Singh* (analyzed in the previous chapter), it was constructed as a self-evident fact rather than a matter of categorization, however—despite the greater individualization of Anne Shen as compared to defendant Malkit Singh. I would insist that the problem with the cultural essentialism involved is not that it is empirically wrong; to be contrasted with some correct version of 'culture' (compare Chapter 1 as well as Part II).[94] Rather, I hold that essentialism naturalizes what is invariably a discursive *construction* of culture as an inherent given. Some of the testimony, along with the questions by which it was elicited, reinforced that construction by validating 'the evidence' as scientifically reliable—in a way complementing the "autobiographical" means of validating the 'cultural evidence' in *People vs. Lopez and Singh*:

Q Was there any significance *in your professional judgment* of [Anne]'s cultural background on September the 9th insofar as her mental state was concerned?[95]

Q What does *the professional literature suggest* are the reasons why a Chinese woman would resort to suicide?[96]

But, ultimately, the difference between the two means of validating the 'evidence' is smaller than it might seem. For, in *People vs. Shen*, too, academic expertise was validated in empiricist terms, which rendered transparent the discourses framing the 'facts' of observation and experience. This was quite apparent from the rather controversial manner in which one 'expert' characterized his discipline, anthropology:

Q Now, returning to the question of anthropology, can you tell us how an anthropologist goes about doing his research?
A Well, the classic anthropological method is what we call participant observations [sic], which involves fairly long-term residence in the country or with *the people that one is interested in studying*. It involves participation in the daily activities of *the people one studies*, as one also attempts to watch and observe what's going on, listen to what people talk about. Listen to the things that people consider to be important, the things that get the people angry, the things that make people happy.
To sum up, I think that *anthropologist* [sic] *are interested in the other*—in trying to understand other people's, *other culture's* [sic] prospectives [sic] from their point of view.
Q So then you as, *an American*, would go to China and *watch Chinese people* living, making comparisons between how Chinese people live and how American people live, your own frame of reference?
A That's right. And part of our mission, I think, is to try to explicate *to our fellow Americans* what that experience teaches one about the lives of *other people*.[97]

The 'expert' is here defining anthropology in terms of the study of *other people*. At least since the 1980s literary turn in that discipline (Clifford and Marcus 1986; Clifford 1988), and the accompanying critique of essentialism and colonial discourse in anthropology, this would be a controversial definition of the subject (compare Loomba et al. 2005a, 30–31).[98] Others would define anthropology in more self-reflexive terms, namely, in terms of the anthropologist's constitutive role in constructing the 'cultures' that she represents—and therefore, in constructing an 'Other'. The construct of 'the Other'—and therefore, the definition of anthropology given by this 'expert'—by the time of his testimony had been subjected to extensive criticism from the point of view of colonial discourse theory, due to that construct's implication in (post-)colonial power relations (Said 1978; Spivak 1988c). Rather than studying people or 'their cultures'—understood as essentialized 'things' or a 'heritage' one possesses—many would have argued already in 1990, the year Shen's trial took place, that it is social *practices*, *relations*, and *processes* that (should) form anthropology's subject (e.g., Clifford 1988; 1989; Appadurai 1990; see also Abu-Lughod 1991;

Thomas 1991; Appadurai 1991; Clifford 1992). But, since the 'expert' last quoted fails to mark the conceptual frame in terms of which he characterizes his discipline *as* a (contestable) conceptual frame, he is reifying—rendering as self-evident and uncontested—the particular, problematic definition of anthropology which he is giving. He thereby renders invisible the discursive work he is himself performing, as well as the power relations entailed in practicing, and defining, anthropology from the position of 'the expert' empowered to 'describe' 'the other'. Instead, his comments about the subject leave the impression that anthropology is a matter of simply observing others (here: 'Chinese', who are again situated outside 'America' as if to be 'American' necessarily meant *not* being 'Chinese')—without any conceptual mediation. Much as this means of validating the testimony as to 'culture' as authoritative differs from the means involved in *People vs. Lopez and Singh* (see Chapter 2), the commonality is that 'observation' of 'culture' was treated as being discursively unmediated by those involved. Consider the following question, put to the same 'expert', and the extract following it—in which 'observation' is appropriated as a means of self-authorization by another 'expert', a clinical psychologist specialized in cross-cultural psychology:[99]

Q Your experience, doctor [sic], or your training and *observations on the scene*, have you become familiar with the subject of the afterlife in Chinese culture?[100]

Q Very well.
I'd like to ask you, please, if you could tell us about the general relationship of Chinese women toward Chinese men as compared with an American culture, as an example.
A Traditionally, Chinese women had little power and little independence by comparison with men, and widely [sic] accepted Confucian principle is that a woman should forever obey first her father, then her husband, and then her adult son.
So there is always a man in position of authority over the woman. And this persists in the minds of Chinese men and women to this day, although, of course, there are modern influences that work as to the weakening of these kinds of attitudes and beliefs.
Q Would you find this relationship between men and women to be common, for example, in 1990 in—
A Oh, yes.
Q —in parts of China?
A Yeah. *I have observed it* on my visits to various parts of China, including Hong Kong.[101]

Volpp (1994) has criticized similar comments made by a white male anthropologist in another trial involving 'cultural evidence'. And certainly, the power relations entailed in statements such as the above heavily implicate that between the subject position of white (male) 'expert' and his 'subjects' of color, as Volpp maintains. But this does not exhaust the power relations involved. For one thing, 'white male' as a discursive *subject position* can also be filled by a person of color—in which case the discourse would entail a form of self-Othering,[102] but would yet contribute to reinforcing white supremacy. But beyond racialized colonial relations of power, the authority of science—popularly associated with objective knowledge—can be appropriated, likewise, for non-hegemonic academic discourses, which may yet be implicated in hegemonic discursive forms. This is illustrated by the following procedure of one 'expert witness' testifying on Anne Shen's behalf on cross-examination, who was qualified as an expert both on grounds of being a psychiatrist with publication experience in transcultural psychiatry, and of being a first-generation immigrant from Taiwan:[103]

A Right. But in that evening [sic] when there was intimate conversation, all of a sudden those information came up like thread to resolve all the puzzles, and at that time she [Anne Shen] start feeling, couldn't breathe. And I call that an oath [sic] of very, very kind of depressed, disappointed, and worrying about what could happen to her son if she went back to Macau.

So she chose to strangulate her son and kill herself together as a kind of common suicide which was quite often observed in Asian culture.

So naturally all this process would have to be taking place. And knowing that many Japanese, for instance, during World War II, when American Marine was invading Saipan, hundred and thousand [sic] of the Japanese families, not just military personnel, but the children, the mothers, ordinary civilian [sic], jump from the cliff to kill themselves. Some of them are out of panic; some of them are out of, stem all of psychological situation [sic].

Q Yes, Doctor. But they were Japanese. This lady is not Japanese.

A Yes. But they are Asian in the same category.

And all the chopstick-using Asian [sic] seem to share a common philosophy, *at risk, you know, are Asian-American psychiatric teaching. We teach our psychiatric* [sic] *in that way.*[104]

This expert justified his sweeping generalizations as to "chopstick-using Asian[s]" by reference to Asian American psychiatry. The latter discipline, or its construction by this particular 'expert', thus does not seem to be immune to reproducing a cultural essentialism that, in turn, plays a central part in stereotyping and colonial discourse. Volpp suggests the contrary in the context of her relatively positive assessment of the 'cultural evidence' presented on Anne Shen's behalf (see above). She relates the greater individualization of Shen as compared to the subjects of another case she analyzes to the fact that, in *Shen*, some of the 'experts' testifying were themselves immigrants (1994, 89), and argues that:

> the 'experts' *were* [original emphasis] experts in the sense that they were immigrants to the United States themselves and were thus invested in representing the experience of immigrants from a subjective position. Their position stands in contrast to the white anthropologist Pasternak [the expert witness in the other trial examined by Volpp, C.B.], whose subjectivity was based on an oppositional position to the 'other,' Dong Lu Chen [the defendant in that other trial, C.B.], veiled behind a pretense of objectivity. / Although advocating that expert witnesses offer a subjective point of view flies in the face of traditional reliance on 'objective' testimony, subjective cultural experts may present a fuller, more human analysis of the defendant. This is especially true because *the "othering" that Pasternak practiced will not transpire.* In other words, *it may be more difficult to obscure the power relations within an immigrant community through a monolithic description of 'culture' if the person doing the describing is from that* [sic] *community.* This increased accuracy may result because the experts' description is more suspect as 'less objective' and therefore more closely examined. *More importantly, someone from an immigrant community may have more difficulty describing another member of that community in a way that completely denies their humanity* (1994, 89, my emphasis).

Elsewhere, Volpp states that:

> I have proposed that, given the culturally racist tropes that frequently are deployed in these cases, we look at the subject position of who is asserting cultural evidence, and whether the assertion of this evidence reifies stereotypes that further subordination (1996, 1612).

Unfortunately, it would appear from Shen's trial (beside other trials in my corpus of cases, including the following chapter's case study) that being from the community of, or a community close to, that of the accused (or the victim/s)—while it is desirable for 'expert testimony'—is no safeguard against either colonial or gendered Othering. Remember, for instance, the following statements by the same 'expert':

Q Well, is there any explanation as to why this Chinese woman would permit or tolerate the man to direct what's to happen with her life?

A I don't want to be too typical [sic], but it is true that many anthropologists would agree that Chinese woman's role is quite different from the Western woman's role.

Their [sic] role of the Asian women is characterized as a passive, submissive role rather than assertive kind of dominant role you might see in this country.[105]

A It was very—*in my expertise as a transcultural psychiatry* [sic], in my familiarity, *with my familiarity with the Chinese cultural* translate [sic] and from the information interview I obtained from [Anne], she thought she was doing that out from the mother's love, mother's responsibility to bring a child together with her when she realized that there was no hope for her or a way for her to survive in this country or on this earth.

Q Well, are you telling us that the death of [Ed] was her act of love?

A Yes. It's a mother's altruism. This may be very difficult for the Westerner to understand . . . [106]

Anne Shen's greater individualization as compared to, e.g., Malkit Singh (see the preceding chapter's case study) did not prevent the expert testimony on her behalf from being framed in terms of the colonialist dichotomy of the West vs. the rest, nor from reproducing patriarchal discourse, then—contrary to Volpp's assessment (which is based on the appellate opinion rather than the trial transcript in full [1994, 85n125]) (see above). Nor did the fact that several of the 'experts' testifying on her behalf were themselves immigrant Asian Americans. Nor, finally, did the gendered and racialized constellation of the case—of a 'cultural defense' offered on behalf of an Asian American woman, who (in Volpp's words) "resisted what she perceived as subordination out of a set of very narrowly defined choices" (1994, 98), in which one might have hoped that the 'evidence' would be presented in more progressive terms. I will discuss in more detail the implications of this conclusion for the politics of culture-based prosecutions and defenses subsequent to the next chapter's—comparative and smaller—case study (namely, in Chapter 5). For the moment I will merely spell out my thesis that the reason for the lack of difference made by the factors just enumerated is the *hegemonic status* of colonial and patriarchal discourse, in general, and of the figure of the Patriarchal Other Culture, in particular. The chief consequence of this is that it is necessary to attend critically to the *discursive quality* of the 'cultural evidence' presented—rather than primarily to who is speaking, or to the constellation of the case (as suggested by Volpp's principle of anti-subordination [1996, 1596, 1612[107]] [see above], which is also defended by Deckha ([2004, 40–42]). In order to do this in a way thoroughly vigilant against discourses that reinforce unequal relations of power, it is necessary to approach the 'information' presented, not merely (or even primarily) with questions of empirical accuracy in mind—as is suggested by Volpp's statement that:

> Compared to Dong Lu Chen's case, [Anne Shen]'s case presents a more compelling reason to admit cultural information and *a more accurate and individualized portrayal of cultural factors influencing the defendant's behavior* (1994, 84, my emphasis).

Rather, it is necessary to approach the 'information' presented in terms of *discourses*, as I have argued throughout—that is, in terms of the conceptual and normative frames by which the representation of 'information' is invariably mediated.

4 'Cultural Defense' II

The *Patriarchal Other*—Third Case Study

The case of *State vs. Cao* poses a significant contrast with Shen's in some respects.[1] Tried in Alabama in 1986, Quang Cao was convicted of capital murder for killing his three children (aged four, six and seven).[2] He had slit their throats alongside his own, but his injuries required only first aid—seemingly an analogous act to Anne Shen's (see the preceding chapter). The defense maintained that Cao had committed it as an act of either insanity or "a legal provocation to the heat of passion from which there was no time to cool"[3] in response to having been left by his wife, who for two days had had been "running around" with another man, or so he suspected.[4]

The defense introduced a witness qualified by the court as an expert in cross-cultural counseling. (Like Cao, he had originally lived in Vietnam.) Among other areas relating to the defendant's experience of the Vietnam war and as a refugee, the expert testified to the effect that, in Vietnam, a wife is considered virtually the property of her husband, who is the head of the family for all purposes; that adultery on her part signifies a loss of face to the entire family, and that a husband's killing himself and his family is a measure of saving face.[5] (The testimony was ambiguous as to whether such an act would be considered acceptable in Vietnam.[6]) There was no explicit proposition that killing one's children is considered an act of extended suicide. Still, the connection made between homicide and suicide by the 'cultural evidence' makes this trial reminiscent of Anne Shen's.

Despite certain analogies, there are significant differences in the gendered articulation of that 'evidence' within each defense strategy—differences that reinforce my point that testimony as to another culture's gendered order may be tailored to a patriarchal normative economy pertinent in the U.S., contrary to the notion that gendered hierarchy is particular to the other culture. First, the main analogies: in both defense strategies, the 'story' was that one spouse had killed the child, or children, he had had with the other spouse in reaction to being rejected by the latter, who was allegedly pursuing another sexual relationship. In both cases, the defense attempted to shift blame to the other spouse. However, the way in which this occurred in *State vs. Cao* was able to benefit from an utterly sexist logic: the allegation that his wife, Jane Cao, had been 'running around' on her husband, i.e., that she had been sexually unfaithful to him, was articulated in such a way that she stood as the person ultimately responsible for the death of her children. In this case, it was Mrs. Cao who was effectively pictured as a bad mother. Both in that she had left her husband and was said to have been 'running around' with another man, and in that, during the two days preceding the killing, she had been hiding from her husband in fear of his violence.[7] (She testified that, in the course of her ten-year relationship with Quang Cao, he had repeatedly threatened physically to hurt or kill, and had actually hurt, both her and their children. The prosecution tried to establish that the killing followed a pattern he had used over years to coerce her back into the relationship, or into having sex with him, in which he had been using the children as pawns.[8]) The defense went so far as to as to blame Jane Cao for her fear of returning home to check on the safety of her children on the night of the killing. (She sent the police to check on them after her husband had told her on the telephone that he would kill them.) That is, one defense attorney literally implied that *she* should have put herself at risk for the sake of protecting her children. Effectively, the argument boiled down to saying that Cao's wife had *driven him* into killing their children by leaving him repeatedly, and by allegedly pursuing new relationships. Suggesting that she had used both her husband and her alleged lover for financial gain, this attorney stated, inter alia:

> What we have, I submit to you, ladies and gentlemen of the jury, is a cold and calculating woman who is going to get her way *at the expense of her children.* / Now, if we are to believe the state's testimony, it came in their argument from [Jane Cao], as to that unfounded child abuse report, as to the machete, as to the fists, as to being scared for her and her children. Scared for her children? What kind of woman leaves her children with a madman? An insane person? And goes away? She knew all about this. . . . [Jane Cao] testified that he changed, but she left him and she left those children there with him.[9]

This line of argument instantiates the characteristic pattern of blaming women for men's violence that has been focused upon much in the debate as to the 'cultural defense' (most commonly in cases of violence against the women concerned) (Rimonte 1991; Spatz 1991; Volpp 1994; Coleman 1996).[10] Ironically, the argument implies something similar to pertain to hegemonic U.S. culture as was stated in this case regarding Vietnam[11]: namely that, in the U.S., too, a wife may be considered her husband's possession. The gender-related 'cultural evidence', which in this trial assumed a very limited place in the defense's argument, merely served to reinforce and legitimize that all too familiar idea. Cao's defense capitalized upon this idea in a way that Anne Shen's defense (see Chapter 3) was unable to do with regard to her husband, because a husband who is unfaithful to his wife (like any man who is 'promiscuous') is not stigmatized to the same extent as in the inverse case. As the prosecution in Cao's trial said, it was as a "prostitute and whore" that his wife was cast by the defense.[12]

The gendered dissimilarity between how the 'cultural evidence' was deployed in both cases was the most apparent in regard to the subject of aggression or anger. As we saw in the preceding chapter, Shen's defense made an effort to picture her act of infanticide as something other than an act of revenge (in part by picturing it as an extended suicide in a way appealing to the myth of the naturally benign, altruistic mother), and her person, as submissive not assertive, and masochistic rather than sadistic. Revenge and, by implication, anger on her part were treated as illegitimate, even though a motive of revenge would have been compatible with the verdict sought by the defense according to the jury instructions (see also n. 14, this Ch.). A very different tendency is evident in the following argument by the defense attorney for Cao, which follows the comments regarding his wife's alleged adultery that I just quoted (an argument in favor of a finding of heat of passion rather than insanity):

> He was provoked by a legal provocation to the heat of passion from which there was no time to cool. . . . And ladies and gentlemen, time to cool is not a matter that is reserved to a clock. Time to cool is in the heart. We are all human beings with grudges and resentments. How long do they last? How long does anger to the point of losing your mind and injuring somebody last? But for the grace of God, I don't know. And I feel real fortunate to be standing at this side of the table. It lasts until it cools down and not one moment before. The Hatfields and the McCoys carried it on for 86 years over much less. You've heard the cultural evidence on adultery, and you folks are occidentals, you're Westerners. Look deep into your hearts, ladies and gentlemen.[13]

Rather than suppressing the dimension of aggression entailed in the child killings, it would appear that the attorney is overtly legitimizing that aggression here. This would be unthinkable in the case of a *woman* who has killed her children. She would not be able to cater for forgiveness on the grounds that she had been 'provoked' into that act by her husband's infidelity.[14] In fact, it is striking that in the trial of Quang Cao, there was very little effort by the defense to construct him as a loving parent, as there was in the case of Anne Shen. The 'cultural expert' did state that "when someone commits suicide in a closed culture, it's not the end of the life as much as the [sic] movement to another life", and that the defendant "believed on one level that he was transporting himself and his children to Vietnam"—implying, as in *Shen*, a notion that death would be followed by a shared existence with his children.[15] But in Cao's case, the killing was not constructed as having been intended beneficially towards his children, or as having occurred with any view at all to what was good for them. Reference was made only to its being a measure of saving face—rather than a fatherly act, or an act of parental responsibility. Instead of any major focus upon the defendant's relationship to his children, it was his wife that was placed center-stage as a traitor to her children; a 'bad mother'. The argument that she was at fault for leaving her children 'with a madman' (see above) implied that a mother has no right to even protect her own physical safety if this might endanger her children—a parallel to the self-effacing devotion to her son in 'the other world' in terms of which Anne Shen's defense constructed her motive for killing her son (see Chapter 3): Both lines of argument indicate that maternal duty, in the hegemonic common sense of the U.S. of the late 20th century, could still be legitimately interpreted as negating any pursuit of self-interest, or even self-preservation, on a woman's part if it is to her children's detriment. In contrast, the construction of Quang Cao by his attorneys and expert witnesses (the 'cultural expert' as well as a psychiatrist) showed no sign of a similar defensive posture vis-à-vis the notions of parental duty, love, and benign intent—let alone altruism.

Even the prosecution followed the patriarchal logic relied upon by Cao's defense to a significant extent. To be sure, during the trial's evidentiary phase, the state was at pains to demonstrate the pattern of threats, coercion and violence involving the children as well as his wife which the defendant had used to control her, and pointed to her fear for her safety as the reason why she had left her husband and had been with another man while leaving the children with Cao during the days before the killings—implying thereby that that fear might excuse her conduct.[16] But in the rebuttal responding to the closing argument by the defense that contained the defense's attacks on Mrs. Cao of which I have quoted some 'highlights', the state made far-reaching concessions to those attacks. It now pictured both parents as having destroyed the family unit at the cost of their children, in a way that partially placed their respective actions on the same level of blame, and that de-legitimized Jane Cao's fear for her safety in the days preceding the killings as a reason for her not to return to the family home to take the children away from her husband.

> Now, I don't know the extent of that marriage over there or so-called marriage between the defendant [Quang Cao] and his so-called wife. . . . I don't know of that relationship, but I will tell you this much: it's not one that we revere or we think of as wholesome. I mean, seven years of living in fear, the attacking of a woman with a baby in her arm with a machete, *running off with some guy to Atlanta when your kids are being murdered.* Do you know what this is all about: the depravity that existed in the relationship between [Quang Cao] and his wife. That's what it's about. The utter and cold, complete destruction of the family unit and the children involved.[17]

Situating both parents as blameworthy in opposition to their innocent children, whom he asked the jury to side with on the motto of the then current *Band Aid* song, "We are the world. We are the children",[18] the prosecutor added later on, referring to the Cao children:

> They didn't have anything but a hope for the future. And their Momma just running around with some guy, and this defendant willing to murder them to get his wife's attention. . . . Who speaks for them? Nobody but you.[19]

There was no comparable move of blaming the second parent in the prosecution strategy in *People vs. Shen* (which I shall examine in Chapter 6). In contrast, in the latter case the state focused upon the loss and hurt that the infanticidal spouse had caused the other parent by killing his only offspring—a theme entirely absent from the transcript material in *State vs. Cao* that I have reviewed.[20] The psychiatrist testifying for the prosecution in Shen's trial, who adjudged her "a very, very manipulative, calculating woman",[21] imputed to her a motive of punishing Mr. Shen for not returning her romantic interest, picturing her as taking pleasure in his pain:

> A It is my opinion, Counsel, that [Anne] wished to witness the discomforture that her killing of [Larry Shen]'s most precious thing in the world for him, the thing she gave him, his son—it's my believe [sic] that that was her chief motivation[22]
>
> That is the reason, of course, why she is still alive is so that she can have the satisfaction of seeing the grief that it caused him.[23]

So, while in Shen's case the prosecution focused upon how, by killing their child, one parent had hurt the other, and pointed to this as an additional source of blame incurred by the defendant, in Cao's case, the state instead colluded with the defense to a significant degree in picturing both parents as evil and, to some extent, responsible. In either case, then, the mother figured as a guilty, bad subject—even in the discourse of a prosecuting party, where it would have seemed close-at-hand to represent her as an additional victim of the infanticide.

The case of Quang Cao thus shows that it was not simply Anne Shen's position as a criminal defendant, or as an infanticidal parent in a gender-neutral sense, that placed her in such a defensive position. The discontinuity between the defense's line of argument in constructing Cao's actions as compared to hers (its legitimation of his aggression vs. its repression in Shen's case, plus the much lesser focus upon Cao's emotions for his children than upon Shen's), and the affinity between the defensive fashion in which Anne Shen was represented, on the one hand, and the sexist attack upon Mrs. Cao, on the other, reinforce the point that the defense strategy in her case, as in

Cao's, was structured in accordance with a gendered, patriarchal discourse, rather than by mere gender-neutral rhetorical resources and strategies.

* * *

EXCURSUS: THE SIGNIFICANCE OF INFANTICIDE CASES' OUTCOMES

The (initial) outcome of the two trials may seem to be contrary to the argument just made: Quang Cao's deed was prosecuted as a capital case by the state of Alabama, and he was sentenced to death. That sentence was imposed almost unanimously in several independent instances: After the jury pronounced a verdict of capital murder (rather than of either a lesser included offense based upon the provocation defense, or an acquittal on grounds of insanity), it recommended by a majority of ten to two that Cao receive the death penalty. The trial judge followed the jury's recommendation.[24] Finally, the appellate judges affirmed the death sentence unanimously.[25] In contrast, in the first trial of Anne Shen, on which my study is based, the state of California pursued only a verdict of second-degree murder, for which no death penalty is imposed (which in principle is legal in California, and was at the time). The jury followed that recommendation.[26]

In fact, Cao's is the only death penalty case in the reduced corpus of twenty-four cases upon which this study is based (see Part III). This, and the more lenient handling of Shen's case, is suggestive of a *less* rather than more punitive attitude towards a mother who kills her own child than towards a father who does so—contrary to what I would have expected. What is more, I am aware of three other cases involving 'cultural evidence' in which a parent killed their child or children. One involved a man who initially was charged with a capital crime:[27]

> [I]n 1997 an Orthodox Jew in New Jersey killed his children in order to prevent his ex-wife from raising them as Christians. Avi Kostner claimed that Judaism required him to kill his children in order to protect them from evil ('better dead than goyim,' he claimed). He was charged with capital murder, but on the eve of the trial, he pled guilty in order to receive a life sentence. Apparently he had learned that the Jewish community refused to support his depiction of Jewish law, thereby undermining his cultural requirement defense (Levine 2003, 65, footnote omitted, citing Wall 1997).

In contrast, I know of two cases of a woman on whose behalf 'their' communities mobilized and who, as a result, each received a mere probationary sentence for allegedly killing their child or children. One is the highly publicized case of *People vs. Kimura*:[28] Another California woman whose children died in the course of a failed suicide attempt on her part, which she committed upon learning of her husband's infidelity, Kimura eventually received the extremely light sentence of one year in jail (which she had already served by the time of sentencing) plus five years probation.[29] (Initially she too was charged "with first-degree murder with special circumstances which could have brought the death penalty" [Renteln 1993, 463]. It was only after "[t]he Japanese-American community gathered a petition with over 25,000 signatures appealing to the Los Angeles County district attorney not to prosecute her, arguing that her actions were based on a different worldview", that the state's position changed and a plea bargain was struck, resulting in the said light sentence [ibid.].) Another woman, in whose case no 'cultural evidence' was presented, and which involved no claim of a suicide attempt, "was sentenced to twenty years for second-degree murder and felonious child abuse" (Volpp 1994, 96) after the death of one of her children (the cause of which was contested at trial) (ibid.).[30] Chong Sun "France was released on parole on December 31, 1992, after a massive campaign organized by Korean women, who pointed out the lack of culturally specific information in her representation" (ibid.). I shall address the significance of communities' mobilization in each case further ahead, in the context of the specific role of 'race' and of 'cultural evidence' in infanticide cases. First, I want to discuss the fact that the apparent bias against *men* who have killed their children which appears to emerge from this set of cases appears to be consistent with the handling of infanticide cases in general, i.e., apart from the matter of 'cultural evidence'. All of these facts may appear to invalidate my claim that women alleged to have killed their child or children are placed in an especially defensive, gender-biased position relative to men alleged to have done so.

Research indicates that, historically as well as today, there has actually been a trend towards a particularly lenient handling of infanticide cases involving the mother as perpetrator. Thus, a British study comparing the disposition of infanticide cases in the 1980s involving mothers as compared to fathers concludes that:

> From this statistical analysis, it is clear not only that mothers and fathers were treated differently by the criminal justice system but that mothers were dealt with more leniently. Mothers were less likely than fathers to be convicted of murder or to be sentenced to imprisonment and were more likely to be given probation and psychiatric dispositions (Wilczynski and Morris 1993, 35, footnote omitted).

Women perpetrators of infanticide tend to be adjudged insane (ibid., 36). The authors reason that, in contrast, male perpetrators of that act "are perceived as 'wicked' and in need of punishment rather than as victims in need of sympathy, support and psychiatric treatment", as are mothers (ibid., 35). For the U.S., Oberman (1996; 2002) has found the same tendency towards excusing infanticidal mothers, even though she offers no comparison with fathers convicted of the same crime.

On the other hand, research has also noted a discrepancy within the legal handling of infanticides committed by mothers: Wilczynski has found a dichotomy, in a British sample, in virtue of which the defendants received either very light convictions and sentences, or harsh punishments. She accounts for this by arguing that it reflects a perception of those defendants in terms of a dichotomy between 'good mothers' and 'bad mothers':

> In 14 cases, the women were seen as 'mad' and as fulfilling the stereotype of having mental or psychiatric problems. These offenders were viewed as essentially good women and mothers, for whom something had gone tragically wrong. Their responsibility was, therefore, lessened, and hence they were treated sympathetically. . . . In the other eight cases the women were perceived as 'bad' and as having behaved in a way inconsistent with the female stereotype (e.g., as neglectful, uncaring or sexual). They were seen to have committed 'wicked' acts for which they were totally responsible and were treated punitively. All were given prison sentences. There did not appear to be anything between these two extremes (Wilczynski 1991, 74).

Similarly, Oberman observes regarding her U.S. sample of women accused of killing their children:

> Yet, it is also clear that not all infanticide defendants are treated with lenience. Instead, it seems that the criminal justice system and the media cast these diverse defendants as either crazy women, who are punished leniently, if at all, or evil women, who are punished rather harshly (1996, 43).

Accordingly,

> the case outcomes are remarkably varied. At one end of the spectrum, at least two women convicted of infanticide have been sentenced to death, while at the other end, there are several women who were convicted, but released without a prison sentence (1996, 42).

In fact, according to a 2004 study, of the 49 women who were on death row in the U.S. as of June 30 that year, nine were convicted for killing their own child or children—four of them in California and one in Alabama, the state where Cao too received the death penalty.[31]

Citing Wilczynski's study relating to Britain, Oberman agrees with her that:

> Unlike the 'mad' infanticide defendants, those who are viewed as 'bad' are portrayed as 'ruthless, selfish, cold, callous, neglectful of their

> children or domestic responsibilities, violent or promiscuous.' In addition to being tried for infanticide, the media 'tries' these women for all 'crimes' relating to their lack of maternal altruism (Oberman 1996, 45).

Not surprisingly, the 'mad/bad' dichotomy in her sample has class and racialized overtones:

> The cases in my sample in which infanticide defendants received particularly harsh sentences (life imprisonment or death) predominantly involved poor women and/or women of color (ibid., 47).

How do I propose to reconcile my interpretation of the cases of Anne Shen and Quang Cao with these findings? While the latter point to a gendered (as well as racial and class) bias in the disposition of infanticide cases, that bias appears to go the other way from what I have suggested, seemingly privileging women over men. And they certainly do at the level of the outcomes of the cases on average. However, I am proposing that women's advantage and men's disadvantage at the pragmatic level of legal results harks back to patriarchal discourse, that is, to a discourse establishing a hierarchy that in fact privileges men over women.

Much as women are held to a norm of parental duty more sternly than are men, there is also a contrary corollary to the fact that their being is defined in terms of their reproductive capacity in a way that men's is not. As is suggested by the research just introduced, the idea that women are 'destined to be mothers'—an idea historically central to Eurocentric discourse—may also produce an offshoot thought to the effect that, if a woman acts contrary to her nature by hurting her child, this must be due to either extreme duress or insanity. Of course, that thought would be in line with just the stereotypes of femininity in terms of which Anne Shen was portrayed by the defense, such as non-violence and altruism (see Chapter 3). Her representation thus could easily have been *both* especially defensive on account of her being a mother rather than a father and, at the same time, able to benefit from gendered stereotypes in a way that Quang Cao's defense was not. A malicious intent might be attributable more readily to a father than to a mother within a Eurocentric patriarchal imagination, or at least that attribution might be less receptive to so-called 'reasonable' doubt, precisely because such an intent would not be taken to be contrary to men's nature to the same extent, as the latter is not fundamentally defined in terms of fatherhood. This would account for the bias in favor of women that is manifested at the level of case dispositions on average. Of course, the construction of parenthood as somehow more definitive of women than of men—i.e., of their imputed nature—in fact privileges men over women. It does so in that it constructs men as autonomous to define themselves, rather than predetermined by an inherent nature—an attribute accorded the highest value in Enlightenment discourse.

Taken together, then, the differences between the trial strategies in the *Shen* and *Cao* cases, respectively, along with the research just discussed, could be interpreted such that a woman defendant in Anne Shen's position is not as such at a disadvantage vis-à-vis a male defendant such as Quang Cao. But that, rather, hegemonic discourse is more charged in a mother's case, albeit in an ambiguous manner—promoting *both* doubt about any malicious intent imputed to her, and an especially punitive impulse in the event that suspicion wins out over doubt.[32] Much as women may capitalize upon patriarchal notions of mothers' inherently benevolent nature, as is so evident in Anne Shen's defense, the starker end of the spectrum of penalties visited upon women convicted of killing their children is consistent with the notion I have put forward that patriarchal discourse as 'we' know it considers especially blameworthy and unjustifiable (or "the most sinful person", in the words of one expert witness quoted in the preceding chapter[33]) for a *woman* to consciously 'betray' the mothering role that that discourse constructs as both inhering in our nature, and our duty. The defensive character of Shen's defense as compared to Cao's is in line with this notion—namely, its tendency to suppress any aggressive or even self-affirmative components in constructing her 'personality' and actions, in favor of imputing to her an altruism and masochism almost to the point of self-effacement (see Chapter 3). As we shall see in Chapter 6, Shen's prosecution evidenced the accusatory counterpart to that idealization of Shen as a mother, capitalizing upon those aspects of her biography that lent themselves to constructing her as 'selfish' and a bad mother in a partially punitive mode. As in Cao's case, Shen's prosecution and defense thus colluded in a shared patriarchal discourse that reinforced the norm of mothers' duty to their children.

Chiu (1994) has contrasted Quang Cao's case with that of Kimura which I mentioned earlier. As I stated, while Cao received the death penalty, Kimura received probation despite a seemingly similar factual constellation of the two defendants' charged acts. Chiu accounts for this by reference to some of the research I have just discussed, maintaining that, in the U.S., women who kill their children tend to be considered insane and as victims, whereas men tend to be condemned as evil (ibid., 1116–1119; see also Wu 2003, 1005; Lee 2007, 951–954). According to her, the stark contrast between the two cases' outcomes is evidence that, in 'cultural defense' cases, "difference collapses into sameness, as influenced by the dominant culture's perception of appropriate gender roles" (Chiu 1994, 1119). Thus she holds that because Western culture tends to pardon women who have killed their children, while being punitive towards men who have done so, the two defendants' similar acts were treated differently. She holds that the "ultra-femininity myth" in terms of which Asian women are constructed in the U.S.—a notion that assimilates Asian women's differences to white men's idea of an ideal, read: submissive femininity (ibid., 1086–1088)—reinforces the perception of an Asian woman who has killed her children in the course of a failed suicide attempt as an unselfish victim (ibid., 1116–1120).

I want to suggest that the more ambiguous gendered pattern I have outlined, according to which "infanticidal" mothers tend to be polarized into the mad vs. the bad, is a more appropriate interpretation of this set of infanticide cases. For one thing, it was only after a campaign on behalf of both Kimura and France—the two women released on parole following those campaigns—organized from within their communities that they received the said light sentences (Woo 1989; Volpp 1994). As I mentioned, Kimura initially was charged with a capital crime, i.e. as a candidate for the death penalty. France had been sentenced to twenty years for second-degree murder and felonious child abuse (Volpp 1994, 96). These initial charging/sentencing decisions, and the fact that it was a Japanese American and a Korean American initiative, respectively, that resulted in the shift towards leniency in these two cases, is contrary to Chiu's thesis of a default apologetic stance towards "infanticidal" mothers in the hegemonic U.S. public.[34]

So is the fact that Anne Shen was not treated with any particular leniency within the criminal justice system, even though she was never a death-penalty candidate as were Cao and Kimura. (In her first trial, upon which my study is based, the jury chose the prosecution's rather than the defense's favored verdict of second-degree murder, and she was sentenced to a prison term of fifteen years to life [Renteln 1993, 473]. Her conviction was overturned on appeal.[35] In her second trial, she was convicted of the lesser offense of voluntary manslaughter, for which she received the maximum possible sentence—eleven years [Renteln 1993, 474].) Shen's treatment as compared to Kimura's may be attributed to the fact that the latter but not the former is easily approximated to the notion of a good, well-meaning mother and a sexually conformist, virtuous woman—in line with the research discussed earlier. Thus while Kimura was publicly constructed as a devoted mother and faithful wife put to shame by her husband's infidelity (Woo 1989), Shen's absence from her son's life, and her 'illicit' sexual relationship with the boy's married father, made it harder to approximate her to such a stereotype. It is my suggestion that this, along with the campaigns that took place on behalf of Kimura as well as France, may account for the fact that the disposition of Shen's case is not one of clear-cut leniency, in contrast with the other two mothers' cases.

It is also necessary to consider whether the cases at hand are set apart from others in virtue of 'race' and the presentation of 'cultural evidence'. Especially in light of Oberman's finding that "[t]he cases in [her] sample in which infanticide defendants received particularly harsh sentences (life imprisonment or death) predominantly involved poor women and/or women of color" (1996, 47; see also Huckerby 2003). The matter seems equivocal to me in the case of Asian *women* defendants in infanticide cases. They might (strategically speaking) either benefit from or be disadvantaged by racist notions such as the 'ultra-femininity myth', depending in part on how convincingly they manage to embody that particular stereotype (Volpp 1994)—which as such may support a construction of the defendant in terms of the notion of the traditional, subordinate woman/mother, as Chiu suggests.[36] But it is easy to see how any bias against *men* who have killed their children would be aggravated by the construct of the Asian patriarch—a principal possibility whenever the notion of Patriarchal Other Cultures is mobilized in defense of a man rather than of a woman. For, whereas that notion serves to construct women as victims (reinforced, in the case of Asian or Asian American women, by the ultra-femininity myth), in however debasing a form, in men's case, its potential for mobilizing an identification along patriarchal lines competes with a potential condemnation of the racialized Other as "not-me", in a way exemplified by the prosecution's procedure in *People vs. Lopez and Singh* (see Chapter 2). So, the sexist defense strategy chosen for Cao's legal representation may have boomeranged for reasons related to 'race' as much as to 'gender'.

I am suggesting, then, that male privilege at the level of trial strategy (the fact that aggression in Cao's case was overtly legitimized, and that his feelings about his children were not in focus, unlike in Shen's trial) may have a detrimental effect for men at the level of case dispositions, which is aggravated if the defendant is viewed as racially Other. It is, nonetheless, a privilege in that the kind of defense strategy offered for Cao would be unthinkable in support of a woman defendant.[37] Whether or not I am correct in thinking that this shows a woman tried for infanticide to be in a particularly defensive position relative to a man: even if this were untrue, that is, if Chiu were correct in arguing that there is a *consistently* greater leniency towards infanticidal mothers than towards fathers, this would still add up to a gendered unevenness in the legal handling of such cases—both at the level of their results, and at that of defense strategy, as evidenced in the comparison of the trials of Shen and Cao. Even then, that unevenness would hark back to a patriarchal logic: If Chiu is right, then the norm of motherly duty is naturalized such that women are *generally* deemed incapable of intentionally harming their children. If I am right, that norm tends to be cited in a prescriptive mode rather than *exclusively* as a naturalization of women as "compulsively" good mothers—meaning that women need to '*evidence*' being good mothers rather than being presumed to be that in advance. Either possibility is consistent with my tenet that the norm of parental duty continues to be more pronounced in mothers' case than in fathers' in the U.S. With this conclusion, I am ready to return to the point of my comparison between the two defense strategies: the relationship between patriarchal discourse and the construction of cultural difference.

* * *

My comparison has shown that the 'cultural evidence' presented in *People vs. Shen* and *State vs. Cao*, respectively, was shaped by gender-differentiated divergent discursive frames that are fully 'native' to U.S. common sense. (In this fundamental point, that comparison fully vindicates Chiu's thesis that, in many 'cultural defense' cases, "difference collapses into sameness, as influenced by the dominant culture's perception of appropriate gender roles" [1994, 1119].) The argument made in each of the two defenses, to the effect that the infanticide was in some sense a culturally specific act associated with an attempted suicide, which was committed in response to intense shame and emotional upheaval being blamed on the defendant's spouse, was articulated, respectively, in accordance with 'feminine' vs. 'masculine' *Euro-American* myths of gender character that entail patriarchal norms. In *People vs. Shen*, on the one hand, that point was constructed such as to buttress a rendering of the defendant as both helpless and altruistic in intention in accordance with hegemonic U.S. norms of femininity that subordinate women, based on an appeal to stereotypes of submissive, oppressed Asian women. In *State vs. Cao*, on the other hand, the 'same' point was used to legitimize, rather than dissimulate, the defendant's aggression against both his wife and their children by making her responsible for it, in accordance with U.S. notions of masculinity that promote male dominance, possessiveness and violence, and a patriarchal concept of the family. In either case, it is a *U.S.* patriarchal discourse that the cultural 'information' as to a patriarchal Asian culture is called upon to buttress, and to which the selection and discursive construction of that 'information' is tailored. The patriarchal character of the argument therefore is not primarily a function of the 'cultural evidence' mobilized. It is a function, instead, of the hegemonic status of patriarchy in the U.S.[38] This point is reinforced by the fact that the prosecution in Cao's trial, which offered no 'cultural evidence', colluded in the patriarchal discourse structuring the ethnicizing defense strategy. As we shall see in some detail in Chapter 6, Shen's prosecution too interlocked with the defense in a shared patriarchal discourse. Something not unusual for prosecutions' discourses of sexual difference within my corpus of cases—especially in rape trials. As Chiu argues, in the 'cultural defense', "[t]he judicial process becomes an opportunity for white society to reify sexism and to reinforce and reconstruct the subordination of women through another culture" (ibid., 1120; see also Phillips 2007, 96–97).

As in Shen's trial (see Chapter 3), the patriarchal character of the U.S. sensibilities to which Cao's 'cultural defense' was appealing was being dissimulated by a colonialist frame of representing the 'evidence' regarding Vietnam, which contrasted Vietnamese gender inequality to an implied gender egalitarianism in the U.S. This occurred chiefly through the expert for cross-cultural counseling—himself initially from Vietnam—who related cultural difference through a paradigm contrasting 'closed societies', with which he identified Vietnam, with 'open societies', in terms of which he classified the U.S.[39] This conceptual scheme forms another variant, of course, of a dichotomy that classifies each social formation in terms of an essence. It is yet another dichotomy consonant with the hierarchizing colonial discourse that contrasts 'the West' and 'the rest' in terms of liberalism vs. despotism (an opposition we have encountered in the trial *People vs. Lopez and Singh* [Chapter 2] in the guise of that between liberalism and illiberalism).[40] Thus, the witness defined a closed society in part by its hierarchical character, specifying that characterization to gender relations. For instance:

Q Now, let's go to cross-cultural comparison. What is a closed society?
A A closed society is a term that anthropologists use to describe a society that is very hierarchical and very structured whereby the rules of the course of conduct by each member in that society is spelled out very very clearly. And that is significant in the sense that the conduct of the husband to a wife is spelled out; the conduct of a wife to a husband is very very much spelled out. And that contrasts with an open society which anthropologists consider the U.S. as an open society where rules or course of conduct are not spelled out that clearly.[41]

Q What is the father's role towards the family in the Vietnamese society?
A To make all decisions concerning the family, and also to be responsible for all of those decisions.[42]

Q Dr. [X], what is the significance of fidelity in the marital relationship in the Vietnamese culture?
A Okay. Let me set the background for you. This comes out of the confusion [sic[43]] analex [sic]. It says when you're a young girl, you listen to your father; when you are of an age to be married, you listen to your husband; and when your husband's deceased, you listen to your eldest son. So, a wife or woman is almost considered, in a sense, the possession of a man when they are married.[44]

The 'open society' vs. 'closed society' opposition in terms of which the 'expert' constructed cultural differences between Vietnamese and 'U.S.' (read: Euro-American) culture, including gendered differences, suggested that the latter is characterized by (more) liberal, flexible sexual arrangements—especially given that his testimony addressed gender-unegalitarian arrangements only in relation to Vietnam, and cast Vietnamese culture as being very different from the U.S., without pointing out any similarities in regard to gendered order:

Q In terms of cross cultural [sic] differences, are there differences between a closed society and an open society?
A Yes. They are very—they contrast with each other. Very much so.[45]

Q . . . When we talk about Vietnam and the culture in Vietnam and the United States, is it or is it not a true statement that it is not the similarities that cause the problems but the differences?
A Yes.
Q And what do you mean by that?
A That unless you can realize on a conscious level what the differences are between the two cultures and work to overcome them and have

> the support system to overcome them, which [Quang] does not, that you indeed have a real serious problem, and it's almost a ticking time bomb.[46]

The anthropological paradigm that the expert witness brought to bear, then, forms another instance of the figure of the Patriarchal Other operative in the trials examined in this study. As in *People vs. Shen* (Chapter 3), that figure functioned within the defense strategy in such a way as to disown the patriarchal character of the latter. In a defense such as Cao's, which mobilizes patriarchal discourse to discredit a woman rather than to raise sympathy for her, and which justifies a man's actions in according fashion, this takes a form of "double speak" posing as tolerance of supposedly 'alien' and 'un-American' cultures, which sanctions the objectification of women without acknowledging (at least explicitly) its affinity to U.S. norms. Maguigan aptly characterizes this dynamic in commenting upon another case of 'cultural defense' on behalf of a male defendant in a rape case, which resulted in a very light sentence:

> Stated simply, the disposition in Kong Moua may be seen as a retreat, under the guise of cultural pluralism, to the dominant culture's view that crimes of violence against women are not serious and that the price of anti-woman violence is not high. Such a view has long been represented in American criminal courts' treatment of rape cases (1995, 66, footnotes omitted).[47]

Due to the disavowal of the identification with the sexism imputed to the Other, however, this identification does not negate the racist devaluation of that Other within the variant of discourse instantiated in *State vs. Cao*. For, the fact that the patriarchal identification with the ethnically Othered remains unacknowledged secures a morally innocent, superior Western/white self who merely extends 'tolerance':

> Culture, when it is taken into account, usually reinforces Anglo-Saxon superiority, as when a male of Polish origin who is found guilty of sexual assault is described sympathetically by the court as being a new immigrant 'perhaps unfamiliar with Canadian social mores or the rules of social interaction' (Razack 1998, 84, footnote omitted; see also Fournier 2002).

This seemingly 'sympathetic' variant of the figure of the Patriarchal Other therefore forms but an inversion of that variant which condemns that Other (compare Koptiuch 1996, 216)—which is implicitly instantiated in *People vs. Shen* (see Chapter 3) and, most pronouncedly so, in prosecutions engaging in 'cultural profiling', such as *People vs. Lopez and Singh* (Chapter 2) (see also Desai 2007, 78–79, 82n23):[48] All of these variants devalue the

Other, postulating a superiority of the West based upon a disavowal of its patriarchal character. Koptiuch sums up the colonialist underpinnings of even the supposedly 'tolerant' version of this discourse:

> In the name of multicultural sensitivity, advocates of a cultural defense urge the court to expand the law's legitimacy through greater flexibility—yet the only cultural alterity they seem willing to countenance is a highly specific, reified Otherness. What counts as 'culture' in this context? The law's own claims of representative *inclusiveness* are premised upon essential, asymmetrical, racially constructed, unified, stable 'traditions' of gender difference and cultural identity, all representations that were initially devised by colonial discourses to *exclude* from equal status those Others whose disqualifying difference from Western culture was carefully classified, coded, and hierarchized by the panoptic, disciplinary technologies that sustained colonial rule (1996, 228, original emphasis, references omitted; see also Deckha 2009, 267; Lawrence 2001, 113; Briggs and Mantini-Briggs 2000, esp. 306, 318).

5 Conclusion

Cultural Information or Gendered Colonial Discourse?

The juxtaposition of *People vs. Lopez and Singh*[1], *People vs. Shen*[2], and *State vs. Cao*[3] in the three preceding chapters (2 through 4) shows that trials encompassing diverse evidentiary constellations and categories of ethnicity, as well as differences in gendered constellation and in the backgrounds of the 'culture witnesses' presented (hegemonic or minority, qualified on biographical or academic grounds) exhibit very similar discursive structures characterized by gendered as well as colonialist concepts that are both hierarchizing and essentializing. Moreover, as shown in Chapter 2, these structures do not transpire only in cases of a 'cultural defense' at all, but have shaped prosecution strategies that relied upon so-called 'cultural evidence' as well. What this indicates is that the construction of patriarchy as something essentially non-Western in which these structures intersect is a hegemonic *discursive figure* in terms of which what is presented as 'cultural information' *in U.S. courts* tends to be framed—rather than a matter of patriarchal norms actually inhering primarily in 'the other culture'.

Reinforcing this point, my discussion of *People vs. Shen* (Chapter 3), and the comparison with *State vs. Cao* (Chapter 4), have shown that a patriarchal deployment of 'cultural evidence' is in no way unique to cases in which a male defendant legitimizes gendered violence by appeal to his cultural background—as some 'feminist' contributors to the debate, such as Rimonte (1991), Goldstein (1994, 162–163), and Cardillo (1997), seem to have assumed. While Anne Shen's 'cultural defense' perhaps was not harmful in the same way as arguments that legitimize male violence (whether against women or otherwise), such as occurred in *State vs. Cao*, the logic of argument is no less patriarchal in character, validating as it does both gender-unegalitarian norms and their reifying inscription as a matter of women's 'nature'. I find it hard to imagine that any self-avowed feminist would want to dispute, in the face of the 'evidence' I have provided in Chapter 3, that it is to the *U.S.* norm of motherly duty that the representation of Shen's 'culture' was tailored to appeal. The patriarchal character of the defenses of both Anne Shen and Quang Cao, then, were a function, in the first place, of the hegemonic status of sexism in the U.S. (see also Phillips 2007, 97; Boulette Taylor 1998, 467; Suri 2000, 139).

Framing the debate about the 'cultural defense' in terms of the question of "whether to permit criminal defendants to introduce cultural evidence" (Maguigan 1995, 36)—the motto under which that debate has been conducted—therefore is utterly inappropriate. It is to render invisible the overarching unegalitarian practices entailed *in the deployment of* cultural 'evidence' in regard to both race and gender and, instead, to repeat the displacement of patriarchy to a realm of cultural Otherness so prevalent in trials where such 'evidence' is used. Feminist as well as antiracist interest commands that, instead of reproducing the dissimulation of hegemonic U.S. patriarchy, and the construction of a morally superior West buttressed by it, the figure of the Patriarchal Other be vigorously questioned in regard to its service to both imperialism and patriarchy. We need to intervene against their *interlocking* agency in that figure.

Just as empiricism served to validate as inhering in 'culture' and 'gender' the hierarchizing, essentialist discourses within the trials examined above, so it also underpins the reification of 'Other cultures' as patriarchal engaged in by writers such as Coleman (1996) and Okin (1999). After all, that reification is rendered possible only by their treatment of 'cultural evidence' as unmediated facts about 'the other culture'. But as shown in Chapter 1, amongst others, that approach is also instantiated in contributions to the debate with which I otherwise sympathize. For instance, we have seen in Chapter 3 that Volpp's empathy for women, such as Anne Shen, who have attempted parent-child suicide apparently tempts her to adopt an empiricist perspective by claiming greater accuracy for the 'cultural evidence' presented on Shen's behalf as compared to that presented for Dong Lu Chen. As I have argued, she does so at the cost of naturalizing the patriarchal norms cited as part of Anne Shen's defense as a matter of Shen's actual character. (Essentially, I would hold that Volpp herself constructs Shen as a 'good' rather than 'bad' mother in a way that reinforces that dichotomy rather than marking it as patriarchal.) This example thus shows the pitfall inherent in an empiricist approach to 'cultural evidence': it tends to reify its constructions as the truth about 'the Other', while naturalizing hierarchizing norms and assumptions in the process. This produces power effects not exclusively at the level of discursive politics, but also at the level of presuming to *know* the individual other involved. Thus one might question whether Volpp, in constructing Anne Shen's portrayal by the defense as more accurate than Dong Lu Chen's, is not imputing to herself a bird's-eye view upon these cases and persons in a way similar to the anthropologist Pasternak whom she criticizes.[4] This double risk—of a political and ethical imperialism—is inherent also in those contributions to the debate which frame the sexist complicities with 'the Other' that occur in many 'cultural defense' cases (such as *State vs. Cao*, as shown in Chapter 4) as a matter of factual cultural similarity (Chiu 1994; Phillips 2007, Ch. 3; Song 2007, Ch. 4)—for instance, when Chiu argues that "Hmong and American sexual concepts are the same" (1994, 1116).

While the epistemological alternative I am proposing may raise problems of its own,[5] it seems to me to be the more cautious approach in dealing with the ignorance vis-à-vis "others" that is endemic to a hegemonic subject position (white/middle-class/male, etc.), but that also emerges *wherever* anyone deals with cultural differences she has no personal experience of. (Moreover, as Narayan has argued, "[e]ven for a purported insider, it is clearly impossible to be omniscient: one knows about a society from particular locations within it" [2003, 295]. A consideration that [amongst others] leads her to question the very dichotomy of 'cultural insiders vs. outsiders'.) Such ignorance certainly is no excuse for accepting colonial and patriarchal constructions as 'facts'—as Phillips may seem to suggest when she states:

> The risk as regards minority cultural practices and traditions is that courts may lack the knowledge to assess the evidence and may be too ready to accept what they are told. Ignorance can lead to gullibility, and exaggerated beliefs about cultural difference can lead people to believe the strangest things about how those from other cultures behave. There is a danger, in other words, that cultural claims might not be adequately scrutinised [sic] (2007, 83).

I am not suggesting, of course, that constructions of 'cultural evidence' may not contain false claims or that they should not be scrutinized for empirical inaccuracies. The infamous trial of *People vs. Dong Lu Chen* (compared by Volpp [1994] to *People vs. Anne Shen* [see Chapter 3]) is a case in point (see also Chen 2009, esp. 252–254; Renteln 2009, 71–74). My position is, rather, that an attention to the hierarchizing quality of the discourses passing themselves off as 'cultural information' will discredit much of such 'information' even in the absence of its empirical falsification—and whether or not it is, in fact, empirically inaccurate (as I argued in examining *People vs. Anne Shen* [Chapter 3]). An approach to 'cultural evidence' that treats it in terms of normatively loaded *constructions* to which there is no unmediated alternative will avoid converting such constructions into 'the truth about the Other'.

The discourse-theoretical, anti-essentialist position which I am trying to formulate here also implies that in assessing 'cultural evidence', we should be vigilantly critical of the discourses drawn upon in *all* court cases—rather than attending primarily to whether the 'evidence' is deployed in favor of a man or a woman, or to what is the racial/sexual classification of those testifying. For, given the hegemonic status of both colonial and patriarchal discourse, their occurrence is to be anticipated in *any* of these constellations. This finding, which has emerged most clearly from my study of *People vs. Anne Shen*, is contrary to optimistic assessments of the use of 'cultural evidence' in cases where its presentation could be viewed as promoting the value of anti-subordination, as Volpp has proposed (1994, 59, 97–99) (see Chapter 3). Volpp has put forward this principle in the spirit of strategic essentialism, well aware of the likely essentializing character of evidence based upon cultural identity (ibid., 90–96; see also Deckha 2004, 40–42).

The case studies presented in this Part also make it apparent that cultural expert testimony by members of a given minority 'community' is not immune to using approaches and concepts with colonialist implications—and with patriarchal implications, we should add. Thus, we have seen in the preceding chapters that both colonialist Othering and gendered Othering do indeed transpire (though perhaps to a lesser degree) in testimony on cultural difference even where it is mobilized from within 'the' community concerned. Nor should we assume that academic experts who are not 'white' are inherently immune to appealing to scientific 'objectivity' to authorize their assertions, as we have seen in Chapter 3. Moreover, the discourse of cultural authenticity based upon biographical experience can serve an empiricist validating function as readily as can academic expertise, much as that function may have racist implications that objectify the 'native' expert at the same time, as we saw in *People vs. Lopez and Singh* (Chapter 2). While I agree with Volpp's position that it is preferable for 'cultural evidence' to be presented by members of the community concerned (and specifically by members of the community "sensitive to the dynamics of power and subordination" within it [1996, 1593–1594; see also Wong 1999, esp. 391]), this does not automatically eliminate a problematic discursive politics. Nor, as we have seen, does the calling of several 'experts' from the community concerned automatically guard against their collusion in a shared hegemonic perspective—contrary to what one might take Song to suggest (2007; compare Chapter 1). None of this is meant to imply that the measures proposed by these commentators—that is, Volpp's principle of antisubordination (1994), and Song's of calling a number of 'experts' from within a given community, and of establishing a code of ethics and a system of peer review for expert witnesses (2007, 107; see also Rosen 1977)—are useless. It is to say, rather, that they are unlikely fundamentally to alleviate what is a problem, in the first place, of a discursive politics so hegemonic as to be nearly paramount in courtroom discourses of cultural difference.

Lawrence's contribution to the debate as to a 'cultural defense' performs a significant shift here (2001; see also Desai 2007). Adding to suggestions similar to Volpp's that pertain to the social positionality of those charged with constructing 'cultural evidence', she proposes, inter alia, that the postcolonial-feminist principle of intersectionality (see Part II) also inform judicial education programs (2001, 130–134), and that these should deconstruct the kind of "cultural racism" (ibid., 130) that opposes 'their culture' to 'our reason'. This is to move in the direction of formulating criteria targeted directly at changing the *discourse* in terms of which 'cultural evidence' is framed and received. While I welcome this step, in itself, in addition, I think that—potentially at least—it paves the way for a recognition of the discursive *character* of such 'evidence', as such. Thus the relational perspective that is implicitly introduced through concepts such as 'intersectionality' and 'cultural racism'—which makes it possible to place power center-stage, including the positioning of the *hegemonic* subject within the relevant constructions—serves to undermine the common reduction of 'culture' to a matter of 'facts about the Other' which seems to be characteristic, too, of judicial education programs as currently practiced (ibid., 129–131; see also Razack 1998). An introduction of this relational perspective would thus hold a potential for rendering problematic the empiricism underlying the latter approach (with its attendant reduction of discursive politics to a matter of accurate vs. distorted representations of 'facts'), while drawing attention, instead, to the normative and conceptual frames in terms of which such 'facts' are *invariably* constructed. (I will address institutional limits to initiatives for discursive change, such as this, in the Conclusion to this work [Part VI].)

The lesson to be drawn from this Part, then, is this: It is not a question of whether or not 'evidence' pertaining to cultural difference should be permissible. As Maguigan (1995, 53) and others have written, excluding such 'evidence' would amount to disadvantaging minority defendants vis-à-vis those from the hegemonic culture in many cases because it may have a bearing upon state of mind.[6] Moreover, it is absurd to consider that question while 'cultural evidence' is used by prosecuting parties, usually as part of proving a minority defendant guilty. Nor can the question be reduced to which categories of "subject" introduce such evidence, or in what gender/race constellations—much as I respect Volpp's proposition that the decision of whether to support its introduction should be guided by whether (considering the gendered and racial constellation of a given case) this would promote the value of anti-subordination or be detrimental to it (1994). What needs to be understood is that, for the purposes of the U.S. criminal justice process, there *is* no 'cultural information' with an identity independent of the discourses in terms of which it is framed and received as 'evidence' in U.S. courts. What is produced in court are *discourses* of difference (cultural, sexual, etc.). It is, first and foremost, the *unegalitarian discourses hegemonic in the U.S.* that must be critiqued and transformed—both regarding the discursive politics of 'cultural evidence', and beyond.

In the next Part, this insight will be given further foundation through a closer inspection of the contributions by the trial's respective participants to reproducing those discourses—the opposing attorneys as well as the different varieties of witnesses. Contrary to Maguigan's injunction for us to rely on the workings of the adversary system, particularly on the critical ability of prosecutors in contesting 'cultural evidence' (1995; see Chapter 1), we will see in the following chapter to just what extent the opposing parties are caught up in the same discourses instead of contesting them at any fundamental level. This should teach us to be cautious of assuming a reason autonomous of discourse, as I will conclude. Before embarking upon this argument, however, I will round off the present Part with a comment on recent trends in the controversy about 'the cultural defense'.

RECENT DEVELOPMENTS IN THE DEBATE: A CRITICAL PERSPECTIVE

In the last few years (especially in 2009), an unprecedented number of texts has appeared that cover the subject of 'cultural evidence' in the legal system—including two collections of articles; one academic (Foblets and Renteln 2009), the other a symposium issue of a judicial journal (*Judicature* 2009). Two developments are noteworthy within the rather linear course that this mini-publishing industry has stirred—which industry, for the most part, continues to trade in ever new, yet astonishingly repetitive additions to what has long ago become a staple stock of "pro" and "contra" arguments (either for vs. against a *formal* 'cultural defense', or regarding other, more specific usages of pertinent 'evidence').

For one thing, we may note an increasing, usually quasi-journalistic interest in surveying the empirical spectrum of cases and forms in which 'cultural evidence' has actually entered the legal system, criminal and otherwise (Renteln 2004; Foblets and Renteln 2009; *Judicature* 2009; Levine 2006; Glass-O'Shea 2009)[7]—aside, that is, from the continuing preoccupation with the normative question of its permissibility (represented most recently by Hallevy 2009, 2010; Held and Fontaine 2009; DePalma 2009; Morgan and Parker 2009; Friedman Ramirez 2009; Cohan 2010; Frischknecht 2009). Partially, though not throughout, however, this more empirical strand of recent scholarly and professional publishing on the subject is characterized either by clear-cut advocacy of the 'pro' position vis-à-vis a (formal) 'cultural defense'—represented by Renteln's many contributions on the subject [see, e.g., References])—or at least by a display of open-mindedness towards 'cultural difference' and the ways in which it may "show up" in the legal system. The latter posture is illustrated by the majority of the contributions to the symposium issue of the journal *Judicature* which I have already mentioned.

Much as this strand of recent writing on the subject tends to associate itself, specifically or more loosely, with what may be called the 'pro' position in the debate, then, *it is fully (if inadvertently) complicit with the very colonial and racialized discourse whose implication in the issue of 'cultural evidence' in the legal system it deflects from systematically.* This applies in at least two respects. One concerns the exclusionary character of the rhetoric engaged by most texts in this category: an uncritical rhetoric framed by terms such as 'cultural differences' and 'pluralism', rather than 'power', which *engages* in Othering those whom it treats as inherent 'cultural others' (whom it is supposedly 'our' mission to 'include') in virtue of that very—patronizing—language. Even as, at the same time, that rhetoric *disavows* its own participation in racialized exclusion and inequality (compare Ch. 1, n. 8, concerning Renteln's major, book-length treatise [2004]).

This duplicity[8] is enabled, while simultaneously being covered over, by the empiricist treatment of 'cultural difference in the legal system' in terms of mere 'facts' about 'others' which I have been critiquing throughout this work. Indeed, the empiricist approach makes for more common ground between proponents and opponents of 'the cultural defense', even aside from the mutual complicity of many of them in constituting the figure of a Patriarchal Other Culture (as demonstrated in this Part, and see Ch. 4, n. 47). What the empiricist approach leaves utterly unthreatened—and, indeed, actively stabilizes—is the position of an implicitly Western, primarily white 'us' that forms the unquestioned normative standard whose imaginary superiority is as much implied as it will (usually) be disavowed when challenged head-on.

As is well illustrated by the 2009 issue of *Judicature* mentioned earlier—especially by its Introduction (Ridgway 2009)—, the 'open-minded' position being adopted here in a pose of what might be called judicial 'armchair anthropology' protects the subjects assuming that position from ever having to face the relational perspective that the empiricist treatment of 'cultural difference in the legal system' occludes from view: that is, the question of what the exclusive focus upon 'cultural facts' about exoticized 'others' accomplishes for the Western, hegemonically white 'self' in terms of power, normativity, and presumed superiority. In this dividing practice (Foucault 1982, 208) of constituting a self in distinction from a cast-out 'other', the imaginary whiteness of the 'us' that results remains unacknowledged within the kind of discourse which I am trying to characterize here—which at most is admitted to be culturally particular (e.g., Renteln 2004; see Ch. 1, n. 8); usually in the form of the (similarly) exclusionary euphemism for 'the Western' that the term 'American' has tended to become. The unavowedly racialized paternalism of this pseudo-pluralist rhetoric—whose condescension may be glossed, ironically speaking, as 'foreigner-friendly'—is aptly analyzed by Razack as follows:

> A knowledge of cultural difference of the Other helps those in dominant groups to classify and manage subordinate groups. The eagerness with which theories of cultural difference are taken up by the justice system, while racism and sexism remain unnamed, is a reminder that culture is a treacherous ground to travel in a white supremacist and patriarchal society (1998, 80).

But there is also a second respect in which most of the "positive" or "open-minded" strand of positions vis-à-vis 'the cultural defense' has been complicit with racialized exclusion. Namely, through the rigorous yet perennially unstated isolationalist focus upon '*the* cultural *defense*' which nearly all contributors to the debate have maintained collaboratively: The controversy, as whole, remains as oblivious as ever to any links one might make between that defense, on the one hand and, on the other, *prosecutions* based upon cultural profiling (which the present work demonstrates to form a parallel practice; see Appendix and Chapter 2).

If the simultaneous occurrence of "cultural prosecutions" was acknowledged, and its implications considered, then it would be impossible for the debate to proceed in the terms in which it has been framed so far: that is, in terms of the question of whether a 'cultural defense' should be permissible at all. For, these terms have wrongly insinuated—while never allowing this presupposition actually to be stated, such that it might be exposed to scrutiny—that 'cultural evidence' will only ever enter the legal system as a potential (pragmatic) *advantage* to 'minority' defendants, rather than also being used *against* them by the state in potentially racialized and discriminatory ways.[9] In posing the question for debate in terms that systematically render this latter fact invisible, even *proponents* of 'the cultural defense' have colluded (inadvertently, I assume, but no less actively for that) in promoting the misleading notion—which is championed overtly by *opponents* of the 'cultural defense'—that allowing the use of 'cultural evidence' in the criminal defense of minority subjects (usually: subjects 'of color') would amount to 'dishing out' some 'special favor' to these; that is, to *privileging* them vis-à-vis so-called 'whites' (compare Chapter 1). (In the European, German-language context, this notion has in fact been rendered explicit through the use of the expression 'culture *discount*' [*kultureller Rabatt*] instead of 'cultural defense'—an expression which, significantly, is being bandied about, not only by opponents of a 'cultural defense', but by at least one proponent as well [Frischknecht 2009; see Braunmühl, forthcoming, for a critique].) In propagating that misleading impression through their systematic silence about the occurrence of cultural profiling by prosecutors, advocates of a 'cultural defense' have contributed to the racist exclusion of those whose cause they profess to champion, and have helped nurture the increasingly unabashed hegemonic *ressentiment* that is more overtly being cultivated against migrants and other people of color as a class, both by opponents of that legal strategy (in particular), and by the overall anti-egalitarian neoliberal/neoconservative project (in general) in which they participate (Vieux 1994; Omi and Winant 1994; Dawson and Schueller 2007; see also Razack 2008). In this way, what—on the face of it—appear to be 'diverse', even mutually antagonistic positions within a controversially conducted 'democratic debate' supposedly characterized by openness to all possible viewpoints, are in fact *united* by an underlying hegemonic consensus that binds together most of the political and social spectrum (i.e., most 'pro' and 'con' positions regarding 'the cultural defense'): a consensus biased against migrants and other racialized minorities (as well as against all women, as explained in the preceding chapters).

It is a mere symptom of that fundamental, shared bias—and, therefore, should not come as a surprise—that recently, there have in fact been calls for 'cultural evidence' to be deployed as an *aggravating*, rather than a mitigating, circumstance in criminal sentencing. Thus, in various European states, demands or even legislative proposals have been made for *higher* sentences to be imposed in cases of honor-related violence or (specifically) honor killings (Siesling and Ten Voorde 2009, 165–167, 158–159; Maier 2009, 244)—even (in the case of German politician Kristina Köhler, now named Kristina Schröder) as a blanket, *mandatory* matter (ibid.). An initiative that would effectively *prohibit any consideration of the individual circumstances of a case* specifically and only in criminal procedures relating to honor-related violence (compare Siesling and Ten Voorde 2009, 167, esp. n102). It would thus set apart *as a class* honor-related violence from all other kinds of (gendered) violence—e.g., from so-called 'crimes of passion'—thus instituting a legally sanctioned ethnicizing dividing practice (Foucault 1982, 208) that arguably would amount to direct discrimination.

Similarly, in the U.S. context, Hallevy has recently posited that:

> culture-based crimes against women, by their very essence, include harsher sentencing factors compared with the same offenses committed in contexts other than culture. Thus, for example, when a man rapes a woman, he deserves punishment. When a man rapes a woman out of cultural ideology, as an act of oppressing women or as an act preserving his culture, he deserves harsher punishment. The specific offense is important for the punishment considerations, but the cultural context is crucial for handing down harsher sentences. Thus, the courts should not only avoid mitigating sentencing in culture-based crimes against women, but also should issue harsher sentences (2010, 466).[10]

These voices, while not (as yet) that great a threat in terms of numbers, fully warrant being marked as the second significant recent development in the "cultural defense debate" for qualitative reasons. For, they spell out in the most overt terms—and thus, make explicit—the anti-migrant/anti-minority, punitive potential of the racialized bias which the debate *as a whole* has instantiated from its very inception, as just explained. (It is telling that the potential availability of a so-called 'culture discount' to migrants has been labeled in a German-language educational text designed for schools, which is made available online by an EU-supported website, as a case of *Zweiklassenjustiz* or 'two-class justice'—even as the text in question, too, calls for honor-related killings to be punished as murder rather than manslaughter *invariably* [Ohlendorf, n.d., 2–3]: that is, without consideration of the specific circumstances of a case that criminal defendants are otherwise supposedly afforded. Such demands for 'cultural evidence' effectively to be used *against* migrants as an aggravating circumstance in sentencing—even as a matter of imposing a blanket sentence specifically in cases of ethnicized crimes commonly attributed to people of color—have nowhere drawn protest against the 'two-class justice', the discriminatory racialization of the law, that *this* would, on the contrary, amount to.)

The constitutive interrelation between two seemingly contrary positions which thus characterizes the academic and popular commentary on 'the cultural defense'—between, on the one hand, a 'pluralist', 'tolerant' and 'sensitive' form of Othering and, on the other, a hostility vis-à-vis people of color that is as open-minded towards measures discriminating against them as it will cry 'reverse discrimination' (or '*Zweiklassenjustiz*') in protest at every move designed to counter such unegalitarian practices—this relationship of mutual indebtedness parallels the oscillation, in the courtroom itself, of 'culture' discourse between a condescending sexist '*toleration*' and an overt, pseudo-feminist *condemnation* of an Other who is, in either variant, freeze-framed as essentially patriarchal (as analyzed at the end of the preceding chapter). Therefore, the same point I have argued in this Part with a view to the in-court use of 'cultural evidence' holds for the academic/professional debate regarding that practice as well: Each pole within the spectrum of the (mainstream, meaning: ethnicizing, power-blind) positions on offer forms but the other side of the coin of its supposed adversary.

As I have been demonstrating in this work so far, that collusion pertains, firstly, to a shared empiricism which renders power relations invisible and, secondly, to an overall racialized bias against people of color, which is embedded in the very way that the debate has—ultimately—figured the migrant presence in the first World as a *problem* (compare Koptiuch 1996). Thirdly, contributors to the debate have, on either side, resorted to gender as a means of stirring that racialized (primarily anti-immigrant) "moral panic" (Volpp 1996, 1602–1603)—paralleling other uses of gender to that same end, as in the 'war on terror' (Volpp 2006, 1634–1635; Razack 2008; see also Römhild 2007, esp. 218–220). In doing so, those concerned have been mutually complicit, not merely in instrumentalizing—ultimately—all women, as I have argued. They have also colluded, particularly, in objectifying women of color: whether as legitimate objects of violent sexist practices (in the 'pluralist' variant 'tolerant' of patriarchy yet supposedly unimplicated in it [compare Ch. 4, n. 47]), *or* as objects of 'protective' advances by white would-be saviors (in pseudo-feminist comments such as Hallevy's [2010]).

Part V

Resistance/Instabilities

The Spectrum of Discursive Politics in Trials Involving 'Cultural Evidence' and the Involuntary Subversion of Hegemonic Discourse

6 Contesting 'Cultural Evidence'

Adversarial Opposition or Mutual Collusion?

Dominance appears most effectively precisely as its 'Other'.

Butler (2000b, 28)

As documented in Chapter 1, Maguigan's thoughtful intervention into the 'cultural defense' debate places faith in the adversary system and the capacity of prosecutors effectually to challenge stereotyped 'cultural evidence' offered by the defense (1995, 96–97, 86; see also Wong 1999, 395–396). However, the present chapter will demonstrate that placing faith in the adversary system and in prosecutors' capacity for critical reasoning is misplaced, considering the strategies of contesting 'cultural evidence' deployed in the corpus of cases upon which this study is based. That conclusion is contrary to the one reached in a recent contribution to the debate—Hoeffel's 2006 article with the promising, but misleading title "Deconstructing the cultural evidence debate". Arguing that the large array of 'cultural defense' cases which she surveys—on the basis of judicial opinions rather than trial transcripts—shows that the admissibility of the 'evidence' in question was handled by judges in accordance with relevancy considerations unrelated to "cultural insensitivity", she concludes that "a more detailed accounting of some of the cases involving cultural evidence belies a pattern of either cultural insensitivity or a gender bias" (2006, 327). She adds that:

> Far from concluding there are no problems in the presentation of the evidence, this Essay has determined that problems do exist, but they do not appear to stem from the cultural insensitivity assumed by the scholars. Rather, they are failures of advocacy and the substantive criminal law (ibid., 344–345).[1]

That conclusion is enabled by a bifurcation on Hoeffel's part of "cultural insensitivity" vs. "common sense and legal judgment", which appears to situate the latter two outside the social and the discursive. This is most explicit in her statement that:

> Looking at four of these cases, it appears that the factfinder used *common sense and legal judgment, and not cultural bias,* to reject evidence

> that was weak, marginally relevant, or unpersuasive (ibid., 321, my emphasis).

This statement assumes that "common sense and legal judgment" are not constituted by discourses of culture and gender. Hoeffel thereby in effect rationalizes common sense and legal judgment as potentially politically neutral. She further depoliticizes court cases involving 'cultural evidence' by treating the 'failures in advocacy' she encountered as purely contingent, i.e. a problem of a particular case (ibid., 314–315). Thus she treats the failure of the prosecution, in the high-profile trial of Dong Lu Chen,[2] vigorously to contest the defense's (sexist and racist) 'cultural evidence' as a moral or, perhaps, a professional failure on the part of the individuals involved (not unlike Maguigan seems to do [1995, 86]; see also Friedman Ramirez 2009, 209–210):

> Hence, the real problem in *Chen* was a breakdown in the adversarial process. If Pasternak's [the expert witness's, C.B.] testimony was patently unreliable, the prosecution should have exposed this to the jury through the tools at its disposal: cross–examination, experts, and jury instructions. The prosecution failed to do so. The criminal justice system is equipped to handle 'shaky' expert evidence (Hoeffel 2006, 314–315).

However, Volpp has shown that the prosecution in *People vs. Dong Lu Chen* did cross-examine the 'cultural expert' presented by the defense—albeit quite ineffectually. Volpp points out that both the prosecutor and the defense 'expert' "accepted a construction of China as a 'closed' or 'conservative' nation slumbering away, as compared to the 'advanced' West" (1994, 72). The prosecutor did so in the form of asking the 'expert' whether China had recently "'embraced Western culture' and if this had a 'liberalizing' or 'awakening' effect" (ibid.). As Volpp asserts, the prosecutor's "method of attack thus depended in part on the same stereotypes he attempted to undermine" (ibid.). He also invoked the concept of assimilation (ibid.)—which problematically pictures diasporic existence in terms of a gradual shedding of one's culture of 'origin'—as a way of distancing the defendant from 'patriarchal Chinese culture'. A move which, as I will argue in this chapter, leaves unquestioned the notion of patriarchy's cultural Otherness. This is to say that the prosecutor's ineffective mode of contesting the 'cultural evidence' was premised upon similar colonialist assumptions as was that 'evidence' itself. That is, this particular "breakdown in the adversarial process" (see the last quote above) was indeed linked immediately to "cultural bias" (Hoeffel 2006, 321) or, as I prefer to say, colonial discourse. As we shall see in this chapter, not only is this a systematic pattern amongst the trials I have studied, but the particular shared colonialist assumptions pointed out by Volpp regarding the *Chen* case are replicated throughout my corpus of 'culture' cases.

Had the prosecution exposed the essentialist, colonialist, and patriarchal logic on which the defense's 'expert evidence' in Dong Lu Chen's trial relied, the judge—who convicted the defendant only of second-degree murder for the killing of his wife, and imposed a mere probationary sentence explicitly on grounds of that 'evidence' (Volpp 1994, 73–74)—might have been more critical of it. However, I would disagree with Hoeffel's assertion, made with reference to this trial, that:

> Unless the prosecution offers its own expert to counter the testimony of a defense expert, a judge cannot be expected to recognize inaccurate stereotyping by the defense expert. For better or worse, factfinders often take their cues from experts. It was not unreasonable for Justice Pincus to assume that Pasternak [the defense's 'expert', C.B.] knew more about Chinese culture than he did (2006, 309).

I disagree because I hope to have shown in the preceding Part that it is principally possible—for both judges and advocates—in the absence of any *information* to the contrary to be critical of the normative, hierarchizing *frames* in terms of which what is offered as 'information' about another culture is presented. However, it is because of the hegemonic status of the pertinent frames for constructing 'culture' and 'gender'—whose conceptual and normative features tend to be naturalized as inhering in cultural and gendered identities/differences—that such critical scrutiny tends not to occur. Thus it is due to the depoliticization of 'cultural evidence' as a matter of mere facts that opposing parties at trial tend to miss out on vigorously contesting such 'information' (whether or not they offer their own 'experts')—as we have seen in Chapter 4 (on *State vs. Cao*[3]), and as will be shown in more detail in the present chapter. Hoeffel in effect rationalizes the judicial treatment of 'cultural evidence' as something unrelated to 'cultural insensitivity' (for instance, in the *Chen* case, in which she blames a seemingly contingent "breakdown in the adversarial process" for the trial's result) because she fails to see that the "common sense and legal judgment" deployed in 'cultural defense' cases—and in ethnicizing prosecutions—are themselves drenched in hegemonic discourses of gender, culture, and race. This will be demonstrated in this chapter in regard to the systematic discursive collusion amongst opposing trial parties, whose respective procedures share in common many of the same assumptions regarding these categories.

There is only one case in the corpus assembled for this study in which the notion of Patriarchal Other Cultures is close to fully deconstructed by an opposing party in a manner compatible with both feminism and postcolonial critique. In the case *People vs. Gonzalez*,[4] in which the defense requested leniency in sentencing on the grounds that the Mexican American defendant had killed his ex-girlfriend in the context of a socialization in accordance with 'machismo', and of believing her a witch,[5] the prosecution responded at the sentencing hearing:

> And it's not a substantial ground for you to consider, Judge, the fact that this defendant comes from a Mexican background, or from the Mexican culture. / You heard the testimony from Dr. [X—a forensic psychologist, C.B.] about the differences in the Mexican culture as to gender roles and to U.S. customs as to the same. / That's insulting, Number 1, Judge, but if you're going to consider it, I ask you to consider the fact that what you heard today from Dr. [X] talks about a man in a Mexican culture, whose self-esteem was lowered. / He turned around, occasionally, and took that out on the victim when he had been drinking apparently. / *That's not unlike what you probably heard in your years on the bench in this court, hearing domestic violence cases about men in the United States culture. / The bottom line is, it's not an accepted behavior in either culture.* And it's not something that excuses what he's done.[6]

The judge sentenced the defendant to fifty years in jail (for first-degree murder) and argued—after acknowledging a potential relevance of culture to sentencing:[7]

> But sadly enough as the State indicated, it happens all too often. Domestic violence, combined with jealousy, in this particular case, she [the victim, C.B.] called her next friend, combined with alcohol, is a deadly combination that caused the death of Ms. [Santiago]. *And that type of violence, jealousy and alcohol, crosses all cultures. It's not unique to the Hispanic culture.*[8]

The prosecutor and, following in her tracks, the judge, here de-ethnicize male violence against women by constructing it as an equally familiar phenomenon in the U.S., beyond Mexican (American) ethnicity (which, the prosecutor claims, does not condone such violence). While not as such constructing domestic violence as a matter of male control over women, and while not deconstructing the essentialist distinction between 'Mexican' and 'United States culture', such violence *is* here rendered as being about gender, and as occurring, likewise, in the latter 'culture'. That is, the patriarchal practice at hand is neither being naturalized in sexist terms (as it is by the defense in *State vs. Cao* [see Chapter 4]), nor is its colonialist ethnicization as 'culturally Other' on the part of Gonzalez's defense left intact. Unlike in other trials in the corpus of cases I have examined, male domination throughout U.S. culture is not even constructed as being *less* pronounced than in Mexican (American) culture. There is no quantifying comparison along such lines at all.

The fact that responses to a (here: sexist) 'cultural defense' such as the above do occur in criminal trials shows that they are possible, as such. I would argue that this kind of response is also strategically viable: why should it be rejected by the judge or jury more readily than would a counter-strategy that replicates colonialist and/or patriarchal assumptions? And yet, as most of this chapter will be devoted to showing, the notion of (more) Patriarchal Other Cultures, and the essentialist and colonialist construction of cultural difference that goes with it, tend to be replicated rather than (fully) questioned in most of the trials within the corpus in which there is any contest at all regarding the 'cultural evidence'. I take this for an indication that the strategic imagination of advocates is being constrained in virtue of the hegemonic status of the normatively loaded assumptions that they fail to question. While it is beyond the scope of this study to try to test whether or not this interpretation holds (as against the possible counter-thesis that strategic considerations account for the predominant absence of more critical counter-discourses), my analysis of the strategies of contestation occurring in the corpus is conducted in line with that interpretation.

The next part of this chapter will examine the defense's counter-strategies in *People vs. Lopez and Singh* (a case discussed above in Chapter 2). Doing so is instructive in part because, due to the involvement of two defendants in this trial, we have the opportunity to observe two different defense attorneys each pursue their own strategy of contesting the same 'cultural evidence' introduced by the prosecution. As I shall argue, one attorney (whom I will call defense attorney 1) attempted a more critical strategy but which was stalled by the prosecution's counter-tactic. Effectively, this attorney's critical endeavor was silenced in virtue of coming up against a boundary of hegemonic reasoning as instantiated in the prosecution's procedure of 'proof'. As a result, the defense attorney dropped his initial strategy and joined the other defense attorney (defense attorney 2) in a discursive strategy that affirmed, rather than questioned, the notion of a more gender-egalitarian West.

PEOPLE VS. LOPEZ AND SINGH[9]

Heterogenization and Universalization

Defense attorney 1's initial strategy in responding to the prosecution's 'cultural evidence' consisted in questioning the homogeneity of 'Sikh culture' that was so central to the state's procedure of proof (see Chapter 2) as well as the 'evidence's' particularity to that 'culture'. The former occurred in the following passages (from the cross-examination of the state's expert witness Joga Kaur), amongst others:

Q Okay. You were asked a number of questions by the district attorney that utilized the term predict.

There was a number of questions that you—that you were asked based on the knowledge of the culture and traditions within the Sikh community, if you assume these facts what could you predict would be—would be the response; do you remember those kinds of questions in general?

A In general, yes.

Q And isn't it a fact that your responses often were, well, you could see this happen, this could happen; do you remember those kinds of responses?

A Yes.

Q You're not saying that there is any kind of scientific level of predictions involved here, where if you know that somebody has grown up in the Sikh community that you can with scientific certainty predict what behavior they're going to engage in; you're not saying that, are you?

A No, I'm not.[10]

Q You just answered a question to the effect that the wife's family will go to any length to try to keep the marriage together; do you remember that question?

A Yes.

Q But that's not every family. There are a great deal of variations of individuality *even* within the Sikh community; isn't that right?

A Yes.[11]

The defense attorney is here questioning the (racialized) cultural determinism upon which the prosecution bases its procedure of proof. His use of the word "even" in the second quote, however, may be taken as an indication of a defensive position; as a concession in the direction of the prosecutor's 'theory' of Sikh culture. Such a tension may also be registered in the following two objections made by the same defense attorney during the direct examination of 'cultural expert' Joga Kaur:

Q In your experience within the Sikh community—well, how can I phrase this?

Assume for the time being that a male child is born within the Sikh community. Thereafter can you tell the ladies and gentlemen of the jury what feelings are engendered in a Sikh father? Obviously, I'm including it as a base. Every father we presume loves his children, as we presume every mother does as well.

Beyond that as a—as a matter of fact, matter of culture, can you tell the jury whether there are any special feelings that you would become familiar with concerning a father's relationship with a male child?

[Counsel for defendant]: Well, I'm going to object. I think this goes too far. *This is asking him to mind read* [sic] *to what the culture might think in a particular situation*. He—he's already testified that variables have changed, this has really gone too far, judge.

The court: Perhaps you could rephrase the question as it relates solely to the Sikh religion.

[Counsel for state]: I will, your Honor.
The court: All right.

Q (By [counsel for state]: The last question, Lieutenant [Kaur], whether there are certain feelings commonly recognized within the Sikh community by you, which pertain to the arrival of the male child, feelings common to Sikh fathers with respect to their sons, and I'm not asking you to speculate as to any particular individual feelings, what I'm asking you for cultural relationships with the father's relationship to the son?
A It's usually stronger than if it was a daughter.[12]

Q (by Mr. [counsel for the prosecution]) Okay. And as I understood your answer you said it was not common for the [Sikh, C.B.] wife's family to seek to prevent a remarriage to someone else?
A Yes.
Q On the other hand, do I understand you correctly or let me say this, let me approach it looking at a new attempt by a wife's family to achieve a reconciliation to get the two marital partners back together as a family unit?
A Yes.
Q In your experience do those efforts continue or can they be expected to continue even after a divorce has been obtained?
A It has been known to continue even after the divorce.
Q Now, let's assume that we've got one of uncommon—[sic]

Mr. [counsel for the defense]: I'm going to move to strike the answer it is not properly within the expertise, *the fact that it may have happened on occasion doesn't have a bearing on the tradition and traits which would have—may arguably have some bearing here.*[13]

In the first of the two quotes above, the defense attorney phrases his objection in a form that apparently undermines what he is trying to assert: It would appear that he is here, again, attempting to question the predictability of Sikhs' conduct—or here: feelings—based upon the notion of an absolutely unitary Sikh culture. But the phrasing he uses for rendering that critique actually affirms the latter notion, as '*culture*' (rather than an individual) is here being pictured as *having thoughts*. This could be taken as an indication that this defense attorney is partially caught up in the very discourse he is seeking to question.

The second quote above poses a similar case. In objecting, the attorney is here attacking the prosecutor's attempt to render as 'cultural' even a conduct that admittedly occurs less than commonly among Sikhs ("It has been known to continue even after the divorce"). Yet, in doing so, the defense attorney uses the term 'trait'—as if talking about a single 'personality' rather than about 'culture'. In other words, the term 'traits' suggests a culture unified to such an extent that it may be thought of in terms of a character exhibiting personality-like traits—an extreme homogenization. Here, too, then, the phrasing somewhat subverts the argumentative direction the attorney is trying to take. I shall return to the role of interpellation (Althusser 1971; see Part II) in arguably restricting this defense attorney's moves shortly. First, I will illustrate his use of a strategy of *universalization* complementary to the one just demonstrated, of trying to heterogenize 'Sikh culture'.

The following are among the relevant extracts here:

Q You said that the father is the dominant member within the Sikh culture?
A Within the family, yes.
Q Within the family?
A Yes.
Q Is that any different from most cultures?
A No.[14]

Q Let me ask you a hypothetical question. You've indicated that the ties to a son, a father to a son, are stronger than they are to a daughter, correct?
A I think it's an unwritten rule, yes.
Q Do you have any reason to believe that that's any different than an American father to his son?
A No.[15]

Q Okay. And do you remember your response was not aggressively hostile, but hostile; do you remember that?
A Yes.
Q Is that different from any other culture on earth when a bride is being dumped by her husband in terms of response to [sic] the family?
A Well, I'm looking at it this over here when I say that, hostile, but aggressive and not hostile it's a continuation of escalation from starting from mere threats to a higher escalation of force, if you want to call it that. That's what I was implying.
Q All right. But—but you are saying by, as I understand it and tell me if this is correct, when you say not aggressively hostile, but hostile, what you're saying is that you would expect that there would be—that the bride's family would be upset with the situation, but it doesn't necessarily escalate to violence?
A Yes.
Q Okay. And that—that is not much different than any other culture in which you would expect the bride's family to be upset that their daughter is being dumped by somebody?
A That is correct.
Q You use the term or the term was used that I think you acknowledged the concept of damaged goods, a daughter, a bride who is divorced by a man in some respect is damaged goods, correct?

A Yes.
Q Is that any different than any other culture?
A No, it's not.
Q I mean, it's true in every culture that families don't want their daughters dumped by their husband; isn't that fair?
A Yes.[16]

I do not necessarily consider overly progressive this strategy of universalizing, in particular, the gender-specific aspects of the 'cultural evidence' introduced by the prosecution. For one thing, patriarchal social relations here are not marked as unegalitarian social arrangements. Rather, they could equally well be read, in the above quotes, in terms of quasi-natural phenomena inhering in all cultures. Secondly and relatedly, universalism of the kind catered to by defense attorney 1 (see n. 15, this Ch.) tends to essentialize about 'culture' just as much as does the kind of racism emphatic upon cultural difference practiced by the prosecution in this case (see Chapter 2): in like fashion, it tends to anthropologize 'culture' as a static second nature inhering in human beings, rather than conceiving of it in terms of shifting practices constitutive of human subjects without determining them in any predictable ways (Butler 1997b).[17] Moreover, such universalism tends to emphasize 'sameness' among 'cultures' at the expense of difference between them. Still, the defense's initial move of universalizing male dominance is preferable in my view to its replicating the notion that only certain (read: Third World) cultures are patriarchal—a strategy it would subsequently adopt in response to a move by the prosecution which I shall detail next.

Restabilizing 'Difference'

The state responded to the defense's above moves by introducing the quantifying notion of 'degrees of difference' (compare Chapter 1). Thus the prosecutor asked Joga Kaur on redirect:

Q . . .
Mr. [counsel for defendant] and Ms. [counsel for codefendant] asked you whether many of the things that you testified to on direct examination were any different from conditions in the United States, do you recall?
A Yes.
Q Are you testifying that the Sikh values and traditions are no different than the values and traditions of American culture?
A No. Yes, I am. They're not that different, you know, some are valued higher than the other ones. I mean, it—they are no different than the others.
Q Okay. Are you talking about a difference in degree?
A You can say that, yes.[18]

This proved to be the model on which the prosecutor was able to re-establish an essentialized cultural difference in a way that appears to have silenced defense attorney 1 (represented in all but one quote under the preceding heading), who subsequently moved on an alternative tack. For instance, the state used the model of a 'cultural difference in degrees' in the following questions pertinent to the notion of (more) Patriarchal Other Cultures:

Q As I understand in answer to some of the questions on cross-examination, you indicated that, oh, let's see, a female family member being divorced then being considered damaged goods.
Some Americans feel the same way about their children; is that what you're testifying?
A Yes.
Q Well, *do you see a difference, a very clear difference in degree as to those feelings?*
A Well, I see the difference of the fact that it's—again, it's an unwritten rule over here that in the East Indian community the female is looked down upon after a divorce. Regardless of what her rank, what her financial capacity is, she's looked down upon.
Q By the community?
A By the community within that—within where she resides.
Q Okay. And in India, in the Punjabi or Punjab area of India, among the Sikh community is the looking down upon a woman who has been divorced by the community even more marked?
A It's more there than it is here, yes.
Q And would you be willing to admit that in the Sikh culture in general that it's a much stronger feeling than in the non-Sikh culture in the United States?
A Yes.[19]

Q (by [counsel for state]) Do you find any difference in the *degree of dominance* of the senior male member of the family in the Sikh culture as opposed to generally in American culture?
A Well, again, it's unwritten rule [sic] that it's more in the Sikh religion than it is in the American culture.
Q Okay.
A The father or the elder member of the family is usually, you know, or the—or the final say so, I guess, in a decision making.[20]

The question in the latter quote in particular will be recognizable to you as deploying the notion that, if male dominance is not unique to the Other culture, it is at least more pronounced there than among 'us'—which notion I concluded in Chapter 1 is, likewise, colonialist in that it provides grounds for hierarchizing 'the West' over and above 'the rest'. In that Chapter, I juxtaposed with this notion one of *qualitative* differences between patriarchal practices, which is not as prone to hierarchizing essentialized 'cultures' one above the other. However, the notion of cultures being *more vs. less* patriarchal seems to exert strong hegemonic appeal—something indicated by the fact that it is a form of restabilizing cultural difference that occurs repeatedly in my corpus of cases in response to developments rendering questionable the notion that *only* the Other culture is patriarchal. Another indication in the same direction is the fact that defense attorney 1 subsequently abandoned his strategy of universalization (rather than resorting to the notion of qualitative cultural differences) in favor of the following:

Americanization as Liberalization

His initial move in this direction shows in the following extract:

Q You talk about the concept of being Americanized?
A Yes, Sir.
Q Would you agree with me that being Americanized is a very subjective term?
A Yes, Sir.
Q I mean, all people come in all different shades [sic] and heights, and beliefs and values, both within and without a given community.
A Yes.
Q And that's true with Sikhs?
A Yes. In fact, what the point that I was trying to make is you become Americanized, that you establish their way of living quarters, their ways of life, but you still try to—there's still practice things and religion [sic].
Q But even in that there are dress [sic] and shades of individuality?
A Yes.
Q And so it's very hard to quantify whether or not a particular individual, because he happens to be a Sikh, whether he personally shares *that value system that would lead to violence*; isn't that true?
A Yes.[21]

In this passage from the re-recross examination of the state's 'expert' Lieutenant Kaur, defense attorney 1 is responding to the prosecution's move—analogous to the ones shown under the preceding heading—of establishing (with the witness's cooperation) the alleged patterns of violent conduct attendant upon divorce among Sikhs as being quantitatively more pronounced than among 'non-Sikhs'.[22] Defense attorney 1 is here making a major concession to the state by saying that the Sikh "value system . . . would lead to violence". He does so against the background of testimony by the same witness according to which Sikh males who wear a turban—like defendant Malkit Singh[23]—are invariably tradition-minded in his experience, rather than 'Americanized'[24]—and hence (as his overall testimony stated), that they are prone to react with potentially deadly violence when a sister's husband decides to leave her (see Chapter 2).

While still pursuing an attempt to individualize the defendant by associating him with 'Americanization', which he seeks to cast as being less clear-cut than simple distinctions between turban wearers and non-turban wearers would suggest, defense attorney 1 now resorts to doing so *in virtue of seeking to distance his client, defendant Singh, from Sikh culture.* He is deploying the concept of Americanization in a binarizing way; as an opposite of Sikh traditionalism, rather than in terms of cultural influences that will merge with elements of 'Sikh culture' in unpredictable and varying ways, without necessarily leading to a dilution of one's orientation to the latter.[25] For, defense attorney 1 here is clearly invoking 'Americanization' as a means of setting his client *apart* from 'the Sikh value system'. In doing so, he is no longer contesting but is fully affirming the prosecution's version of a unitary, essential Sikh "value system"[26] in terms of which (traditional) Sikhs' conduct is predictable, including in regard to violent behavior (see Chapter 2). His means of distancing his client from the violent conduct alleged now is to identify him with 'America' rather than with 'Sikh culture'. He thereby implicitly replicates the binarism set up by the prosecution between a (singular) liberal 'American culture' and an illiberal (violent; coercive) 'Sikh culture' (see Chapter 2).

This is the strategy which defense attorney 2, counsel for defendant Samuel Lopez, pursued from the beginning. Thus, she had replicated the binarism between 'Sikh' and 'American' cultures (each framed in unitary terms) by trying to mark expert witness Joga Kaur as less than fully Sikh in virtue of his imputed 'Americanization'. She apparently did so in order to render him as 'inauthentic' and therefore, as less than fully competent qua 'expert' on Sikh culture:

Q Would it be fair to say that as an adult you have not practiced the Sikh cultural—that is aside from going to church, the culture of the Sikh religion has not been a significant part of your life, has it?
A Yes, it has.[27]

Defense attorney 2 also pursued this strategy as a way of distancing defendant Singh and his sister from 'Sikh tradition'. Thus, where the prosecution tried to mark out the Singh family as 'traditional' rather than 'Americanized' on grounds of their being first-generation immigrants,[28] and of Singh's wearing a turban and the traditional beard,[29] defense attorney 2 did the opposite, highlighting the duration of their stay in the U.S.:

Q Now, one thing that I'd like to understand and that is the fact of being in the United States on one's beliefs. You talked about—you use the term Americanization of people, correct me if I'm wrong, but it's almost a dilution of the beliefs or the practices of it; isn't that true?

A Yes.
Q And you yourself are a product of that to a certain extent?
A Yes.
Q Would it be fair to say that the Sikhs that you know of your generation, that is who have come to the United States in their youth, have become fairly Americanized?
A Lot of them have, yes.[30]

Both sides thereby colluded in constructing cultural identity in terms of an "either/or"; dichotomizing 'Sikh' and 'American' identities against each other. Defense attorney 2 thereby left uncontested the prosecution's characterization of Sikh culture as such—both as regards its imputed internal homogeneity, and its characterization in terms of a coercive illiberalism. This applies also to the gendered aspects of the prosecution's 'cultural theory', and hence, to the notion of patriarchal social relations being particular to the Other(ed) culture. Thus defense attorney 2 tried to dissociate Singh's sister, Jaswinder (who was only ever referred to by first name by the attorneys, unlike the defendant himself), from the notion that she would be considered 'damaged goods' if divorced by her husband, or that she would be affected by being so considered within the Sikh community, in a way illustrated by the following extract from Lieutenant Kaur's cross-examination. (This was an indirect attempt to eliminate the murder motive imputed to her brother, defendant Singh.)

Q Suppose you have a woman who has a profession, has her own job and her own life, are you saying that she would then be subjected to some kind of demeaningness [sic] [sic]—that's not a word—she would be stigmatized because she had previously been divorced?
A I think it would be there within the community, yes.
Q Suppose she went outside the community?
A I don't think that that would be a problem, no.
Q There are Sikh women that will marry American men, aren't there?
A Yes.
Q That's not prohibited?[31]

The hypothetical rendered in this quote was applicable to 'Jaswinder', defendant Singh's sister—who was working full-time and living with two sisters, rather than being a "burden on the family" with no place of her own to go to, as the prosecution alleged of divorced Sikh women.[32] What is striking about this extract is that the only way for Sikh women to rid themselves of, or to struggle against, gendered oppression that it envisages is for them to leave their community and, by implication, to join 'American culture'. Since, at the same time, 'American culture' was not associated by this defense attorney with patriarchal social relations (unlike, arguably, in the other defense attorney's initial strategy of universalization),[33] it stood as the avenue to women's freedom and self-determination in opposition to 'Sikh culture', the only source of women's subordination rendered apparent. (Notwithstanding the attorney's invocation of the norm of heterosexual marriage in the above extract, which of course is not being marked as a matter of gendered oppression.) This was, obviously, to pursue a strategy of contesting the prosecution's case that *reproduced the notion of patriarchy's Otherness to U.S. society* (or 'culture') which was central to that case (as part of the state's overall rendering of 'Sikh culture' in terms of an illiberalism opposed to U.S. liberalism) (Chapter 2).

It was this strategy that defense attorney 1 joined after abandoning the initial, more progressive strategy described further above. His subsequent procedure actually perfected the opposition between a patriarchal Sikh culture and a U.S. culture liberating to women in the following passages—which stem, respectively, from Joga Kaur's recross-examination, from another Sikh witness's recross-examination, and from his closing argument (where defense attorney 1 is characterizing 'expert' Kaur's testimony):

Q How about Sikh women who—who have jobs outside the home; do you see that?
A Yes.
Q Do you see Sikh women who live alone and have their own living place?
A Not very many.
Q You see Sikh women who move away from the predominant Sikh group up in [county X]?
A Yes.
Q And live alone?
A That I don't know.
Q You don't really know about the independence of Sikh women who do not live within the [county X] area?
A No.
Q Okay. *So you don't really know about how Americanized Sikh women living in [city X] would be?*
A No.[34]

Q [by counsel for the prosecution, C.B.] From what you could see with [Jaswinder], could she appear to be one Sikh woman in the United States who adhered to the traditions and the culture as it was in the old country?
A Yes.
. . .
Q [by defense attorney 1, C.B.] Well, do women in the old country work at plants like [company X], as single women?
A Well, they don't have [company X] in India.
Q Okay. Well don't women in India pretty much work in the home and take care of the kids?

A Yes, they usually do.
Q That's not the way [Jaswinder] was living her life; isn't that right?
A Well, she was thinking the same way, but in India [sic].[35]

> Women are not necessarily tarnished if she has her [sic] own life and if she lives outside the community, like [Jaswinder].[36]

In the first of the above three quotes, Sikh women's independence is being correlated with their Americanization. In the second extract (which specifies a specific industrial plant because 'Jaswinder' had once worked there), being a housewife is—ironically, given its still-hegemonic status as a life course for middle-class women in the U.S.—associated with India and hence, with Sikh tradition. This combination of moves renders an 'independent' existence as a working single as *the* characteristic life course for 'American women'—reinforcing the opposition between a Patriarchal Other Culture and a gender-egalitarian West set up by the state and the second defense attorney. The shift in strategy pursued by defense attorney 1 (the one last cited) may be attributed to his having been silenced by the prosecution's introduction of the notion of quantitative degrees of cultural difference, according to which male domination is at least more pronounced in 'Sikh culture' than in a fictive unitary 'American culture'. Arguably, this defense attorney could have benefited from constructing Sikh culture as *differently* and not necessarily *more* patriarchal than U.S. culture, as a way of de-stigmatizing it. (I attribute much of both defense attorneys' procedures to an attempt on their parts to remove from the defendants the stigma that the state cast upon 'Sikh culture'.) I interpret his silence about gendered domination outside Sikh culture following the prosecution's establishment of the model of quantitative degrees of cultural difference in terms of his having come up against the limits of his strategic imagination, to which the notion of qualitative cultural differences not necessarily amenable to a quantifying hierarchization was not available. Of course, it could be argued that he dropped his initial strategy, of heterogenizing Sikh culture and universalizing male domination, out of strategic considerations in the face of the prosecution's counter-tactic. Even if strategic, however, his shift in strategy would attest to the hegemonic status of the quantifying notion of differing degrees of male domination (with non-Western 'cultures' being higher up on the scale of intensity than Western ones), which defense attorney 1 may have felt it was fruitless to contest due to its persuasive power—i.e., to its interpellative force (compare Part II).

Defense attorney 1 could, likewise, have constructed Sikh tradition, as such, as a heterogeneous set of variable and mutually relatively independent norms and practices, as a way of subverting the notion of a unitary Sikh 'value system' and a predictability of Sikh persons' conduct based upon it. As I have argued above, however, in this regard too he was struggling in trying to transgress the boundaries of the hegemonic discourse of 'culture' operated by the prosecution, which pictures its object in essentialist terms akin to the model of a 'personality' exhibiting 'character traits', and which resorts to a stark cultural determinism in regard to the 'cultures' of the formerly colonized and enslaved. As I argued, this struggle is indicated, amongst other things, by his objections using a self-subverting phrasing as well as by the fact that he ultimately conceded that the Sikh "value system" (constructed through the same unitary term used by the prosecution) leads to violence. Here too, though, even if we assume that this concession was strategically motivated on the grounds that the jury would find this assumption more persuasive than an anti-essentialist attempt to question the unified character of 'Sikh culture', this would attest to the power of hegemonic discourse to render some constructions more compelling than others, based upon their familiarity and interpellative force. I will return to these two possibilities of interpreting the procedure of defense attorney 1 at the end of this chapter.

Ontologizing 'Cultural Evidence'

The baseline discursive frame that circumscribed all of the defense's strategies of contesting the state's 'cultural evidence' was its own empiricist approach to 'culture'—i.e., its rendering of the latter as a matter of potentially unmediated facts rather than invariably of discursive constructions. The empiricist perspective upon 'culture' (whose distinguishing mark is that it treats itself as no perspective at all) is, of course, suggested by the very framework for eliciting 'evidence' at trial—a point to which I will return in the Conclusion to this work (Part VI). On the part of defense attorney 1, the empiricist approach is most evident when he objects to 'expert' Kaur's testimony (on direct examination) based upon its imputed subjectivity, as opposed to the putatively more "objective dissertation" a 'real expert' would supposedly provide:

Q Can you explain to the jury in your own terms perhaps generally the basic tenets of the Sikh faith, what the Sikh religion is comprised of?
A Basically to my—the way I interpret it is just—
[Counsel for defendant]: Well, I object. I don't think it's proper that we get your interpretation. If he's an expert in—as to what the traditions are he can give an objective dissertation, but he's—
The court: That's sufficient. I think that the objection is properly sustained, that it should be generally accepted beliefs within the religion.[37]

Defense attorney 1 is here implying that it is possible to give an "objective dissertation" about Sikh culture that would be devoid of "interpretation" or, as I would say, of discursive mediation.[38] Affirming this assumption, which renders Sikh culture as a matter of potentially neutral facts, arguably made it more difficult for the defense attorney to undermine the intuitive credibility (in virtue of their hegemonic status) of the prosecutor's specific constructions of 'Sikh culture', both in terms of its unified character and Sikh persons' predictability, and of its substantively illiberal, coercive 'character'. For, these constructions' familiarity in terms of stereotype makes this particular rendering of 'facts' about the cultural 'Other' seem more real than competing ones, so long as their basic status of an objective given is uncontested.

Circumscribed Critique

It is within the limits of the collusions with the prosecution's discourse which I have described that the critical moves made by the defense attorneys must be evaluated. (They look more radical when considered in isolation than when considered in context.) Thus defense attorney 1 (counsel for Malkit Singh) made these remarks in his opening statement and his closing argument, respectively:

> And the final concept I would like to leave you with, whenever you hear the word consistent, a red flag should go up because a lot of the district attorney's case is built around the fact of consistency. If I were to offer evidence that someone who is six foot three, white male, in a blue suit committed this crime, one could ask, is that consistent with Mr. [counsel for the prosecution] being the perpetrator, I'd answer yes, yeah, it is consistent with Mr. [counsel for the prosecution] being the perpetrator. At the time [sic] does it prove that he is the perpetrator, no, it doesn't.[39]

> I said to you yesterday that the district attorney gets to have rebuttal and you're going to get, I can see a good couple hours of rebuttal coming back at you and he's going to hit you and he's going to come at you, *and he's going to say, look, just use your common sense, just fill-in* [sic] *all the gaps here, use your common sense. You know what the phone calls are all about. / He's going to talk about the cultural evidence.* Even though it wasn't supported by his own witnesses, *he's still got this theory that my client is driven by his culture*, to seek out revenge, get his former brother-in-law, and he'll see this symbolic death here with this knife and this hammer. / I want you to see this client not as a stereotype, and we can get into a stereotype. If you're here from Italy and you came from Sicily everyone must be in the Mafia, if you are an Arab you must be a terrorist. I don't want you to see my client in the stereotype that he is being portrayed. Mr. [Singh] is a human being and he's an individual.[40]

The first extract above may be viewed as pinpointing the logic of racial/cultural profiling pursued by the state (see Chapter 2), in that the prosecutor is here racialized as 'white' in a kind of substitution test (compare Lawrence 2001, 130–132; Morrison 1993, 57, 79; see also Morrison 1997, xii–xiii) seemingly intended to clarify to a hegemonic audience what is at stake in such profiling—which is more commonly targeted at '(young) black males' or 'Muslims'. Similarly, the reference to the state's appeal to the jury's common sense may be understood as alluding to the racialized character of the kind of 'gap-filling' being invoked—namely, a stereotyped notion "that my client is driven by his culture", i.e., a racialized form of cultural determinism. While these allusions to the dehumanizing racism underpinning the prosecution's procedure of proof are commendable in my opinion, they must be viewed in the context of the defense's overall strategies of contesting the 'cultural evidence', which only partially questioned the state's construction of that 'evidence', and in fact affirmed much of it, as we have seen. These remarks certainly would have acquired more rhetorical strength if that construction had been questioned more thoroughly.

PEOPLE VS. SHEN[41]

In this section, I want to establish that constructing Westernization as the (sole) source of women's liberation, rather than (also) of specific forms of gendered inequality, is a widespread maneuver in my corpus of cases. As a means of establishing this, I will here account for the shape this maneuver took in *People vs. Anne Shen*. We shall see that this maneuver varies in detail rather than in principle from the strategy of contestation which won out in *People vs. Lopez and Singh*, and that it appears to have made little difference that the contesting party was the defense in the latter case and, in the former, the prosecution. In a way analogous to the three case studies presented in Part IV, I hope that by juxtaposing these two cases, I can give you a sense of the commonalities and some particularities of the said problematic strategy of contestation followed in different individual cases.

'Cosmopolitan' Identity as Women's Liberty

As shown in Chapter 3, the defense in *People vs. Shen* pictured her as an utterly subjected, subservient woman in virtue of her imputed traditional Chinese identity, which was constructed implicitly and explicitly in opposition to supposedly assertive, even dominant 'American women' by the defense attorney and his expert witnesses. As argued in that chapter, the defense's hypostatization of the defendant's gendered oppression was serviceable to picturing her as an inwardly devoted mother who was prevented by social pressures (namely, Chinese patriarchy) from outwardly fulfilling the role of a 'good mother' during her son's lifetime. Shen's killing of her son was constructed as having been intended by her as a way of fulfilling motherly duty. I have posited that the defense, in pursuing this argumentative strategy, defensively mobilized a U.S. patriarchal discourse of motherhood, in tension with its colonialist construction of patriarchy as being specific to Chinese culture.

The prosecution in *People vs. Shen* systematically colluded in both the patriarchal and the colonial discourse operated by the defense. It attempted to dispute the defendant's gendered oppression as such, as a way of undermining the potential empathy/pity for her on the part of the jury to which the 'cultural evidence' was catering (compare Chapter 3). In a way analogous to the defense's procedure in *People vs. Lopez and Singh*, Shen's prosecution sought to dispute her oppression on the basis of distancing her from Chinese culture/tradition—here, in virtue of constructing the defendant as 'cosmopolitan' rather than 'traditional'. (A functional equivalent to the opposition between Americanization vs. traditionalism in *Lopez and Singh*.) Setting up a dichotomy between the traditional and the cosmopolitan (which was implicitly being associated with Westernization), the state identified the former with gendered oppression and the latter, with women's absolute self-determination in a way that faithfully reproduced the dichotomies constructed by the defense between submissive (traditional) Chinese women and assertive American women (and hence, between Chinese and Western cultures). Thus the state, in cross-examining one defense 'expert', sought to distance Hong Kong (where Anne Shen had worked) and Macau (where she had lived most of her adult life) from 'Chinese tradition' on grounds of its cosmopolitan and 'worldly' character—thereby associating 'tradition' with mainland China (where she had grown up):

Q Hong Kong is a pretty cosmopolitan city?
A Right. But because it's also over 90 percent Chinese, the kind of folk Buddhism that I talk [sic] about, which is a, a mixture of Confucianism, Taoism and Buddhism is, is very prevalent.
Q And Macau, too? Same thing?
A Macau, very similar.[42]

Q Is Macau like a Las Vegas of the Orient? Those are my words. If it's not right, say so.
A No. There are a few casinos there.
Q A few?
A A few large ones. And—in the city. And that's one of their major source [sic] of revenue. Another major source is certainly being what they call an entry port. Things that come from China to there or things that come from there to China.
Q A lot of smuggling going on between Mainland China and Macau?
A That I couldn't tell.
Q Fair? [sic]
Lot of bars and racetracks in Macau?
A There is a hound track.

Q A what?
A Greyhound track.
Q Dog?
A Dog racing, yeah.
Q Lot of bars there, too?
A That I couldn't tell you, no: a lot. There are bars there.[43]

The point of these questions is apparent in the following extract:

Q Doctor, you described the defendant, [Anne Shen], as a traditional Chinese woman, that she was subservient and not assertive.
By "traditionally"—we're not talking here about a lady who lived her whole life in Mainland [sic] China; are we?
A No.
Q We're talking about her, about a lady who left Mainland [sic] China when she was about 19 years old. Right?
A That's correct.
Q And lived in a cosmopolitan city, Hong Kong, and/or partially anyway, and apparently a greater time in Macau, which is also a modern cosmopolitan area; is it not?
A That would not be a fair description of Macau.
Q You tell me, then. You tell me what Macau is like.
A Macau is—there are—it's quite traditional. It's not cosmopolitan. I hate to put on record saying it's sort of backward compared to Hong Kong.
Q Sort of what, sir?
A Backward. But, you know, essentially that's, that's how it is. So it maintains even more of the traditional cultures. And even in Hong Kong, it is very traditional Chinese culture, mixed in with Western culture. And in that sense cosmopolitan. But Chinese traditional influences are very strong there still.[44]

Whereas the defense witness—though servicing a colonial discourse that associates (Third World) tradition with backwardness—here constructs Chinese tradition and the cosmopolitan/Western as being "mixed in" with each other, the prosecution clearly seeks to dichotomize the two against one another. The binary contrasts constructed by the state are the most evident in the following passage from its closing argument (in which "Ed" refers to Shen's deceased son and "Larry Shen", to Ed's father):

> The defendant in this case, ladies and gentlemen, made a series of choices. We all make choices in this world. She made a series of them, not to beat this to death, but she came to the United States in 1979 to be with [Larry Shen]. She knew [Larry Shen] had a wife, that was no secret to her. She had a child by [Larry Shen]. . . . / After 70 days, that is 70 days after [Ed] was born, she left, did not see [Ed] again for seven

> years. In December—strike that, January of '81, to January of 88 [sic], seven years. And that time, what did she do if anything to correspond with the little boy? Is that important? Does that focus on the relationship she had with [Ed]? Sure it does. When I asked her, why didn't you just get on an airplane and fly to [California] and see him, her answer, I am a Chinese woman, quote unquote. I said to her, what does that have to do with it? Look at the passport. Look at the visa stamps. She had been to France. She been to Italy [sic]. She had been to Canada. She had been to the United States on two occasions. This lady is not someone who was a peasant in mainland China behind—in a rice patty with a water buffalo tilling the rice patty. She was the opposite of that. She was a cosmopolitan person who traveled around the world. And there was no reason that she couldn't have come here to visit her son.[45]

'Cosmopolitan' and Chinese identities are here set up as absolute opposites, with the cosmopolitan being associated with 'the West' (France, Italy, Canada, U.S.A.). So are gendered oppression and women's self-determination, any amount of which is being equated with an absence of oppression—both at the level of practices of self-determination, such as traveling, and at that of inner attitudes: making choices negates the presence of any tendencies towards subservience. In virtue of this, agency and oppression, too, are set up as mutually exclusive possibilities—just as they tended to be divorced from each other in the defense's discourse: Where the defense reduced Shen to her gendered oppression, eliminating agency, the state dissociated the agency imputed to her (and, indeed, demanded of her on the grounds that she had mothered a child) from any context of oppression—thereby eliminating any feminist perspective upon such agency.

A move of evaluating any manifestation of agency or transgressive behavior as a proof that the woman concerned is not affected by a misogynist culture has been noted by several authors to occur in judicial discourse (Phillips 2007, 87–89; Razack 1998, Ch. 4; see also Volpp 1994, 90–91). Razack, in the context of Canadian asylum hearings regarding gender-based persecution, writes:

> [R]acist constructs operate on the logic that women of the Third World are to be pitied, and pity is unlikely to emerge when the women in question demonstrate that they are also strong individuals who can make decisions to flee and survive (1998, 113).

Similarly, Phillips observes:

> It seems that culture becomes available to female defendants when they can be shown to conform to images of the subservient non-Western wife. When they deviate in some way from that stereotype, they can not so easily figure as emblems of culture (Phillips 2007, 87).

> Honour [sic], by implication, attaches to the sexually chaste or the dutiful wife, while those exhibiting a capacity for action cannot hope to be believed when they say they were constrained by shame or fear. . . . A woman cannot, it seems, be both strong willed and abused by others; she has to be either the helpless victim wronged by others or capable of wrongdoing herself (ibid., 88–89).

Within the corpus of cases I have examined, the dichotomization between oppression and agency forms a regular pattern. This pattern of contesting 'cultural evidence' that instantiates the motif of patriarchy as being culturally Other replicates that motif, in that it admits of gendered oppression only in an absolute form (which is identified with the Other culture)—thereby reinforcing the totalizing image of the Oppressed Third World Woman defined in opposition to 'Western Woman', who accordingly is defined as being totally self-determined (compare my discussion in Chapter 1). In the prosecution's strategy of contesting the 'cultural evidence' offered by Anne Shen's defense (and especially in the above-cited passage from the state's closing argument), gendered and colonial discourse map onto one another in such a way that 'the West'/the cosmopolitan stands as 'post-patriarchal' while gendered oppression is being confined to an imaginary rural setting in mainland China—reproducing the notion that patriarchy is peculiar to the Other culture which is constitutive of the 'cultural evidence' being contested.

The 'Bad Mother'

But this is not the only complicity between prosecution and defense in Anne Shen's case. Rather, both sides here actively collaborated in replicating patriarchal discourse, particularly the norm of maternal self-sacrifice. The state's procedure of contesting the 'cultural evidence' did have a critical, de-essentializing aspect. Thus, the state posed the following questions to defense expert witnesses (in the first of which the prosecutor is referring to a phrasing used in a report written by the 'expert' being cross-examined):

> Q Doctor, regarding the comment, "and continuing the close and caring relationship with her son," are you aware that she left her son when he was about 70 days old and did not see him for seven years? What close and caring relationship are you talking about?[46]

> Q Doctor—Okay. But what evidence do we have in this case that there was that strong physical bond between [Anne Shen] and [Ed Shen] for the first 70 days of his life?
> A We don't have such information. It's just the inference on what mothering typically involved in the cultural setting—
> Q Okay.

A —from which Mrs. [Shen] has come.
Q But you don't know in fact whether Mrs. [Shen] was one of a mother [sic] who held a lot or not much; is that right?[47]

In these extracts, the state—without thereby affirming patriarchal norms—is questioning the defense's idealizing construction of Anne Shen as being utterly devoted to her son, and the use of generalizing 'cultural evidence' as an essentialist stand-in for evidence relating to the defendant's conduct individually. But at other points, the prosecution did cite the norm of motherly duty affirmatively—for instance, by accusing Shen of selfishness for having left her son to grow up with his father. (The following quotes are taken from the defendant's cross-examination.)

Q (by Mr. [counsel for the prosecution]) Mrs. [Shen], I think you told us that you felt shame because you had the son and were not married; is that true?
A Yes.
Q And in the summer of 1981 when you asked to see your son, you still weren't married; were you?
A Yes. But really, I really missed my son very much. So I didn't pay attention to too [sic] much.
Q Then why didn't you get on an airplane and fly to America to see him?
A I would only come if there was a status.
Q *Were you more interested in status or in seeing your son?*
A I was interested in both.[48]

Q What countries did you visit in the summer of '88?
A Canada.
Q Where else?
A United States.
Q Whereabouts in the United States?
A Las Vegas.
Q Did you stop by and see [Larry] and [Ed] in the summer of '88?
A I called [Ed] and [Larry], but I did not come to see them.
Q How come?
A Because that time there wasn't enough time. I had to hurry back. Also I was not married. Also I called and talked to [Larry]'s mother and [Sherry] [his sister, C.B.].
Q How long did you stay in Las Vegas in the summer of '88?
A Three to five days.
Q And did you call [Ed] on the first day or on the last day?
A I called [Ed] many times.
Q From Las Vegas?
A La [sic] Vegas and Canada.
Q And you didn't have time to stop by and see him [Ed]; is that right?

A I had to leave anyway, even if I saw them. And then I would be very painful when I leave.
Also they said things. The things that they said made me didn't want to come.
Q Did [Ed] say things to you or [Larry]?
A [Larry]'s family.
Q Let's talk about [Ed] first.
When you talked to [Ed] on the phone from Las Vegas in the summer of '88, did he indicate he wanted to see you?[49]

Like the defense (see Chapter 3), the prosecution in these quotes is actually implying that patriarchal oppression is no good-enough reason not to fulfill the maternal role—a role entirely naturalized in the prosecution's discourse (rather than being marked as patriarchal), just as it was in the defense's (see Chapter 3). Both parties to the trial, then, colluded not merely in a colonial discourse that disavows patriarchal order in the West, but (in tension with that discourse) also in a patriarchal discourse of motherhood—with the defense picturing Anne Shen as an essentially 'good mother' and the state, as the opposite. An opposition defined by the norm of maternal self-sacrifice.

The 'Scorned Woman'

In addition, the prosecution used other gendered counter-stereotypes to those stereotypes of femininity circulated by the defense. I will merely focus upon one of them. Where the defense rendered Shen as being devoted to her son to the point of self-effacement, tending somewhat to suppress self-interested aspects of her behavior (see Chapter 3), the state pictured her in terms of the notion of the vengeful 'scorned woman' (Sanday 1997). In referencing the notion of the 'scorned woman'—which is more commonly deployed in the context of trials of acquaintance rape (ibid.), where it serves to render the woman as a false accuser intent upon revenge for having been rejected—the state dissociated the anger it attributed to the defendant from her situation of gendered oppression (as portrayed by the defense), freezing that emotion in the terms of a power-blind discourse of Woman's jealous and vengeful Nature:

A . . . She was trying to maintain peaceful relationship with [Larry], even though she was very angry, disappointed, and depressed.
Q She was very angry with [Larry]. Right?
A Yes.
Q Okay. Go ahead.
A No doubt about that emotional component of the anger.
Q So you're telling us that you have no doubt [Anne Shen] was angry at [Larry] on the 9th of September?

A Right. Angry, disappointed, and sad, depressed.[50]

Q All right. And on September 9 when [Ed] tells your client about [Linda] and apparently makes—at least according to your client says something to the effect that, "[Linda] is Dad's girlfriend"—the old adage, "Hell has no fury like a woman scorned"—at that point don't you think your client was real mad at [Larry Shen], angry at [Larry Shen]?
A There are a few things there. The first thing was what was contained in [Anne]'s report was not so much that it was her anger. What the statement of [Larry]'s relationship with [Linda], which was, it seemed to be foremost in her mind, was that, was [Ed]'s statement that [Larry] loved [Linda] more than [Larry] loved [Ed].
Q That's part of it, undoubtedly. All right. But—
A Yes. There are some feelings, certainly, between, that would likely be between [Larry] and [Anne].
Q After all, [Anne] had just married him on September the first, and on September the 9th, the boy says, "Oh, by the way, Daddy has a girlfriend," essentially.
A Yes.
Q That would irritate, I assume, the new wife?
A Although [Anne] knew of [Linda]'s presence a long time ago.[51]

As argued in Chapter 3, whether or not the defendant was angry at her husband on September 9, 1989—the night of the killing—was legally irrelevant to the verdict according to the jury instructions given at the conclusion of Shen's first trial (see also Ch. 4, n. 14).[52] Irrespectively of whether or not one agrees with this analysis, however, the discursive struggle between the competing parties—which, in either case, was (also) a struggle for the jury's sympathy—was conducted in gendered terms. In the first of the above quotes, the state seeks to isolate the anger imputed to Shen from the feelings of sadness/depression emphasized by the defense. In the second, the state articulates that anger to the patriarchal stereotype of the vengeful woman, so as to make out the killing as an act of revenge against the child's father. 'Patriarchal' because that stereotype, in dissociating a woman's anger from her subordination (and in Shen's case, from her exploitation by Larry Shen [see Chapter 3]), eliminates any feminist perspective upon that emotion, and upon acts based on it. The two parties, then, jointly divided up the defendant in terms of a gendered dichotomy between the passive-submissive, altruistic woman (or 'good girl') devoid of agency vs. the assertive, egoistic woman (or 'bad girl') floating free of any context of oppression. Whereas one side of that gendered dichotomy was being supported, on the defense's part, by the culturalizing notion of the Oppressed Third World Woman, the other side was couched by the state in equally essentialist *universalizing* terms that stripped the defendant's predicament and motives of any particularity of context: While the defense hypostatized Anne Shen's cultural difference (in virtue of emphasizing her 'traditional' Chinese identity) (see Chapter 3), the state brushed aside any significance of cultural difference, constructing her as 'essentially the same':

Q Is it a fair statement to say that women, divorced women with children who commit suicide do it for about the same reasons in San Francisco as they do in Boston as they do in Hong Kong?[53]

Q All right. Do you agree that all of us get depressed from time to time? And isn't it true that many people who are very depressed—and I'm using a layman's term, but very depressed—don't go out and commit crimes, that they don't go out and kill their children, that they don't even attempt to commit, or either attempt suicide or make a suicide gesture? Is that a fair statement?
A Correct.
Q And is it a fair statement that people whose husbands cheat on them, women who have marital problems, don't necessarily kill their children because of that, do they?[54]

Both sides' procedures thereby stripped the defendant's experience and situation of any complexity, either encapsulating her in a totalized cultural particularity that hypostatized difference (Chapter 3), or eliminating social context—and differences—entirely.

To summarize: Anne Shen's defense and prosecution colluded with each other in regard to both patriarchal and colonial discourse. In regard to patriarchal discourse, in that they countered each other's strategy by resort to gendered stereotypes that jointly affirmed normatively loaded dichotomies central to patriarchal discourse—chiefly, the dichotomy of good vs. bad mother which is premised upon the norm of maternal duty. In regard to colonial discourse, in that both sides affirmed the notion that patriarchal social relations are (largely) confined to Third-World settings such as China. This latter collusion closely resonates with that demonstrated in the preceding section of this chapter to have united prosecution and defense in *People vs. Lopez and Singh*: The strategy of contesting 'cultural evidence' instantiating the figure of a cultural Otherness of patriarchy by means of distancing a defendant (or, in other cases, putative victim/s) from the culture in question by resort to a notion of Westernization, while leaving intact the other's side's construction of that culture, and of the West, in terms of the dichotomy between patriarchal oppression and women's liberation, is standard currency in the corpus of 'culture cases' I have examined. This is apart, of course, from the opponents' collusion in an empiricist discourse of 'culture' which treats the latter in terms of unmediated ontological givens, rather than of discursive constructions—not merely in *Lopez and Singh* (see the preceding section), but also in *Shen* as well as the other trials making up the corpus.

CONCLUSION

Much as the adversary system in principle offers a lot of scope for controversy over 'cultural evidence', and much as such 'evidence' is sometimes vigorously contested (as in the trials examined above), such contest within the sample of cases I have examined tends to affirm, rather than subvert, certain premises central to colonial and gendered discourse—most centrally, the notion that only Other cultures are starkly patriarchal.[55] This collusion amongst opposing trial parties might be attributed either to strategic considerations, or to attorneys' own interpellation by the relevant discourses, or to a combination of both. Strategic considerations might cause attorneys to reason that hegemonic narratives will convince juries more readily because of *their* probable interpellation by the discourses in question. This interpretation has been advanced in some of the literature as to a 'cultural defense': it has been suggested that questioning certain hegemonic narratives may endanger a client's case (Razack 1998; Volpp 1996, 1615–1616; see also Volpp, n.d.; Lee 2003; Nunn 2006)—an assumption that should not be taken for granted, as I will argue in the Conclusion to this work (Part VI).[56] Based upon the above analysis, I favor the second interpretation, according to which most attorneys' strategic imagination is itself constrained by hegemonic discourses, such that they miss out on perfectly feasible strategic options. I think that the example from *People vs. Gonzalez*, from which at the beginning of this chapter I quoted a "counter-hegemonic" strategy of contesting the figure of Patriarchal Other Cultures, provides such a feasible option. I also tried to show that, in the trial *People vs. Lopez and Singh*, defense attorney 1 could have been more successful with his initial strategy of countering his client's racialized stigmatization had he attacked the notion that cultural differences are necessarily measurable in quantitative degrees, rather than being a matter of *qualitative* difference—including in regard to patriarchal practices. That option may have been discursively unavailable to him. Certainly, we have seen that his attempts to object to the racialized essentialism of the prosecution's procedure of proof contained certain self-subverting phrasings, indicating that he was encountering a boundary in his capacity for critical reasoning.

If my interpretation is correct, then the problem cuts deeper than what Maguigan suggests when she appeals to prosecutors' "obligation" to critically contest stereotypes (1995, 92–93; see the beginning of this chapter)—namely, that this is a mere question of motivation (Maguigan 1995, 86) and thus, of the will. Then prosecutors' and defense attorneys' trial strategies would not be a matter of entirely voluntary choices. Even if the other interpretation holds (or a combination of the two), however, it would mean, likewise, that hegemonic discourse tends to circumscribe the boundaries of critical contest at trial. This finding is contrary to the widespread optimism about the workings of the adversary system in "sorting out" stereotyped 'cultural evidence' which I have reported in Part IV. It is also contrary to the optimistic intuition articulated by Burns (1999, 58, 60–61, 68, 132) that the narratives making up the U.S. trial—particularly direct vs. cross-examination—tend mutually to deconstruct one another.[57] Far from amounting to a deconstruction of the opponent's procedure, strategy and counter-strategy tend to be united by shared assumptions deriving from a hegemonic consensus that itself remains unquestioned and taken for granted. In the following chapter, we will see that consensus circumscribing most of the contributions made to trial discourse by witnesses.

7 Witnesses and Hegemonic Consensus

I will begin this chapter with an account of a few of the most radical examples of resistance encountered in the corpus of cases. Thereafter, I will turn to discursive practices more common among witnesses: firstly, the strategic use of colonialist essentialism by subjects who are themselves devalued by it. Next, I offer a more systematic account of witnesses' discursive politics of constructing 'cultural evidence', based upon individual examples—starting with the category of witnesses functioning, as I write, as 'Native Informants' (Spivak 1990, 66), and proceeding subsequently to the category of witnesses introduced at trial as academic experts. The final section offers my conclusion to this chapter. As in the preceding chapter, my examples will be drawn largely from two trials with which I have already acquainted you in detail: *People vs. Shen*[1] and *People vs. Lopez and Singh*.[2]

RADICAL RESISTANCE

Subverting 'Essential Difference' I

There are some rare moments in the corpus of trials that amount to a radical disruption of hegemonic discourse in my judgment. The first example takes us back to the trial *People vs. Lopez and Singh*; specifically to the testimony of Lieutenant Joga Kaur, the prosecution's expert witness. We have seen in the preceding chapter that this witness was caught up between the prosecutor and two defense attorneys, each of whom tried to shape his testimony in terms of the opposite project: where the state sought to establish a unitary Sikh 'value system' allowing for a prediction of Sikhs' conduct, defense attorney 1 (counsel for Malkit Singh) attempted to de-particularize Sikh culture by comparing it to others and by individualizing Sikh people. Where both defense counsel (eventually) sought to distance the defendant and his family from 'Sikh tradition' by emphasizing the 'Americanization' of many Sikhs, and by constructing 'Americanization' as a binary opposite of 'tradition', the prosecution emphasized the traditionalism of many Sikhs in the U.S., especially among first-generation migrants who (as males) continue to wear a turban. (It did so based upon the same opposition between 'tradition' and 'Americanization' that was propagated by the defense). Lieutenant Kaur's testimony regarding the magnitude of cultural difference shifted significantly depending on who he was talking to—conceding major differences when questioned by the prosecution, while partially minimizing or even negating difference when 'examined' by the defense. Against this backdrop, he was asked by one defense attorney:

Q Lieutenant, do you think that in the course of your testimony that [sic] you may have waffled a little bit here on some of your opinions about the presence or absence of violence in the Sikh community?
A I tried not to.
Q You told us that there was no particular difference, the presence of violence or the absence of violence in the Sikh community than any other community this morning; do you remember that?
A Yes.
Q Are you saying by that statement—
A To a certain point, yes.
Q Well, to a certain point are you withdrawing your—your opinion from that statement?
A I'm saying that it is not that much difference, however there is still a little bit of a difference between one culture versus the other.[3]

The prosecution's introduction of a model of 'difference in degree', or of 'quantifiable difference' (which, as I argued in the preceding chapter, brought to rest defense attorney 1's relatively progressive initial strategy of contestation, since he found no means to contest that hegemonic model), eventually "solved" the said tension within this witness's testimony, between asserting cultural difference and negating it. That tension was apparent especially at the moment when the prosecutor first introduced this model:

Q . . .
Mr. [counsel for defendant] and Ms. [counsel for codefendant] asked you whether many of the things that you testified to on direct examination were any different from conditions in the United States, do you recall?
A Yes.
Q Are you testifying that the Sikh values and traditions are no different than the values and traditions of American culture?
A No. *Yes, I am. They're not that different, you know, some are valued higher than the other ones. I mean, it—they are no different than the others.*
Q Okay. Are you talking about a difference in degree?
A You can say that, yes.[4]

The second-last answer in this quote shifts back and forth between the options of asserting and negating difference—arguably a result of the binary options the witness was presented with by the different attorneys, of either essentializing *difference*, or *sameness* across cultures (likewise a problematic option, as I argued in the preceding chapter). These options were also presented in the variant of an either/or choice between being 'traditional' vs. 'Americanized'—especially once defense attorney 1 had abandoned his strategy of universalization, and had joined the other attorney (counsel for Samuel Lopez) in seeking to distance the Singh family from 'Sikh culture' (see the preceding chapter). The binary character imputed by the attorneys on all sides (one for the state, two for the defendants) to the relationship between 'Sikh culture' and 'Americanization' may be said to silence experiences and practices that do not fit this neat schema. I would interpret Lieutenant Kaur's "waffling" (see the second-last quote above) on the subject as being symptomatic of that silencing. At one point, however, he responded proactively to the dividing practice (Foucault 1982, 208) constitutive of the mode of his courtroom examinations. This was when defense attorney 2 applied the schema in question to the witness himself, trying to push him exclusively in one of the two directions in virtue of suggesting that, being Americanized and having a 'white' wife,[5] he was no 'real (or authentic) Sikh' (and therefore, not a competent expert on Sikh culture). (At the same time, the following questions by this attorney may be taken for an attempt to render the witness an example of a Sikh who has largely left his culture behind, as she tried to suggest of defendant Singh and his family.)

Q Would it be fair to say that as an adult you have not practiced the Sikh cultural—that is aside from going to church, the culture of the Sikh religion has not been a significant part of your life, has it?
A Yes, it has.[6]

A short time later, this exchange transpired:

Q Okay. I know I understand what you're saying that you have followed the Sikh religion, but correct me if I'm wrong, but as far as your day-to-day living that you have experienced has not followed the strict Sikh cultural tenets?
A When you're talking about strict, counselor [sic], could you elaborate a little bit more so maybe I can answer.

When I go to work I am [Joga Kaur], I'm doing my job as a law enforcement officer. When I come home, you know, I have both worlds so I try to stay within those boundaries, but trying to raise my children more towards the Sikh religion which is more mine than my wife's. But it doesn't—it doesn't require any certain—in other words, I don't go over here and do something else, the Sikh religion is there. I practice

> it, you know, what I mean, if I want. *What you are asking maybe I—I can't give you, okay.*[7]

Lieutenant Kaur here is clearly rejecting the binary options with which the defense counsel has presented him. His last sentence may be taken for a statement that what he is trying to say cannot be articulated in the terms of such discourse. Disrupting the discourse of essential cultural difference (as well as that of essential sameness), his remarks allude to a transcultural life world much more fluid, every day, and *devoid, precisely, of essential* difference: "I don't go over here and do something else, the Sikh religion is there". It is my sense that Lieutenant Kaur's response also undermines the Othering of Sikh culture, i.e., colonial discourse. That Othering is manifest in the notion of "strict Sikh cultural tenets" circulated by the attorney—a notion she fails in any way to explain or to fill with substance. Without any such substantiation, the (hegemonic) 'intuition' that 'Sikh tenets' are in some way *strict* seems to feed off the construction of Sikh culture as essentially illiberal (in contrast to American liberalism) promoted by the prosecution, and reproduced in the defense strategy overall (see Chapters 2 and 6, respectively). My sense of the questions put to Lieutenant Kaur which I just quoted is that they also project Sikh culture as something somehow more definite, more marked than 'American culture', which may be identified with the everyday life the attorney is invoking. This amounts to the exact exoticization of Sikh culture, and to the hegemonic un-marking of the 'American' (read: 'white') as devoid of anything so particular as 'culture', that are characteristic of colonial discourse. In saying, "When you're talking about strict, counselor [sic], could you elaborate a little bit more so maybe I can answer", Lieutenant Kaur challenges these moves and arguably marks the emptiness of the signifier 'strict', exposing it as lacking any denotative content and as, instead, serving merely to connote 'difference' as such—or rather, 'illiberalism'—as the unspecific Otherness that serves to buttress the construction of a hegemonic, white American liberal self.[8] This particular sentence therefore may also be taken to question the characterization of 'Sikh culture' as essentially 'illiberal' in opposition to 'American culture' which was at the bottom of the prosecution and defense strategies in this trial.

We shall return to Joga Kaur's testimony in a later section of this chapter. For my next example of a moment of fundamental resistance to hegemonic discourse, I will turn to the subversion performed by another witness in *Lopez and Singh*—the homicide victim's mother.

Subverting 'Essential Difference' II

Inberit Johl, who testified early on in the trial along with her husband and one son, was portrayed by the prosecution as a quintessential traditional Sikh. Not only did the state highlight her lesser education (and her husband's) compared to that of their college-educated sons, but also her 'Indianness': the victim's parents had resided in India for as long as he was alive.[9] In the trial as a whole, India/its Punjab state was cast as the locale of Sikh culture in its most 'traditional' form. Sikh Americans were being linked to tradition in the form of being linked to India. I cite two examples showing this for both the prosecution's and the defense's procedures of proof—the first extract being from the state's redirect examination of Joga Kaur; the second, from the redirect and recross-examinations of another Sikh witness (we encountered both extracts in the preceding chapter):

A Well, I see the difference of the fact that it's—again, it's an unwritten rule over here that in the East Indian community the female is looked down upon after a divorce. Regardless of what her rank, what her financial capacity is, she's looked down upon.
Q By the community?
A By the community within that—within where she resides.
Q Okay. *And in India, in the Punjabi or Punjab area of India, among the Sikh community is the looking down upon a woman who has been divorced by the community even more marked*?
A *It's more there than it is here, yes.*[10]

Q [by counsel for the prosecution, C.B.] From what you could see with [Jaswinder], could she appear to be one Sikh woman in the United States *who adhered to the traditions and the culture as it was in the old country*?
A Yes.
. . .
Q [by defense attorney 1, C.B.] Well, do women in the old country work at plants like [company X], as single women?
A Well, they don't have [company X] in India.
Q Okay. *Well don't women in India pretty much work in the home and take care of the kids*?
A Yes, they usually do.
Q That's not the way [Jaswinder] was living her life; isn't that right?
A Well, *she was thinking the same way, but in India* [sic].[11]

In these quotes, the witnesses and attorneys jointly identify 'Sikh tradition' with India. And we saw in the preceding chapter that 'Americanization' was identified with 'liberalization' by the defense (as it was by the prosecution[12]). By implication, India in the trial was identified with conservatism. In the following passage from Inberit Johl's direct examination, the contrast between 'Americanization' and 'traditional India' is rendered even stronger through the prosecutor's attempt to mark out the rural Punjab (where the victim grew up[13]) as even more quintessentially conservative/traditional:

Q Am I correct that you, yourself, were also raised in the Sikh faith?
A Yes.
Q And in the area of India where you were raised, are there certain values, certain beliefs of the Sikh people that are traditionally followed?
A Yes.
. . .
Q In the Punjab, are there both cities as well as small villages?
A Yes.
Q *And the traditional values of the Sikh people in your experience, have they remained more traditional and more geared to that* [sic[14]] *in the villages perhaps than in the large cities?*
A Yes. *We respect all religions, but because the life is the same for everybody.*
Q In the—when you were raising your family, when [Sardeep] was growing up in India, did you live in a city or in a rural village?
A In the village.[15]

The function of marking out Sardeep Johl's mother and father as quintessentially traditional was apparently to render them as particularly competent to testify about 'the' Sikh 'value system' in virtue of their cultural authenticity. Inberit Johl's italicized reply in the above quote is, however, utterly at odds with both that attempt and the underlying discursive grid that opposes an authentic Sikh tradition (situated in India) with an Americanization conceived of in terms of 'progress to Westernization' (see n. 12, this Ch.), and hence, as monopolizing 'the modern'.[16] The witness here seems essentially to be invoking multiculturalism as well as a form of universalist humanism that asserts that "life is the same for everybody".[17] This must strike a sensibility constituted by the said discursive grid as confusing for, it upsets its orderly division of the world according to which such cosmopolitan concepts 'belong' in the West and are certainly least expected to be familiar to a *woman* from rural India testifying through an interpreter (see n. 15, this Ch.). The fact that the Indian state is organized as a parliamentary democracy and that multiculturalism is at the heart of Indian politics must be withheld from that discursive order if it is to be maintained.

Exposing Institutional Racism

I will end the present subsection of this chapter with a final, very brief example of radical resistance from another trial which I have not as yet addressed.[18] 'Radical' at least in the context of the criminal trials I have studied, where exposing racism, especially in an institutional form, is indeed a rare act. It is not necessary here to go into the details of that trial except for the following: Another case in which the notion of the Oppressed Third

World Woman was invoked in support of a woman defendant (compare Chapter 3 as well as the Appendix), the state produced yet another version of that strategy of contesting 'cultural evidence' of this kind whereby the person in question is portrayed as 'Westernized' (rather than as 'traditional', as she is by the other party) (see Chapter 6)—here: as a 'modern woman'—as a means of distancing her from the 'Third world culture' concerned. In this context, the prosecution asked the defense's 'cultural expert'—a senior lecturer of Arabic language and literature and Islamic studies at a U.S. university who had spent his life in Egypt prior to migrating to the United States:[19]

Q And there is one truism that people change, don't they?
A Absolutely.
Q So, for instance, by living in the United States for the last ten years, that's changed you in many respects, hasn't it?
A Yes, but also you have to consider the factor that I live on campus, I live on university [sic] and I have to change, otherwise I won't be promoted.[20]

The latter answer, while open to various interpretations, may be read as a statement that, to get promoted in so supposedly 'enlightened' a setting as a (renowned) university, means that one cannot simply remain the person one was prior to the experience of migration because there is an expectation that one *should* change, on the part of those from whom one hopes for a promotion. On this reading, the statement alleges that 'cultural difference' constitutes a problem to a university institution—i.e., that there is assimilatory pressure. This reading of the reply in question makes it reminiscent of hooks's [sic] description of the experience of working in academia as an experience of "white supremacy" (1995; see also Cook 1997; Christian 1994).

The above statement may be compared to the ones by Malkit Singh's defense attorney, discussed in the preceding chapter, which expose the racism underpinning the procedure of proof deployed by the state in Singh's trial.[21] Unfortunately, the above and other similarly progressive statements by the 'expert' I just quoted occur within an overall frame of a highly essentialist discourse of culture—just as the critique made by Singh's attorney was highly circumscribed by colonial discourse. In similar fashion, other moments of resistance (like the ones treated earlier in this section) occur amid moves by the same speakers which advance colonial and/or patriarchal discourse. Before treating this point in more detail, I will turn—in the next section of this chapter—specifically to moments of *resistance* that deploy hegemonic discourse in an affirmative rather than subversive or critical manner. This is what I mean by "strategic essentialism" (a concept usually associated with Spivak [1988c, Ch. 12]).

STRATEGIC ESSENTIALISM

The point of doing so is to show that, while there is a lot of antagonism between attorneys and witnesses, such antagonism—and even a witness's resistance to an attorney's agenda—has nothing to do necessarily with resisting hegemonic discourse. The corpus of cases I have examined is replete with instances in which just the opposite occurs. In giving two examples of practices of this kind, I want to "demystify" the notion of resistance, disidentifying it from its common association with progressive politics.[22] Of course, the strategic deployment of stereotyped (colonialist/patriarchal) 'cultural evidence' by subjects who are themselves devalued by it occurs in the context and under the pressure of the power relations entailed in the highly consequential matters negotiated by defendants, victims, and witnesses in criminal court, and in the fact that the decision-makers and personnel involved are often (mostly) 'white'—such that they may be assessed by those subjects to be more receptive to hegemonic than to counter-hegemonic strategies. However, as in the preceding chapter regarding attorneys, so here too must the possibility be considered that—over and above any strategic considerations that might dispose witnesses to deliberately deploy colonial/patriarchal discourse in hopes of achieving a more favorable result thereby—they might themselves be (partially) interpellated by those discourses. Therefore, it is an open question to what extent, in 'strategic essentialism', subjects deploy the relevant discourses, or to what extent the latter in fact deploy the subjects enunciating them.

We have witnessed one example of strategic essentialism in Chapter 3: Anne Shen's utterance "I'm a Chinese woman".[23] She made that utterance a few times during her testimony; I will here quote just one instance, from her cross-examination:

Q Did you apply for a visa to come back to America in the next year?
A No.
Q At the time did you have a Portuguese passport?
A Yes.
Q And you had to go to the American consulate in Hong Kong and get a visa; is that right?
A Yes.
Q Why didn't you do that?
A Because I was waiting for him [Larry Shen, C.B.] to marry me.
Q How could he marry you when you were in Hong Kong and he was in [town X, California]?
A He could come back and marry me.
Q You also could go to [town X] and marry him; right?
A *But I did not want to do that.*
Q Why not?

A Because he promised me that he would marry me.
Q Don't you agree it takes two people to get married?
A Yes.
Q Why didn't you just get on the airplane and fly back to [town X] and marry him?
A Because I'm a Chinese woman.
Q What does that have to do with it?
A The initiative should be with the man. If I came just like that, *it would have been very shameful for me*, because I was already shamed the first time.[24]

The defendant is here resisting the prosecutor's move of brushing aside her gendered subordination—in the form of a social norm against women's initiating the subject of marriage—as insignificant or nonexistent. Against the backdrop of the (U.S.) norm of mothers' duty to their children, which (as shown in Chapters 3 and 6, respectively; see esp. n. 48, Ch. 6) was cited affirmatively *to* the defendant (and to women generally) by both the defense and the prosecution, Anne Shen is here asserting her interest in avoiding being shamed. In stating, "I'm a Chinese woman", she is asserting her subjection to a gendered norm. But, in doing so in this particular form, she is, of course, engaging in a form of self-exoticization in the eyes of an 'American', possibly largely or wholly 'white', audience—appropriating an identity label that, at least on the side of the reception of that statement, situates her within colonial and patriarchal discourses as an essentialized subject and an Other. This throws into relief the power relations that make a discursive move of this kind potentially beneficial, in that the essentializing label deployed may help render the defendant credible with the jury precisely because it is evocative of the stereotype of passive, submissive Chinese women (one variant of the figure of the Oppressed Third World Woman [see Chapter 1]).

My second example of strategic essentialism shows how it is sometimes deployed to devalue somebody else—in this instance, by Anne Shen's husband, Larry Shen, to devalue her. Mr. Shen in a few sequences of his testimony appears to have presented himself as 'pro-American' in attitude. In contrast, he imputed to his wife a dislike of the U.S., in a way that may be interpreted as catering to assimilationist discourse—such that he stood as a 'good', assimilated citizen, while the defendant was positioned as anti-American and, by implication, an 'inassimilable alien'. The last of the following sections of transcript combines these arguable moves with appealing to patriarchal discourse by representing Anne Shen as a 'bad mother' and a (female 'foreign') pleasure seeker. "Ed" in the following quotes refers to the homicide victim, the spouses' child:

Q Did you talk to her [Anne Shen] about, you know, what religion you were going to bring [Ed] up in or anything like that?

A I say leave it to [Ed] to America way, you know, because he's born here. He's America citizen. You know, whatever he going to school, he will follow American people.[25]

Q Did you ever have to get [Ed] up earlier than normal so that you could pick up [Linda Fernandez]'s kids to school?
A About five or ten minutes. And I also explain to [Ed], too, I teach him, too, I say, "If you have a friend, you have to help each other," you know. . . . Then [Ed] understands very well America way: have to help each other.[26]

Q Okay. How long after [Ed]'s born [sic] do you and [Anne] and [Ed] live together?
A About three months.
Q Then what happens?
A Then she definitely, she don't like United States life, the life, because she's from very motor city [sic] called Macau, is gambling place just similar like Las Vegas.
Q You've been to Macau several times?
A Yes.
Q Can you tell us what it was like then?
A Similar like Las Vegas. They have lots of restaurant open 24 hours, nightclub open 24 hours, and casino open 24 hours. And lots of tourists people. Weekend, you know, so busy, you know.
Q Okay. Well, then, why did [Anne] decide to leave America and go back to Macau?
Mr. [counsel for defendant]: Objection to the form of the question as calling for a conclusion of this witness.
The court: Rephrase your question.
Q (by Mr. [counsel for state]) Did [Anne] leave America and go back to Macau?
Answer yes or no.
A Yes.
Q Why?
A She say, "I don't want to take care of the baby because a lot of responsible," and she don't like United States life.[27]

While Larry Shen is not immediately resisting an attorney here, he is deploying assimilationist discourse as a way of discrediting the defendant. As such, he is resisting the defense's project of rendering Anne Shen sympathetic to the jurors. It is as part of this agenda that he is resorting to what may therefore justifiably be called 'strategic essentialism'. Of course, Larry Shen here is not merely devaluing his wife. Rather, in arguably appealing to a distinction between 'good foreigner' and 'bad foreigner', he is ultimately devaluing himself, too. As argued above, it is an open question to what extent the subject deploys a given discourse with full consciousness of its implications, or to what extent s/he may (also) be said to be "used" by a discourse.

I hope to have clarified through the above examples that neither political resistance (as occurs in the first one) nor (as in the second) resilience against an attorney's project is necessarily associated with progressive politics—much as it does involve strategies of self-empowerment. While there is much in my corpus of cases in the way of uncooperativeness with attorneys as well as criticism of, and resistance against, specific discursive strategies on their part, very few of these practices actually sabotage hegemonic discourse (as I say of the examples given in the first section of this chapter, headed 'Radical Resistance').

THE OVERALL SPECTRUM OF DISCURSIVE POLITICS

This section aims to give an overall picture of the role of witnesses in buttressing vs. undermining hegemonic discourse. I divide it into subsections on, respectively, discourses instantiating the figure of the Native Informant (Spivak 1990, 66) as the grounds of their validity, and discourses relying on the authority of academic knowledge. (Of course, some 'cultural experts' were being qualified as such on both grounds at once.) I do so because each variety of authorization of 'cultural evidence' organizes power relations in different ways—with the academic 'expert' being positioned on at least an equal footing with the audience and her examiners in my judgment, whereas I perceive those positioned as non-academic 'Native Informants' as being subjected to a very asymmetrical relation of power, as I explain in the following subsection.

'Native Informant' Discourse

I invoke Spivak's capitalized expression "Native Informant" (1990, 66) so as to indicate that subjects called at trial as 'experts' on their own cultures function as part of a discourse continuous with colonial ethnography. The audience at trial is positioned as the culturally unmarked observer while the spotlight is cast exclusively upon the Other culture—in a way well characterized by the following appropriation of Butler by Hill:

> Judith Butler suggests that the white racist imaginary 'postures [itself] as if it were the unmarked frame of the visible field, laying claim to the authority of 'direct perception." White privilege is, thus, the omniscient and invisible force which does the 'framing' without eventually taking its turn at, as it were, being 'framed' (Hill 1997, 159).

Observed (through a seemingly 'direct perception') from this position of unmarked privilege, the 'Native Informant' tends to be positioned as less than a full subject—a transparent window unto the truth of the Other culture. (Something highly apparent in the trial *People vs. Lopez and Singh*, to which I will return instantly.[28]) This is how I understand the following remarks by Spivak:

> One hears, for example, that some of the theoretical stuff that's produced, let's say, in France, is naturally accessible to people from Africa, from India, from these so-called natural places. If one looks at the history of post-Enlightenment theory, the major problem has been the problem of autobiography: how subjective structures can, in fact, give objective truth. During these same centuries, the Native Informant, who was found in these other places, his stuff was unquestioningly treated as the objective evidence for the founding of so-called sciences like ethnography, ethno-linguistics, comparative religion, and so on. So that, once again, the theoretical problems only relate to the person who knows. The person who *knows* has all of the problems of selfhood. The person who is *known*, somehow seems not to have a problematic self. These days, it is the same kind of agenda that is at work. Only the dominant self can be problematic; the self of the Other is authentic without a problem (Spivak 1990: 66; original emphasis).

Returning to the case *People vs. Lopez and Singh*, I have shown in the first section of this chapter that expert witness Lieutenant Joga Kaur—who was accepted as an 'expert' by the judge on grounds of his Sikh 'identity' and of his career in law enforcement, during which he had handled cases involving Sikhs—resisted the prosecution's and the defense's attempts to form his testimony in ways mutually opposed to each other only partially; at one specific point. Otherwise, he did cooperate with both parties some of the time, changing back and forth, for instance, between affirming and negating cultural difference. Fundamentally, however, his testimony formed the heart of the state's 'cultural' case, and—rather than merely being "bullied" by mutually opposing attorneys—Kaur actively testified in a way that helped build that case. In some instances, his insistence upon testifying in a way which, overall, was definitely favorable to the prosecution rather than to the defense (even though he was a subpoenaed witness with no choice but to testify, rather than a voluntary witness for the state[29]), actively frustrated the defense's attempts at undermining the state's racialized 'cultural theory' of the case. For instance, after Sikh men's wearing of a turban had been coded as a sign of a traditional orientation on direct examination, one defense attorney tried to question the reliability of that correlation:

Q Let me ask you another question. Have you, in your experience, encountered any Sikh men who may wear a turban, but yet not be strict followers of the Sikh culture and the tenets?

A Not that I know of.[30]

In so responding, Kaur advanced the state's thesis that any Sikh man's attitudes are predictable from his wearing a turban, while undermining the defense's attempt to question such predictability. Similarly, he answered as follows to a series of questions on redirect examination which, after he had relativized the alleged predictability of Sikh families' policing of marriages on "cross", sought to re-establish an absolute predictability according to which a Sikh woman's extended family will not accept a husband's intent to divorce under any circumstances (compare Chapter 2):

Q With respect now with [sic] the issue of violence attendant to divorce as a specific area of inquiry, can you tell the ladies and gentlemen of the jury whether you find violence in the Sikh community in that regard to be the same or different than violence in the rest of the American community in general?

A Well, I think it is the same to a certain point, if it is agreeable on both parties, *but it's never been that case* to my knowledge since I've been in—a law enforcement officer. The fact that *when a female, when there is a divorce there's always revenge, if you want to call it or retribution against the husband for the divorce.*

Q And in terms of that particular reason for divorce do you find that to be the same or different in general than situations of divorce that don't—that do not involve members of the Sikh community?

A Well, I think it's different the fact that once it's divorce you go on your merry way, if you want to call it, whereas because of the East Indian tradition and staying within the community it's usually taken a little bit more seriously than, let's say, here in America.

Q When you say a little bit more seriously you mean a very small amount of difference, or is there an appreciable quantifiable difference in the level of violence that you expect in a Sikh marriage [sic]; is there an issue as opposed to a non-Sikh marriage?

A I believe I stated earlier that *it goes through the escalation process that where it starts not too intimidating, if you want to call it, but it progresses if things are not back to normal and/or the individuals are not reconciled.*[31]

Kaur also testified on direct examination as follows:

A Could lead—could start from as far as threats and it could escalate to almost anything from the part of the family of the bride's side.

Q Including death?

A Yes.

Q Is that something that you've personally observed within the Sikh community?

A Yes, I have.[32]

Kaur made these statements—which make violent retribution seem inevitable in all cases where the husband goes through with his plans for divorce—even though he conceded on cross-examination that it was not common, once a divorce is final, for the wife's family to continue to achieve a reconciliation; that he knew women divorced and remarried within the Sikh community,[33] and that he was aware of only one case of a killing on these grounds within the U.S.—which had involved Muslims and not Sikhs.[34] In other words, there must have been some level of generalization involved in his formulation of a quasi-law of conduct applicable to Sikhs—a generalization which fed into the prosecution's method of racialized cultural profiling, and without which the state would have had a much weaker case against defendant Singh (see Chapter 2).

I want to make two points with this discussion: One is that speakers in the corpus of cases under study do not necessarily engage in a consistent discursive politics. Thus, Lieutenant Kaur is the enunciating subject of both one of the most radical moments of resistance in the corpus (as discussed in the first subsection of this chapter), and of a most essentialist, criminalizing discourse of Sikh culture. Secondly, his testimony overall may be viewed as representing the span of discursive politics involved in the corpus as regards witnesses represented at trial as 'Native Informants'. While at one point (as discussed in the subsection just specified) he questioned fundamental premises of colonial discourse—namely, the concept of essential cultural difference and the Othering of Sikh culture—overall, his testimony buttressed rather than weakened these very discursive features.

Academic Discourse

In this subsection, I will exemplify the spectrum of academically based discursive politics encountered in my corpus of cases using the example of *People vs. Anne Shen*, a trial I discussed in detail in Chapters 3 (defense's case) and 6 (state's case), respectively. It will be apparent from these earlier discussions that the expert witnesses testifying for the defense—all of them qualified on an academic basis—contributed just as fundamentally to the Othering of Anne Shen, and of Chinese women generally, as did Joga Kaur to the Othering of Malkit Singh and of Sikh culture generally (see the preceding subsection). I will begin, however, with one of the more progressive aspects of the expert testimony in *People vs. Shen*. This was present in the account of one anthropologist concerning the historical role of suicide for Chinese women. While making substantially the same assertions about Chinese women's disempowerment as did the other three 'cultural' expert witnesses for the defense, in the sort of theoretical language he used, this did not amount to constructing Chinese women as tragic, passive, hapless objects of oppression, as it very largely did in the other testimonies (see Chapter 3). In Dr. Miller's account, as I will call him, suicide came across as, historically, a matter of agency and even resistance for Chinese women. Moreover, women's suicide in his testimony was not being linked with infanticide (as in parent-child suicide). Rather, Chinese women were here constructed as acting on their own behalf—unlike in some other testimony for the defense which suggested that the defendant may have tried to kill herself *in order to* take care of her son in the afterlife, thereby catering to the patriarchal norm of maternal self-sacrifice (see Chapter 3). Dr. Miller testified:

Q What does the professional literature suggest are the reasons why a Chinese woman would resort to suicide?

A Well, in traditional Chinese society the relationship between men and women was what we might call asymmetrical one [sic]. The cards were stacked on behalf of the men in society. A man could send a wife back to her family for a variety of reasons. If she failed to produce an heir he could divorce her. If he felt that she was insufficiently honoring his parents, he could send her back for a variety of reasons. If he felt she was too difficult or too hard to handle. He could send her back for virtually any reason he chose. Whereas a woman had very few options in traditional Chinese society. If she—remember, marriage [sic] in Chinese society are arranged marriages, traditionally.

. . .

A But a woman who had married—whose marriage will be arranged and who, for one reason or another, found her husband detestable or despicable or absolutely, you know, horrendous or just would have no choice but to—to commit suicide. There were no other options. She could not sue for divorce in traditional China [sic] society.[35]

My sense of this passage is that 'Chinese women' here do come across as subjects (of experience) and agents (of action) rather than as mere objects of oppression. This testimony reminds me of Gilroy's construction of slaves' voluntary death as an act of freedom—in fact, a pursuit of the only path to agency, and to a liberation from oppression and exploitation, that may have been left open in certain situations (1993, 63, 68).

Another positive aspect of this testimony is that, in historicizing the role of suicide for 'Chinese women', and in relating it specifically to arranged marriage (which, Dr. Miller stated, has fallen into disuse in contemporary China[36]), he clearly differentiated the historical female agents of suicide from the defendant and her situation. In doing so, he declined to render his testimony fully serviceable to the defense's project. The expert testimonies in the corpus of cases under study differ quite strongly by whether or not they are partial to the side the witness testifies for. Obviously, partial testimony will tend to smoothen over any conflicts between particular 'facts' and the strategic goals of a given trial party. In contrast, the fact that Dr. Miller limited his assertions regarding suicide to women whose marriages were arranged, while emphasizing changes in gender relations since 1949 (see below), undermined what I interpret as an attempt on the defense's part to render more credible the defendant's alleged suicide attempt—which the state maintained had been faked[37]—as a genuine attempt on her own life. It made it harder to fit Anne Shen into a smooth stereotype that would have papered over historical discontinuity. Such discontinuity was emphasized by Dr. Miller as regards gender relations both in Hong Kong and Macau (where the defendant had worked and lived, respectively) and in mainland China after 1949 (where she had grown up):

Q Marriages commonly today arranged in Hong Kong and Macau—
A No.
Q —still?
A They are not.
Q That practice stopped when, sir [sic]?
A Well, I don't think there was any official time. It's just became [sic] increasingly—became less and less common as Hong Kong has become more and more cosmopolitan, and as young people have become somewhat more independent of their families, and also because Hong Kong is primarily an area of refugees, many of the people in Hong Kong are rather distant from the kinds of extended family relationships that would have been common in traditional times and, therefore, somewhat freer in their inter-actions [sic] with members of the opposite sex than they might have been were they continuing to live in villages with large numbers of relatives monitoring their behavior very closely.[38]

Q All right. On the subject of suicide for Chinese women, is it a common or uncommon phenomenon?
A It is common phenomenon [sic], in traditional China.
Q What did you mean by traditional China?
A Pre 1949 [sic] China.
Q How does that affect today's China?
A Well, certainly 2,000 years of history and tradition continue to have an effect on the contemporary scene, but there was quite a number of things about traditional Chinese family organization, pre 1949 [sic] family organizations [sic], that have changed the status of women. For example, in Chinese society has improved substantially [sic] since the establishment of the People's Republic of China in 1949. *Prior to 1949, women were really in a—in a horribly subordinate position. I mean, as compared to women in our own society, there* [sic] *status was much, much, much, much lower.*[39]

Despite the politically valuable aspects of Dr. Miller's testimony which I have pointed out, these occur within narrowly circumscribed confines. Thus, beyond the fact that Chinese women's historical oppression seems to be pictured in very totalizing and homogenizing terms in his testimony, begging the question of whether he is omitting areas of self-determination that may likewise have existed for some of them, this expert witness joined the others by picturing women's historical situation in the U.S. as much better, and in equally homogenizing terms. Given that racial segregation was still current in the pre-1949 U.S., and that for African American women, for instance, racist subordination has gone hand in hand with sexual exploitation, it seems likely that Miller was tailoring his generalization primarily to white women. Be that as it may, the comparison made by him in the last quote above deploys the quantifying model of picturing patriarchal relations in the U.S. as *less pronounced* rather than as differing *in quality* from patriarchal relations in the various 'Chinas'—which model, in Chapter 1, I designated as furthering both colonial and patriarchal discourse. His testimony, then, contributed to the even starker portrayal of Western women as utterly self-determined present in several other experts' testimonies in this trial (see Chapter 3).

Moreover, in Chapter 3 I criticized this 'expert's' construction of his scholarly discipline, anthropology, for its empiricist rendering as a matter of unmediated observation of '*the other*'—as if any such thing as an 'other' could exist prediscursively. It is a characteristic of all of the academic expert testimony on 'culture' within my corpus of cases that the perspectival character of academic disciplines and theoretical sub-schools—that is, their entanglement in discursive politics—remains unaddressed. The empiricist assumptions underpinning attorneys' questions such as the following (put to Dr. Miller) remain undisturbed:

Q Your experience, doctor [sic], or your training and *observations on the scene*, have you become familiar with the subject of the afterlife in Chinese culture?[40]

Therefore, the particular discursive politics entailed in those theoretical/disciplinary perspectives by which academic expert witnesses' testimony is framed remain unexposed as "choices" that occur (wittingly or not) to the exclusion of other possibilities. Instead, those politics receive the sanction of 'objective knowledge'—read: normatively neutral descriptions of 'facts'—that is popularly attached to 'science'. As for the specific perspectives brought to bear, there are more and less essentializing variants of academic 'culture talk' within my corpus. Beside the repression of the perspectival, constitutive character of all discourse of the social, however, the following are among the central assumptions underlying colonial discourse that remain unquestioned throughout the academic expert testimony—except in the rare moments of a fundamental transgression of hegemonic discourse of which I have given examples in the first section of this chapter (see also the Appendix): an essential, dichotomously organized cultural difference pertaining between 'the West' (or 'America') and the rest of the world; an equally binary division between being 'tradition-minded' vs. 'Americanized'; an essential homogeneity of 'Other cultures', and the West's implicit superiority to them in virtue of its identification with 'modernity'/'progress'—based in part on its supposedly greater degree of gender equality.[41]

CONCLUSION

Apart from a few rare "gems" of radical resistance within the corpus, the assumptions just detailed also remain uncriticized in the discourses of *non*-academic witnesses on 'culture', whether designated by the court as 'experts' or not. (Most of them fall within the category of 'Native Informant' discourse treated earlier in this chapter.) That is to say, but for a few exceptions these assumptions remain unquestioned in the case corpus as a whole.

One factor that may account for the lack of fundamental contest over such assumptions is that trial testimony functions within a framework in which two competing parties pursue specific and contrary practical outcomes. The binary arrangement of the adversary trial may well reinforce the usually hierarchical binary oppositions (Hall 1996, 5, citing Laclau) constitutive of colonial and patriarchal discourses. Attorneys, in focusing on a particular agenda, tend to frame their questions regarding 'culture' (as well as 'gender') with a pragmatic goal in mind—for instance, that of either distancing or fully identifying a given person from/with a given, 'traditional' culture, so as to distance or fully identify them from/with gendered inequality. In-between options that render subjects, their situations and contexts in complex terms may be judged too ambiguous to "sway" the jury or judge to support the desired trial result (compare Bennett and Feldman 1981, 167; Taslitz 1999, 107; Burns 1999, 46, 51, 55–56, 175–176). Moreover, the framework for receiving 'evidence' at trial is, per se, suggestive of an empiricist epistemology, as I will argue in more detail in the Conclusion to this work (Part VI): This surely advances the empiricist rendering of 'culture' as a matter of unmediated 'facts' that occurs throughout the trials I have studied, and likely places limits upon attorneys' courage to introduce some form of constructionism into trial discourse (see Part VI).

But, as I have stated at various points, the overwhelming reproduction of colonialist and patriarchal assumptions within my corpus of cases—both by attorneys and by witnesses from quite diverse sociocultural and educational backgrounds—seems to me to point beyond a mere salience of strategic considerations that would advantage hegemonic discursive options vis-à-vis more critical ones. For one thing, as I have argued in the preceding chapter, one should not necessarily assume that fundamentally critical discursive strategies are per se less effective with a jury or judge—a point to which I will return in the Conclusion (Part VI). I would question, for instance, whether radical strategies such as those considered in the first section of this chapter are necessarily ineffective in upsetting basic hegemonic assumptions. Beyond this, the fact that the discursive figure of patriarchy being (more) particular to non-Western 'cultures' is circulated virtually without contest throughout the corpus, as are cultural essentialism and an empiricist rendering of 'culture'—as this work so far has been devoted to showing—should make us consider the possibility that speakers are themselves at least partially interpellated by those discursive frames. Just as attorneys' strategic imagination may be constrained by hegemonic discourses, as I argued in the preceding chapter, so might more critical discursive options 'simply' not occur to many witnesses testifying at trial.

Whether it is interpellation, strategic considerations, or both that accounts for the very largely hegemonic discursive politics of trial testimony found in the corpus: I hope to have shown that the problem with 'cultural evidence' provided by experts is not merely a matter of *inaccurate information* due to either partiality or lack of qualification on their part—as Renteln and Volpp suggest, respectively:

> Because there may be concern about the ethical conduct of expert witnesses who appear to be 'hired guns' for lawyers on either side, a code of ethics for expert witnesses would be advisable. Not only would this *ensure that the information presented to the court is accurate*, but it would also help preserve the reputation of the expert witness as a researcher (Renteln 2004, 206, my emphasis).

> What is at issue in cases involving cultural evidence is the weight it is given, the responsibility of prosecutors to introduce additional evidence regarding culture *so that perceptions of culture are not distorted*, judicial training on cultural issues, *and the question of qualifications of expert witnesses who testify about cultural practices* (Volpp 2000, 105n93, my emphasis).

Rather, the chief problem consists in the hegemonic politics that frame both academic and other testimonies on 'culture'. (Academic testimonies at least to the extent to which the theoretical schools or even the entire disciplines brought to bear are themselves framed by such politics—as evidenced by the set of assumptions listed at the end of the preceding section that remains largely uncontested throughout the case corpus.) As argued in Part IV, colonial and patriarchal discourse need not *distort* 'facts', or even to overgeneralize, in order to contribute to social inequality: instead, they operate in large part by *framing* the construction of cultural 'facts'—which is invariably normatively mediated—in hierarchizing ways. Therefore, '*information*' provided even by '*qualified*' experts must not be relied upon per se for a politically progressive rendering of (gendered) 'cultural evidence', or for a progressive strategy of rebutting such 'evidence'—contrary to the call for experts uttered also by Maguigan (1995), Winkelman (1996, 159), Song (2007, 107), Renteln (2009, 81–82), Friedman Ramirez (2009, 210, 211), Frischknecht (2009, 259–262), and Donovan and Garth:

> A principled use of the culture defense in any formulation will require an increased reliance upon the kinds of specialized knowledge available from cultural and legal anthropologists, among others (Donovan and Garth 2007, 138).

The following statement by Razack about "education for social change" is highly apt in this context too: like such education, a critical discourse of (gendered) cultural difference—whether in court or elsewhere—"is not so much about new information as it is about disrupting the hegemonic ways of seeing through which subjects make themselves dominant" (1998, 10). This chapter has shown that—like attorneys (see Chapter 6)—witnesses testifying about 'culture', whether as academic experts or otherwise, are as likely as they are not to stabilize rather than disrupt such "ways of seeing". What is lacking, in the first place, is a wider spread of truly critical discursive strategies—both among attorneys (whose methods of cross-examination are at least as important as their calling rebuttal witnesses) and among the 'experts' they identify. Nothing is won per se by calling an 'expert' to rebut 'cultural evidence' if s/he colludes with its hegemonic discursive framing rather than challenging it.

In the next step of my analysis, we will broaden our perspective beyond an exclusive consideration of intentional strategies of (de-)constructing gendered 'cultural evidence', so as to appreciate as well the weight of unintentional instabilities generated in the course of the citation of the colonial and patriarchal discourses that frame the trials under study. As I shall argue in the following chapter, in accumulation, the diverse modes in which hegemonic discourse is subject to destabilization in criminal court do make a difference—provided that we move beyond an exclusive consideration of subversive events clearly identifiable as *practices of resistance* which could be attributed to an intending author-subject. In my Conclusion to this work (Part VI), I shall return to the theoretical question as to why the latter concept provides a limited and problematic discursive frame for conceiving of, and conducting, counter-hegemonic politics (see also Part I).

8 Beyond Mere 'Resistance'

The Spectrum of Instabilities Fracturing Hegemonic Trial Discourse and What Difference They Make

In this chapter, we shall see that developments readable as destabilizing to the gendered colonialist constructions circulating at trial, or as shifting those constructions in a politically more progressive direction, occur in other forms beside their direct, articulated challenge by a speaker. This highlights the fact that hegemonic discourses circulating in the courtroom are subject to destabilization from sources operating independently of, or even against, participants' intentions. That is significant particularly given how rarely the overwhelmingly hegemonic trial strategies making up the corpus (as shown in Part IV) are challenged or rearticulated in their fundamentals in ways clearly identifiable as counter-hegemonic *resistance* (the subject of Chapters 6 and 7). It means that, even in the absence of radical resistance, the stability of hegemonic discourses of gender and ethnicity/race at trial is not guaranteed.

As a start into this chapter, I want to provide a brief illustration of the vulnerability of discursive practices to a destabilization unintended by the subject who enunciates them. In the instance at hand, this occurs by way of self-contradiction—which, assuming that we all aspire to be taken seriously, can be taken to be self-undermining *involuntarily* rather than intentionally. The example presented is drawn from *People vs. Shen*, a trial I have already illuminated from a number of different angles in Chapters 3, 6, and 7. Following this brief initial section of the Chapter, I will embark upon a final, more detailed case study, returning for the last time to *People vs. Lopez and Singh* (compare Chapters 2, 6, and 7). Based upon this case study, I shall demonstrate and assess the cumulative impact—and hence, the overall political significance—of the various forms of intentional and (possibly) unintentional instability that rupture, if only momentarily, the hegemonic discourses at the center of this work; at least in some of the trials I have examined (compare Part III). I shall consider the significance of such destabilizing developments explicitly in light of the fact that the disturbances in question tend not to affect the trial's material results, and even tend to be ignored—or actively "repaired" for—by most participants.

PEOPLE VS. SHEN[1]

> *[T]here is no ritual without disruptions, lapses and flaws . . . [There is] something constantly infecting the dominant ideology, even from within the practices in which it tends to be realised* [sic] *. . . fleeting forms of appearance of something 'of a different order',* minute victories that for a flash thwart the ruling ideology by taking advantage of its faltering.
>
> Pêcheux (1982, 217–218, footnote omitted, my emphasis)

A fundamental tension in the strategy of Anne Shen's defense is that between the patriarchal discourse framing the 'cultural evidence', and the construction of patriarchal norms as being (more) particular to the Other culture (in this instance: Chinese) (compare Chapter 3). That is, the notion of Other cultures being more patriarchal than Western/hegemonic U.S. culture is subverted by the patriarchal character of the defense's own discourse. Many of the numerous developments in Anne Shen's trial, and in other similar trials in my corpus of cases, which I read as being politically subversive hinge upon this fundamental tension, which they bring into specific focus. One example was provided by an expert witness who testified in Anne Shen's defense—an 'expert' in transcultural psychiatry originally from Taiwan. Here is the relevant excerpt from his direct examination:

Q Well, is there any explanation as to why this Chinese woman would permit or tolerate the man to direct what's to happen with her life?

A I don't want to be too typical [sic], but it is true that many anthropologists would agree that Chinese woman's [sic] role is characterized as a passive, submissive role rather than assertive kind of dominant role you might see in this country.

Q All right.

A For instance, to give you an example, Japanese Emperor's wife would never walk together with the Emperor side by side. It is a custom and social acceptable behavior to walk behind the husband.

And I can also give you some example which was told as a joke quite often.

One day I was in UCLA Medical Center in the elevator. And there was a couple, a Japanese couple, visiting professor and his wife, in the elevator. And obviously he did not know I understood the Japanese [sic].

So he was responding to his wife, saying, "This is the last time I'm opening the door for you, Button. We are in Japan, and I never do it to you again."

That would dramatize how the ladies first was done in the United States but not in Asia. And I am having a problem in Taipei in the last week because I am so accustomed to the American culture, I kept telling the Chinese secretary to walk ahead when we are passing through the door or elevator, and they say, "No. No. Please, you first."

So I'm suddenly realizing that this is Taiwan, not America.

Q Well, did [Anne] tell you what she did, then, when she told [Larry] she wanted to go to Macau and he said, "Go ahead"?

A She just cried. She couldn't be assertive like American women usually do.

In other word [sic], Chinese women are not so much trained, raise up with kind of verbal communication to express their own, or assert their own desire.[2]

The 'expert's' intention clearly is for the U.S. convention phrased 'ladies first' to serve as an example supportive of his construction of American gender relations as (more) egalitarian compared to gender relations in China. But arguably, this construction of his argument misfires. For, there is an alternative coding to this 'preferred meaning' (Hall 1980, 134; see Part II) of 'ladies first'—namely, its coding by U.S. feminism as a patriarchal convention. Due to this competing meaning of the convention, the example provided may actually be read as being supportive of the notion of *qualitatively* different patriarchal orders not easily ranked in terms of a hierarchy of *more vs. less* gender inequality, which I have advanced in Chapter 1: For women to walk ahead of men (who open the door for them), vs. for women to walk behind men, may be read simply as constituting two qualitatively differing patriarchal conventions. The former is patriarchal in that it feeds into the Western norm for women to be weak and, therefore, dependent upon men. Therefore, the 'expert''s choice of example may be read as unintentionally subverting the construction, to which he is contributing in the above quote, of Chinese gender relations as being more patriarchal than those in 'America'.

This is merely one instance from among the many events which register in the corpus of trial transcripts I have examined that may be analyzed as subverting colonial and/or patriarchal discourse in the absence of any manifest intention on a speaker's part of doing so—or even, as in the case at hand, actually *contrary* to the speaker's apparent ("hegemonic") intentions. Such instabilities further highlight—as does the role of our interpellation by hegemonic discourses, which was in focus in the previous two chapters—the involuntary aspect of discursive practices, in virtue of which they can generate effects that either exceed our intent, or even actively undermine it. As such, the above example illustrates and underscores (in line with poststructuralist theory) the limits of the control exercised by speakers over their own discourse; even in so seemingly strategic and controlled a setting as the courtroom; in so supposedly logically coherent and rationally organized an 'order of discourse' (Foucault 1984) as that which frames the U.S. criminal trial. A theme I shall return to in my Conclusion to this book (Part VI).

PEOPLE VS. LOPEZ & SINGH[3]

> *The very necessity to police and monitor, and to denigrate those who do not conform, indicates the instability of the racial sign 'black' and its refusal to be contained and codified; this seems, in turn, to produce more attempts at closure.*
>
> Young (2000, 427)

So far in this work, we have encountered both the colonial and (oftentimes) patriarchal character of the discourses constitutive of trials involving 'cultural evidence', and certain—intentional as well as unintentional—instabilities that register in the course of their citation. I now want to integrate the different strands of this study by means of a case study that, firstly, considers the cumulative effect of various instances of destabilization within a single trial. This also forms an opportunity to relativize the previously made distinction between sources of intentional and unintentional instability. For, many statements made by witnesses in particular are ambiguous as to whether the relevant effect was intended or not, or to what degree. And certainly, effects of both kinds are closely intertwined in many instances. The second purpose of the following case study is to place those instabilities in perspective. It does so in virtue of attending *at once* to their theoretically destabilizing force *and* to their limited practical significance. This case study shows how—on the one hand—participants to trial discourse paper over such destabilizing effects either by ignoring them, or by engaging in restabilizing exercises. On the other hand, it demonstrates that the damages wrought are not truly repaired thereby. Instead, as I shall argue, they linger on in ways that do unsettle what is handled by participants as being a coherent, rational discourse. They do so in that the assumption of that discourse's coherence and rationality is brought to crisis.

People vs. Lopez and Singh forms the appropriate choice of case study for the purposes just specified because it instantiates, both one of the most extremely Othering discourses of 'culture' in my corpus of cases, and that trial in which the greatest amount of destabilization occurred. In virtue of this, *Lopez and Singh* contrasts with other trials in the corpus in which I have been able to identity very little in the way of destabilizing events or features (compare Part III). This case is thus particularly suited to highlighting the difference made by such instances of destabilization. In what follows, I will focus upon the state's direct examination of its first and only official expert witness on 'culture', Lieutenant Joga Kaur—which was perhaps the most crisis-ridden of all the culture-related examinations in this case—to give you an appreciation of the combined impact of some of the strongest moments of instability that registered here. This direct examination also stands out in that participants sometimes responded actively to the relevant developments—if only by dismissing as nonexistent the threat emanating from them—rather than ignoring them altogether, as occurs in many other such developments as identified within my corpus of cases. It thus offers an opportunity to assess the practical significance of such threats to the coherence of hegemonic discourse.

As recounted in detail in Chapter 2, the state's strategy of proof in regards to defendant Malkit Singh relied upon an extremely homogenizing notion of Sikh culture. The prosecutor aimed to buttress the individualized evidence implicating Singh in the murder of Sardeep Johl by claiming the conduct imputed to the former to conform with 'the Sikh value system' and certain 'patterns of conduct' cast as being so uniform as to be followed 'predictably' by (tradition-minded) Sikh men and their extended families in a given situation. But the prosecutor's attempt to establish 'Sikh identity' in terms of a cultural particularity essentially different from 'the American' was rather crisis-ridden from the start:

Q Can you explain to the jury in your own terms perhaps generally the basic tenets of the Sikh faith, what the Sikh religion is comprised of?
A Basically to my—the way I interpret it is just—

Mr. [counsel for defendant]: Well, I object. I don't think it's proper that we get your interpretation. If he's an expert in—as to what the traditions are he can give an objective dissertation, but he's—

The court: That's sufficient. I think that the objection is properly sustained, that it should be generally accepted beliefs within the religion.[4]

What irrupted in the witness's reply—even though it was immediately repressed, both by the character of the defense attorney's objection, and the judge's response—was the possibility that 'Sikh culture' is always already a construction. While the witness may not have been thinking of discourse theory in giving this reply, the latter would seem to entail an assumption that what the Sikh religion "is comprised of" is a matter of interpretation, and that there are diverging interpretations. This would, of course, undermine the conception, propagated by the prosecution, of Sikh culture as a self-same essence, and of Sikhs, as interchangeable exemplars rather than subjects of that culture (see Chapter 2).

The defense attorney, in phrasing his objection, restabilized the first of these notions (of Sikh culture as a self-same essence)—even as he questioned the second one (of Sikhs as interchangeable exemplars), in virtue of casting non-academic renderings of Sikh culture as unduly interpretative/subjective. But by opposing such subjectivity to the notion of an "objective dissertation" on Sikh culture, which he implied would be devoid of interpretation, he stabilized the assumption that there is such a thing as a self-same essence of Sikh culture (rather than so many interpreted versions of it). The judge's response, too, restabilized that assumption, along with the idea that any Sikh could in principle render that essence in identical fashion. It did so by introducing a similar opposition, between particular, 'subjective' interpretations of Sikh culture vs. "generally accepted beliefs within the religion"—the existence of which he presupposed rather than tested. This fiction—that Sikh culture is so uniform as to be unproblematically generalizable—formed the largely unexamined premise of the entire 'cultural' expert testimony in *People vs. Lopez and Singh*.

Next, the prosecutor engaged in a rather active exercise in re-establishing that fiction, counseling his 'expert' to affirm rather than to examine it. The degree of effort made by him may be taken as a measure of the destabilizing impact of the witness's above response. The following excerpt immediately follows the one last quoted:

Q (by Mr. [counsel for the prosecution]) Sorry for using imprecise terminology. The Sikh values and beliefs that you and your family have followed and been raised in, based on your own personal knowledge are those the values and beliefs in cultural traditions that are common to the Sikh people *in general*?

A Yes.

Q In other words, the Sikh faith that you have been raised in and thus have personal knowledge of is that *the same* as the Sikh values and opinions in the Punjabi [sic]?

A Yes.

Q And as those values and traditions have been *transplanted* to the Sikh population in California you have continued to be conversant with those values and beliefs, because they are your own?

A Yes.

Q With that understanding then, and also *if my question at any point seems to be asking for* either *speculation on your part* or a personal belief that is at odds with *the commonly accepted values* within the Sikh population here in the United States, I would ask you at this point to be advised that my questions are intended to elicit information about the Sikh traditions and values here in California *in general* as you know them to be. With that understanding then can you give a brief introduction to the jury as to the *general tenets* of the Sikh culture and faith?[5]

As I write in Chapter 2, the contentious assumption here is that it is, indeed, possible to make such generalizations about Sikh culture without speculating. If one assumes that all Sikh subjects will not construct Sikh culture in the same way, the level of generalization which the witness is here counseled to engage in necessarily requires him to make arbitrary assertions pertaining to that fiction, 'Sikh culture in general'. An exercise whose speculative character was systematically repressed by moves restabilizing to colonial discourse such as those by the prosecutor, judge, and defense attorney recorded above. Still, inasmuch as the said contentious assumptions remained untested, these agents' ventures of removing the question mark with which the witness's initial move of exposing the interpretative character of definitions of 'Sikh culture' marked those assumptions were less than wholly successful.

In the subsequent course of Kaur's direct examination, the attempt to lend substance to the notion of 'Sikh culture' being established—and therefore, to harden the sense of its particularity—remained subject to difficulties. Following his acceptance by the judge "as an expert in the Sikh religion",[6] the examination resumed in the following manner:

Q I think there was a question pending.
If you can give a brief description to the jury concerning the Sikh faith and traditions as *you have personally observed those things from your own personal experience*, and assume for the time being that no member of our lay jury is in fact a member of the Sikh community?
A Believe in God, follow the—basically the guidance of your parents, basically that's about it.
Q In the area of the Punjabi [sic] where the Sikh people are concentrated, as I understand it are the Sikhs a majority or a minority of the population of that area of India?
A Once again, can you repeat the question?
Q In the Punjabi [sic] are the Sikh people a minority or majority?
A No, they're minorities [sic].
Q How does the Sikh religion differ from the majority religion in India in that area which is, as I understand it, Hindu?
A Hindu. Different cultures, that's about the only way I can explain it.
Q Well, can you tell the ladies and gentlemen of the jury how the family structure fits into the overall value system of the Sikh culture?
A I don't follow you.
Q Well, is there—are there predominant values within the Sikh culture that—concerning the family unit and how it's construed and who has responsibility and things like that?
A Usually *the eldest family member, which would be the father, has the—is the dominant or is in charge*, I guess, of the family out there, if I'm understanding your question.
Q Well, it's intended to be as general a question as possible to allow—to explain to the jury *the differences between the Sikh culture and in general culture here in the United States in terms of family structure*?[7]

The witness's initial reply is conspicuously vague: presumably, any (monotheistic) religion could be characterized in these terms at least by its more conservative adherents. Even when the prosecutor seeks to facilitate the attempt to provide 'Sikh culture' with substance by way of contrast with Hinduism, no specifics are forthcoming. And when, finally, a specific detail is mentioned, it is one that could, again, easily be invoked as a characterization of 'U.S. culture': namely, that the father is considered the head of the family. Thus the state's attempt to establish "the differences between the Sikh culture and in general culture here in the United States" is not altogether successful. These initial difficulties in making credible 'Sikh difference' and particularity may be taken to destabilize those notions, in that cultural difference (and hence, identity) here comes across as rather more slippery and vague than cultural essentialism (in general) and colonial discourse (in particular) would have it.

When, subsequently, the prosecutor brought up arranged marriage, the role of the extended family, and religious attire for Sikh men, he was more successful in constructing a particular identity for 'Sikh culture'.[8] Yet even these markers of 'Sikh difference' were relativized in the course of Kaur's examination. Thus, Malkit Singh's defense attorney on cross-examination successfully relativized the opposition between arranged marriage and 'love marriage' by foregrounding financial considerations that may play into maintaining 'love marriages' *as well as* arranged marriages (as the prosecution had held regarding the latter specifically), and by suggesting that arranged marriages too may involve love.[9] The defense attorney also held that, in 'love marriage' too, relatives may react in a hostile manner when the wife or 'bride' (as he said) is "being dumped by her husband".[10] Finally, while the witness insisted that for a Sikh man to wear a turban is a reliable sign of his being tradition-minded, he maintained that wearing a turban and a beard is not required for Sikhs of the younger generation.[11] In all of these cases, then, the prosecutor's moves at establishing Sikh culture in terms of a distinct profile were only partially successful.

To return to the subject of the necessarily speculative character of witness Kaur's generalizations about Sikh culture, sometime later during his direct examination the following exchange transpired:

Q . . .
Getting back to another topic, let's assume for the time being that a Sikh woman married to a Sikh man here in the United States and bearing children, then is divorced by that man, what affect [sic], if any, on the wife's family in terms of actual support, in maintenance of that woman, what affect [sic], if any, is created by the breakup of the marital relationship?
A Usually the woman ends up back with the parents, looked at as used merchandise, and I guess the responsibility or the welfare of the female is back on the parents again.
Q And you use the term, "I guess". Was that a figure of speech or was that in fact actually a guess on your part?
A A guess on my part.
[Counsel for codefendant]: I would move to strike it as speculation then.
[Counsel for defendant]: I will join.
The court: *I'm not sure if the answer was a guess on your part, Lieutenant.*

The witness: Yes, yes.

The court: Then the answer is ordered to be stricken. The jury is ordered to disregard it as speculative.[12]

It would appear that the prosecutor's inquiry as to whether Lieutenant Kaur had actually been guessing in his initial reply was directed at gaining the witness's affirmation that he had *not* been speculating. The fact that this move backfired may be read as exposing the guesswork character of most of Kaur's testimony as to 'Sikh culture in general'. After all, he was being counseled *throughout* the direct examination to testify at this level of generality. (On cross-examination, the witness admitted that he had based this particular guess upon the assumption that the woman in question would be a housewife—a status not applicable to all Sikh women, as he conceded.[13]) The judge in the above excerpt aims at re-establishing the official status of the testimony as something other than speculative by encouraging the witness to retract the concession that his last response had been based upon a guess. Yet, to my mind, his instruction to the jury to disregard this particular answer as speculative, likewise, raises the question of how the latter differs from the rest of Lieutenant Kaur's testimony. In other words, it arguably contributes to exposing the guesswork character of that testimony as a whole. The threat to its status of empirically valid assertions was thus *both* treated as nonexistent by the judge (and, arguably, by the other participants, who ignored it), *and* was not, ultimately, contained.

A similar instance occurred sometime earlier during the same direct examination:

Q In your experience within the Sikh community—well, how can I phrase this?

Assume for the time being that a male child is born within the Sikh community. Thereafter can you tell the ladies and gentlemen of the jury what feelings are engendered in a Sikh father? Obviously, I'm including it as a base. Every father we presume loves his children, as we presume every mother does as well.

Beyond that as a—as a matter of fact, matter of culture, can you tell the jury whether there are any special feelings that you would become familiar with concerning a father's relationship with a male child?

Mr. [counsel for defendant]: Well, I'm going to object. I think this goes too far. This is asking him to mind read to [sic] what the culture might think in a particular situation. He—he's already testified that variables have changed, this has really gone too far, judge.

The court: Perhaps you could rephrase the question as it relates solely to the Sikh religion.

Mr. [counsel for the prosecution]: I will, your Honor.

The court: All right.

Q (By Mr. [counsel for state]) The last question, Lieutenant [Kaur], whether there are certain feelings commonly recognized within the Sikh community by you, which pertain to the arrival of the male child, feelings common to Sikh fathers with respect to their sons, *and I'm not asking you to speculate as to any particular individual feelings*, what I'm asking you for [sic] cultural relationships with the father's relationship to the son?

A It's usually stronger than if it was a daughter.

Q And in your experience, from both being raised within the Sikh community as well as being a law enforcement officer encountered with the—with a large Sikh population, can you tell the ladies and gentlemen of the jury whether there is any *predictable* or common value in terms of a Sikh father wanting to personally maintain the presence of the son and instill in him personal values of the Sikh culture?

A If I'm reading your question, it usually as I stated, it tends to be stronger that the father usually wants to keep the child with him regardless of what the consequences or what happens, okay, during a marriage. They're usually a lot stronger towards the son than it is towards the daughter, not that it's not there either, okay.

Q Okay. I want to make sure that my question is clear to you so that the answer can be equally clear, *is this a matter of culture*?

A Yes.

Q —something you've *seen culture-wise*?

A Yes, it is.[14]

The defense attorney's objection—while phrased in a self-subverting form (see Chapter 6)—would appear to question the prosecutor's move of extrapolating from generalizations about 'Sikh culture' to the feelings of a given Sikh individual. In other words, by speaking of 'mindreading', the attorney is questioning the predictability of Sikh people. The judge's answer and ruling entirely bypass the point of the objection. So, too, does the prosecutor ignore that point in his next question, where he claims that "I'm not asking you to speculate as to any particular individual feelings". He does so based upon a dichotomy between seemingly un-cultural *individual* feelings, and feelings that are "a matter of culture" and apparently therefore shared in identical form by all of its human 'exemplars'.[15] That dichotomy in the trial maps onto the opposition between (individual) Americans and Sikhs as a homogenized group. That is, it harks back to the notion of Sikhs' being determined in predictable fashion by culture in implied contrast to 'Americans' (read: 'whites'). But this dichotomy is precisely what had been questioned by the defense attorney. Therefore, the prosecutor's claim not to be asking for speculation may be read as a denial; a mere disavowal of the fact that this is exactly what he is doing. The subsequent course of the testimony continues as if no embarrassment had occurred: with the objection having been (implicitly) overruled, the witness's ensuing answers continue to engage in generalizations and predictions as if doing so had not been exposed as problematic.

The prosecutor's final two questions in the above excerpt engage in further restabilizing exercises, partly by ontologizing as a matter of observable fact the dichotomy between culture and individuality invoked earlier: whether the feelings and (implicitly:) the conduct imputed to Sikh fathers are 'cultural'—surely a question of conceptualizing culture—is now treated as a matter for an *eyewitness's sensual experience*. This serves to validate the 'expert's' testimony as both neutral and incontrovertible from an empiricist perspective—as in 'I've seen it with my own eyes'. And yet, the judge's, the prosecutor's, and the witness's joint behavior *as if* they were dealing with purely observational testimony rather than with speculation cannot ultimately cover over the damage done to the state's project by the defense attorney's objection (no matter that it has been overruled)—which, ultimately, may be taken to suggest that the arbitrary character of the testimony makes what comes to figure as 'evidence' about Sikh culture in this trial a fairly contingent matter (see below). From this perspective, validating exercises such as the one definitive of the last two questions in the above excerpt—as well as of the first three questions in the one that follow—may be read as marks of anxiety and as seeking reassurance (by empiricist means) in the face of possible disbelief (compare Butler, e.g., 1997b, Ch. 5).

Joga Kaur's direct examination culminated in an attempt by the prosecution to establish as 'cultural' even a conduct purported to be exceptional among Sikhs. (Something I have no qualms with in principle, given that I take the position that there *is* no conduct autonomous from 'culture' or discourses—but which meant that the state was digressing from its initial notion of culture as making Sikhs' conduct predictable.) This was a tactical move that occurred in response to Kaur's insistence that—while Sikh families will seek to prevent male in-laws from divorcing a female member of the family—it is not unknown, but not common either for them to continue to seek a reconciliation after the divorce has been instituted.[16] The witness also insisted that it was uncommon for families to seek to prevent an ex-husband from remarrying.[17] These were assertions fitting uncomfortably with the case-related 'evidence', according to which the killing at the center of the trial had occurred years after the relevant divorce. They also sat uncomfortably with the fact that the state in its opening statement had tried to make out what could have been an attempt by the homicide victim to seek a new wife in India shortly before he was assassinated as a motive for the Singh family to have him murdered.[18] Here is one of the relevant excerpts:

Q (by Mr. [counsel for the prosecution]) Let me once again, Lieutenant [Kaur], ascertain whether or not the answers that you're giving to these questions are based on the totality of your knowledge of the Sikh community both from being raised in that community yourself and having observed it over the course of your law enforcement career?

A Yes, it is.

Q And that's, I presume, correct me if I ever deviate from that, but I presume that's the basis of your answers to the questions that have been asked at this point?

A Yes, Sir.

Q And with that proviso now with your knowledge and personal experience within the Sikh community—

A Yes.

Q —you've indicated that efforts to seek a reconciliation of the two parties even after a divorce has become final are not—that's not something that's unknown in your experience?

A Yes, Sir.

Q Because there are, as I understand it then, some families, some Sikh families who *for whatever reason* will continue to attempt to achieve a reconciliation of the husband and wife even after the law says they're legally no longer married?

A Yes.

Q And I think then the question that I was attempting to rephrase to you after the objection ruling, is whether the *reasons in your experience* behind a family's continuing to seek a reconciliation of the husband and wife even after a divorce are based on cultural values of the Sikh people?

A Yes.

Mr. [counsel for defendant]: I object. I think this is beyond expertise, *the fact that he may know someone within that culture who acted in a particular way and then to speculate based on the broader traits as being the motivating force* is beyond what you can do as an expert in this area.

The court: Well, that's proper cross-examination, Mr. [counsel for defendant], but repeat the question as within the framework that I've requested, Mr. [counsel for the prosecution].[19]

In effect, the prosecutor here makes out "*whatever reason*" may be motivating an assertedly unusual course of action among Sikhs to be based upon culture—as the defense attorney points out in his objection. This is arguably to stretch the dichotomy the state had introduced earlier—between (uncultural) individual feelings/conduct vs. feelings/conduct based upon culture that can be 'expected' (as the prosecutor often suggested[20]) to occur 'in' all Sikhs, or at least in all 'traditional Sikhs'—to a point where it is effectively abandoned. At the very least, it is to explode the notion that (traditional) Sikhs' conduct is predictable in certain instances. It is to explode it *in the very act* of seeking to rescue it in modified form: While the prosecutor seems to be suggesting here that Sikhs' actions are explicable in terms of culture *whatever their form* (unlike 'non-Sikh' Americans' conduct, which on redirect examination he implicitly described, in the context of family violence, in terms of a mere "normal emotion of anger" in contrast with the "family values" on which violence on the part of Sikh families is supposedly predicated[21]), this is to concede that they are not predictably uniform. With this, the notion of culture as determining (Sikhs') conduct and feelings *in invariant form* is abandoned. Or, put differently, the state at this point is contradicting its own earlier construction of 'Sikh culture'.

Even so, 'culture' continues to be ontologized as a purely empirical matter—here in the form of constructing reasons for action as being based upon culture *as a matter of experience* rather than definition. But the defense attorney reverses that ontologization by framing the prosecutor's move as calling for speculation (rather than, implicitly, for a faithful rendering of experience). The judge once again bypasses the point made in the defense attorney's objection: his invocation of a framework he had requested refers, precisely, to his earlier ruling that the witness must testify solely to matters within "his personal knowledge of the culture".[22] So, his injunction simply ignores the defense attorney's point that reference to 'cultural reasons' for a given conduct is subject to conceptual questions (or, as he says, to speculation) as much as to experience. Of course, the judge's reaction merely *papers over* the embarrassment of the prosecutor's self-contradiction in constructing Sikh culture—which exposes the conceptual nature of that construction, contrary to the judge's implicit insistence upon culture's unmediated perceptual status.

That embarrassment grew towards the end of the direct examination, when the state began "fishing" around for just about any motives for an ex-wife's family to achieve reconciliation even after a divorce, or to prevent the ex-husband from remarrying, that the witness would come up with:

Q (by Mr. [counsel for the prosecution]) I sure apologize for asking long convoluted questions, but I'll probably continue doing it.

We were talking about how common or uncommon it is in the Sikh culture, based on your experience, for a family to make some effort to try to prevent the remarriage of a divorced Sikh male.

Do you remember that general area?

A Yes.

Q Do you have an opinion or do you have knowledge of *the* Sikh cultures [sic] and traditions *which* would explain such activity taken by a wife's family in those—on those occasions when such action is taken?

A Well, I think it's not common for the family members, again, to try and reconcile the marriage for—could be a lot of reasons, could be one of the biggest things is to keep faith within the community.

Could be, you know, a lot of other things over there that we don't see could be behind closed doors whether it's financial and other—

Q Well, let me ask you this, you indicated that one possible area of concern or one possible area of analysis would be financial. Explain the ability [sic] of the term financial to this particular question?[23]

The witness explained that, in the arrangement of marriages among Sikhs, the prospective spouse's earning power is a central factor.

Q Is it your testimony then that in the arranged marriage that the goals of the parties arranging the marriage are not necessarily just to achieve a love interest between a husband and wife?
A Not usually.
Q It goes to other things such as how much money the prospective new addition to the family might be able to bring in?
A Sure.
Q Okay. Is that a factor that plays then in [sic] the decision of a family to attempt to achieve a reconciliation where a marriage has gone awry?
A *It's a possibility.*
Q *And when you say "a possibility", is that something that you've seen personally* over the course of your years, not only of practicing Sikh faith, but also enforcing the law in [county X]?
A Yes.
Q As I understand it then the families having made a good bargain and brought a good money earner to the family feels [sic] some stake in having that person remain a part of their—
A Yes.
Q —family member's life?
A Yes.[24]

As the defense attorney would point out on cross-examination, financial motives for trying to maintain a marriage would hardly seem to be culturally particular to Sikhs.[25] Effectively, one could argue that the state's attempt to establish as 'cultural' any motives that defendant Singh and his family could have had in allegedly having Sardeep Johl murdered years after he had divorced Singh's sister had failed dismally by the end of the direct examination of Joga Kaur. Arguably, this served to render less plausible the discursive logic that prompted the prosecution to make out as 'cultural' the conduct imputed to the Singhs: namely, its reliance, in constructing a motive for the murder, upon a racialized sense of potentially criminal conformity among the adherents of Sikh culture.

The plausibility of that racialized project diminished not least because, within the development of the direct examination examined in this section, the state's procedure of proof turned out to be circular: After initially having tried to extrapolate from generalizations about 'Sikh culture' to the conduct and feelings of individual Sikhs (compare Chapter 2), the prosecutor subsequently tried to extrapolate generalizations about Sikh culture from a conduct imputed to the occasional Sikh individual—only in order to extrapolate, in turn, that the Singh family may have acted as a number of Sikhs allegedly had. This was to read both 'culture' off individuals, and individuals off 'culture' (compare Phillips 2003, 13).

But not only did the state engage in a reasoning whose circularity could be clouded only by the racist premise of the utterly culturally determined character of 'the Other'. Lieutenant Kaur's direct examination also came to expose the utter contingency of what assumed the status of 'cultural evidence' in this case. Not only was his testimony contingent upon the particularities of his own experiences of, and generalizations about, 'Sikh culture', and upon the prosecutor's rather obvious attempts at influencing those generalizations in a particular direction. What came to figure as 'evidence' in this case was also contingent upon judicial rulings that systematically ignored, and thus covered over, the arbitrary and incoherent character of the state's procedure of proof. Apart from the examples we have already encountered, the judge in one instance first ruled a question by the prosecutor (which I cited earlier) improper in form, only to subsequently allow the answer to stand, contrary to the request of one defense attorney.[26] It was because of this latter ruling that the remainder of the direct examination could take the direction of officially establishing as 'culturally Sikh' any murder motive that the witness would speculatively come up with (as we saw above).

To summarize: During Lieutenant Kaur's direct examination, numerous points of instability surfaced. Of course, the fundamental instability was *inherent* in the project pursued by the state—as I have argued analogously of another case (*People vs. Shen*) in the preceding section of this chapter. Thus *one* way of reading the prosecutor's generalizing questions is, precisely, as trying to advance a criminal prosecution based upon ludicrous stereotyping. (For instance, nearly all of the state's attempts at making credible the existence of a fundamentally 'different' Sikh culture are vulnerable to comparison with similar features attributable to Euro-American culture—as in the question: " . . . marriage is intended to be a permanent state; is that correct?"[27]). But destabilizing developments such as those discussed in this section serve to bring such fundamental instability, or vulnerability to disbelief, into focus.

In the instances considered above, the destabilizations resulted from diverse sources—not all of which are readily categorizable according to whether they were intentional or not: critical statements made by the objecting defense attorney (hampered by phrasings that tended to undermine his apparent propositional intent, as I argued in Chapter 6); a response by the witness (regarding the interpretation of Sikh religion) whose critical impact may or may not have been intended by him, or which may have been intended to some degree. More answers by Kaur that failed to suit the state's project, whether intentionally or not, and a tactically infelicitous move by the prosecutor which was intended to repair for the witness's use of the phrase "I guess", but which (due to the answer provided by the latter) ended up magnifying the untoward effect of that phrase. There was also the state's self-contradictory tactical shift in "theorizing" Sikh culture—presumably an intentional tactical step but which is unlikely to have been consciously self-undermining. Thus, it appears that the instances of destabilization analyzed in this case study combine intentional and (possibly) unintentional discursive effects, as well as including different sorts of hybrids of the two: for instance, a *critical* intent subverted by a phrasing more in keeping with hegemonic discourse (in the case of the defense attorney), or (in the prosecutor's) an attempt at restabilizing that discourse—by constructing it as being based on experience rather than guesswork—which, in yielding an (intentionally critical?) reply, backfired. The above case study thus illustrates that intentional and unintentional aspects of developments destabilizing to hegemonic (here: colonial) discourse at trial are closely intertwined.

As for the combined effect of these destabilizing occurrences, they could be judged very differently depending on one's vantage point. On the one hand, their discursive effects are extremely destabilizing in my judgment—to the point that the entire direct examination of Lieutenant Joga Kaur (the state's only formally recognized 'cultural expert' in this trial[28]) could be seen as wholly discrediting to the prosecution's project. On the other, the judge, the prosecutor, and in some instances, the defense attorneys clearly treated those discursive effects as nonexistent. And it is worth remembering here that defendant Malkit Singh was convicted of first-degree murder with a special circumstance, as the prosecution had requested.[29] It is, likewise, worth reminding ourselves that the appeals process went up to the U.S. Supreme Court, which denied review—technically not an affirmation of Singh's conviction, but arguably a statement that the infringement of his constitutional right to due process which the defense alleged was not serious enough to warrant intervention.[30] At a practical level, then, even the numerous and severely damaging occurrences during Kaur's direct examination which I have discussed made no difference to the *material* effects of the citation of racialized colonial discourse constitutive of his prosecution's trial strategy. Yet, from the discourse-theoretical perspective which I have adopted in this work, they form embarrassments that shatter the pretense to rationality and discursive coherence upheld by the participants as if nothing had happened—and hence, shatter the authority of their discourse. Potentially, they render more difficult a reception of the 'cultural evidence' in line with hegemonic discourses than would be the case in their absence.

Part VI

Conclusion

Practical/Theoretical Implications

> *During the 150 or 200 years that Europe has been setting up its new penal systems, the judges have gradually, by means of a process that goes back very far indeed, taken to judging something other than crimes, namely, the 'soul' of the criminal.*
>
> Foucault (1977, 19)

In this Part, I consider some practical and theoretical implications of the preceding study. I begin with the more practical aspect, reflection on which in turn requires a minimum of further grounding in social theory (see also Part II). In particular, I want to address the question of what alternative narratives to be told at trial might look like, and what stands in the way of offering such narratives. For, after all, the subversive effects occasioned as part of the negotiation of 'cultural evidence' in criminal court (see Chapter 8) are but the underside of the depressing reality of its persistent discursive framing in terms of a hegemonic consensus, which we have witnessed throughout this book. Our political desire should, obviously, be directed towards a fundamental *displacement* of that consensus within criminal court hearings (as elsewhere). Yet, criminal justice itself is constructed in terms of discursive frames that set limits to the counter-hegemonic narratives that can be told at trial, even provided that participants will come up with any. Thus, I find it hard to imagine that many judges will tolerate discursive strategies that expose as racialized and/or patriarchal, not just a given trial opponent, but the state itself (see also D'hondt 2009, 824–826). (In trial transcript after transcript I have studied, parties try to interpellate jurors as citizens of a democratic state that is the incarnation of justice.)

For one thing, not only do essentializing discourses of culture, race, and sex rely upon an empiricist epistemology, but so does the trial's very framework for constructing 'evidence' (Twining 1990, 39–40, 72–74): that notion in itself would appear to assume an ontology that is devoid of discursive constitution. For, the idea that 'evidence' serves to prove *facts* harks back to a conception of facts as existing independently of their discursive construction. If it did not, what is constructed at trial would have to be considered (as it has been in this work) as just that: discursive *constructions*. This would make it impossible to render the kinds of decisions taken at trial, which cannot but presuppose an independent existence of the social world. Moreover, as Burns explains the 'received view' of trial evidence, it entails the assumption that the factual and the normative are separate realms, such that it is possible to limit trial evidence to a reconstruction of *neutral* facts that will be 'imprinted' with norms only after having been 'found' as such by the jury or judge, and only with the *legal* norms (1999, Ch. 1, esp. ibid., 24). Quite apart from the fact that the law, too, contains racialized and gendered norms, this is to ontologize any extra-legal racialized and gendered normative assumptions, including the very concepts of racialized, cultural, and sexual difference—which tend to be constructed in hierarchizing ways in hegemonic discourse, namely, in ways advancing notions of white/European, male, and heterosexual superiority (see Part II). The empiricist epistemology in terms of which trial 'evidence' is framed thus cannot fully acknowledge the unegalitarian character of the discourses that underwrite the construction of even the most minute evidentiary details: for, to do so would be to acknowledge their discursive character. The empiricist epistemology that governs the trial thus circumscribes the tolerance likely to be extended to a deconstruction of discursive objects such as cultural or sexual difference.

A second factor that militates against their radical deconstruction at trial is the fact that "identity" is taken to be foundational of subjects' practices not merely in the context of 'cultural evidence', but of criminal justice in general. Volpp has argued that presenting 'cultural evidence' in court is problematic to the extent that it places the focus on who somebody is rather than on what she has done (1994, 90–95). But according to Foucault (1977), this is just what characterizes modern criminal justice as such. As he demonstrates, the criminal justice system has come to focus increasingly upon the delinquent rather than her actions, within a juridical discourse that—in overlapping strongly with disciplines like psychiatry, psychology, and criminology—produces as one of its chief effects a subjected individual. The idea here is that what parades as a humanization of punishment in modern times—one not only officially devoid of physical torture, but in which the human being as a whole is considered for her benefit (e.g., in virtue of the notion of mitigating circumstances, or of psychologizing criminal defenses that place a defendant's biography center-stage)—has come to legitimize an intensification in the surveillance and control of individuals, and the establishment of a separate class of 'delinquents' understood in terms of an essential criminality imputed to them as a matter of character rather than of specific actions.

> The criminal's soul is not referred to in the trial merely to explain his crime and as a factor in the juridical apportioning of responsibility; if

> it is brought before the court, with such pomp and circumstance, such concern to understand and such 'scientific' application, it is because it too, as well as the crime itself, is to be judged and to share in the punishment. . . . The additional factor of the defendant's soul, which the legal system has laid hold of, is only apparently explanatory and limitative . . . During the 150 or 200 years that Europe has been setting up its new penal systems, the judges have gradually, by means of a process that goes back very far indeed, taken to judging something other than crimes, namely, the 'soul' of the criminal (Foucault 1977, 18–19).

> Certainly the 'crimes' and 'offences' [sic] on which judgement [sic] is passed are juridical objects defined by the code, but judgement [sic] is also passed on the passions, instincts, anomalies, infirmities, maladjustments, effects of environment or heredity; acts of aggression are punished, so also, through them, is aggressivity; rape, but at the same time perversions; murders, but also drives and desires (ibid., 17, original emphasis).

As one example 'evidencing' the fact that it is the subject rather than her actions that is being judged today, Foucault mentions the higher punishment meted out to repeat offenders.[1] Convincingly, I think, he argues regarding the historical introduction of their treatment as a separate class:

> Now, through the repetition of the crime, what one was aiming at was not the author of an act defined by law, but the delinquent subject himself, a certain will that manifested his intrinsically criminal character. Gradually, as criminality, rather than crime, became the object of penal intervention, the opposition between first offender and recidivist tended to become more important (ibid., 100).

Foucault's analysis, however, extends beyond the prison system to a thesis that discipline and surveillance combine into a modern microphysics of power that extends through the social as a whole—covering institutions such as schools, hospitals, asylums—and that produces us as subjects *subjected* by notions of norm vs. deviance:

> It would be wrong to say that the soul is an illusion, or an ideological effect. On the contrary, it exists, it has a reality, it is produced permanently around, on, within the body by the functioning of a power that is exercised [sic] on those punished—and, in a more general way, on those one supervises, trains and corrects, over madmen, children at home and at school, the colonised [sic], over those who are stuck at a machine and supervised for the rest of their lives (ibid., 29).

Following Foucault, then, we might question whether *individualizing* subjects—something widely demanded in the literature as to a 'cultural defense' as a measure against racialized stereotyping (e.g., Volpp 1994; 2000; Suri 2000; see also D'hondt 2009, 816–817)—is a sufficiently radical strategy towards undoing racist, colonial and patriarchal discourses. *De-essentializing* the subject might be the more fundamental political goal. Thus, consider—in the light of the following critique of the psychologizing notion of the 'biographical' by Foucault—the statements by writers on 'the cultural defense' cited thereafter:

> The introduction of the 'biographical' is important in the history of penality [sic]. Because it establishes the 'criminal' as existing before the crime and even outside it. And, for this reason, a psychological causality, duplicating the juridical attribution of responsibility, confuses its effects. At this point one enters the 'criminological' labyrinth from which we have certainly not yet emerged: any determining cause, because it reduces responsibility, marks the author of the offence [sic] with a criminality all the more formidable and demands penitentiary measures that are all the more strict. As the biography of the criminal duplicates in penal practice the analysis of circumstances used in gauging the crime, so one sees penal discourse and psychiatric discourse crossing each other's frontiers; and there, at their point of junction, is formed the notion of the *'dangerous' individual*, which makes it possible to draw up a network of causality in terms of an entire biography and to present a verdict of punishment-correction (Foucault 1977, 252, my emphasis).

> I argue that any testimony about a defendant's cultural background must embody an accurate and personal portrayal of cultural factors used to explain an individual's state of mind and should not be used to fit an individual's behavior into perceptions about group behavior (Volpp 1994, 58).

> To determine whether a defendant had the requisite purpose and knowledge when committing the criminal act, *the judicial system must probe the psyche*; the judge and jury must know what the person was likely to think or perceive given his or her specific circumstances. . . . If, in fact, the criminal justice system values individualized justice, such that people are punished only for the crimes they actually committed, then the full story must include both the battered woman's story and the immigrant's cultural story (Suri 2000, 135, footnote omitted, my emphasis).

As I have done throughout this work, I am suggesting that treating 'the immigrant's' (or anyone's) story, whether framed as a story about 'culture' or otherwise, as transparent rather than as inherently a discursive construction on the part of those empowered to represent the subjects concerned—and a construction that inescapably excludes alternative discursive possibilities—risks colluding in a colonization of those represented (Spivak 1988a):

whether they are framed as ethnicized 'Others' *or as 'individuals'* characterized in some way or other. Representing subjects in de-essentializing terms would, by contrast, entail questioning *any* ontology that reifies such representation as the inherent truth about those concerned—thereby acknowledging our inescapable implication, as narrators, in power and politics.

But modern discourses of the subject/individual must be reflected upon critically at an even more fundamental level than the one just addressed: Beside the determinist, psychologizing and essentializing variant of it characterized by the Foucauldian analysis just presented—an analysis of what he terms 'disciplinary' society—, the very idea (constitutive of legal discourse) that people are accountable for their actions presupposes a subject constituted in advance of her discursive and other practices, as their author, rather than their performative effect (compare Part II). This is a presupposition which we may be unable to do without in practice, but which has been questioned in theory (Butler 1997b). Thus, in the context of the legal prosecution of hate speech, Butler writes:

> Would this not be something like the effort to prosecute a history that, by its very temporality, cannot be called to trial? If the function of the subject as fictive origin is to occlude the genealogy by which that subject is formed, the subject is also installed in order to assume the burden of responsibility for the very history that subject dissimulates; the juridicalization of history, then, is achieved precisely through the search for subjects to prosecute who might be held accountable and, hence, temporarily resolve the problem of a fundamentally unprosecutable history (Butler 1997a, 50).

In other words, whether we assume a *self*-determined, morally accountable subject or one causally determined by environment and/or genes (as Foucault argues that an increasingly pedagogized and medicalized criminal justice does [1977, 18, 251–252]): either variant, by definition, presumes a subject whose character or being *underwrites* her discourses and actions. As against a subject *constituted* by socio-discursive processes that implicate her in power and norms at the level of her very being—which is thus understood, in the alternative, poststructuralist perspective being sketched here, as being coterminous with our socially organized, yet historically contingent self-understanding (compare Part II). In Butler's analysis, juridical discourse renders this most fundamental level of our subjection to political power invisible by picturing us as entering into social relations, politics, and power as *already-constituted* subjects equipped with a prediscursive 'nature' and an autonomous will (1999, 4–5).

In my view, this analysis suggests that 'self-determination' and what Kant (1959) termed 'external determination' (whether genetic or environmental) form mere variants of a discourse that reifies the subject in terms of a prediscursive ontology which would fix as eternal what, from the theoretical perspective taken in this work (compare Part II), amounts to a historically contingent constitution of 'the human' *in terms of* these options, understood as *discursive* options—each of which is as essentializing as the other—to the exclusion of alternative possibilities of conceiving of ourselves, and thus, of being. This latter, third theoretical perspective has the benefit of rendering the workings of power in our very constitution as subjects apparent to the fullest extent possible. By the same token, it eschews any notion of *human nature* that would ontologize as inhering in us what might turn out to be an effect of particular socio-discursive arrangements. It thereby maximally politicizes our construction of ourselves, and maximizes the potential for change that we can envision (compare Butler 2000a; 2000b).

But there is a further, related reason for skepticism towards the alternative notions of a self-determined, morally accountable subject vs. one determined 'externally' by environment and/or genes: *Qua* alternatives between which modern discourses of the subject have been oscillating, they also have a fundamentally exclusionary potential, as briefly addressed in Part II. To spell out more fully the line of reasoning touched upon there: The alternatives of self-determination vs. 'external' determination, or autonomy vs. dependency, have often been opposed to one another in ways privileging the first term, in association with further hierarchical dichotomies such as mind vs. body and culture vs. nature. The pole respectively treated as inferior, within this list of binary oppositions, in fact plays the part of *constitutive outside* (compare Part II) to the term deemed superior and independent or self-generated (compare Hall 1996, 4–5): Identified with autonomy, mind, and culture, the (full) subject deemed *capable* of governing, or determining, himself—historically figured as 'white', 'male', 'middle-class', 'heterosexual', and 'able-bodied'—has constituted himself as such in opposition to a simultaneously constituted sphere of abjected beings (his Others in these various respects) defined in terms of dependency, body, and nature, and consigned to the status of "the inhuman, the beyond the human, the less than human, the border that secures the human in its ostensible reality", to borrow Butler's words (2004, 218). Alternatively, within the discourse according to which *all* humans are determined genetically and/or biographically, at least to some extent, rather than (entirely) autonomous—as detailed in the Foucauldian analysis of disciplinary society—, counting fully and without question for an *individual*, whether he be classified as normal or abnormal (Foucault 2003), and however unself-determined he is taken to be *qua individual*, still tends to be a 'white' and 'male' (etc.) privilege. A privilege that marks apart the category of normal/abnormal *individual* from that of supposedly interchangeable exemplars of racialized/sexed inferiority, who are deemed determined *collectively*, whether by 'culture' or 'genes' (compare Chapter 2 and Vaughan 1991, esp. 11; 2007, esp. 7). In either discursive variant, then, Enlightenment discourse has positioned its Others ambiguously in the border zone between the categories of "subject" and "object"—oscillating between defining human beings *inclusively* in terms of our mastery over an object world of 'nature', on the one hand and, on the other, *excluding* women/people of color/the unemployed etc. from that definition of the human by opposing them to the white, middle-class male as part of what is (to be) mastered (compare Valverde 1996, 362). (Indeed, the present study purports to provide another example of how easily these two sides of Enlightenment discourse—one of them the official legal discourse of individual rights, the other a racialized colonial/gendered discourse that co-exists with it side by side—slide into one another.)

One possible conclusion from this association of the norms of autonomy and individuality with such exclusionary moves—which position some of us as unfit (as yet) for self-governance (compare Parts II and III; Spindler 2006, Ch. 16)—is that these terms always already imply their Other; that Othering is historically, if not logically, *built into* the notions of autonomy/individuality. Which would mean that these notions are just as fundamentally racialized, gendered etc., as is their shared conceptual counterpart or co-construct, of the unindividualized Other—of color, "etc."—imagined as being determined 'externally' and qua group membership (whether by 'culture' or otherwise); the figure that rears its head time and again in the trial transcripts we have encountered in this study. In my view, this possibility contributes further to discrediting the kinds of individualism to which several of the politically most progressive writers to have commented upon the 'cultural defense' debate have been appealing as the appropriate alternative to the hegemonic de-individualization of gendered, ethnicized/racialized Others—an alternative shaped either by notions of agency, self-determination, and moral accountability or, alternatively, by the concept of an *individual* (rather than racial or cultural) social/biographical determination.

Yet—and this brings me, finally, to the second discursive frame alluded to earlier that circumscribes, not merely 'cultural evidence' in court, in particular, but criminal justice, in general—the de-essentializing narrative of the (human) subject which I have recommended as a preferable alternative to its hegemonic essentialization may well be incompatible with the very conception of criminal justice. For, any tale that introduces a performative theory of the human subject which undermines the notion of a doer behind the deed (Butler 1997a, 45–46; 1999, 181)—and thereby renders questionable the very concept of moral accountability—is likely to exceed the bounds of permissible argument at trial. This is quite apart from the fact that such an account, like an anti-empiricist rendering of epistemology, would, in radically subverting the practical purposes of the trial, also subvert the practical interests of the client. It is more likely, then, that trial narratives directed at undermining racist/colonial/patriarchal discourse will resort to an essentializing account of the human subject that individualizes the persons concerned, and that might put to work a determinist notion of biography of the kind criticized by Foucault (along the lines of the quotes from Volpp [1994] and Suri [2000] given further above).

Despite these structural limits to how hegemonic discourse may be transgressed at trial (provided that participants' strategic imaginations are able to do so, in the first place), it is worth experimenting at the boundaries of tolerance. Instead of introducing ever more identity-related, essentializing evidence that oftentimes reinforces marginalized subjects' pathologization (such as 'evidence' of syndromes like rape trauma syndrome or the battered woman syndrome [Volpp 1994, 90–95]), for instance, narrative at trial might work on exposing and questioning the norms and assumptions constitutive of their marginalization (see also Desai 2007, 80–81). That is, instead of (merely) constructing subjects in terms of a particular, 'different' culture, narrative might focus upon problematic dominant *assumptions* regarding cultural difference. (E.g., the notion of 'other' cultures being especially patriarchal, and its white-supremacist implication [see Chapter 1].) I want to take the position here that constructing counter-hegemonic trial strategies as standing less chance of winning over the judicial audience than do discursive strategies affirmative of the hegemonic (e.g., Suri 2000; Nunn 2006, xvi–xvii; Lee 2007) risks rationalizing the latter as the pragmatically most appropriate option. If what it is instrumentally rational to do is itself defined within discourses—as I shall be arguing shortly—, then it is principally open to being reconstituted. To the extent that participants to the trial are able to imagine strategies critical of colonial and other unegalitarian discourses, they should work to reconstitute in counter-hegemonic terms what it is 'reasonable' to think and to do, and to win over the jurors/the judge to alternative interpellations. If interpellation involves fantasy and identifications that may shift—as Hall (1995) and Mercer (1994, esp. 280) have argued (see Part II)—then the struggle for hegemony waged on the terrain of the criminal trial has not been decided for good.

This point about rationality links the above discussion to the more academic implications of this work, to which we shall be turning now (and with which, as we have seen, the practical implications, as addressed thus far, are very much interwoven): I hope to have shown that the discourse-theoretical, poststructuralist perspective which has enabled this study affords much insight, not merely regarding the specific subject matter of this book—i.e., 'cultural evidence' in criminal court and the debate pertaining to it—, but also at a more general theoretical level. Thus, in focusing upon the capacity of the concept of interpellation to account for the discursive practices of (opposing) attorneys and other participants to criminal court hearings that involve 'cultural evidence', I have foregrounded the limits of the practical rationality in terms of which most of microsociology conceives of social action and discursive practice. My angle of vision is contrary, in particular, to the approach taken within the literature associated with the notion of *law in action*—the dominant sociological approach to trials, which is broadly identified with ethnomethodology and conversation analysis. In line with these approaches, the focus of this literature is overwhelmingly upon subjects' or 'members'' practices as they intend them, and upon their artful 'accomplishments'/'achievements'. Thus, the literature has focused to a great extent upon the art of cross-examining witnesses effectfully as well as upon witnesses' artful methods of countering such strategies (Atkinson and Drew 1979; Drew 1997; Matoesian 1993; 2001; 2005; 2008; Lynch and Bogen 1996).[2] Successes achieved, and the means by which they are accomplished, are much more prominent in these studies than are options missed out on, or strategic failures and the reasons for them (but see Matoesian 2001, Ch. 1)—consolidating a picture of 'members'' *competence* that largely excludes discursive strictures upon their agency. Unintentional effects are virtually ignored. Where challenges to practices of domination are examined, these too are reduced to intentional resistance (Matoesian 2001, Chs. 2, 4, 5; 1993, Ch. 5; Drew 1997)—which is not scrutinized for the extent to which it may be caught up in the very hegemonic discourses it is struggling against (but see Ehrlich 2001, Ch. 4).[3] This bias pinpoints a voluntarist concept of the human subject, in line with the notion of self-determination critiqued earlier in this Part: a subject whose discursive practices are assumed to be based upon informed choice, and who is implied to be (largely) in control of the discursive effects s/he produces.

In this sense, that concept also entails a rationalist bias—contrary to the idea underpinning the notion of interpellation, according to which discourses circumscribe (and enable) in historically contingent ways our strategic imagination; the field of choices we can envisage as being open to us: Once we take the power implications of discursive constructions into account, the instrumental or practical rationality of many of our practices is thrown into relief. Thus, is it self-evident that strategic essentialism (see Chapter 7) is instrumentally rational even if it degrades me by implying my inferiority as, e.g., a white woman or a woman/man of color? Is it instrumentally more rational for an attorney to construct her client in hegemonic terms that inferiorize her than to deploy discursive practices that abstain from doing so? These questions clarify that what is considered 'instrumentally rational' is itself a matter of discursive construction, that is, a matter of assigning priorities somewhat arbitrarily—in the sense that there would have been alternatives that could, likewise, be justified in terms of some conceivable account. This would imply that there is no inherent rationality to the practical choices we make.

What about theoretical reason? In Chapter 8, I focused in part upon the role of logical incoherence in destabilizing colonial and patriarchal discourses. At the level of explicit acknowledgment, this theoretical dimension of rationality is dearer to philosophers than to (micro-)sociologists—who tend to rest content with claiming a *strategic* rationality for 'members' or 'agents'. But I would insist that the philosophical, deconstructive insight into the subversive potential of logical incoherence—an insight in the absence of which the entire undertaking of deconstruction would be pointless—is also extremely fruitful for social inquiry (and, of course, for struggles for radically democratic and egalitarian social transformation). For, as with the questionable character of the concept of instrumental rationality pointed out above, this insight, too, poses an utter threat to the notion of the autonomous subject critiqued earlier in this Part, which remains so cherished within sociology. Thus, the fact that logical incoherence pervades our reasoning practices—as this study suggests regarding colonial and patriarchal discourses of 'culture' as deployed in U.S. criminal courts (see esp. Chapter 8)—undermines our necessary, if implicit, claim to be practicing discourses that are coherent, not just strategically, but also logically.[4] This claim is necessary to our being intelligible, and thus, to being taken seriously at all, by ourselves as well as others. Yet, to the extent that the validity of this necessary claim to our own rationality can be shown to be questionable—as it is in this book with respect to juridical discourse and the institution of criminal justice—this places their authority and legitimation under threat. While this embarrassment to rationalism fails to affect in a politically progressive manner the practical outcomes of court cases involving 'cultural evidence' (as we saw in Chapter 8)—whose mode of construction is, on the contrary, overwhelmingly detrimental to both racialized minorities and all women, as I have argued (for, the relevant constructions shield from view women's subordination by hegemonic, 'Western' patriarchal order)—, it does expose as such what may be considered a mere rationalist façade of such discourses and institutions. The avowal of their own putative theoretical reason on the part of legal actors as well as other parties involved in legal proceedings, whether as defendants, (alleged) victims, or witnesses, may be read in terms of a mere denial, in the psychoanalytic sense, of the lack of rationality of the racialized and gendered discourses that they put to work (compare Chapter 8) and—in the final analysis—of the social order shaped as well as legitimized by unegalitarian discourses such as these.

Ultimately, then, the theoretical and political import of this work extends beyond its immediate subject matter—of the legal use of 'cultural evidence' and the debate pertaining to it. At its most fundamental, this study challenges the rationalism which frames much sociological theorizing and research; with respect to both theoretical and strategic, instrumental, rationality. As such, it contributes to the endeavor of decentering the subject that is at the heart of poststructuralism—an endeavor grounded in the larger project of subverting an account of the subject that would obfuscate social relations of power by presenting his historical forms as our inherent nature (see also Part II), and would claim mastery for the subject at the cost of those figuring, if not as mere objects to him, then at least as "infrahuman" (Gilroy 2004) (compare Part II).

For the most part, that project thus far has been carried out at the level of theoretical (Butler, Derrida, Lacan) or macro-historical (Foucault) analysis. The present study, by contrast, has accentuated those aspects of socio-discursive practices at the micro-level of trial interaction that expose gaps in the rationality of those practices both at the strategic (Chapters 6 and 7) and the theoretical (Chapter 8) levels. I suggest that the failure of 'reason' in both respects may be as much a part of our practices and predicament as either theoretical coherence or instrumental rationality.

If I criticize the rationalism that is so closely associated with what might be termed "theoretical narcissism"—a narcissism that insists that the subject is self-identical and in control, or (in Freudian coinage) 'master in his own house'—then I do so inspired, first and foremost, by the deconstructive ethos exemplified by some of Gayatri Spivak's writings (compare Part II). That is to say, I do so on the understanding that to critique rationalism is not necessarily synonymous with cultivating the illusion that we could dispose of it entirely. But that, on the contrary, it can mean critiquing 'reason' by resort to one of its own central tools (compare Spivak 1988a, 295; 1990, 33): that of logic.

Appendix
Overview of the Cases (with Commentary)

I here specify cases according to their title at appellate level rather than trial level (as in the table of cases found under the heading, "Cases, Constitutional Amendments, Rules of Evidence, and Statutes Cited", but unlike in Tables III.1 and III.2). For a formalized overview of the cases (by jurisdiction tried in, year of hearing, form in which 'culture' was introduced, etc.), see those Tables. The following case summaries are confined to the arguments respectively made by the party introducing the matter of 'culture'.

[Cao] vs. State, 551 So.2d 1094 (Alabama 1988)

The defendant was convicted of capital murder for killing his three children (aged four, six and seven). The defense introduced a witness qualified by the court as an expert in cross-cultural counseling. (Like Cao, he had originally lived in Vietnam.) Among other areas relating to the defendant's experience of the Vietnam war and as a refugee, the 'expert' testified to the effect that, in Vietnam, a wife is considered virtually the property of her husband, who is the head of the family for all purposes; that adultery on her part signifies a loss of face to the entire family, and that a husband's killing himself and his family is a measure of saving face. The defense maintained that Cao had committed the killings as an act of either insanity or 'a legal provocation to the heat of passion from which there was no time to cool' in response to having been left by his wife, who allegedly had had been 'running around' with another man. The 'cultural expert' treated Vietnam as an instance of a 'closed society', which he described in terms of static hierarchies, and the U.S. as one of an 'open society'. As an example illustrating the difference, he referred to gendered inequality in Vietnamese society.

[Chemmanoor] vs. State, 892 S.W.2d 186 (Texas 1994)

The defendant was convicted of murder for having burnt his wife to death. Both had migrated from India to the United States. Chemmanoor disputed having been the person to have set her on fire, and alleged that she had committed suicide instead. In his opening statement, the prosecutor argued that fire is as common a weapon in India as a gun is in 'America', and "[t]hat fire is often used in India to get rid of one's wife. That's the method of divorce."[1] The state questioned several 'lay' witnesses about the place of women in Indian culture, about the frequency of wife burning there, about the 'ritualistic' use of fire, and other related subjects. It also presented an 'expert' on the matter of culture. Among other things, the 'expert' established the dowry system as well as inequality of the sexes as principal reasons for the frequency of wife-burning in India. In his closing and rebuttal arguments, the prosecutor commented extensively upon 'Indian culture'. His statements included the following: "Maybe that's what happens in Indian [sic]. But women are not possessions in America, something that can just be thrown gasoline on and torched when we get tired of them in our middle age."[2] And, with reference to the victim: "She loved this country. If there was any of those two people that were Americanized, it was [the victim]. Because she took the ability to become an American citizen, she took the ability to raise that hand and say, yes, I will abide by the Constitution of the United States. Did this defendant ever do that? No. He is tied to his traditions over in India. The No. 1 way that wives are killed is tied to that."[3]

[Chung] vs. State, 423 S.E.2d 249 (Georgia 1992)

The defendant was convicted of the felony murder of his ex-wife's lover. An 'expert'—a Professor of Anthropology and East Asian Studies—whose testimony was ruled inadmissible, but was elicited in front of the judge, maintained the following in pertinent part (i.e., as relates to gendered domination and culture): that women's role in Chinese culture is subordinate; that they are considered virtually their husbands' property; that adultery on the woman's part causes a loss of face to the husband vis-à-vis his family; that a son is considered much more important than a daughter. This 'cultural evidence' was supposed to illuminate the case-related evidence, which indicated that the defendant's wife had borne him only daughters and no son; that they had divorced, partially in connection with this, and that his ex-wife had had an affair with the victim. The 'expert' compared 20th-century Chinese culture to 19th-century England in regard to the prevalence of resistance against women's pursuing an education, and noted that China was 'developing' much more slowly than the U.S. with regard to the equalization of gender relations. He located U.S. sexism largely in the Southern states and portrayed U.S. culture overall as harboring a strong norm against sexism.

[Le] vs. State, 520 S.E.2d 907 (Georgia 1999)

The defendant was convicted of aggravated assault for shooting and wounding her husband and stepdaughter. Her attorney asserted the defense of self-defense. He sought, unsuccessfully, to introduce expert testimony as to battered person syndrome and to Le's Vietnamese cultural background. The defense maintained that she had been disrespected and verbally threatened both by her husband and by his children from a first marriage, who lived in the same household. The defense wanted to explain her sense of being threatened by this behavior to the point of physically attacking these family members partially in cultural terms. On the one hand, Le and her attorney suggested that her husband had dominated and controlled her—a claim which the attorney ethnicized in the following way, for instance: "He [Le's husband] worked at [Corporation X] and worked different shifts than she did, and it was his practice to call home during breaks to make sure that she was at the house because he wanted to control her. That was their culture. That was the way he was raised to act, and that's the way he acted. He controlled Mrs. [Le]."[4] On the other hand, the defense presented the judge with a 'cultural expert' who introduced a more complex 'cultural' theory of the case—and who compared Vietnamese culture's patriarchal character to that of U.S. culture (a move that is very rare in the corpus of cases), rather than treating it as a matter of cultural Otherness. The 'expert', whose testimony was ruled inadmissible in front of the jury, testified that, for a Vietnamese wife to be disrespected by the children is a severe violation of her dignified position within the family, and absolutely requires the husband's intervention to restore that position—something Le's husband had allegedly failed to do. Her sense of being threatened, the prospective expert testimony suggested, related in great part to the idea that being shamed in this way will bring bad karma—something that could both bring illness or other negative events to the person herself or to family members, and could have implications in terms of being reincarnated at a lower level. In other words, the defense arguably sought to introduce a concept of being threatened alternative to the Eurocentric legal limitation of threats considered to authorize self-defense to *imminent bodily* harm. Apparently as a way of explaining the wife's dependence upon her husband to safeguard her dignified position in the household, the prospective 'expert' introduced the notion of male domination in Vietnamese culture. *Inter alia*, she testified that 'females' in Vietnamese culture rank at the bottom of the hierarchy, and that, within the family, a wife is subject to the full authority of the husband and the mother-in-law. She stated: "At first glance, a typical or traditional Vietnamese family would appear very much like nuclear families that we're quite familiar with. Vietnamese families are patriarchal, and what that means is the father is the head of the household. Vietnamese families are also patrilineal, and that means that we trace our heritage through the father's side. There are some subtle similarities. . . ."[5] While interrupted at this point by the trial judge, she added later on that the traditional Vietnamese family unit is "very similar in nature to what we would otherwise observe within the context of an American culture [sic]."[6]

People vs. [Gonzalez], 659 N.E.2d 398 (Illinois 1994)

The defendant was convicted of first-degree murder for having killed his ex-girlfriend. At trial, the judge ruled inadmissible the testimony of a clinical and social psychologist who would have addressed the 'cross-cultural' aspects of the case. (Both the defendant and the victim had lived in Illinois as well as Mexico.) At the sentencing hearing, the 'expert' was, however, allowed to testify for the defense. Among other things, she asserted that Mexico is considered a very masculine society in social psychology; that 'U.S. culture' is more flexible than 'Mexican culture'; that gender roles and distinctions between the masculine and the feminine are more fluid in the U.S. than in Mexico, and that men in the latter state tend to have more authority vis-à-vis women than in the former one. She added that for men to beat women may be more common and more accepted in Mexico than in the U.S.—even though it is not strictly approved of there either—and that violence (generally) may be even more pronounced in the Mexican-American community. The victim's behavior (of allegedly calling an ex-boyfriend on the telephone) had hurt his sense of manhood for cultural reasons, she suggested. (In addition, the defense asserted that the defendant had been told by relatives that the victim was a 'bruja' or witch, who may have cast a spell on him.) The judge interpreted the expert testimony as having related in part to 'machismo'.

People vs. [Lopez] and [Singh]: see [Singh] vs. Cambra

People vs. [Merlino], 176 Cal. Rptr. 477 (California 1981)

The defendant, who offered an insanity defense at his jury trial, was found guilty of second-degree murder and found to have been legally sane at the time of killing his girlfriend. During the cross-examination of a psychiatric expert witness for the defense, the latter maintained that psychotic behavior tends to be deviant from the group. The prosecutor asked: "Doctor, supposing I lived in a society where women were almost chattel, and women were simply either like children or like property, and you beat them as you beat your horse and you displayed them as you would a very tiny child, and I beat my wife. Would I be abnormal?"[7] As the appellate court stated, it was the prosecutor's purpose to establish "that appellant's violent attitudes and conduct toward the victim, and women in general, were not symptomatic of mental disease, but merely the normal responses of a man raised in a traditional Italian culture".[8] The prosecutor also pursued this strategy in his closing argument during the trial's sanity phase. Another one of his statements was the following, made with reference to New York's "Little Italy" and a city in California, respectively: "in downtown New York on Mott Street women are not considered the same as they are in white middle-class San Jose".[9]

People vs. [Shen], 286 Cal. Rptr. 868 (California 1991), depublished by order, Jan. 23, 1992

The defendant was convicted of second-degree murder for killing her eight-year-old son. The defense maintained that she had done so out of maternal altruism in the course of a failed suicide attempt. Allegedly, this was in line with a practice of parent-child suicide established in Eastern Asia, meant to prevent the possibility that the child will be uncared for in the future in the event of a parent's suicide. The prosecution emphasized, however, that the defendant had barely fulfilled the maternal role towards her son during his lifetime, as a way of rendering uncredible the motive for the killing offered by the defense. The latter explained this fact, through its several 'cultural experts', in terms of Shen's subordinate and subservient socialization qua traditional Chinese woman, which it contrasted with women's 'emancipated' position in the U.S. The defendant had separated from her 'illegitimate', U.S.-born son, who grew up with his father, and had returned to live in Macau (her place of residence prior to her visit to the father in the U.S., where she bore the child), to avoid a 'Chinese' stigma against 'illegitimate' motherhood, the defense maintained. Both that stigma and her submissive mentality had allegedly prevented her from fighting for custody. This mentality was also invoked by the defense to explain additional evidentiary particulars. Moreover, it argued that Chinese mothers may feel more attached to their children than Western mothers, to the point that they feel they know what their child is thinking. This claim served to suggest that Shen's emotional bond with her son had been strong despite their physical separation and lack of direct contact during most of his lifetime.

People vs. [Xiong], 499 N.Y.S.2d 823 (New York 1986)

The defendant was convicted of the second-degree murder of his wife. He asserted a defense of extreme emotional disturbance. The testimony of two expert witnesses on Laotian culture and on refugees' experiences was ruled inadmissible. However, 'culture' was addressed as part of the defendant's testimony as well as of the defense's cross-examination of the victim's sisters, who testified for the state. (All the protagonists were refugees from Laos.) The defense asserted that, by Laotian standards, the defendant's wife had behaved disrespectfully towards him by accepting phone calls from another man, and by telling him about that man's achievements. In virtue of these acts, she had caused him a loss of face. Given his cultural make-up, these acts were sufficient to provoke an extreme emotional disturbance in Xiong, the defense maintained. The defendant testified that Laotian women must obey their husbands, and must obtain their authorization in advance of their actions. Arguably, then, the upshot of this 'cultural defense' was the suggestion that, in failing to fulfill the deferent role expected of a Laotian wife, the homicide victim had provoked the defendant into killing her. Given that gendered relations in other U.S. 'cultures' remained unaddressed at trial, the defense's argument would appear to have implied that a Laotian(-American) man would be provoked more readily by unsubmissive conduct on his wife's part than would other American men.

[Singh] vs. Cambra, 204 F.2d 964 (U.S. 2000, California)

Two defendants were tried jointly for having killed Sardeep Johl. Defendant Malkit Singh was convicted of first-degree murder with the attendant special circumstance that the murder had been committed after lying in wait. Singh was accused of having hired Samuel Lopez, the other defendant, to kill Johl. The defendants disputed all involvement in that deed. 'Culture' was invoked by the prosecution to prove that Singh had acted as charged. The homicide victim had divorced Malkit Singh's sister years before he was killed. According to the prosecution, women divorced against their will in Sikh culture are considered 'damaged goods' difficult to remarry, and a financial 'burden on the family'. This will cause a loss of face to the entire family. The extended family of the woman will pressurize the husband to maintain the marriage—violently, should other means fail. This was what had allegedly occurred in this case. Malkit Singh was argued to have been at the head of the family conspiracy against the victim, and to have arranged the murder for hire, based upon individualized evidence as well as the 'cultural evidence' that he was the divorced woman's brother (presumably, the oldest brother). The 'cultural evidence' further established that the Sikh family is male-dominated, and that decisions and actions on behalf of the family tend to be taken by elder males.

State vs. [Arrisgado], 917 P.2d 370 (Hawaii 1996)

The defendant was convicted of first-degree murder, amongst other charges. It was not disputed that he had physically attacked his wife, their son, her parents, and members of the extended family of her lover, killing several of them. The defense highlighted the fact that his wife had left him, had begun an affair with another man, and had allegedly taunted him about his manhood. It also presented two 'cultural experts'. One subject of their testimony was the notion of 'amok'. The expert testimony was contradictory as to whether this is to be understood as a culture-bound psychiatric syndrome applicable to South-East Asians in particular, or as a transcultural phenomenon that merely had once been culture-bound (prior to the 20th century). One of the expert witnesses, qualified by the trial judge as an 'expert' on Filipino values, testified (*inter alia*) about Filipino concepts of masculinity. While he emphasized that, behind the public façade, women in the Philippines (where the defendant was originally from) exert a lot of power within their families, he also asserted that Filipino society is characterized by sexism—nothing similar to which was mentioned in regard to U.S. society in his testimony. (Unusually within the corpus of cases described in this Appendix, however, the 'expert' accounted for this in part by Spanish and American-Protestant influences which, according to him, had been partially misinterpreted and been grafted onto Malay culture. This contrasts with the essentialization of Third-World 'cultures' as 'Other' to the West that is otherwise characteristic of the corpus.) The expert witness testified that when the public image of a proper family, according to which the husband/father is in charge, is questioned, this negatively affects his sense of self, and that sexism in the Philippines entails a double standard according to which men but not women can have extramarital affairs. For women to do so would be interpreted in the public as a failure on the husband's part to control his wife. The tension in which this would place the man concerned may well be intensified for Filipinos who live in the U.S., where traditional 'solutions' such as wife-beating are less accepted, the 'expert' opined. The defense invoked the above 'evidence' in support of its claim that Arrisgado had committed the acts on trial under the influence of extreme mental or emotional disturbance for which there is a reasonable explanation from the point of view of a person in the defendant's situation under the circumstances as he believed them to be at the time of those acts.

State vs. [Galicia], 537 N.W.2d 147 (Wisconsin 1995)

The defendant was convicted of first-degree intentional homicide while armed as well as attempted first-degree intentional homicide while armed. He had shot dead three men, and critically wounded another, after he had been physically thrown out of a bar following a verbal altercation with a woman there. An 'expert' in clinical psychology testified for the defense, assessing the defendant as having been unable to conform his behavior to the law at the time of the homicides due to a mental disease. Suggesting an alternative explanation of the defendant's acts, the prosecutor on cross-examination introduced the concept of machismo, on which he elaborated by use of the term chauvinism. He asked, inter alia: "So it's your testimony that you don't see it as at all significant that [the defendant] was rejected by a female patron of the bar and ejected by a female owner of the bar?"[10] The 'expert' responded that "[i]t had no significance."[11] Prior to this, the prosecutor had asked: "If, in fact, the defendant had a macho orientation, wouldn't the fact that it was a female that rebuffed him make a difference?"[12] As the defendant's brief on appeal states, these comments "were based on a stereotypical and racially motivated assumption that Hispanic males have an inclination towards having a 'macho' orientation."[13] Note that the state imputed a chauvinistic inclination specifically to men culturally oriented towards machismo.

State vs. [Her], 494 N.W.2d 475 (Minnesota 1992)

The defendant was convicted of third-degree criminal sexual conduct for three separate rapes of two women. 'Hmong culture' was extensively addressed by both the prosecution and the defense. Both sides presented expert testimony as to that culture, which included 'information' about the social position of women in Hmong society (the defendant and the victims were refugees from Laos) and upon migration to the U.S.; about what consequences follow from rape (the prosecution's allegation) and from adultery (the defense presented a consent defense), respectively, especially for the women concerned, and about standards of propriety for married Hmong women. (Both alleged victims were married.) The defense maintained that the victims were falsely alleging rape because Her had refused to pay the fine for adultery that would have been customary in Hmong culture. The defense's 'expert' presented as 'Hmong' notions of rape highly reminiscent of the dictum in the U.S. that 'no means yes', and generally reminiscent of rape myths prevalent in the U.S. to the effect that women are always already to be blamed for unwanted sexual advances, such that what they allege to be rape is always already considered a consensual sexual affair. This testimony seems to have been offered on the rationale that, if 'the Hmong' would disbelieve a Hmong woman's claim of rape and would punish her as an adulteress instead, 'Americans' too should disbelieve the allegations. While the defense did not code as patriarchal either this rationale, or Hmong norms as to rape and adultery themselves, the state did. Capitalizing upon the familiarity of the obvious sexism entailed in the defense's expert testimony, the state made it out as a matter of cultural difference—emphasizing a gender-egalitarian, seemingly power-critical approach to sexual violence in contrast to what it portrayed as a specifically *Hmong* patriarchal order. The prosecutor called the Hmong a relatively repressive society for women and maintained that a woman in the Hmong community is much more powerless than a traditional American woman. The state's own expert testimony suggested that it was unlikely that a Hmong woman would commit adultery, considering the heavy social sanctions imposed for this upon women, and entailed an assessment of the alleged victims as credible. The testimony also explained what the prosecution alleged was a 'gullibility or naivete' in one of the victims' conduct of accompanying Her to allegedly suspicious places, by the fact that he was a community leader whom she had no reason to distrust. In addition, the prosecution presented the testimony of a state's attorney who had successfully prosecuted another rape case involving Hmong on both sides. This testimony was geared towards rebutting the defense's claim that delayed reporting of a rape, which occurred in both cases, would make that report uncredible to Hmong—and, by implication, should make it uncredible to a U.S. jury. The state very largely explained the reporting delay in the case on trial in terms of gendered power dynamics within the Hmong community, which had initially scared one of the alleged victims away from telling others of her experience. Arguably, the introduction of such 'cultural evidence' enabled the prosecution to abstain from exposing and attacking *U.S.* rape myths and gendered norms that seem quite similar to the Hmong notions that it coded as oppressive towards women—myths and norms that, instead, the state reproduced as such *in virtue of* constructing Hmong women as exceptions to their validity. For instance, the idea that any raped woman—other than a Hmong woman—will immediately report to police, or else should be disbelieved. Or the notion entailed in the state's argument that women should bear in mind the possibility that their male company might try to rape them, and should thereby be intimidated into taking 'appropriate' cautionary measures.

State vs. [Ku], 1995 Ohio App. LEXIS 5862 (Ohio 1995)

The defendant was convicted of assault. Allegedly he had sexually harassed a woman employee of his, and upon her having complained of this, had struck her with a golf club. From the opening statement onwards, the prosecution made an issue of the fact that both the defendant and the alleged victim were members of the Korean-American community. It theorized that the alleged victim's having stood up to the sexual harassment had been felt by the defendant to be an insult, and her informing the authorities of the alleged assault, a provocation as well to other male members of the Korean American community—some of whom were present in the courtroom, as the state pointed out. The prosecutor stated, for instance (with reference to the anticipated testimony of the police officer whom the alleged victim had called to the scene): "Officer [X] will also tell you about how Ms. [alleged victim] was very afraid to do anything in this instance, explaining to her how women do not stand up to men in that culture, how a man is to be respected; man can do anything he wants to to [sic] a woman, basically that kind of a thing, and how she was afraid to do anything."[14] The alleged victim partially supported and partially relativized this representation. Thus, she responded as follows to the state's question, "In the Korean culture, are men expected to be—supposed to keep women in control, keep them in line?"[15]: "Not so much nowadays; but in the past, yes, it was."[16] Sexual harassment and male domination of women were addressed exclusively in connection with Korean culture in this trial.

State vs. [Kubicek], 871 S.W.2d 600 (Missouri 1994)

The defendant was convicted of conspiracy to commit murder in the first degree, amongst other offenses, for planning to kill his wife after she had separated from him. During *voir dire* of prospective jurors, the prosecutor used a peremptory challenge on one man "who appeared to be of Indian or Pakistani descent",[17] according to the appellate opinion—meaning that the prosecutor excluded that man from serving on the jury for Kubicek's trial. When questioned by the judge as to why, she stated in pertinent part: "Second reason I struck him, which is not really a racial reason, but more a cultural reason, is from my general knowledge and from my own personal knowledge about the Middle Eastern cultures or [sic] which my family is. I do know that they have, although, [sic] they profess to have great respect for women in those cultures, I do know that the women are not treated as equal [sic] or I feel that they are not treated equally in those cultures. If, in fact, he is Indian there have been reports and newspaper articles and documentaries about Indian men murdering their wives, because divorce is not appropriate in their culture and for that reason—for those two reasons I struck him."[18]

State vs. [Lee], 606 N.W.2d 719 (Minnesota 2000)

The defendant was convicted on several counts of criminal sexual conduct (first and third degree), amongst other counts, for repeatedly raping his ex-wife. He presented a consent defense, according to which the sexual acts alleged had occurred with her agreement. His ex-wife maintained that Lee had beaten and raped her many times both during and after their marriage. The prosecution elicited testimony about Hmong culture from both the alleged victim and several defense witnesses, as well as from an expert witness whom it offered specifically for that purpose. (Both the alleged victim and the defendant were presented as members of the Hmong community at trial.) A major subject of the 'cultural testimony' was the male domination of Hmong culture. It was apparently invoked, both to suggest a proclivity to gendered violence on the part of Hmong men, and hence, the defendant, and to explain why his ex-wife had hesitated for years until she informed police of the violence he had been subjecting her to—namely, by the fact that there was heavy pressure from within the Hmong community not to involve the U.S. state in such matters. In its closing argument, the prosecution portrayed U.S. society as a haven of safety and protection for the alleged victim, with the only apparent source of oppression to her in the state's rendition emanating from within the Hmong community. The alleged victim herself supported that representation. When the defense attorney asked the prosecution's 'cultural' expert witness (a Euro-American police officer with professional experience relating to the Hmong community) whether male domination *in the past* had not also been a feature of 'American' culture, the expert denied this.

State vs. [Saidani], 634 N.E.2d 700 (Ohio 1994)

The defendant was convicted of felonious assault for running over two women, who had been arguing in the street, with his car, injuring them. On cross-examination of a defense witness, the state introduced the subject of 'culture' by asking him questions about how women are regarded among Muslims in Morocco, where the witness was originally from. (While the defendant was originally from Algeria.) In the rebuttal part of his closing argument, the prosecutor stated: "Why would anybody do this? And that was the only reason for asking questions about the cultural mind-set that exists in another part of the world in terms of attitude towards women, and I think that could be part of this. I don't know. / But [the relevant witness] sat there and said that in our part of the world we don't have this. Women don't fight in the street. You never see that. / This man became impatient."[19]

State vs. [Seyoum], 652 A.2d 150 (New Hampshire 1994)

The defendant was convicted of first-degree murder for the killing of his fiancé and a friend of hers. The killing had occurred a few days after his fiancé had told him that she was ending their engagement. The defense attempted, unsuccessfully, to have the trial judge admit 'cultural evidence' relating to Ethiopia—the state from which both Seyoum and the homicide victims had migrated, respectively, to Sweden and to the U.S. (The defendant had killed the victims while visiting them in the U.S.) A neighbor of the victims testified, however, that Seyoum's fiancé had changed in the course of their acquaintance, and had apparently begun to consider other options than that of returning to Ethiopia upon completion of her graduate studies in the U.S. In his closing argument, the defense attorney stated that: "We heard [the relevant witness] talk, one of the few people that really knew [victim 1] that spoke at this trial, and he talked about how [victim 1] had gotten a taste of America and how you could see how she could become torn about whether to go back or whether to stay. What future is there for a woman in Ethiopia?"[20] (There was no basis in the 'evidence' for this gendered statement.) I take the latter for an instantiation of the figure whereby a male-dominated Third World 'culture' is contrasted with a U.S. that supposedly offers more opportunities to women.

State vs. [Smith], 551 N.W.2d 870 (Wisconsin 1996)

The defendant, who was eventually convicted of first-degree intentional homicide, alongside additional convictions, unsuccessfully asserted a mitigating defense of adequate provocation and complete loss of self-control. (If successful, that defense would have resulted in a jury verdict of second-degree intentional homicide.) He admitted to having killed his girlfriend and her daughter. The defense sought to introduce the testimony of several 'experts' in regards to the matter of self-control, but the judge ruled the expert testimony inadmissible. Among other experts, the defense intended to "call an Anger Management Specialist [to] testify about the dynamics of domestic violence and how men are trained not to control their temper in our society and that the concept of 'manhood' in the African-American culture is directly connected to the degree to which an ordinarily constituted person under these circumstances would loose [sic] control."[21] Note that, while domestic violence is here constructed as a 'male' problem in 'our society', generally, that problem is implied to be more severe among African-American men.

State vs. [Vue], 510 N.W.2d 218 (Minnesota 1994)

The defendant was convicted of first-degree criminal sexual conduct for the rape of a woman. He presented a consent defense, according to which the alleged victim had initiated the sexual acts that had transpired between the two. At trial (both in argument and in the testimony), the prosecution made much of the fact that both protagonists were Hmong. Among other things, the state argued that the alleged victim and her family had been easily exploitable by the defendant due to differentials in education, English-speaking skills and duration of stay in the U.S.—differentials which had made the alleged victim place her trust in Vue initially, and had intimidated her and her family once the rape had occurred. According to the state, the alleged victim and her family had also been economically dependent upon the defendant—an employment counselor who, it was testified, had threatened that the family's welfare benefits would be cut off if the alleged victim would not accompany him on the trip that allegedly ended in a rape (a trip that he supposedly pretended to be taking place in search of a job for the woman). The prosecution also highlighted traditional Hmong ways of dealing with rape and adultery, and that for the alleged victim to have initiated sex—as the defendant testified she had—was improbable in the face of norms of social conduct as applicable to married Hmong women. In particular, the state argued that the response of the family of the alleged victim indicated that they believed she had been raped, rather than trusting in the defendant's version of a consensual sexual affair. Had they believed the defendant, the state argued, they would have expelled the alleged victim from the household. This was despite the fact that, as the prosecution emphasized, Hmong traditionally tend to punish the woman even in the event of a rape because she will not be believed, and will be suspected of having committed adultery instead. In this context, the prosecutor asked the defendant on cross-examination: "And in your culture, Mr. [Vue], if a woman is raped it could still be considered her fault, couldn't it?" To which he replied: "In my culture there is no such thing as rape."[22] In her closing argument, the prosecutor commented: "When the defendant testified here he said, 'In my country [sic] there is no such thing as rape.' But this is not his country, this is our country. And in this country a man who forces a woman to have sex, a man who inflicts injury on a woman to have sex, a man who threatens her life to have sex has committed rape."[23] She added: "[The alleged victim] and her family have chosen to resolve this problem in our law and in our system, and they have placed their faith in it" and asked the jury to convict the defendant.[24] Statements which, I would argue, disavow the fact that U.S. rape myths entail a similar logic, according to which a woman's 'no' always already means 'yes'. In fact, the 'evidence' as to standards of conduct for married Hmong women arguably assumed importance to the state's case precisely in virtue of serving to counter the skepticism against women's allegations of rape so widespread in hegemonic U.S. culture. That is, it was arguably in the face of patriarchal rape myths prevalent *in the U.S.* that the state invoked a sexist *Hmong* society.

U.S. vs. [García] et al., 936 F.2d 661 (U.S. 1991, New York)

Defendant Castillo and her co-defendants "pled guilty to a count that charged the conduct of a financial transaction involving the proceeds of narcotics distribution with the intent to promote that unlawful activity".[25] At the sentencing hearing, one male defendant stated to the judge with reference to fellow defendant Castillo: "I would like Your Honor to be aware of lifestyle in Columbia [sic] [sic]. We Columbians [sic] [sic] are machos—we always like to tell our women what to do. I want my woman to do what I tell her. So, what I'm asking is for you to please be compassionate with her. . . . If possible, I'll serve her time."[26] The judge, in departing downwards from the sentence range recommended by the Sentencing Guidelines, stated in part that he had taken that comment into account.[27]

U.S. vs. [Ibrahim] et al., 53 F.3d 1426 (U.S. 1995, Illinois)

This case involved federal charges of conspiracy, bankruptcy fraud, mail fraud, wire fraud, and Currency Transaction Reporting Act violation against several people, most of whom were members of the same family. The trial in question was against four defendants. They were accused of having conspired to operate a so-called "bust-out" scheme, that is, of having defrauded trade creditors of a company set up specifically for that purpose. "The scheme involved (1) ordering on credit large quantities of goods and services worth more than $3.1 million, for which the defendants did not intend to pay; (2) selling those goods for less than their cost; (3) diverting approximately $1.7 million of the proceeds from the sale of those goods to bank accounts held by various family members, and eventually out of the United States to Jordan; and (4) concealing the diversion."[28] In the remaining counts, "the indictment alleged the fraudulent activities by which the defendants carried out their scheme."[29] Among the defendants was a married couple. For the wife (the only female accused), a 'cultural defense' was presented. The prosecution sought to prove that she had known of the scheme and had actively participated in it by conducting some of the financial transactions through which sales proceeds were diverted from the creditors and through which that diversion was being concealed. Her defense conceded that she had engaged in the transactions alleged, but disputed that she had contributed to the fraud scheme to which they had been instrumental 'knowingly and intentionally'—mental states that were necessary elements of the crimes attributed to her. The defense maintained that the accused had acted at her husband's instruction and (hovering somewhat ambiguously between two possibilities) that she had either not known of the fraud scheme, or (to the extent that she had suspected some illegal activity on her husband's part) had not dared resist him. In support of those claims, it constructed for her an identity of 'traditional subjugated Arabic woman'.

U.S. vs. [Okute] & [Onyekachi], 1995 U.S. Dist. LEXIS 6037 (U.S. 1995, New Jersey)

The defendant was indicted for conspiracy to distribute and to possess with the intent to distribute heroin. Pretrial, a hearing was held on the admissibility (at trial) of expert testimony on her culture as well as on Battered Woman Syndrome (BWS). The trial judge denied the motion for an admission of that testimony—following which the defendant pleaded guilty. The defense's position was that Onyekachi had been coerced, by her estranged husband, into dealing with heroin. At the hearing in question, two separate prospective expert witnesses were heard—one, with reference to BWS and the other, to the defendant's culture. The latter 'expert' was originally from Nigeria (like defendant Onyekachi) and, as holder of a Ph.D. degree and consultant with organizations, specialized in 'her' culture, Igbo culture. In relation to gender roles in Nigerian and especially in Igbo culture, his testimony held that the man plays a dominating role, and that Igbo marital relationships often entail physical abuse of the wife as well as forced sex. He maintained that the defendant's marital relationship had followed that pattern and that Onyekachi was very dependent upon her husband. On cross-examination, the 'expert' granted that the defendant had been exposed to Catholic and American culture both at an early age and in her adult years—in response to questions which implied these to have been 'liberating' influences. He did point out, however, that Christian moral beliefs, too, tend to support a submissiveness of women to men. In response, the prosecution maintained this to be a universal phenomenon cutting across cultures. Yet, the examination subsequently returned to the theme of the defendant's exposure to U.S. culture (following her migration there) as a potential influence that would have made her less susceptible to subservience vis-à-vis her husband.

U.S. vs. [Perea], 804 F. Supp. 476 (U.S. 1992, New York)

The defendant pleaded guilty to knowingly and intentionally possessing cocaine with intent to distribute. Based on a confidential psychiatric report on the defendant, the judge in sentencing her departed downward from the

Sentencing Guidelines to the statutory minimum "[b]ecause of subservience to her husband who was himself primarily responsible for her acts".[30] In his written opinion, the judge based this assessment on the fact that Perea's husband had regularly beaten her, and had "insisted that she assist him in his drug operation".[31] While there is no indication (in either the written opinion or the sentencing transcript) that the confidential report upon which the judge based his sentencing decision raised the issue of ethnicity, I am unable to verify whether or not, in fact, it did. Be that as it may, the judge treated the matter in terms of a gendered pattern of subservience, in general, and as a cultural phenomenon relating to the defendant's upbringing in Colombia, in particular. At the sentencing hearing, he merely stated that: "I'm going to depart downward . . . on the ground that based on the information now available this defendant was coerced. She was not sufficiently coerced to constitute a defense to the charge. But she was coerced by her husband as well as by the relationship between males and females in her culture and the circumstances. So that she was acting under the influence of the husband which she could not escape by any reasonable means. While at the same time being guilty, technically, since she had the necessary mens rea."[32] The published opinion elaborates upon this statement in the following way: "Women reared and living in traditional cultures, in which gender roles are often highly determined and women are more likely than in the United States to be relegated to a subservient status, are particularly susceptible to patterns of dependence, domination and victimization. . . . Women reared in traditional Latin American cultures are likely to be subjected to male domination that often includes physical abuse. . . . The level of reported violence against women in Colombia [sic] is extremely high."[33]

U.S. vs. [Ramírez-Arellano], 879 F.2d 391 (U.S. 1989, Missouri)

The defendant pleaded guilty to distribution of cocaine. Her romantic partner, who had allegedly cooperated with her in this trade, and whom she allegedly considered her husband, pleaded guilty to conspiracy to distribute cocaine. Ramírez-Arellano had been born and raised in Puerto Rico. At her sentencing hearing, her attorney argued, inter alia, that "in her culture essentially the wife or the woman does what her husband says",[34] and that "she did what he told her to do. And that is why we are here right now".[35] Contrasting the defendant to herself, the attorney stated: "If my husband told me to go jump off the cliff, I would laugh and tell him he was crazy. If her husband told her to do it, she would do it."[36] This was offered as an argument in support of the defense's request to the judge to depart downward from the Sentencing Guidelines in sentencing Ramírez-Arellano.

Cases, Constitutional Amendments, Rules of Evidence, and Statutes Cited

Cases are cited by appellate case name, the most common law reporter in which the appellate opinion was published, and by state and year of the appellate court's opinion. In the case of federal cases, I cite the state in which the criminal matter initially arose. Unless otherwise noted, the appellate court in question is a criminal appeals court, or the appellate division of a criminal court. The particular appellate courts involved are specified in the opinions cited below.

THE CORPUS OF CASES

[Cao] vs. State, 551 So.2d 1094 (Alabama 1988); see also *[Cao] vs. Haley*, 279 F.3d 1327 (U.S. 2002, Alabama), *withdrawn* 321 F.3d 1304 (U.S. 2003, Alabama); In re *State vs. [Cao]*, 888 So.2d 1227 (Alabama 2004)
[Chemmanoor] vs. State, 892 S.W.2d 186 (Texas 1994)
[Chung] vs. State, 423 S.E.2d 249 (Georgia 1992)
[Le] vs. State, 520 S.E.2d 907 (Georgia 1999)
People vs. [Gonzalez], 659 N.E.2d 398 (Illinois 1994)
People vs. [Lopez] & [Singh]: see [Singh] vs. Cambra
People vs. [Merlino], 176 Cal. Rptr. 477 (California 1981)
People vs. [Shen], 286 Cal. Rptr. 868 (California 1991), depublished by order, Jan. 23, 1992
People vs. [Xiong], 499 N.Y.S.2d 823 (New York 1986)
[Singh] vs. Cambra, 204 F.2d 964 (U.S. 2000, California); see also 69 U.S.L.W. 3380 (U.S. 2000)
State vs. [Arrisgado], 917 P.2d 370 (Hawaii 1996)
State vs. [Galicia], 537 N.W.2d 147 (Wisconsin 1995)
State vs. [Her], 494 N.W.2d 475 (Minnesota 1992)
State vs. [Ku], 1995 Ohio App. LEXIS 5862 (Ohio 1995)
State vs. [Kubicek], 871 S.W.2d 600 (Missouri 1994)
State vs. [Lee], 606 N.W.2d 719 (Minesota 2000)
State vs. [Saidani], 634 N.E.2d 700 (Ohio 1994)
State vs. [Seyoum], 652 A.2d 150 (New Hampshire 1994)
State vs. [Smith], 551 N.W.2d 870 (Wisconsin 1996)
State vs. [Vue], 510 N.W.2d 218 (Minnesota 1994)
U.S. vs. [García] et al., 936 F.2d 661 (U.S. 1991, New York)
U.S. vs. [Ibrahim] et al., 53 F.3d 1426 (U.S. 1995, Illinois)
U.S. vs. [Okute] & [Onyekachi], 1995 U.S. Dist. LEXIS 6037 (U.S. 1995, New Jersey)

U.S. vs. [Perea], 804 F. Supp. 476 (U.S. 1992, New York)
U.S. vs. [Ramírez-Arellano], 879 F.2d 391 (U.S. 1989, Missouri)

ENLARGED CORPUS—ADDITIONAL CASES (SEE PART III)

Bates vs. U.S., 2000 D.C. App. LEXIS 143 (District of Columbia 2000)
Blakely vs. State, 344 So.2d 812 (Alabama 1977)
Bryant vs. State, 2000 Tex. App. LEXIS 5835 (Texas 2000)
Carter vs. Rafferty, 621 F. Supp. 533 (U.S. 1985, New Jersey)
Clifford vs. Commonwealth, 7 S.W.3d 371 (Kentucky 2000)
Coleman vs. State, 621 P.2d 869 (Alaska 1980)
Commonwealth vs. Ligambi: see *Commonwealth vs. Scarfo*
Commonwealth vs. Mahdi, 448 N.E.2d 704 (Massachusetts 1983)
Commonwealth vs. Morgan, 401 A.2d 1182 (Pennsylvania 1979)
Commonwealth vs. Phoenix, 567 N.E.2d 193 (Massachusetts 1991)
Commonwealth vs. Richardson, 473 A.2d 1361 (Pennsylvania 1984)
Commonwealth vs. Scarfo, 611 A.2d 242 (Pennsylvania 1992)
Commonwealth vs. Tirado, 375 A.2d 336 (Pennsylvania 1977)
Commonwealth vs. Washington, 549 N.E.2d 446 (Massachusetts 1990)
Griffin vs. Wainwright, 760 F.2d 1505 (U.S. 1985, Florida)
Harris vs. People, 888 P.2d 259 (Colorado 1995)
Hilburn vs. State, 765 P.2d 1382 (Alaska 1988)
Joyner vs. State, 2000 Ind. LEXIS 950 (Indiana 2000)
Kelly vs. Stone, 514 F.2d 18 (U.S. 1975, California)
Kornegay et al. vs. State, 329 S.E.2d 601 (Georgia 1985)
McDonald vs. State, 578 So.2d 371 (Florida 1991)
Majid vs. State, 713 S.W.2d 405 (Texas 1986)
Miller vs. North Carolina, 583 F.2d 701 (U.S. 1978, North Carolina)
Owens vs. Hanks, 1996 U.S. App. LEXIS 15465 (U.S. 1996, Indiana)
Palmer vs. State, 288 N.E.2d 739 (Indiana 1972)
People vs. Anderson & Stinson, 421 N.W.2d 200 (Michigan 1988)
People vs. Bain, 489 P.2d 564 (California 1971)
People vs. Brown, 524 N.E.2d 742 (Illinois 1988)
People vs. Cooper, 601 N.W.2d 409 (Michigan 1999)
People vs. Cudjo, 863 P.2d 635 (California 1993)
People vs. Dien, 554 N.Y.S.2d 581 (New York 1990)
People vs. Fearon: see *People vs. Williams*
People vs. Glenn, 592 N.Y.S.2d 175 (New York 1992)
People vs. Green, 453 N.Y.S.2d 228 (New York 1982)
People vs. Lurry, 395 N.E.2d 1234 (Illinois 1979)
People vs. Poddar, 518 P.2d 342 (California 1974)
People vs. Rhines, 182 Cal. Rptr. 478 (California 1982)
People vs. Richardson, 363 N.E.2d 924 (Illinois 1977)
People vs. Sales, 502 N.E.2d 1221 (Illinois 1986)
People vs. Springs, 300 N.W.2d 315 (Michigan 1980)
People vs. Sylvers, 540 N.Y.S.2d 52 (New York 1989)
People vs. Thomas, 514 N.Y.S.2d 91 (New York 1987)
People vs. Thomas, 561 N.E.2d 57 (Illinois 1990)
People vs. Turner, 367 N.E.2d 1365 (Illinois 1977)
People vs. Watson, 490 N.Y.S.2d 33 (New York 1985)
People vs. Williams, 614 N.E.2d 730 (New York 1993)
Reynolds vs. Commonwealth, 367 S.E.2d 176 (Virginia 1988)
Reynolds vs. State, 580 So.2d 254 (Florida 1991)

Rhoden vs. State, 274 So.2d 630 (Alabama 1973)
Riley vs. State, 429 P2.d 59 (Nevada 1967)
Roberson vs. State, 276 S.E.2d 115 (Georgia 1981)
Robinson vs. State, 520 So.2d 1 (Florida 1988)
Sattayarak vs. State, 887 P.2d 1326 (Oklahoma 1994)
Smith vs. State, 510 S.E.2d 1 (Georgia 1998)
State vs. Bautista, 514 P.2d 530 (Utah 1973)
State vs. Burks, 1997 Ohio App. LEXIS 2841 (Ohio 1997)
State vs. Cotton, 394 S.E.2d 456 (North Carolina 1991)
State vs. Davis, 415 N.W.2d 861 (Wisconsin 1987)
State vs. Escobedo, 573 N.W.2d 271 (Iowa 1997)
State vs. Finlayson, 956 P.2d 283 (Utah 1998)
State vs. Garrett, 681 A.2d 362 (Connecticut 1996)
State vs. Gotur, 1997 Wash. App. LEXIS 1528 (Washington 1997)
State vs. Greene, 542 So.2d 156 (Louisiana 1989)
State vs. Haque, 726 A.2d 205 (Maine 1999)
State vs. Hernandez, 462 S.W.2d 790 (Missouri 1971)
State vs. Maldonado, 675 P.2d 735 (Arizona 1983)
State vs. Mayhue, 653 S.W.2d 227 (Missouri 1983)
State vs. Miller et al.: see *Miller vs. North Carolina*
State vs. Ortiz, 831 P.2d 1060 (Washington 1992)
State vs. Richmond, 904 P.2d 974 (Kansas 1995)
State vs. Terry, 582 S.W.2d 337 (Missouri 1979)
State vs. Thomas, 777 P.2d 445 (Utah 1989)
State vs. Thompson, 654 P.2d 453 (Kansas 1982)
State vs. Trammell, 1999 Ohio App. LEXIS 780 (Ohio 1999)
State vs. Vaughn, 431 So.2d 358 (Louisiana 1982)
State vs. Vinson, 1990 Mo. App. LEXIS 456 (Missouri 1990)
State vs. Wanrow, 538 P.2d 849 (Washington 1975)
State vs. Weaver, 386 S.E.2d 496 (West Virginia 1989)
State vs. Yelloweyes, 1995 Tenn. Crim. App. LEXIS 396 (Tennessee 1995)
Stephens vs. State, 431 S.E.2d 422 (Georgia 1993)
Trujillo-Garcia vs. Rowland, 1992 U.S. Dist. LEXIS 6199 (U.S. 1992, California)
U.S. ex rel. Haynes vs. McKendrick, 481 F.2d 152 (U.S. 1973, New York)
U.S. vs. Calvin, 1995 WL 755285 (U.S. Air Force Court of Criminal Appeals 1995)
U.S. vs. Hickman: see *U.S. vs. Washington*
U.S. vs. Mansfield, 1991 CMR LEXIS 1523 (U.S. Air Force Court of Military Review 1991)
U.S. vs. Ojo, 1997 WL 66725 (U.S. Air Force Court of Criminal Appeals 1997)
U.S. vs. Owens, 1998 CCA LEXIS 349 (U.S. Air Force Court of Criminal Appeals 1998)
U.S. vs. Robertson, 430 F.Supp. 444 (U.S. 1977, District of Columbia)
U.S. vs. Thompson, 37 M.J. 1023 (U.S. Army Court of Military Review 1993)
U.S. vs. Washington, 836 F.Supp. 192 (U.S. 1993, Vermont)
U.S. vs. Wheeler, 434 F.2d 1195 (U.S. 1970)
Villacres vs. U.S., 357 A.2d 423 (District of Columbia 1976)
Weddington vs. State, 545 A.2d 607 (Delaware 1988)

OTHER CASES CITED

Daubert vs. Merrell Dow Pharmaceuticals, Inc., 113 S. Ct. 2786 (U.S. 1993)
Loving vs. Virginia, 388 U.S. 1 (U.S. 1967)
People vs. Berry, 18 Cal.3d 509 (California 1976)

People vs. Chen, No. 87–7774 (N. Y. Supr. Ct. 1988, New York, unpublished decision)
People vs. Hanikei, No. LA013768 (Super. Ct. Los Angeles County, California, 1994, unpublished decision)
People vs. Kimura, No. A-091133 (Super. Ct. Los Angeles County, California, 1985, unpublished decision)
People vs. Moua, No. 315972–0 (Super. Ct. Fresno County, California, 1985, unpublished decision)
People vs. Valentine, 28 Cal.2d 121 (California 1946)
People vs. Wickersham, 32 Cal.3d 307 (California 1982)
Reed vs. State, 59 S.W.2d 122 (Texas 1933)
State vs. France, 379 S.E.2d 701 (North Carolina 1989)

CONSTITUTIONAL AMENDMENTS, RULES OF EVIDENCE, AND STATUTES CITED

Ala. Code §13A-5–40(10)
Fed. Rules Evid. 401
U.S. Const. amend. V
U.S. Const. amend. XIV, 1

Abbreviations

A.2d	(West's) Atlantic Reporter, Second Series
Ala.	Alabama
Cal.2d	(West's) California Reports, Second Series
Cal.3d	(West's) California Reports, Third Series
Cal. Rptr.	(West's) California Reporter
Cir.	Circuit
Ct.	Court
Cty.	County
Dist.	District
Div.	Division
F.2d	(West's) Federal Reporter, Second Series
F.3rd	(West's) Federal Reporter, Third Series
F. Supp.	(West's) Federal Supplement, Second Series
M.J.	(West's) Military Justice Reporter
N.Y.S.2d	(West's) New York Supplement, Second Series
P.2d	(West's) Pacific Reporter, Second Series
S.E.2d	(West's) South-Eastern Reporter, Second Series
So.2d	(West's) Southern Reporter, Second Series
Super.	Superior
Supr.	Supreme
S.W.2d	(West's) South-Western Reporter, Second Series
U.S.L.W.	United States Law Week

Notes

NOTES TO PART I

1. In addition, I have collected cases in which 'cultural'/'racial' and 'sexual difference' were otherwise addressed in connection with each other at a trial court hearing. See Part III for details on how the corpus of cases upon which this study is based came to be composed.
2. In fact, the only other qualitative empirical studies of the in-court negotiation of 'cultural evidence' of which I am aware are two recent articles by D'hondt (2009; 2010) concerning Belgian cases. Apart from these, Volpp (1994, 64–76) provides a pertinent, very useful mini-discourse analysis pertaining to the U.S. context (compare Chapter 6). I find both authors' perspective to be circumscribed, however, by a juridical discourse of individuality that tends to naturalize the latter notion (along with those of the psyche, agency, and rationality)—contrary to the problematization of those concepts by Foucault (1977; 1990) and Butler (e.g., 1993; 1997b; 1999), which will be briefly elucidated in my Conclusion (Part VI). In virtue of the juridical discourse by which her writings on 'cultural evidence' are framed, Volpp appears to treat as problematic only or primarily culturalizations/racializations of 'deviance' that *negate* the 'individuality', 'rationality', and 'agency' (if not, indeed, the 'normality')—imputed, within racialized discourse, to 'whites only'—of people of color. Rather, that is, than questioning those notions in themselves. While D'hondt goes further in that he problematizes the notion of 'deviance', more generally, as well as forms of pathologizing defendants other than in the form of cultural Othering (see esp. 2010, 94–95; 2009, 817), like Volpp, he stops short of questioning the very opposition between (Othering, pathologizing, potentially racializing, etc.) determinism vs. (individualizing, rationalizing) voluntarism, as such (see esp. D'hondt 2009, 816–817). As I can merely allude in the present work (see Part VI), that opposition arguably has, in and of itself, been fundamental to racializing, to gendering, and to structuring in further unegalitarian, exclusionary ways, modern discourse. Butler's work, as a whole (see References), provides a third theoretical option to the unhelpful alternatives—of being either 'externally' or self-*determined*—to which the said opposition confines our imagination; an alternative anchored in the notion of contingency.
3. Citing *Daubert vs. Merrell Dow Pharmaceuticals, Inc.*, 113 S. Ct. 2786, 1798 (U.S. 1993).
4. Koptiuch has attempted to do so (see esp. 1996, 230) in a different way. Her focus is the more macro-level one of the role of the colonial discourse underwriting the 'cultural defense' in "the contemporary disciplinary practices of the postmodern state" (ibid., 221). She reads the 'cultural defense'

as "a technology for the production of gendered, 'disciplinary individuals'" (ibid.); "a method of 'training' for immigrants" (ibid.) whose effect it "is to primitivize the inhabitants of Pacific Rim nations, chief competitors of the United States in the global economy" (ibid., 223). Koptiuch observes in this context that Asians figure prominently in cultural defense cases (ibid.). For a seemingly discursive approach to 'culture' in the courtroom, see also the brief text by Nunn (2006). By contrast, while Razack's approach is highly power-conscious and expressly critical of notions of 'cultural information', I would understand it as being closer to ideology critique than to discourse theory. (See especially the last chapter of her 1998 book.) The same holds for Lawrence (2001) and Desai (2007).

5. However, Maeda has called upon us to attend to the destabilizing moments in constructions of 'culture' informing 'the cultural defense'—for instance, by recourse to Bhabha's (1994) notion of hybridity, or by exposing the contradiction between the assimilationist notion of an 'American culture' endangered by immigration and the idea that U.S. law is culturally neutral (Maeda 2000, 97–99): "Justice is to be both neutral and American. This contradiction reveals the assumed but unnamed superiority of American culture that objectively measures higher than other cultures, especially Eastern ones" (ibid., 98).

NOTES TO PART II

1. In using the term 'patriarchy', I do not mean to signify the latter as a uniform, universal structure. Rather, I am suggesting that the diverse forms male domination can take in (to invoke that problematic construct) 'the West' *share* those features which I have attributed to 'patriarchal discourse'. Compare the position of Laclau and Mouffe, according to whom "[t]he ensemble of social practices, of institutions and discourses which produce woman as a category, are not completely isolated but mutually reinforce and act upon one another" (1985, 118), such that "overdetermination among the diverse sexual differences produces a systematic effect of sexual *division*" (ibid., 117, original emphasis). An overall effect that entails a subordination of 'the feminine' to 'the masculine' (ibid., 117–18).
2. Especially since 9/11/2001, mass-media and political representations of 'the West'/the U.S. have increasingly come to encompass people of color.
3. Spivak barely elaborates on her notion of a "theoretical fiction" (1990, 148), except to circumscribe it as "a necessary theoretical presupposition" (ibid.). She does state, however (after saying that "the proletarian is a theoretical fiction" [ibid.]): "it is absolutely necessary to assume him, it is absolutely dangerous to naturalize him" (ibid.)—adding that: "claiming to be a member of that naturalized group is politically harmful" (ibid.). I take it that the upshot of these remarks is that we cannot forgo making certain essentializing presuppositions, but which we should nonetheless treat as problematic (in the sense of keeping in mind that they really are discursive constructions), rather than actually 'believing' in their essential or prediscursive character.
4. Foucault calls his archeology "a method of analysis purged of all anthropologism" (1972, 16), which is designed to undermine the (hegemonic) attempt "to preserve, against all decenterings, the sovereignty of the subject, and the twin figures of anthropology and humanism" (ibid., 12).
5. Foucault writes that "it is not possible for us to describe our own archive, since it is from within these rules that we speak" (1972, 130)—the archive

being "the law of what can be said" at a given spatio-temporal conjuncture (ibid., 129), as he puts it in rather structuralist coinage.

6. The account in this paragraph is influenced by Fairclough (1989, Ch. 4), but uses different terminology than he does.
7. "Antagonistic indebtedness" is a phrasing that I owe to Paul Gilroy and/or Vikki Bell. I believe it appears in the description of a course offered by them jointly at Goldsmiths College, University of London, some time between 1996 and 1998.
8. An endeavor that will inevitably produce constitutive exclusions of its own, of which I may be unaware.
9. "For the defence [sic] of the interests of the workers not to be made at the expense of the rights of women, immigrants or consumers, it is necessary to establish an equivalence between these different struggles. It is only on this condition that struggles against power become truly democratic, and that the demanding of rights is not carried out on the basis of an individualistic problematic, but in the context of respect for the rights to equality of other subordinated groups" (Laclau and Mouffe 1985, 184).
10. Laclau and Mouffe write: "There are not, for example, necessary links between anti-sexism and anti-capitalism, and a unity between the two can only be the result of a hegemonic articulation" (1985, 178).

NOTES TO PART III

1. With reference to where to draw the line that 'concluded' the 'story' of the Civil Rights Movement, Birnbaum and Taylor write:

    Some journalists and historians point to the 1965 Voting Rights Act or the assassination of Martin Luther King, Jr., in 1968. Others argue that the movement ended when the objectives of some of its participants changed from integration and interracial coalition protest to black power politics. Still others say the end came with the backlash of the 1970s and 1980s (2000, 1).

   Houck and Dixon, in their collection of documents pertaining to *Rhetoric, Religion, and the Civil Rights Movement*, assert that:

    Most periodizing schemes are necessary fictions, ours included. But by beginning in 1954 and ending in 1965, we have simply borrowed from the civil rights orthodoxy (2006, 7; see also ibid., 7–8; Newman 2004, Ch.3; Davis 1998, 385–386; Verney 2000).

2. Omi and Winant describe the post-civil rights societal consensus thus:

    The accomplishments of the 1960s could not simply be reversed. Since 1965, for example, it has become impossible to argue *for* segregation or *against* racial equality. Any 'legitimate' politics must claim to favor racial equality *in the abstract*, even if specific egalitarian measures are condemned. To argue for a return to the explicitly racist ideology of pre-civil rights movement days is to move to the proto-fascist fringes of the far right (1994, 140, original emphasis).

3. Generous funding of my acquisition of those materials was provided by the DFG (Deutsche Forschungsgemeinschaft/German Research Foundation), which partially covered both travel expenses and expenses for the materials themselves. A few trial transcripts were kindly provided to me for free by prosecutor's or defense attorney's offices.
4. In the U.S., an acquittal cannot be appealed by the state in virtue of the double jeopardy clause of the Fifth Amendment to the Constitution (U.S.

Const. amend. V). Therefore, only convictions will be appealed on the part of the defense.

The one exception in my corpus concerns a trial of several defendants, most of whom were convicted (and appealed) but one of whom—the one of relevance to this study, because she received a 'cultural defense'—was acquitted (see Table III.1).

5. By using this term, I mean to *mark* the racist character of the notion of sexuality across the 'color bar' conveyed by it, rather than to repeat that racism.
6. In one case, the ethnicizing category in question is 'Italian'; in the other, 'Hispanic'—which could refer either to a person of Latin American or Spanish/Portuguese ancestry. See Table III.2.
7. I have mostly chosen names identified in the Internet with the relevant ethnicizing categories. Any mistakes or inappropriate choices will, I hope, form an embarrassment to me rather than to the persons I have renamed, as they reflect upon my ignorance of the relevant conventions.

NOTES TO CHAPTER 1

1. There are a few lone exceptions to this trend—which mention the prosecutorial use of 'cultural evidence', but fail to consider its implications for the debate. See Chung (2004), Martin and Thompson (2002, 253–259), Beger and Hein (2001, 39, 47, 53–54, 56, 58), Boulette Taylor (1998, 451–452), Song (2007, 111–112), Kim (1997, 113), and Frischknecht (2009). Siesling's and Ten Voorde's remarks, in the Dutch and Swedish contexts, regarding advocates of a use of 'cultural evidence' as an aggravating (rather than mitigating) circumstance in sentencing are also relevant here (2009, 158–159, 165–169; see also Greenawalt 2008, 302–303).

   In my corpus of twenty-four cases, the trials involving a use of 'cultural evidence' by the prosecution include *[Chemmanoor] vs. State*, 892 S.W.2d 186 (Texas 1994); *People vs. [Lopez] and [Singh]/[Singh] vs. Cambra*, 204 F.3d 964 (U.S. 2000, California); *State vs. [Her]*, 494 N.W.2d 668 (Minnesota 1992), and *State vs. [Lee]*, 606 N.W.2d 719 (Minnesota 2000). In addition, references to a male-dominated Other culture were made as part of a prosecutor's argument or questioning in the following cases: *People vs. [Merlino]*, 177 Cal. Rptr. 899 (California 1981); *State vs. [Galicia]*, 537 N.W.2d 147 (Wisconsin 1995); *State vs. [Ku]*, 1995 Ohio App. LEXIS 5862 (Ohio 1995); *State vs. [Kubicek]*, 871 S.W.2d 600 (Missouri 1994); *State vs. [Saidani]*, 634 N.E.2d 700 (Ohio 1994); *State vs. [Vue]*, 510 N.W.2d 218 (Minnesota 1994). All of these cases except that of Merlino and, possibly, of Galicia (who was only categorized as 'Hispanic'), involve defendants classified by 'Third World' ethnic categories; Merlino involved an Italian-American man. A good source for additional relevant cases up to the present, and including ones unrelated to gender, is 70 A.L.R.4th 664 (American Law Reports, with regular update in pocket part) (Landis 1989).
2. See the References for many more examples.
3. As inscribed in the Fourteenth Amendment to the U.S. Constitution (U.S. Const. amend. XIV, 1).
4. Coleman comes close to the latter claim when she writes:

   > While American culture during the nineteenth century provided a limited role for women, our culture has since evolved to provide a more expansive one. Our culture has evolved in this respect, *for the most part leaving behind* conventions, traditions, and customs—all derived from the various cultures that make up the American anthropological

landscape—that subjugated and dehumanized women (1996, 1164, footnotes omitted, my emphasis).

5. FGM is a common abbreviation for "female genital mutilation".
6. Volpp writes:

> What I call for is not a refusal to criticize, but a more careful examination of the particularity of women's relationships to *specific patriarchies*, as well as to geopolitical and economic relationships. Attempts to make normative judgments and to change behavior must be premised on the understanding that cultures, including our own, are patriarchal—*not more or less so, but differently patriarchal* (2001, 1217, my emphasis).

She gives an example that drives home the ease with which the practice of hierarchizing Othered cultured as more, rather than differently, patriarchal rests on the fallacy of constructing them as *essentially* patriarchal: in a letter to the editor commenting upon a newspaper article's reference to a husband's stabbing death as a pitfall of arranged marriage, the letter's author draws an analogy by "calling the death of Nicole Brown Simpson a 'pitfall of dating'" (ibid., 1189n38). Nicole Brown Simpson was the murdered wife of O.J. Simpson.

Honig nicely captures what I would hold a qualitative understanding of differing patriarchal practices to require of white/Western women, namely, a

> willingness of Western feminists to hold their own practices up to the same critical scrutiny they apply to Others, to hear the plural voices of women everywhere and to learn from them, while also refusing to prejudge the merits of practices that are unfamiliar or threatening to those of us raised in bourgeois liberal societies. For the sake of a future solidarity of women as feminists, the question of what constitutes gender (in)-equality [sic] must be kept disturbingly open to perpetual reinterrogation (1999, 40).

As an example of such prejudgment, Honig invokes polygamy, questioning whether monogamy necessarily functions in less patriarchal a manner in all contexts (ibid., 38).

7. For instance, Coleman writes of the victims of crimes regarding which a 'cultural defense' is then offered: "They are denied the protection of the criminal laws because their assailants generally go free, either immediately or within a relatively brief period of time" (1996, 1095). This false generalization appears to be drawn from the media's and the academic literature's (including Coleman's own) excessive focus specifically on 'cultural defense' cases in which the sentence *was* unusually low. The bias entailed in this—which intensifies the anti-immigrant bias instantiated in the debate's one-sided focus upon cultural *defenses* at the expense of culture-based prosecutions, inasmuch as it makes it possible to picture immigrants (mainly men) as walking virtually free based upon 'cultural excuses' for violent crimes—is indicative of what Volpp has called a "moral panic" incited a propos the 'cultural defense' (1996, 1602–1603).
8. Renteln's book-length treatise on "The Cultural Defense" (2004) is another instance of this tendency ("Stereotypes can be true or false. The problem arises with the transmission and reinforcement of false stereotypes" [2004, 315n30; see also 197–198]). Her methodology of reviewing the empirical evidence, as she calls it (ibid., 7–8), is not, of course, a discursively unmediated procedure—contrary to what that claim may be taken to suggest. Rather, Renteln's approach to 'the cultural defense' is shaped by a particular perspective. Namely, a liberal-pluralist (e.g., ibid., 218–219) and relativist perspective which is devoid of a critical dimension regarding gender and race. As a result, while Renteln's approach of recounting the 'evidence' presented

as cultural in a great many cases has its merits, she has nothing to say in regard to unegalitarian discourses of gender or race that may shape such presentations. For instance, she quotes a highly racialized British legal opinion without commenting in any way on the Othering, devaluing mode of cultural 'tolerance' performed by it (ibid., 116–117). She also insists that the gendered, highly problematic legal defense of provocation (compare Ch. 4, n. 14) be made accessible to members of minorities, rather than arguing that it should be abolished or altered in general on grounds of its sexist operation (2004, 36; contra Song 2007, 102–106). Thus, Renteln's pluralism is effectively androcentric, privileging culture over gender. Moreover, her treatment of culture purely as a matter of facts (rather than of discourse and power) is arguably power-blind, too, with respect to neocolonial relations of domination, as the said example involving a British opinion indicates.

9. See, e.g., Suri:

   > [I]nstead of trying to make the evidence fit into a certain stereotype of what culture is and who a battered woman is supposed to be, the defendants can provide evidence of their particular backgrounds (2000, 137).

   As we shall see in Chapter 3, individualization is no guarantee against constructions of a defendant in stereotyped, demeaning terms.
10. *People vs. [Lopez] & [Singh]*, No. 152775 (Super. Ct. Santa Clara County, California, 1993); 204 F.3d 964 (9th Cir. Cal. 2000).
11. 204 F.3d (9th Cir. Cal. 2000), 971, 974–978; Brief of Appellant, U.S. Court of Appeals for the Ninth Circuit, No. 98–17223 at 35.
12. *State vs. [Cao]*, No. CC-86-647-PR (Montgomery Cir. Ct., Alabama, 1986); 551 So. 2d 1094 (Ala. Ct. App. 1988).
13. *People vs. [Shen]*, No. ICR-12873 (Super. Ct. Riverside County, California, 1990); 286 Cal. Rptr. 868 (1991), depublished by order, Jan. 23, 1992.

NOTES TO CHAPTER 2

1. *People vs. [Lopez] & [Singh]*, No. 152775 (Super. Ct. Sta. Clara County, California, 1993); 204 F.3d 964 (U.S. 2000, California).
2. 204 F.3d (U.S. 2000, California) at 967. The circumstance was "that the murder had been committed after lying in wait" (ibid.).
3. 69 U.S.L.W. 3380 (U.S. 2000). Denial of the writ is not technically an affirmation of the lower court's judgment, which in this case denied the defendant's petition for a writ of habeas corpus (204 F.3d 964 [U.S. 2000, California]). But the refusal to grant review may, of course, be seen as a refusal to consider to be of sufficient importance the infringement of constitutional rights alleged in the petition. Brief of Appellant, U.S. Court of Appeals for the Ninth Circuit, No. 98–17223.
4. 204 F.3d (U.S. 2000, California), 971, 974–978; Brief of Appellant, U.S. Court of Appeals for the Ninth Circuit, No. 98–17223 at 35.
5. *People vs. [Lopez] & [Singh]*, op. cit., Reporter's Transcript on Appeal, 636, 1669.
6. Ibid., 1664.
7. Ibid., 1663–1665.
8. Ibid., 1673–1682, 1934.
9. I have not been able to find a specific claim in the trial transcript that he was the oldest brother. I infer this from the fact that, beside gender, birth order was made a significant issue in regard to who takes decisions in Sikh families (ibid., 1662). There was no mention made of a father to the defendant and his sister. Only a grandfather was made reference to, as "the patriarch" (ibid.,

3659)—a man possibly too old to actually arrange for the murder for hire. Outside the presence of the jury, the prosecutor referred to Malkit Singh as "the dominant male family member" (ibid., 1124).

10. Ibid., 1652, 1662.
11. Ibid., 671.
12. Ibid., 636.
13. Ibid., 731–732, 786–787, 1018–1023, 1029–1033, 3654–3660.
14. Ibid., 1934, 1936, 1945.
15. The twin-brother of defendant Lopez, who was also a suspect, had fled the country. Ibid., 3848.
16. Ibid., 659–668.
17. Ibid., 645.
18. Ibid., 673. By his own admission, the relevant witness routinely informed to authorities in return for favors. Supposedly, he had not received any in this instance; he had, however, inquired about that possibility after making the relevant assertions to police. The defense maintained that he had made up the alleged confession, and could have gleaned relevant details about the crime Singh had been charged with by secretly accessing his case file. Ibid., 2559–2742, 3349.
19. Ibid. 1713, 1715–1724, 1728. For instance:

    Q And I want you to focus now on the Sikh community as you became familiar with it here in the United States, the violence that you had an opportunity to become familiar with firsthand.

    Can you tell the ladies and gentlemen of the jury whether there's a distinct identifiable difference in that violence and the violence that you normally see in the non-Sikh community?

    Ibid., 1728. The prosecutor also tried to ask its 'cultural expert' about violent events among Sikhs in India, but was prevented from eliciting answers to those questions (ibid., 1715–1723). This prosecution tactic culminated in its assertion, in the closing argument: "You don't want to know the culture involved. That by itself has been known in some instances to lead to death." Ibid., 3668.
20. In addition, it was held that a son is esteemed more highly than a daughter, and that a father will cultivate an especially close bond with a male child (ibid., 1658–1660).
21. Ibid., 632, 634, 640, 3651–3652.
22. Ibid., 1691, 1984.
23. Ibid., 1649.
24. Ibid., 1655, 1955.
25. Ibid., 1660–1662.
26. Ibid., 3852.
27. A construction which, while equally discursive, would be more progressive in political trajectory.
28. E.g., *People vs. [Lopez] & [Singh]*, op. cit., Reporter's Transcript on Appeal, 632, 637.
29. Ibid., 1660–1662.
30. Ibid., 632.
31. Ibid., 637.
32. Ibid., 1654.
33. Ibid., 1939–1940.
34. Ibid., 1695.
35. "Mr. [Singh] also said that his turban and beard were important to him, but they were also a source of antagonism toward him in the workplace. He said that, you know, people made fun of him, because of the turban and wearing

of a beard and it was something that he had to continue doing because it was in his culture, it was in his religion, he was, in short, still part of a traditional Sikh family." Ibid., 3652–3653 (prosecutor's closing argument).

36. Ibid., 1730.
37. Ibid., 3651–3652.
38. Ibid., 1664, my emphasis.
39. Ibid., 1673–1677.
40. Ibid., 1679–1680, my emphasis.
41. Ibid., 1680.
42. Ibid., 1681–1682.
43. Ibid., 1680.
44. Ibid., 3854. "D.A." stands for "District Attorney", i.e., for the prosecutor.
45. Ibid., 3849.
46. Ibid., 1661–1662, my emphasis.
47. Ibid., 1725, my emphasis.
48. Ibid., 1647–1648, my emphasis. The discursive instabilities entailed in this extract, and in the remaining ones cited in this section, will be discussed in Chapter 8.
49. Ibid., 1659–1660, my emphasis.
50. Ibid., 1677–2678, my emphasis.
51. Ibid., 1116.
52. Ibid., 1103–1105, 1129–1130, 3514.
53. Ibid., 1108, 1120–1121.
54. Ibid., 3514–3515.
55. Ibid., 1676–1677.
56. Ibid., 3653–3654.
57. Ibid., 3884.
58. Ibid., 3668.
59. Ibid., 1654–1655, my emphasis.
60. Ibid., 1729–1730, my emphasis.
61. Ibid., 3852, my emphasis.
62. Anti–'miscegenation' laws were struck down as unconstitutional nationwide by the U.S. Supreme Court in 1967 (Loving vs. Virginia, 388 U.S. 1 [U.S. 1967]). Fifteen states still had such laws just prior to that decision (Lay 1993, 175). Their institution in what would become the United States was no carryover from English law, for at the time of the establishment of the American colonies, there was no ban on 'miscegenation' at common law or by statutes in England (ibid., 165).
63. *People vs. [Lopez] & [Singh]*, op. cit., Reporter's Transcript on Appeal, 1668.
64. Ibid., 3654.
65. Ibid., 632–633.
66. Ibid., 637.
67. Ibid., 635.
68. Ibid., 636.
69. Ibid., 1656.
70. Ibid., 1652.
71. Ibid., 1711.
72. Ibid., my emphasis.
73. Ibid., 749–750.
74. Ibid., 3854, my emphasis. "D.A." stands for "District Attorney", i.e., for the prosecutor.
75. Ibid., 1709–1710.
76. Ibid., 1661–1662.

77. Ibid., 1672–1673, my emphasis. Note how the lengthy question in the above quote simply presumes what is to be proven: that the violence committed upon Sardeep Johl was the result of the breakup of his relationship to his ex-wife—i.e., that the ex-wife's extended family was in some way connected to his murder. That is, the prosecutor's question presupposes, rather than contributing to a proof of, the state's theory of the case.

NOTES TO CHAPTER 3

1. *People vs. [Shen]*, No. ICR-12873 (Super. Ct. Riverside County, California, 1990); 286 Cal. Rptr. 868 (California 1991), depublished by order, Jan. 23, 1992.
2. *People vs. [Shen]*, op.cit., Reporter's Transcript on Appeal: 1624; 1672–1673; Clerk's Transcript on Appeal: 76–77; 84–87; 93–94.
3. Shen's conviction was overturned on appeal and the case was remanded for a new trial. *People vs. [Shen]*, 286 Cal. Rptr. 868 (California 1991), depublished by order, Jan. 23, 1992. For that trial's outcome and the sentences received each time, see Ch. 4, n. 26.
4. *People vs. [Shen]*, 286 Cal. Rptr. at 879–887.
5. E.g., *People vs. [Shen]*, op.cit., Reporter's Transcript on Appeal, 880–882.
6. Ibid., 265, 284–285, 862–863, 868, 1450–1451.
7. "[T]he existence of heat of passion at the time of the killing . . . eliminates malice and reduces an intentional killing to voluntary manslaughter." *People vs. [Shen]*, 286 Cal.Rptr. at 883. Here the Court of Appeal is in agreement with the jury instructions given at Shen's first trial. See CALJIC 8.40, given at trial, which in part contains this text: "There is no malice aforethought if the killing occurred upon a sudden quarrel or heat of passion." *People vs. [Shen]*, op.cit., Clerk's Transcript on Appeal, 85. See also CALJIC 8.50, which was given at trial in the following form (see ibid., 93):

   > The distinction between murder and manslaughter is that murder requires malice while manslaughter does not. / When the act causing the death, though unlawful, is done in the heat of passion the offense is manslaughter. In such a case, even if an intent to kill exists, the law is that malice which is an essential element of murder, is absent. / To establish that a killing is murder and not manslaughter, the burden is on the People to prove beyond a reasonable doubt each of the elements of murder and that the act which caused the death was not done in the heat of passion.

   Ibid.
8. *People vs. [Shen]*, 286 Cal. Rptr. at 883, my emphasis; citing *People vs. Wickersham* (California 1982), 32 Cal.3d 307 at 326, which in turn quotes *People vs. Berry* (California 1976), 18 Cal.3d 509, 515, which quotes *People vs. Valentine* (California 1946), 28 Cal.2d 121, 139.
9. *People vs. [Shen]*, op.cit., Clerk's Transcript on Appeal, 89, citing CALJIC 8.44 as having been "given as requested" "by defendant" (ibid.). (The Court of Appeal acknowledges that this instruction was given to the jury. See 286 Cal. Rptr. at 881.) Likewise, CALJIC 8.11 states regarding malice aforethought, the mental state which forms a necessary element of second-degree murder: "The mental state constituting malice aforethought does not necessarily require any ill will or hatred of the person killed." *People vs. [Shen]*, op.cit., Clerk's Transcript on Appeal, 77. In other words, the decision between murder and manslaughter is to be neutral as to the sort of emotion or the moral quality of the motive involved.

10. *People vs. [Shen]*, op.cit., Reporter's Transcript on Appeal, 1652, 1693–1698. See Ch. 4, n. 14 for some relevant quotes.
11. The California Court of Appeal appears to agree with this in that its opinion states:

    Initially, we note that the facts presented at trial, while not in conflict as to certain specific events, did vary considerably as to whether defendant had 'motherly' feelings toward the victim, her son, whether she was a 'traditional' Chinese woman, and, based on the above noted [sic] factors, whether the motive for his death was a desire for revenge against [Ed]'s father or guilt over not having taken good care of the child and fear that he would be ill-treated in the future.

    286 Cal. Rptr. at 870.
12. This may be fully apparent only once we consider the specific 'evidence' offered in this case. As I read the jury instructions offered in Shen's initial trial, the legal questions to be answered by the jury pertained in significant part to whether (a) an intent to kill (see Clerk's Transcript on Appeal, 85, citing CALJIC 8.40) her son had formed in the defendant's mind upon reflection *or* upon a provocation sufficient to prompt her to carry out that act impulsively (ibid., 86–87, citing CALJIC 8.42), and (b)—as a an additional question affecting the answer to (a)—*when* that intent had formed; more specifically, whether "sufficient time [had] elapsed between the provocation and the fatal blow for passion to subside and reason to return" (ibid.; see also ibid., 88, citing CALJIC 8.43). According to 'the evidence' introduced at trial, the moral quality of Shen's motive in killing the child was *neutral* as to both (a) and (b). For, there was 'evidence' supportive of either theory of the case (the prosecution's vs. the defense's)—*each* of which would have been reconcilable, *both* with a motive of revenge and, alternatively, with one of benevolence towards the victim. In other words, in this particular case, the timing and (hence) the "reflexivity" vs. spontaneity of the formation of the intent to kill on the defendant's part (the presence of which neither party disputed) was unrelated to what had *motivated* this intent and its fatal consequence.

    However, none of this is to say that the 'cultural evidence' admitted in the trial was legally irrelevant *as a whole*. As to this question, I do not commit myself. What I am contesting is merely the view, as articulated by the Court of Appeal of California, that Shen's *motive* (of revenge, benevolence, or—potentially—some ambiguous, more nuanced *constellation* of motives) could be construed as having been legally relevant according to the instructions received by the jury—and hence, that those aspects of the 'cultural evidence' which pertained to the moral quality of her intentions could be.
13. *People vs. [Shen]*, op.cit., Reporter's Transcript on Appeal, 224–225, 686–687, 1023–1024.
14. Ibid., 219, 792–793, 795.
15. Ibid., 275–276, 1147, 1162.
16. Ibid., 871, 1098, 1114–1115.
17. Ibid., 209, 211.
18. Ibid., 274–275, 277–278, 1180–1181.
19. Ibid., 1075.
20. Ibid., 198.
21. Ibid., 788, 1164–1165.
22. Ibid., 1077–1078.
23. Ibid., 1083.
24. Ibid., 595–599.
25. Ibid., 200–202, 787–789.
26. Ibid., 789.

27. Ibid., 1096, 1112–1113, 1170.
28. Ibid., 1115, 1168, 1170, 1179.
29. Ibid, 212, 275.
30. Ibid., 1142–1143.
31. Ibid., 1141, 1199.
32. Ibid., 213.
33. Ibid., 1122–2113.
34. Ibid., 279.
35. Ibid., 207–208, 272–273, 871.
36. Ibid., 214, 1127.
37. Ibid., 1129, 1190.
38. Ibid., 217–218, 256, 794, 1204.
39. E.g., ibid., 786, 791, 903.
40. Ibid., 862–863, 868–869.
41. Ibid., 1016, 1019–1020.
42. Ibid., 1020–1021.
43. Ibid., e.g. 1019, 1043.
44. Ibid., 1006–1007, 1037–1039.
45. Ibid., 1006–1007, 1037–1038, 1051.
46. Ibid., 184, 190, 191.
47. Ibid., 768, 769, 774.
48. Ibid., 192, 239, 775–777.
49. Ibid., 994, 996, 1018, 1025.
50. Ibid.: 1071–1072.
51. Ibid., 1496–1498.
52. Ibid., 238, 812, 1029.
53. Ibid., 222–323, my emphasis.
54. Ibid., 224–325.
55. Ibid., 686–687, my emphasis.
56. Ibid., 219, my emphasis.
57. Ibid., 220, my emphasis.
58. Ibid., 223, my emphasis.
59. Ibid., 794, my emphasis.
60. See ibid. (998–999):

    Q Is that customary in China to produce a child for a fatherless man—I mean a childless father [sic]?
    A They do.
    Q And that's what you were falling back on: the Chinese custom to have this woman bear a child for you, even though you're married to another woman?
    A In Hong Kong, the rich men, they have two, three wives.
    Q My question is: were you falling back on a Chinese custom?
    A No. I just falling, my thought.
    Q Was that an American thought that you had?
    A Yes.
    Q So you thought it would be okay since you were not Americanized if you had a wife and a child from a lover on the side; is that right?
    A Child from other woman.
    Q A child from another woman?
    A Right.
    Q For whom you had love, some love; right?
    A It's not really love. Okay.
    Q Not really love?
    A Yes.

Q Just passion?
A Because I feel, you know, I love children. Okay?
Q So in other words, the child was more important than [Anne]; right?
A Yes.
Q The child was more important than [Larry Shen's wife]; right?
A Yes.

61. As stated before, I have changed the names of defendants and others involved in the trials I discuss. It will be obvious to those familiar with the literature about the 'cultural defense' who the pseudonym *Anne Shen* stands for.
62. *People vs. [Shen]*, op.cit., Reporter's Transcript on Appeal, 1006.
63. Ibid., 1007.
64. I surmise that the word intended was "empirical".
65. *People vs. [Shen]*, op.cit., Reporter's Transcript on Appeal, 1036–1037, my emphasis.
66. Ibid., 1019–1020.
67. Ibid., 202, my emphasis.
68. Ibid., 1067, my emphasis.
69. As pointed out in Chapter 1, erasing the agency of women of color is a constitutive ingredient to the construct of the Oppressed Third World Woman.
70. *People vs. [Shen]*, op.cit., Reporter's Transcript on Appeal, 1022–1023, my emphasis.
71. Ibid., 787–788.
72. Ibid., 1083; see also 1086, 1164.
73. Ibid., 1049.
74. Ibid., 1019.
75. Ibid., 1021.
76. Ibid., 1152.
77. Ibid., 1680, my emphasis.
78. Ibid., 1016, 1020.
79. Ibid., 1160.
80. Ibid., 786, my emphasis.
81. Ibid., 216, 283.
82. Ibid., 214–215, my emphasis.
83. Shen had a daughter in Macau from her first marriage. I am not certain of the intended meaning of the plural form of the phrase, "for the sake of her children".
84. Ibid., 804.
85. Ibid., 841–842.
86. Ibid., 863–864, my emphasis.
87. Ibid., 1011.
88. Ibid., 1012–1013, 1044.
89. Ibid., 1013.
90. Ibid., 1053–1054.
91. Ibid., 1066.
92. *State vs. [Cao]*, No. CC-86–647-PR (Montgomery Cir. Ct., Alabama, 1986); 551 So. 2d 1094 (Alabama 1988).
93. *People vs. [Shen]*, op.cit., Reporter's Transcript on Appeal, 1000, my emphasis.
94. Contra Volpp:

> Essentializing narratives about particular cultures can often serve to *mask reality*. For example, a battered woman who is an immigrant may have failed to call the police, not because her culture condones passivity on the part of women, but because her partner was a police officer in her country of origin, because she has witnessed a failure of police protection and practices of police brutality, and because the police in

> her present location do not speak her language. Granting explanatory power to essentialized depictions of 'culture,' as purportedly made up of unchanging rituals that cement the subordinate location of women in a fixed system of social practices, will inevitably fail *to accurately describe* the relationship of culture, difference, and domestic violence

(2003, 399, my emphasis).

95. *People vs. [Shen]*, op.cit., Reporter's Transcript on Appeal, 785, my emphasis.
96. Ibid., 1508, my emphasis.
97. Ibid., 1498–1489, my emphasis.
98. As anthropologist Clifford asserted in his introduction to a pertinent work published in 1986, "no one can write about others any longer as if they were discrete objects or texts" (1986, 25).
99. *People vs. [Shen]*, op.cit., Reporter's Transcript on Appeal, 994, 996.
100. Ibid., 1500, my emphasis.
101. Ibid., 1008 (my emphasis).
102. On self-Othering, or 'alteritism', as he calls it, see Appiah (1992, 156–157), who maintains (with reference to the African context) that "there are those who will not see themselves as Other" (ibid., 157).
103. *People vs. [Shen]*, op.cit., Reporter's Transcript on Appeal, 184, 190–191.
104. Ibid., 293–294, my emphasis.
105. Ibid., 202.
106. Ibid., 224, my emphasis.
107. Volpp advocates "using the principle of antisubordination to examine and challenge *who* makes claims to cultural authority in these cases, and what that culture is claimed to be" (1996, 1596, my emphasis).

NOTES TO CHAPTER 4

1. *State vs. [Cao]*, No. CC-86–647-PR (Montgomery Cir. Ct., Alabama, 1986); 551 So. 2d 1094 (Alabama 1988).
2. In Alabama, murder is charged as a capital offense when accompanied by certain aggravating circumstances. One of them is specified as "[m]urder wherein two or more persons are murdered by the defendant by one act or pursuant to one scheme or course of conduct". Ala. Code §13A-5–40(10).
3. *State vs. [Cao]*, op.cit., trial transcript, 1162 (defense's closing argument). See also Renteln 1993, 475n148.
4. 551 So. 2d at 1099. From the materials I have studied, I see no evidence that this was anything more than an unfounded suspicion—an extremely weak basis for the allegation that the defendant had been 'provoked' by his wife's conduct. My account here is based upon the appellate opinion as well as the following portions of the trial transcript: the testimony of the defendant's wife, Jane Cao; of a psychiatric expert witness for the defense, and of the expert in cross-cultural counseling through whom the 'cultural evidence' was introduced; the closing and rebuttal arguments of both sides at the trial's guilt phase. (The defendant in this case did not testify.) It is possible that the repeated innuendo suggesting that Jane Cao was 'unfaithful' was based upon evidence contained elsewhere in the trial record.
5. *State vs. [Cao]*, op.cit., trial transcript, 1006–1058.
6. The expert testified on cross-examination that he knew of no laws against such acts in Vietnam. On the other hand, he attributed the defendant's act to the fact that he was a refugee with no family in the United States, and who was insulated from the local Vietnamese American community. (He had apparently married into a family of different cultural affiliation, but which

was never specified in those parts of the trial transcript that I am familiar with [see n. 4, this Ch.].) In Vietnam, the expert maintained, the extended family could have 'taken care' of the matter, and would traditionally have returned the unfaithful wife to her family of birth. *State vs. [Cao]*, op.cit., trial transcript, 1023–1024, 1045, 1052.

7. Ibid., 1144–1145, 1159–1163, 807–809, 822.
8. Ibid., 704, 708–711, 752–765, 783–792.
9. Ibid., 1161–1162, my emphasis.
10. Among the three cases mentioned the most in the literature are two involving male violence against women: *People vs. Chen*, No. 87–7774 (N. Y. Supr. Ct., New York, 1988, unpublished decision), and *People vs. Moua*, No. 315972–0 (Super. Ct. Fresno County, California, 1985, unpublished decision). At least one of them (*Chen*) involved blaming the woman murdered for the deadly violence her husband had brought against her, on grounds of her alleged adultery.
11. *State vs. [Cao]*, op.cit., trial transcript, 1045.
12. Ibid., 1175 (rebuttal). The statement was: "Now, they want to attack [Jane Cao]. . . . Oh, if she had talked all about these nightmares and all of these Vietnam movies, do you think [Jane Cao] would have been cast to be the prostitute and whore she is by these people if she had gone along with the plan and scheme to deceive you?" Ibid., 1175–1176.
13. Ibid., 1162–1163.
14. The argument as construed in *State vs. Cao* forms a classic instance of the legal defense of 'provocation to the heat of passion'—except that it is here used to excuse the killing of one's children, rather than of a partner and/or her lover. (A finding that a killing was committed in a heat of passion resulting from provocation reduces a verdict from murder to manslaughter, which carries a lighter sentence [Coker 1992, 72].) In U.S. as well as English law and legal scholarship, the case of a husband who catches his wife *in flagrante delicto* and instantly kills either or both partners in response is repeatedly treated "as *the* paradigm example of provocation adequate enough to mitigate what would otherwise be murder to a voluntary manslaughter conviction" (ibid., 72, original emphasis; see also ibid., 72n5). This is despite the fact that adultery "is the only major traditional category of 'adequate provocation' that does not involve an actual or threatened physical assault" (ibid., 73). As Coker shows, the privilege that the allegation of a wife's adultery is legally accorded as a 'provocation' sufficient to excuse a killing is strongly resonant with the patriarchal construction of male violence as being due to a loss of control that is blamed upon the woman's exercise of independence, rather than as an *exercise* of control *over* her. That this line of legal reasoning places part of the blame with the victim (if identical with the adulterer), Coker argues, is apparent in part from the fact that courts, by contrast, *reject* "claims that the behavior of a child or of a 'resisting victim' [in robbery cases, C.B.] can provide 'adequate' provocation to render a killing voluntary manslaughter" (ibid., 101). Unlike a child's actions or those of a victim resisting robbery, a spouse's adultery, in being deemed 'adequate provocation', is constructed as *justifying* a lethal response to some extent (ibid., 105–106). This is effectively to make those engaged in adultery responsible for the violence brought against them.

    Of particular interest to a comparison of the *Cao* and *Shen* cases is the fact that: "If adultery is the 'paradigm' heat of passion event, anger is the paradigm heat of passion emotion. Traditionally and modernly in many jurisdictions, anger is the *only* recognized 'heat-of-passion' emotion" (ibid., 102, original emphasis). Cao's defense was consistent with this. However, as shown in Chapter 3, Shen's defense—while also a defense of heat of passion (op.cit., Reporter's Transcript on Appeal, 1657–1660, 1684–1686)—did not construct her deed in terms of legitimate aggression in a state of 'heat of passion' but, instead, sought to eliminate any moment of (outward) aggression from it. This is all the more notable considering that Shen's jury was given the following instruction of law, named CALJIC 8.44:

> Neither fear, *revenge*, nor the emotion induced by and accompanying or following an intent to commit a felony, nor any or all of these emotional states, in and of themselves, constitute the heat of passion referred to in the law of manslaughter. *Any or all of such emotions may be involved in a heat of passion* that causes judgment to give way to impulse and rashness. Also any or more of them may exist in the mind of a person who acts deliberately and from choice, whether such choice is reasonable or unreasonable.

People vs. [Shen], op.cit., Clerk's Transcript on Appeal, 89 (my emphasis). In other words (as argued in the preceding chapter), whether Shen killed her son with a benign motive or as a matter of revenge was irrelevant to the verdicts that the jury had to decide between (murder, as advocated by the prosecution, or manslaughter, as asked for by the defense), according to the version of the law in terms of which the trial was conducted. That version (i.e., the quoted instruction) is contrary to received doctrine as recognized by Shen's judges on appeal—according to which a motivation of revenge, as distinguished from anger, negates heat of passion since it is taken to indicate premeditation (286 Cal. Rptr. 868 at 883 [California 1991], depublished by order, Jan. 23, 1992; compare Coker 1992, 79–80). Nonetheless, this was the version of the law that the trial parties treated as valid. Thus, both prosecution and defense affirmed it in closing argument—the defense, by citing the above jury instruction, which was given at its request (Clerk's Transcript on Appeal, 89; Reporter's Transcript on Appeal, 1660); the prosecution, in saying:

> I submit to you that the evidence is supportive of two different views. One, she [Anne Shen] did it out of the desire to save [Ed] from this horrible life that he was leading, that's one view. The other view is she did it out of revenge to get back at [Larry], okay. Is it important that you have to adopt either view? Can you adopt a little of both views? Does it really matter as to the intent to kill [Ed] or not?

Ibid., 1693–1694.

> In this case, have the evidence [sic] of what [Anne Shen] intended to do, she fully intended to kill herself, or at least looks that way. She intended to take [Ed] with her. You want to adopt that view? To do that she had to kill him first. She had to form the specific intent to kill. *Doesn't make any difference for the purpose of that case whether there was an altruistic feeling on her part or not*, that is, I'll take him with me because this is such a horrible place that he lives in.

Ibid., 1696, my emphasis.

In terms of the law as constructed at Anne Shen's trial, then, there was *less* rather than more reason in her case than in Quang Cao's for the defense to be apologetic about the accused's anger. This is a strong indication that the divergence between the two defense strategies is based upon gender, as argued in the main text.

One court decision cited in Coker's feminist analysis of heat of passion doctrine indicates, likewise, that—at least historically—it was tailored to condoning anger and deadly violence specifically in *men* positioned as jealous lovers, rather than gender-neutrally: The 1933 decision *Reed vs. State*, 59 S.W.2d 122 (Texas 1933) ruled "that a wife who killed her husband's lover could not receive the benefit of a state statute that provided that a husband's homicide of 'one taken in the act of adultery with his wife' was justifiable homicide" (Coker 1992, 81n41)—i.e., not a crime. Coker points out: "When men kill their present or former wives or lovers, they bring excuses and justifications to law that reflect societal understandings of *male* rage and *female* provocation. These justifications and excuses resonate with and find expression in the heat-of-passion doctrine" (ibid., 94, my emphasis).

15. *State vs. [Cao]*, op.cit., trial transcript, 1033–1034.
16. Ibid., 750–765, 783–792, 807–809, 822. My source here is the state's cross-examination of the defendant's wife.
17. Ibid., 1178–1179, my emphasis.
18. Ibid., 1192.
19. Ibid.
20. I have not accessed the entire trial transcript (see n. 4, this Ch., for details).

    To be sure, there are other factors besides gendered discursive structures that may account for the differences between the trial strategies in *State vs. Cao* and *People vs. Shen*. In this instance, it seems relevant that Jane Cao positioned herself towards her husband in a highly ambiguous manner. Thus she testified for the defense. While she made certain statements that utterly destroyed its case, she also said that Quang Cao was a loving father, and trivialized his prior acts of violence against his children. She testified, too, that she had visited him in jail regularly (ibid., 692, 763–767). In contrast, Mr. Shen, who testified for the prosecution, utterly opposed himself to his wife in the witness stand and was clearly determined to picture her in the most negative ways.
21. *People vs. [Shen]*, op. cit., Reporter's Transcript on Appeal, 1373.
22. Ibid., 1450–1451.
23. Ibid., 1380.
24. 551 So.2d at 1098. I take the term "capital murder" from the prosecutor's closing argument. *State vs. [Cao]*, op.cit., trial transcript, 1190–1192.
25. This assertion pertains to Cao's appeal at state level. More than fifteen years after his initial conviction, his petition for habeas corpus at federal level was granted and the case was remanded for a new trial. *[Cao] vs. Haley*, 279 F.3d 1327 (U.S. 2002, Alabama), *withdrawn* 321 F.3d 1304 (U.S. 2003, Alabama).
26. In her initial trial, Anne Shen was sentenced to a prison term of fifteen years to life (Renteln 1993, 473). Her conviction was overturned on appeal. *People vs. [Shen]*, 286 Cal. Rptr. 868 (California 1991), depublished by order, Jan. 23, 1992. In her second trial, she was convicted of the lesser offense of voluntary manslaughter, for which she received the maximum possible sentence—eleven years (Renteln 1993, 474).
27. *People vs. Hanikei*, No. LA013768 (Super. Ct. Los Angeles County, California, 1994, unpublished decision).
28. *People vs. Kimura*, No. A-091133 (Super. Ct. Los Angeles County, California, 1985, unpublished decision).
29. I follow Renteln (1993) here. According to Chiu, Kimura received a pure probation sentence (1994, 1116).
30. *State vs. France*, 379 S.E.2d 701 (North Carolina 1989).
31. Streib 2004, 15–20 (Appendix B). In addition, two of the 49 women had allegedly killed their children as well as their partner. Two more women of the fifteen women on death row in California as of June 30, 2004 were convicted of killing their young niece or grandchildren, bringing the share of women who killed child relatives to more than a third of the women awaiting the death sentence in California at that time. Ibid. The report offers no comparison pertaining to male death-row inmates.

32. Two journalistic articles observe that while the U.S. media focused excessively upon the infanticide committed by Andrea Yates in 2001 (who was tried in 2002), infanticides committed by fathers in the same period were barely given attention (Ostrowski 2002; Skinner 2002). Interestingly, the articles give contrary interpretations to this—with Ostrowski suspecting that the media limelight placed upon the 'Killer Mom' indicates that she is condemned more readily than the men, while Skinner complains of feminist and other public empathy extended to her. I am suggesting that there may be an ambiguity at work which encompasses both of these tendencies.
33. *People vs. [Shen]*, op.cit., Reporter's Transcript on Appeal, 223.
34. Chiu, who discusses only Kimura's case, leaves unmentioned the fact that the initiative on behalf of Kimura originated in the Japanese American community (Woo 1989, 404–405, who is cited by Chiu), and actually suggests the contrary when she refers to the signatures gathered to support her statement that "[t]he public viewed Kimura with sympathy and felt that her sentence of probation was appropriate"—as if referring to a hegemonic, predominantly white public (1994, 1116 and n386).
35. *People vs. [Shen]*, 286 Cal. Rptr. 868 (California 1991), depublished by order, Jan. 23, 1992.
36. "In the results of these cases we can see the ultra-femininity assimilationist construct at work. . . . For white men, threatened by white feminists, this Asian woman becomes the true woman. . . . This construction of the true woman informs the results of the cultural defense cases previously discussed. The judicial process becomes an opportunity for white society to reify sexism and to reinforce and reconstruct the subordination of women through another culture" (Chiu 1994, 1119–1120).
37. Of course, it may be argued that even in a man's case it was a poorly devised strategy, strategically speaking. In my judgment, nothing would have militated against offering a construction of Cao similar to that offered of Anne Shen, i.e., as a loving father. Apart from the gendered aspects of the defense strategy, in comparing individual cases' outcomes, it is conceivable that other factors were involved too. Additional factors that could account for the discrepancy between the two trials' results include differences in each case's specific evidentiary constellation, and between other aspects of the defense strategies pursued (beside contingencies such as the particular attitudes of those who partook in producing the trials' respective outcomes). Thus, in my judgment Cao's defense was harmed in part by a very effective cross-examination of the psychiatrist who testified on his behalf, in conjunction with an utterly ill-prepared and inarticulate performance by that expert witness. (*State vs. [Cao]*, op.cit., trial transcript, 929–90, 994–1002.)
38. It is pertinent to this context that, as Volpp writes, "what is often referred to as a sign of the barbarity and misogyny of Asia—that 'Asian men kill their wives for looking at other men'—is in fact encoded into our common law as justifiable" (1994, 90n143). A claim such as "that 'American' men would react less violently than 'Chinese' men to the belief [that] their wives were having affairs is belied by the very encoding of the manslaughter/provocation doctrine in American law, which is explicitly premised upon a *violent* reaction to this knowledge" (ibid., 67n45). Compare n. 14, this Ch.
39. *State vs. [Cao]*, op.cit., trial transcript, 1030–1034, 1050.
40. Chiu observes that the notion of "the power-hungry despot" is among the stereotypes associated specifically with Asians / Asian Americans (1994, 1071–1072).
41. *State vs. [Cao]*, op.cit., trial transcript, 1030–1031.
42. Ibid., 1035.

43. The term should be "Confucian".
44. Ibid., 1045.
45. Ibid., 1031–1032.
46. Ibid., 1054–1055.
47. This sexist variant of colonialist Othering is also represented in the literature about the 'cultural defense'. Examples include Anonymous (1986), Winkelman (1996), Van Broeck (2001), Donovan and Garth (2007), and Frischknecht (2009, esp. 76, 347, 360–361). Caughey (2009, 30–33) arguably forms another, albeit more subtle, case in point.

    It should not be necessary to point out that sexist Othering is not limited to colonialist variants but can surface as readily in texts critical of colonial discourse. Here one example from the literature as to 'the cultural defense' is Humphrey (2007, esp. 21).
48. In fact, the continuum between sexist 'sympathy' for the ethnically Othered and his overtly racist condemnation may account for the penalty of death imposed upon Quang Cao.

NOTES TO CHAPTER 5

1. *People vs. [Lopez] & [Singh]*, No. 152775 (Super. Ct. Santa Clara County, California, 1993); 204 F.3d 964 (9th Cir. Cal. 2000).
2. *People vs. [Shen]*, No. ICR-12873 (Super. Ct. Riverside County, California, 1990); 286 Cal. Rptr. 868 (1991), depublished by order, Jan. 23, 1992.
3. *State vs. [Cao]*, No. CC-86–647-PR (Montgomery Cir. Ct., Alabama, 1986); 551 So. 2d 1094 (Ala. Ct. App. 1988).
4. Volpp makes such an ascription to Pasternak in the following passage, in which she contrasts his testimony in the trial against defendant Dong Lu Chen with the testimony of the immigrant expert witnesses in *People vs. Anne Shen* (see Chapter 3):

    > [T]he 'experts' [in Anne Shen's trial, C.B.] *were* [original emphasis] experts in the sense that they were immigrants to the United States themselves and were thus invested in representing the experience of immigrants from a subjective position. Their position stands in contrast to the white anthropologist Pasternak, whose subjectivity was based on an oppositional position to the 'other,' Dong Lu Chen [the defendant in that other trial, C.B.], *veiled behind a pretense of objectivity*

    (1994, 89, my emphasis).
5. Its chief problem consists in the need, in order to follow through with this approach, to bracket our sense of reality, including as regards cultural differences. At a phenomenological and practical level, by contrast, we are compelled to essentialize difference, i.e., to construct it in one form or other as 'ontological'. See Part II.
6. The fact that I hold the specific 'cultural evidence' as to *motive* presented by Anne Shen's defense to have been legally irrelevant according to the version of the law rendered in the jury instructions given at her first trial (Chapter 3) does not invalidate the argument as to the potential relevance of 'cultural evidence' to state of mind.
7. For the most part, this attention so far has taken what, from a sociological perspective at least, amounts to a rather superficial form—in that it has been concerned primarily with a quantitatively exhaustive coverage of pertinent cases, accompanied or not by purely legalistic analysis (see also Friedman Ramirez 2010). Thus the publications mentioned above are closer to documentation than to qualitative social research (see esp. Renteln 2004;

compare Ch. 1, n. 8). By the latter term I am referring to research that is theoretically informed and reflexive at least to some extent, and that entails in-depth empirical analysis. D'hondt (2009; 2010) provides laudable examples with respect to our subject. To my knowledge, his studies have been the first to be based on substantial qualitative data, such as (in his case) ethnographic fieldwork in the courtroom or (in mine) trial transcripts—rather than being limited (largely) to the sketchy case summaries provided by judicial opinions.

8. I am not attributing duplicity to the authors of the texts under discussion in terms of their intentions. Rather, I characterize as duplicitous the argumentative logic of the discourse which they engage.
9. This applies even to that article in the said symposium issue of *Judicature* which is specifically on "Prosecutorial discretion in cross-cultural cases" (Kenny 2009). While the text may be read as *alluding* to the possibility of a prosecutorial use of 'cultural evidence' that is adverse to a (potential) defendant, it abstains from any explicit recognition of this possibility—as if 'culture' will only ever count in favor of persons so positioned.
10. Needless to say, Hallevy's statement—and his argument as a whole—make the untenable presupposition that there could be any such thing as acts *not* based upon culture. The notion that rape is ever something other than "an act of oppressing women", or that it is ever *not* committed "out of cultural ideology" in some other way (see main text above), would, of course, be contested by most feminists.

NOTES TO CHAPTER 6

1. By "failures of . . . the substantive criminal law", Hoeffel is referring to patriarchal notions entailed in the available legal defenses and in statutory definitions of the crimes of rape and manslaughter (2006, 316–320).
2. *People vs. Chen*, No. 87–7774 (N. Y. Supr. Ct., New York, 1988, unpublished decision).
3. *State vs. [Cao]*, No. CC-86–647-PR (Montgomery Cir. Ct., Alabama, 1986); 551 So. 2d 1094 (Ala. Ct. App. 1988).
4. *People vs. [Gonzalez]*, Gen. No. 92 CF 679 (Cir. Ct. Lake County, Illinois, 1993); 659 N.E.2d 398 (Illinois 1994).
5. *People vs. [Gonzalez]*, op.cit., Report [Transcript] of Proceedings, March 15, 1993.
6. Ibid., 154–155, my emphasis.
7. The sentence was overturned on appeal on the grounds that the trial judge had considered impermissible aggravating factors in determining the sentence, and had made reference to "witchcraft trials, child abuse, ritualistic facial scaring [sic], supernatural beliefs, rape, incest and severing an arm" which may have impacted the sentence. 659 N.E.2d at 15. These references were made in the context of the trial judge's assertion that U.S. courts should be sensitive to cultural differences (*People vs. [Gonzalez]*, op.cit., Report [Transcript] of Proceedings, March 15, 1993, 179–180), and that: "I think that in fact the Court system must accept and understand cross-cultural defenses. And this Court, in particular, has always kept an open mind, and I must follow the law, but there are many cultures that have emphasis on such things as Dr. [X] indicated, like machismo." Ibid., 179.
8. Ibid., 184, my emphasis.
9. *People vs. [Lopez] & [Singh]*, No. 152775 (Super. Ct. Santa Clara County, California, 1993); 204 F.3d 964 (U.S. 2000, California).

10. *People vs. [Lopez] & [Singh]*, op. cit., Reporter's Transcript on Appeal, 1684.
11. Ibid., 1742, my emphasis.
12. Ibid., 1659–1660, my emphasis.
13. Ibid., 1676, my emphasis.
14. Ibid., 1687–1688.
15. Ibid., 1698. This question was posed by defense attorney 2, whereas in general I am here treating the initial strategy of defense attorney attorney 1. I include this question by the other attorney because my interest is, ultimately, in the modes of discursive strategy pursued, whether they are enunciated by different subjects or just one of them. This is to say that my unit of analysis is discursive strategies, not their speakers.
16. Ibid., 1685–1686.
17. An alternative construction which, while likewise discursive, would be more progressive in political trajectory.
18. Ibid., 1709.
19. Ibid., 1709–1710, my emphasis.
20. Ibid., 1711, my emphasis.
21. Ibid., 1735, my emphasis.
22. Ibid., 1712–1729.
23. Ibid., 3652–3653.
24. Ibid., 1730.
25. Which would be a more progressive construction as it subverts the essentialism that underpins colonialist cultural hierarchies. Compare Torry (1999, 134–139) on the role of the binarism between assimilation and "separation" within the debate about the 'cultural defense'. He writes: "Lives thus embedded in crosscutting cultural worlds elude the global dichotomy of assimilation and separation. In reality many people are multiply cultured, in turns assimilated and unassimilated, depending on context and vantage point" (ibid., 139). Volpp (1996, 1589–1590) critiques such a binarism in Coleman's (1996) article.
26. E.g., *People vs. [Lopez] & [Singh]*, op. cit., Reporter's Transcript on Appeal, 632, 637 (prosecutor's opening statement).
27. Ibid., 1692.
28. Ibid., 1668.
29. Ibid., 3652–3653.
30. Ibid., 1695–1696.
31. Ibid., 1702.
32. Ibid., 636, 1668–1670, 1958–1959.
33. The only arguable exception pertaining to defense attorney 2 is the following passage, which I quoted earlier:

    Q Let me ask you a hypothetical question. You've indicated that the ties to a son, a father to a son, are stronger than they are to a daughter, correct?
    A I think it's an unwritten rule, yes.
    Q Do you have any reason to believe that that's any different than an American father to his son?
    A No.

    Ibid., 1698. However, nothing in this extract marks the situation referred to as patriarchal rather than 'simply natural'.
34. Ibid., 1736, my emphasis.
35. Ibid., 1982.
36. Ibid., 3730.
37. Ibid., 1647, my emphasis.
38. Arguably, however, that premise is being subverted by Lieutenant Kaur's invocation of his interpretation of Sikh culture, inasmuch as it may be taken

to allude that there is no such thing as a rendering of Sikh culture devoid of interpretation. I pursue this argument in Chapter 8.

39. *People vs. [Lopez] & [Singh]*, op. cit., Reporter's Transcript on Appeal, 676. The term "district attorney" refers to the prosecutor.
40. Ibid., 3754–3755, my emphasis. The term "district attorney" refers to the prosecutor.
41. *People vs. [Shen]*, No. ICR–12873 (Super. Ct. Riverside County, California, 1990); 286 Cal. Rptr. 868 (California 1991), depublished by order, Jan. 23, 1992.
42. *People vs. [Shen]*, op.cit., Reporter's Transcript on Appeal, 857.
43. Ibid., 858.
44. Ibid., 991–992.
45. Ibid., 1692–1693. The statement, "I am a Chinese woman", had been made by Anne Shen in the following context:

    Q Did you apply for a visa to come back to America in the next year?
    A No.
    Q At the time did you have a Portuguese passport?
    A Yes.
    Q And you had to go to the American consulate in Hong Kong and get a visa; is that right?
    A Yes.
    Q Why didn't you do that?
    A Because I was waiting for him to marry me.
    Q How could he marry you when you were in Hong Kong and he was in [town X, California]?
    A He could come back and marry me.
    Q You also could go to [town X] and marry him; right?
    A But I did not want to do that.
    Q Why not?
    A Because he promised me that he would marry me.
    Q Don't you agree it takes two people to get married?
    A Yes.
    Q Why didn't you just get on the airplane and fly back to [town X] and marry him?
    A Because I'm a Chinese woman.
    Q What does that have to do with it?
    A The initiative should be with the man. If I came just like that, it would have been very shameful for me, because I was already shamed the first time.

    Ibid., 1163–1164. As in some quotes cited in the main text, the prosecution in this passage brushes aside any relevance of gendered oppression to the defendant's conduct.
46. Ibid., 1033.
47. Ibid., 1037–1038.
48. Ibid., 1167, my emphasis. Ironically, the prosecutor's suggestion that Shen could (psychologically), and should, have been *insubordinate* vis-à-vis the alleged Chinese patriarchal norms in issue ("Then why didn't you get on an airplane and fly to America to see him?") really amounted to saying that she should have *submitted* to the norm of maternal self-sacrifice hegemonic in the U.S., too. That is, it amounted to stigmatizing her defiance of *that* norm. In the prosecution's procedure, then, sexist logic trumped the performance of a West alienated at 'patriarchal China'.

    In the response last quoted in the main text ("I was interested in both"), Anne Shen—in a defiant mode that was singular in her testimony—actively exposed the patriarchal collusion between prosecution and defense (as demonstrated in this chapter and in Chapter 3, respectively), and therefore also, the hypocrisy of their collaborative displacement of patriarchal order to 'Chinese tradition': Her unapologetic affirmation of her interest in protecting herself from stigmatization juxtaposed *her* assertiveness to *their* encouragement of subservience in her. In virtue of her response, the defendant also refused the alternative versions of her that were championed by prosecution and defense, respectively—that is, being stereotyped as either self-effacing or devoid of feeling for the child. All of this, of course, subverted her perception as a 'servile Chinese woman'.

49. Ibid., 1180–1181. The trip at issue had been financed by a woman friend whom Shen was accompanying. That friend testified that she had told Shen that there was no time for her to visit Ed. Ibid., 933–934; see also 1180–1182.
50. *People vs. [Shen]*, op.cit., Reporter's Transcript on Appeal, 284–285
51. Ibid., 868–869.
52. Shen's conviction was overturned on appeal on other grounds and the case was remanded for a new trial. *People vs. [Shen]*, 286 Cal. Rptr. 868 (California 1991), depublished by order, Jan. 23, 1992. For that trial's outcome and the sentences received each time, see Ch. 4, n. 26.
53. *People vs. [Shen]*, op.cit., Reporter's Transcript on Appeal, 1045.
54. Ibid., 250–251.
55. Here I need to take issue with Maguigan's mention of two cases encompassed within my corpus of which she claims that they involved an effective contestation of the defense's 'cultural evidence' (1995, 93n213)—namely, *[Cao] vs. State*, 551 So.2d 1094 (Alabama 1988), the horrendously sexist counterstrategy in which I treated in Chapter 4, and *State vs. [Her]*, 494 N.W.2d 475 (Minnesota 1992). Such misjudgment is probably based in part on the limited information contained in the judicial opinions upon which commentators about cases involving 'cultural evidence' usually base their assessment of trial strategies. It must also be realized that judicial opinions tend to rationalize that particular side of a case in favor of which they find.
56. Razack (1998) and Volpp (1996) opt for constructing more critical narratives nonetheless, while acknowledging the risks involved.
57. Burns writes:

    > Cross-examination can shock a jury into understanding that there exists a series of (often unasked) questions the answers to which will transform the reliability and the meaning of a particular account. It can provide a jury with the experience of a radical reconceptualization of an account of what occurred, reminding them that, finally, they may rely only on their own assessment of what happened and how it should be judged (1999, 61).

    Burns' account overlooks that a set of shared premises limits what the competing parties will question about each other's perspectives.

NOTES TO CHAPTER 7

1. *People vs. [Shen]*, No. ICR-12873 (Super. Ct. Riverside County, California, 1990); 286 Cal. Rptr. 868 (1991), depublished by order, Jan. 23, 1992.
2. *People vs. [Lopez] & [Singh]*, No. 152775 (Super. Ct. Santa Clara County, California, 1993); 204 F.3d 964 (9th Cir. Cal. 2000).
3. *People vs. [Lopez] & [Singh]*, op. cit., Reporter's Transcript on Appeal, 1732.
4. Ibid., 1709, my emphasis.

5. Ibid., 1690, 1693.
6. Ibid., 1692.
7. Ibid., 1693–1694, my emphasis.
8. In distinguishing between the denotative and connotative aspects of a sign, I follow Barthes (1968b; 1968a, 89–92). See also Jameson (1985, 376).
9. *People vs. [Lopez] & [Singh]*, op. cit., Reporter's Transcript on Appeal, 637, 718–719. As to whether they remained there subsequent to his death or not I have no information. He was killed in 1990; the trial took place in 1993.
10. Ibid., 1709–1710, my emphasis.
11. Ibid., 1982, my emphasis.
12. See the following extract from Lieutenant Kaur's direct examination:

    Q In respect to one of the questions asked by Ms. [counsel for the co-defendant] you've indicated that members of the Sikh community here in the United States have *progressed somewhat towards Westernization*, I guess, would be the appropriate term, do not feel compelled to wear the traditional garb, the traditional beard, okay, et cetera, but seem to have assimilated to one degree or another into Western societies; is that correct?

    A Yes.

    Q Did I understand you correctly however that those—those members of the Sikh community who continue to wear the turban and honor the other manifestations of the traditional Sikh culture, in your opinion fall within the more *conservative* or tradition-following members of the community?

    Ibid., 1729–1730, my emphasis.
13. Ibid., 717–718.
14. There is no reference to this "that" in the trial transcript.
15. Ibid., 717–718, my emphasis. Since the second reply, which I discuss in the main text, may be perceived to be somewhat unresponsive, I should point out that some of the witness's answers as translated from Punjabi into English were so obviously unrelated in subject to the questions, as posed in English before being translated to her, that it must be assumed that severe mistranslations were involved. Therefore, what was received by the jury as being Inberit Johl's responses bears an uncertain degree of proximity to what she had actually said (or understood the question to be). None of the legal personnel involved raised the possibility of a mistranslation; instead, she was reacted to by attorneys and judge as being unresponsive. This is outrageous as it made her look as if she were no adult person. But her reply, "We respect all religions, but because the life is the same for everybody", whether or not the result of a proper translation, can certainly be read as subverting this portrayal of her—as part of the overall subversion I attribute to it in the main text.
16. The notion that Westernization constitutes progress (see the extract quoted in n. 12, this Ch.) defines 'the West' in terms of 'the modern'.
17. I am reminded here of Gilroy's characterization of "the humanistic outlook which anchors [George Orwell]'s impatient universalism" (2004, 86). See his remarks about Orwell's essay, "A Hanging" (ibid., 86–87).
18. *U.S. vs. [Ibrahim] et al.*, No. 92 CR 438 (U.S. Dist. Ct., Northern Dist. of Illinois, Eastern Div., Illinois, 1993); 53 F.3d 1426 (U.S. 1995, Illinois).
19. *U.S. vs. [Ibrahim] et al.*, op.cit., Transcript of Proceedings, 1701–1704. He identified himself as a senior lecturer in, and Director of, the program of African and Asian languages at the relevant university. Ibid., 1701–1702.
20. Ibid., 1718.
21. *People vs. [Lopez] & [Singh]*, No. 152775 (Super. Ct. Santa Clara County, California. 1993); 204 F.3d 964 (U.S. 2000, California).

22. For instance, in Matoesian's studies of trial discourse in the context of rape (1993; 2001), victims' resistance is analyzed, but without any distinction as to whether it deploys or subverts hegemonic discourse. To be sure, both can be the case at the same time.
23. *People vs. [Shen]*, No. ICR-12873 (Super. Ct. Riverside County, California, 1990); 286 Cal. Rptr. 868 (California 1991), depublished by order, Jan. 23, 1992.
24. Ibid., 1163–1164, my emphasis.
25. Ibid., 507.
26. Ibid., 560–561.
27. Ibid., 508–509.
28. See Chapter 2. In part this was apparent from the fact that the Sikh witnesses in this trial were partially treated as objects rather than subjects (or mediums) of 'the evidence', in that they were used as *examples* of Sikh identity—for instance, of an 'Americanized (and therefore, no longer a *real*) Sikh'. This practice was engaged in both by the prosecution and the defense.

    My 'finding' that such objectification is not dependent upon a use of professional 'experts' (or upon attorneys posing as 'experts') on Othered 'cultures'—and Spivak's analogous observation regarding the colonialist genealogy of certain academic disciplines—show that other commentators have not cut deeply enough when they have presumed or at least suggested (apparently extrapolating from individual cases) that such Othering is contingent upon a deployment of so-called 'cultural experts' (D'hondt 2010, esp. 72–73, 89–91), let alone a deployment of 'experts' classified as 'white' (Volpp 1994). Their analyses may, at the very least, be taken to imply that having subjects testify about *their own* 'cultures'—even if those subjects are themselves involved in a case, whether or not as defendants or (alleged) crime victims—would be a sufficient measure against such (self-)Othering. Spivak has cautioned, time and again, against the empiricist presumption underlying that idea: namely, the idea that there is some authentic 'voice' or 'self' that could be heard when so-called 'natives' speak 'for themselves' (see, for instance, the next quotation in the main text accompanying the present note). Indeed, she has problematized what she has glossed as a (hegemonic) desire to hear 'the native's voice' as itself potentially colonialist. See, e.g., Spivak 1993, 60; 1988a, esp. 294; 1986, 262–264.
29. *People vs. [Lopez] & [Singh]*, op. cit., Reporter's Transcript on Appeal, 1691.
30. Ibid., 1698.
31. Ibid., 1725, my emphasis.
32. Ibid., 1665.
33. Ibid., 1690, 1695.
34. Ibid., 1687.
35. Ibid., 1508–1509.
36. Ibid., 1508–1509, 1613–1614.
37. Ibid., 1266–1272.
38. Ibid., 1513–1514 (cross-examination).
39. Ibid., 1508 (direct examination), my emphasis.
40. Ibid., 1500, my emphasis.
41. Contra Good (2008), who lays down the entire "blame" for cultural essentialism in anthropological expert testimony presented within the legal system at the feet of that system, while (in my view) tending to idealize academic experts' social science knowledge in general, and anthropological knowledge in particular, as utterly self-reflexive and theoretically well-grounded per se. I envisage a more active (partially constitutive) role for 'expert' discourse in legal proceedings such as those examined here (see also the final

section of Chapter 3) than is suggested by Good's portrayal of "the hapless anthropologist" (2008, S47). It would, for instance, seem to me to border on the irresponsible to apply that characterization to the anthropologist Burton Pasternak, whose performance as an 'expert witness' in the trial of Dong Lu Chen (see Ch. 6, n. 2) provoked outrage on the part of feminist activists and other women from the 'community' whose 'culture' he had 'described' to Chen's judge—a performance whose simultaneously sexist and colonialist character is exposed by Volpp (1994). Compare my discussion at the beginning of Chapter 6.

NOTES TO CHAPTER 8

1. *People vs. [Shen]*, No. ICR-12873 (Super. Ct. Riverside County, California, 1990); 286 Cal. Rptr. 868 (1991), depublished by order, Jan. 23, 1992.
2. *People vs. [Shen]*, op.cit., Reporter's Transcript on Appeal, 202–203, my emphasis.
3. *People vs. [Lopez] & [Singh]*, No. 152775 (Super. Ct. Santa Clara County, California, 1993); 204 F.3d 964 (U.S. 2000, California).
4. *People vs. [Lopez] & [Singh]*, op. cit., Reporter's Transcript on Appeal, 1647, my emphasis.
5. Ibid., 1647–1648, my emphasis.
6. Ibid., 1649.
7. Ibid., 1649–1651, my emphasis.
8. Ibid., 1651–1653.
9. Ibid., 1680–1683, 1735–1736.
10. Ibid., 1685–1686.
11. Ibid., 1653, 1698.
12. Ibid., 1668–1669, my emphasis.
13. Ibid., 1700–1701.
14. Ibid, 1659–1660, my emphasis.
15. I write 'exemplars' because this seems to me to capture the racist objectification of human subjects which is entailed in the notion of Sikhs' predictability advanced by the state. Compare Chapter 2.
16. *People vs. [Lopez] & [Singh]*, op. cit., Reporter's Transcript on Appeal, 1676, 1679.
17. Ibid., 1673–1676.
18. Ibid., 637–638.
19. Ibid., 1677–1678, my emphasis.
20. E.g., ibid., 1651, 1652, 1655, 1556, 1663, 1664, 1665, 1666, 1676.
21. Q In terms of the violence attendant to divorce in the Sikh community, can you tell the ladies and gentlemen of the jury whether there are some Sikh, specific [sic] family values upon which the violence can then be predicated that are different or separate from *just the normal emotion of anger* that might come up in a hot family situation?

    Ibid., 1726, my emphasis.
22. Ibid., 1676–1677.
23. Ibid., 1679–1680, my emphasis.
24. Ibid., 1681–1682.
25. Ibid., 1683.
26. Q And I think then the question that I was attempting to rephrase to you after the objection ruling, is whether the *reasons in your experience* behind a family's continuing to seek a reconciliation of the husband and wife even after a divorce are based on cultural values of the Sikh people?

A Yes.
Mr. [counsel for defendant]: I object. I think this is beyond expertise, *the fact that he may know someone within that culture who acted in a particular way and then to speculate based on the broader traits as being the motivating force* is beyond what you can do as an expert in this area.
The court: Well, that's proper cross-examination, Mr. [counsel for defendant], but repeat the question as within the framework that I've requested, Mr. [counsel for the prosecution].
Mr. [counsel for the prosecution]: I will try to do so, your Honor.
Q (by Mr. [counsel for the prosecution]) First of all, do you understand the question that I just asked?
A I lost the question, I'm sorry.
Ms. [counsel for the co-defendant]: And I would move to strike the answer which had actually been answered [sic].
Mr. [counsel for the prosecution]: Well, we didn't have an answer even though the question's now been asked about three times.
Ms. [counsel for the co-defendant]: I bet you there was an answer, because I heard it out of his mouth. Excuse me.
The court: All right. Why don't we have the question read back and the answer. If it's taken, Madame Reporter.
Mr. [counsel for the prosecution]: Thank you, your Honor.
The court: Would you do that for me?
(Whereupon, the record was read by the reporter.)
The court: Answer is proper although the question is somewhat long. And on that happy note we'll take the morning recess for 15 minutes, ladies and gentlemen, once again, you're admonished not to form or express any opinion concerning the matter or discuss it among yourselves or with any other person. Thank you.
(Whereupon, a short recess was taken.)

Ibid., 1678–1679, my emphasis. This passage dramatizes in the most concrete form the painful rift between the utterly contingent and theoretically confused character of what came to figure as 'cultural evidence' in this case, and the practical closure effected by the judge's rulings as to its propriety.

The sequence immediately following this excerpt is cited above, in the main text accompanying n. 23, this Ch.

27. *People vs. [Lopez] & [Singh]*, op. cit., Reporter's Transcript on Appeal, 1663.
28. Ibid., 1649.
29. 204 F.3d (U.S. 2000, California) at 967. The circumstance was "that the murder had been committed after lying in wait" (ibid.).
30. 69 U.S.L.W. 3380 (U.S. 2000); 204 F.3d (U.S. 2000, California), 971, 974–978; Brief of Appellant, U.S. Court of Appeals for the Ninth Circuit, No. 98–17223 at 35.

NOTES TO PART VI

1. This is dramatized by the 'three strikes' or habitual offender laws—"statutes enacted by state governments in the United States which require the state courts to hand down a mandatory and extended period of incarceration to persons who have been convicted of a serious criminal offense on three or more separate occasions", to quote from the Wikipedia (http://en.wikipedia.org/wiki/Three_strikes_law; access date: July 24, 2011).

2. While each of these references could serve to exemplify that focus, I want merely to single out Lynch and Bogen. For, in their study of the Iran-contra hearings, they frame Lieutenant-Colonel Oliver North as an "applied deconstructionist" (1996, 153) for his articulate, witty moves as a witness at the hearings of turning the tables on his interrogators, of deploying equivocity in his favor, and of questioning the truth value of documentary evidence. This attribution of the term 'deconstruction' to the strategies pursued by an individual 'hero' (see esp. ibid., 257) is noteworthy (and in my view, questionable) considering that deconstruction directs itself in significant part at questioning the foundational and controlling character of our intentions in regard to the production of meaning (Derrida 1982, 326).
3. To comment upon the (socio-)linguistic literature about trials would be beyond the scope of this work. Beside Ehrlich (2001) see, e.g., O'Barr (1982), Stygall (1994), Jaquemet (1996), Heffer (2005), Conley and O'Barr (2005), and Azuelos-Atias (2007).
4. I owe my awareness of this claim, and of its inescapability, to Peter Grönert, my former partner, whose intellectual formation as a philosopher has, in turn, shaped mine—probably in more ways than those transparent to me.

NOTES TO THE APPENDIX

1. *State vs. [Chemmanoor]*, No. 92-1222-A (Dist. Ct. 16th Judicial Dist., Denton County, Texas, 1993), Statement of Facts [= Trial Transcript, C.B.], Vol. I, 99.
2. Ibid., Vol. VIII, 1484.
3. Ibid., 1481.
4. *State vs. [Le]*, No. 96CR44750 (Super. Ct. Bibb County, Georgia, 1997), [Transcript of Trial Proceedings], Vol. I, 34-35.
5. Ibid., Vol. II, 193.
6. Ibid., 245.
7. *People vs. [Merlino]*, No. 71614 (Super. Ct. Sta. Clara County, California, 1979), Reporter's Transcript of Proceedings, Vol. IV, 833.
8. *People vs. [Merlino]*, 125 Cal. App. 3d 275 at 287.
9. *People vs. [Merlino]*, No. 71614 (Super. Ct. Sta. Clara County, California, 1979), Reporter's Transcript of Proceedings, Vol. IV, 834-835.
10. *State vs. [Galicia]*, No. F-910054 (Cir. Ct. Milwaukee County, Wisconsin, 1992), Jury Trial – Phase II [Transcript of Proceedings], June 5, 1992, 141.
11. Ibid., 142.
12. Ibid., 140, my emphasis.
13. *State vs. [Galicia]*, No. 94-0193-CR (Wisc. Ct. App., Dist. I, Wisconsin, 1995), Brief and Appendix of Defendant-Appellant, 14-15.
14. *State vs. [Ku]*, No. M9411CRB-28786 (Municipal Ct. Franklin County, Ohio, 1995), Transcript of Proceedings, [Vol. 1], 181.
15. Ibid., Vol. II, 288.
16. Ibid.
17. *State vs. [Kubicek]*, 871 S.W.2d at 603.
18. Ibid.
19. *State vs. [Saidani]*, No. B-925460 (Court of Common Pleas, Hamilton County, Ohio, undated), Complete Transcript of Proceedings for Appeal, Vol. 4, 502.
20. *State vs. [Seyoum]*, No. 91-S-191, 192 (Super. Ct. Grafton County, New Hampshire, 1993), Transcript of Jury Trial Proceedings, Vol. XVII, 16.

21. *State vs. [Smith]*, No. F-940663 (Cir. Ct. Milwaukee County, Wisconsin, 1994), Motion in Limine to Admit Expert and Lay Testimony Regarding the Issue of the Absence of Mitigation, 3.
22. *State vs. [Vue]*, No. 9000827 (Dist. Ct. Ramsey County, Minnesota, 1990), Transcript of Proceedings, Vol. I, 296.
23. Ibid., Vol. II, 36-37.
24. Ibid., 37.
25. *U.S. vs. [García] et al.*, 936 F.2d at 664.
26. Ibid. at 670.
27. Ibid.
28. *U.S. vs. [Ibrahim] et al.*, 53 F.3d 1426 at 1430.
29. Ibid.
30. *U.S. vs. [Perea]*, 804 F.Supp. 476 at 476.
31. Ibid. at 477.
32. *U.S. vs. [Perea]*, No. 89-CR-901 (U.S. Dist. Ct., Eastern Dist. of N.Y, New York, 1992), Transcript of Criminal Cause for Sentencing, 5.
33. *U.S. vs. [Perea]*, 804 F.Supp. 476 at 479-80, references omitted.
34. *U.S. vs. [Ramírez-Arellano]*, No. 88-00054-02-CR-W-6 (U.S. Dist. Ct., Western Dist. of Missouri, Western Div., Missouri, 1988), Transcript of [Sentencing] Proceedings, Sept. 8, 1988, 10.
35. Ibid., 14.
36. Ibid., 10-11.

Glossary of Legal Terms

In explaining the entries in this Glossary, I have drawn on a number of glossaries published on U.S. courts' websites and the website of the Naval Inspector General, namely:

http://www.uscourts.gov/library/glossary.html
http://www.id.uscourts.gov/glossary.htm
http://www.nycourts.gov/lawlibraries/glossary.shtml
http://www.ig.navy.mil/Documents/InvestigationsGuide/AppendixA.pdf

These websites were visited on September 26, October 16, and October 29, 2008. Any mistakes contained in the following Glossary are likely to be my own.

Italicized terms indicate other entries within this Glossary.

appellate (e.g.: brief; court; opinion). About appeals; an appellate court has the power to review the judgment of a lower court (see *trial court*) or tribunal. For example, the U.S. circuit courts of appeals review the decisions of the U.S. district courts.

brief. A written or printed document prepared by the lawyers on each side of a dispute and submitted to the court in a trial or *appellate* proceeding. Contains a summary of the facts of the case, pertinent laws, and an argument of how the law applies to the fact situation. Also called a memorandum of law.

capital offense / crime / murder. Punishable by death.

case law. Law established by previous decisions of *appellate* courts.

***certiorari*.** A writ of review issued by a higher court to a lower court. A means of getting an appellate court to review a lower court's decision. If an appellate court grants a writ of *certiorari*, it agrees to take the appeal. See also *writ*, *appellate*, and *trial court*.

clerk of court. The court officer who oversees administrative functions, especially managing the flow of cases through the court.

Clerk's Transcript on Appeal. The collection of administrative papers that accumulate in a criminal case file on appeal. Among other things, the

Clerk's Transcript on Appeal consulted for one of the cases in this work contains the instructions of law given to the jury at trial.

closing argument. The closing statement, by counsel, to the jury or judge after all parties have concluded their presentation of evidence. Here the parties may state an argument as to what facts the evidence proves, and as to how the law to be provided in the *jury instructions* applies to those facts. A specific *verdict* may be requested based upon that argument. See also *rebuttal* and *opening statement.*

citation. In the sense in which the term is used in the present work, it is a reference to a legal appellate opinion which specifies in what publication the opinion may be found. See also *appellate* and *opinion.*

court-martial. The exercise of military jurisdiction over criminal offenses as prescribed by law and regulation. Conviction by a general or special court-martial creates a federal criminal record.

cross-examination. The questioning of a witness testifying for the other party. It follows that party's *direct examination* of the witness, and may be repeated after the other party has engaged in *redirect examination*—in which case it is called "re-cross".

direct examination. The first interrogation of a witness by the party on whose behalf the witness is called. See also *cross-examination* and *redirect examination.*

double jeopardy. Putting a person on trial more than once for the same crime. It is forbidden by the Fifth Amendment to the U.S. Constitution.

due process (of law). The right of all persons to receive the guarantees and safeguards of the law and the judicial process. It includes such constitutional requirements as adequate notice, assistance of counsel, and the rights to remain silent, to a speedy and public trial, to an impartial jury, and to confront and secure witnesses.

equal protection (of the laws). The guarantee in the Fourteenth Amendment to the U.S. Constitution that all persons be treated equally by the law.

Fifth Amendment. See *double jeopardy.*

Fourteenth Amendment. See *equal protection.*

grand jury. Twenty-three people empaneled to hear evidence presented by a prosecutor to determine if there is enough evidence to bring a person to trial for a crime.

guilty plea. A criminal defendant's positive answer to the charges made in the *indictment* or information, as against the negative answer of "not guilty". The latter answer will usually result in a trial, whereas the former often occurs as part of a *plea bargain.*

habeas corpus. A *writ* of habeas corpus generally is a judicial order forcing law enforcement authorities to produce a prisoner they are holding, and to justify the prisoner's continued confinement. Federal judges receive petitions for a writ of habeas corpus from state prison inmates who say their state prosecutions violated federally protected rights in some way.

indictment. The formal process of charging a person with a crime. In most contexts, the word is used when a *grand jury* determines that there is enough evidence to proceed to trial.

jury instructions. A judge's directions to the jury before it begins deliberations regarding the factual questions it must answer and the legal rules that it must apply. Jury instructions are usually given at the close of the criminal trial, following the parties' *closing arguments* and the *rebuttal*.

jury nullification. A jury's refusal to follow the law as received in the *jury instructions* in favor of basing its *verdict* upon some alternative notion of what is right or to be willed in the context at hand.

manslaughter. The unlawful killing of another without intent to kill; either voluntary (upon a sudden impulse) or involuntary (during the commission of an unlawful act not ordinarily expected to result in great bodily harm). See also *murder*.

***mens rea*.** Criminal intent. The state of mind indicating culpability which is required by *statute* as an element of a crime.

murder. The unlawful killing of a human being with deliberate intent to kill: (1) murder in the first degree is characterized by premeditation; (2) murder in the second degree is characterized by a sudden and instantaneous intent to kill or to cause injury without caring whether the injury kills or not. See also *manslaughter*.

opening statement. The initial statement made by attorneys for each side, outlining the facts each intends to establish during the trial. Opening statements are followed by the trial's evidentiary phase, after which the parties present their *closing arguments* and *rebuttal*. This is usually followed by the *jury instructions* provided by the judge.

opinion. The written explanation of a court's decision in a matter.

parole. Supervised release of a prisoner from imprisonment on certain prescribed conditions which entitle her to termination of her sentence.

peremptory challenge or peremptory strike. Request by a party that a judge not allow a certain prospective juror as a member of the jury. No reason or cause need be stated. However, if a question arises as to whether a given peremptory challenge is based upon race, the judge may require the party exercising the challenge to offer grounds for the latter.

plea. See *guilty plea* and *plea bargain*.

plea bargain. Process whereby the accused and the prosecutor in a criminal case work out a 'compromise' disposition of the case, usually by the accused agreeing to plead guilty to a lesser offense. Such bargains are not binding on the court, but will usually result in a lesser sentence than the criminal defendant would risk receiving were he to be convicted in a trial. See also *guilty plea*.

rebuttal. (a) Evidence disproving other evidence previously given or reestablishing the credibility of challenged evidence. See also *redirect examination*. (b) The argument offered by the prosecution after the evidentiary phase of a criminal trial, and following the state's as well as the defense's *closing arguments*—the latter of which the rebuttal aims to refute. See also *closing argument* and *opening statement.*

redirect examination. Opportunity to present *rebuttal* evidence after one's witness has been subjected to *cross-examination*. Redirect examination is accomplished by means of questioning the same witness again. See also *direct examination*.

Sentencing Guidelines. A set of rules and principles established by the U.S. Sentencing Commission that trial judges use to determine the sentence for a convicted defendant.

statute. A law passed by a legislature.

subpoena. A command, issued under a court's authority, to a witness to appear and give testimony.

trial court. The U.S. legal system is divided into the trial and the appellate levels. Courts at the appellate level review the decisions taken at trial level, at which defendants plead guilty (see *guilty plea*), are convicted of a given criminal charge by jury or judge, or are acquitted of criminal charges by either of these bodies.

trial transcript. A written, word-for-word record of what was said in a trial proceeding.

verdict. The decision of a trial jury or a judge that determines the guilt or innocence of a criminal defendant, or that determines the final outcome of a civil case.

***voir dire*.** Jury selection process of questioning prospective jurors, to ascertain their qualifications and determine any basis for challenge. See also *peremptory challenge or strike*.

writ. A judicial order directing a person to do something. See also *certiorari* and *habeas corpus*.

References

Abu-Lughod, Lila. 1991. "Writing Against Culture." In *Recapturing Anthropology: Working in the Present*, edited by Richard Fox, 137–162. Santa Fe: School of American Research Press.

Althusser, Louis. 1971. "Ideology and Ideological State Apparatuses." In *Lenin and Philosophy, and Other Essays* by Louis Althusser, translated by Ben Brewster, 123–173. London: New Left Books.

Anonymous. 1986. "The Cultural Defense in the Criminal Law." *Harvard Law Review* 99 (April): 1293–1311.

Appadurai, Arjun. 1990. "Disjuncture and Difference in the Global Cultural Economy." *Public Culture* 2 (2): 1–23.

———. 1991. "Global Ethnoscapes: Notes and Queries for a Transnational Anthropology." In *Recapturing Anthropology: Working in the Present*, edited by Richard Fox, 191–210. Santa Fe: School of American Research Press.

Appiah, Kwame A. 1992. *In My Father's House: Africa In the Philosophy of Culture.* New York and Oxford: Oxford University Press.

Atkinson, J. Maxwell, and Paul Drew. 1979. *Order in Court: The Organisation* [sic] *of Verbal Interaction in Judicial Settings.* London and Basingstoke: The Macmillan Press Ltd.

Azuelos-Atias, Sol. 2007. *A Pragmatic Analysis of Legal Proofs of Criminal Intent.* Amsterdam: Benjamins Publishing Company.

Balram, Indira K. 2005. "The Evolving, Yet Still Inadequate, Legal Protections Afforded Battered Immigrant Women." *University of Maryland Law Journal of Race, Religion, Gender and Class* 5: 387–410.

Barrett, Michèle. 1991. *The Politics of Truth: From Marx to Foucault.* Cambridge: Polity Press.

Barthes, Roland. 1968a. *Elements of Semiology.* Translated by Annette Lavers and Colin Smith. New York: Hill and Wang.

———. 1968b. "L'effet de réel." *Communications* 11: 84–89.

Beger, Randall R., and Jeremy Hein. 2001. "Immigrants, Culture, and American Courts: A Typology of Legal Strategies and Issues in Cases Involving Vietnamese and Hmong Litigants." *Criminal Justice Review* 26 (1), Spring: 38–61.

Benjamin, Jessica. 1988. *The Bonds of Love: Psychoanalysis, Feminism, and the Problem of Domination.* New York: Pantheon Books.

Bennett, W. Lance, and Martha S. Feldman. 1981. *Reconstructing Reality in the Courtroom: Justice and Judgment in American Culture.* New Brunswick: Rutgers University Press.

Bhabha, Homi K. 1994. *The Location of Culture.* London and New York: Routledge.

———. 1995. "The Commitment to Theory." In *Cultural Remix: Theories of Politics and the Popular*, edited by Erica Carter, James Donald, and Judith Squires, 3–27. London: New Formations/Lawrence and Wishart.

Birnbaum, Jonathan, and Clarence Taylor. 2000. "Introduction: It Didn't Start in 1954." In *Civil Rights Since 1787: A Reader on the Black Struggle*, edited by Jonathan Birnbaum and Clarence Taylor, 1–3. New York and London: New York University Press.

Boulette Taylor, Deborah M. 1998. "Paying Attention to the Little Man Behind the Curtain: Destroying the Myth of the Liberal's Dilemma." *Maine Law Review* 50: 445–470.

Braunmühl, Caroline. Forthcoming. "'*Kultureller Rabatt*' ('Culture Discount')? The Debate About a 'Cultural Defence' [sic] in the Criminal Law, and What Gender Has Got To Do With It." In *Interdependencies of Social Categorisations* [sic], edited by Daniela Célleri, Julia Schramm, Tobias Schwarz, and Bea Wittger. Frankfurt and Madrid: Vevuert/Iberoamericana.

Briggs, Charles L., and Clara Mantini-Briggs. 2000. "'Bad Mothers' and the Threat to Civil Society: Race, Cultural Reasoning, and the Institutionalization of Social Inequality in a Venezuelan Infanticide Trial." *Law and Social Inquiry* 25: 299–354.

Burns, Robert P. 1999. *A Theory of the Trial*. Princeton: Princeton University Press.

Burns, Stacy L. 2004. "Pursuing 'Deep Pockets': Insurance-Related Issues in Judicial Settlement Work." *Journal of Contemporary Ethnography* 33 (2), April: 111–153.

———. 2008. "Demonstrating 'Reasonable Fear' At Trial: Is It Science Or Junk Science?" *Human Studies* 31 (2), June: 107–131.

Butler, Judith. 1993. *Bodies that Matter: On the Discursive Limits of 'Sex'*. New York: Routledge.

———. 1997a. *Excitable Speech: A Politics of the Performative*. New York: Routledge.

———. 1997b. *The Psychic Life of Power: Theories in Subjection*. Stanford: Stanford University Press.

———. 1999. *Gender Trouble: Feminism and the Subversion of Identity*. New York and London: Routledge.

———. 2000a. "Competing Universalities." In *Contingency, Hegemony, Universality: Contemporary Dialogues [sic] on the Left* by Judith Butler, Ernesto Laclau, and Slavoj Zizek, 136–181. London and New York: Verso.

———. 2000b. "Restaging the Universal: Hegemony and the Limits of Formalism." In *Contingency, Hegemony, Universality: Contemporary Dialogues [sic] on the Left* by Judith Butler, Ernesto Laclau, and Slavoj Zizek, 11–43. London and New York: Verso.

———. 2003. *Kritik der ethischen Gewalt: Adorno-Vorlesungen 2002*. Translated by Reiner Ansén. Frankfurt a.M.: Suhrkamp Verlag.

———. 2004. *Undoing Gender*. New York and London: Routledge.

Cardillo, Cathy C. 1997. "Violence Against Chinese Women: Defining the Cultural Role." *Women's Rights Law Reporter* 19 (Fall): 85–96.

Caughey, John L. 2009. "The Anthropologist As Expert Witness: The Case of a Murder in Maine." In *Multicultural Jurisprudence: Comparative Perspectives on the Cultural Defense*, edited by Marie-Claire Foblets and Alison Dundes Renteln, 321–334. Oxford and Portland: Hart Publishing.

Chen, Cher W. (2009), "A Critique of 'Loss of Face' Arguments in Cultural Defense Cases: A Comparative Study." In *Multicultural Jurisprudence: Comparative Perspectives on the Cultural Defense*, edited by Marie-Claire Foblets and Alison Dundes Renteln, 247–259. Oxford and Portland: Hart Publishing.

Chiu, Daina C. 1994. "The Cultural Defense: Beyond Exclusion, Assimilation, and Guilty Liberalism." *California Law Review* 82 (July): 1053–1125.

Christian, Barbara. 1994. "Diminishing Returns: Can Black Feminism(s) Survive the Academy?" In *Multiculturalism: A Critical Reader*, edited by David T. Goldberg, 168–180. Oxford and Cambridge: Blackwell.

Chung, Peter. 2004. "Standard of Review for Prosecutorial Use of Race Evidence during Trial." *University of Michigan Journal of Law Reform* 38 (Fall): 237–272.

Clifford, James. 1986. "Introduction: Partial Truths." In *Writing Culture: The Poetics and Politics of Ethnography*, edited by James Clifford and George E. Marcus, 1–26. Berkeley etc.: University of California Press.

———. 1988. *The Predicament of Culture: Twentieth-Century Ethnography, Literature, and Art.* Cambridge etc.: Harvard University Press.

———. 1989. "Notes on Travel and Theory." *Inscriptions* 5: 177–188.

———. 1992. "Traveling Cultures." In *Cultural Studies*, edited by Lawrence Grossberg, Cary Nelson, and Paula A. Treichler, 96–116. New York: Routledge.

Clifford, James, and George E. Marcus, eds. 1986. *Writing Culture: The Poetics and Politics of Ethnography.* Berkeley etc.: University of California Press.

Cohan, John A. 2010. "Honor Killings and the Cultural Defense." *California Western International Law Journal* 40 (2), Spring: 177–252.

Coker, Donna K. 1992. "Heat of Passion and Wife Killing: Men Who Batter / Men Who Kill." *Southern California Review of Law and Women's Studies* 2(1), Fall: 71–130.

Coleman, Doriane L. 1996. "Individualizing Justice through Multiculturalism: The Liberal's Dilemma." *Columbia Law Review* 96 (June): 1093–1167.

———. 2001. "Culture, Cloaked in *Mens Rea*." *South Atlantic Quarterly* 100 (Fall): 981–1004.

Conley, John M., and William O'Barr. 2005. *Just Words: Law, Language, and Power.* Second edition. Chicago and London: The University of Chicago Press.

Cook, Donelda. 1997. "The Art of Survival in White Academia: Black Women Faculty Finding Where They Belong." In *Off White: Readings on Race, Power, and Society*, edited by Michelle Fine, Lois Weis, Linda C. Powell, and L. Mun Wong, 100–109. New York and London: Routledge.

Crenshaw, Kimberlé. 1991. "Mapping the Margins: Intersectionality, Identity Politics, and Violence Against Women of Color." *Stanford Law Review* 43 (6): 1241–1299.

Crockett, Hannah Y. 2006. "Cultural Defenses in Georgia: Cultural Pluralism and Justice—Can Georgia Have Both?" *Georgia State University Law Review* 22: 665–688.

Davis, Townsend. 1998. *Weary Feet, Rested Souls: A Guided History of the Civil Rights Movement.* New York and London: W.W. Norton and Company.

Dawson, Ashley, and Malini Johar Schueller. 2007. "Introduction: Rethinking Imperialism Today." In *Exceptional State: Contemporary U.S. Culture and the New Imperialism*, edited by Ashley Dawson and Malini Johar Schueller, 1–33. Durham: Duke University Press.

Deckha, Maneesha. 2004. "Is Culture Taboo? Feminism, Intersectionality, and Culture Talk in Law." *Canadian Journal of Women and the Law* 16 (1): 14–53.

———. 2009. "The Paradox of the Cultural Defence [sic]: Gender and Cultural Othering in Canada." In *Multicultural Jurisprudence: Comparative Perspectives on the Cultural Defense*, edited by Marie-Claire Foblets and Alison Dundes Renteln, 261–284. Oxford and Portland: Hart Publishing.

Demian, Melissa. 2008. "Fictions of Intention in the 'Cultural Defense'." *American Anthropologist* 110 (4): 432–442.

DePalma, Aahren R. 2009. "I Couldn't Help Myself—My Culture Made Me Do It: The Use of Cultural Evidence in the Heat of Passion Defense." *Chicana/o-Latina/o Law Review* 28: 1–18.

Derrida, Jaques. 1982. "Signature Event Context." In *Margins of Philosophy* by Jaques Derrida, translated by Alan Bass, 307–330. Chicago: University of Chicago Press.

Desai, Gaurav. 2007. "Traveling Culture and the 'Cultural Defense'." In *Sexual Justice/Cultural Justice: Critical Perspectives in Political Theory and Practice*, edited by Barbara Arneil, Monique Deveaux, and Rita Dhamoon, 69–85. London and New York: Routledge.

D'hondt, Sigurd. 2009. "Others on Trial: The Construction of Cultural Otherness in Belgian First Instance Criminal Hearings." *Journal of Pragmatics* 41: 806–828.

———. 2010. "The Cultural Defense as a Courtroom Drama: The Enactment of Identity, Sameness, and Difference in Criminal Trial Discourse." *Law and Social Inquiry* 35 (1), Winter: 67–98.

Donovan, James M., and Garth, John Stuart. 2007. "Delimiting the Culture Defense." *Quinnipiac Law Review* 26: 109–146.

Drew, Paul. 1997. "Contested Evidence in Courtroom Cross-Examination: The Case of a Trial for Rape." In *Law in Action: Ethnomethodological and Conversation Analytic Approaches to Law*, edited by Max Travers and John F. Manzo, 51–76. Aldershot etc.: Dartmouth / Ashgate.

Dustin, Moira, and Anne Phillips. 2008. "Whose Agenda Is It?: Abuses of Women and Abuses of 'Culture' in Britain." *Ethnicities* 8: 405–424.

Ehrlich, Susan. 2001. *Representing Rape: Language and Sexual Consent*. London and New York: Routledge.

Fairclough, Norman. 1989. *Language and Power*. London: Longman.

Foblets, Marie-Claire, and Alison Dundes Renteln, eds. 2009. *Multicultural Jurisprudence: Comparative Perspectives on the Cultural Defense*. Oxford and Portland: Hart Publishing.

Foucault, Michel. 1972. *The Archeology of Knowledge*. Translated by A. Sheridan Smith. London: Tavistock Publications.

———. 1977. *Discipline and Punish: The Birth of the Prison*. Translated by Alan Sheridan. London: Penguin Books.

———. 1980a. "Truth and Power." In *Power/Knowledge: Selected Interviews and Other Writings, 1972–1977* by Michel Foucault, edited by Colin Gordon, translated by Colin Gordon, 109–133. New York: Pantheon Books.

———. 1980b. "Two Lectures." In *Power/Knowledge: Selected Interviews and Other Writings, 1972–1977* by Michel Foucault, edited by Colin Gordon, translated by Colin Gordon, 78–108. New York: Pantheon Books.

———. 1982. "Afterword: The Subject and Power." In Hubert L. Dreyfus and Paul Rabinow, *Michel Foucault. Beyond Structuralism and Hermeneutics*. Chicago: University of Chicago Press, 208–226.

———. 1984. "The Order of Discourse." In *Language and Politics*, edited by Michael J. Shapiro, 108–138. New York: New York University Press.

———. 1990. *The History of Sexuality, Vol. 1: An Introduction*. Translated by Robert Hurley. London: Penguin.

———. 2002. *The Order of Things: An Archeology of the Human Sciences*. Translated from the French. London and New York: Routledge.

———. 2003. *Abnormal: Lectures at the Collège de France, 1974–1975*. Translated by Graham Burchell. New York: Picador.

Fournier, Pascale. 2002. "The Ghettoisation [sic] of Differences in Canada: 'Rape by Culture' and the Danger of a 'Cultural Defense' in Criminal Law Trials." *Manitoba Law Journal* 29 (1): 1–39.

Friedman Ramirez, Linda. 2009. "The Virtues of the Cultural Defense." *Judicature* 92 (5), March–April: 207, 209–211, 247.

———, ed. 2010. *Cultural Issues in Criminal Defense*. Third edition. Huntington: Juris Publishing.

Frischknecht, Tom. 2009. *'Kultureller Rabatt': Überlegungen zu Strafausschluss und Strafermässigung bei kultureller Differenz*. Bern, Stuttgart and Wien: Haupt Verlag.

Gallin, Alice J. 1994. "The Cultural Defense: Undermining the Policies Against Domestic Violence." *Boston College Law Review* 35: 723–745.

Gates, Henry L., Jr. 1991. "Critical Fanonism." *Critical Inquiry* 17 (Spring): 457–470.

Gaynes, Elizabeth A. 1993. "The Urban Criminal Justice System: Where Young + Black + Male = Probable Cause." *Fordham Urban Law Journal* 20 (3): 621–640.

Gilroy, Paul. 1987. *'There Ain't No Black in the Union Jack': The Cultural Politics of Race and Nation*. London: Hutchinson.

———. 1993. *The Black Atlantic: Modernity and Double Consciousness*. Cambridge: Harvard University Press.

———. 2004. *After Empire: Melancholia or Convivial Culture?* London: Routledge.

Gilroy, Paul, Lawrence Grossberg, and Angela McRobbie, eds. 2000. *Without Guarantees: In Honour* [sic] *of Stuart Hall*. London and New York: Verso.

Glass-O'Shea, Brooke. 2009. "The Cultural Offense: How Plaintiffs Use Cultural Claims in U.S. Courts." *Journal of Law and Society* 10: 56–98.

Goldstein, Taryn F. 1994. "Cultural Conflicts in Court: Should the American Criminal Justice System Formally Recognize a 'Cultural Defense'?" *Dickinson Law Review* 99: 141–168.

Good, Anthony. 2008. "Cultural Evidence in Courts of Law." *Journal of the Royal Anthropological Institute* 14, March Supplement: S47–S60.

Greenawalt, Kent. 2008. "The Cultural Defense: Reflections in Light of the Model Penal Code and the Religious Freedom Restoration Act." *Ohio State Journal of Criminal Law* 6 (1), Fall: 299–321.

Hall, Stuart. 1980. "Encoding/Decoding." In *Culture, Media, Language: Working Papers in Cultural Studies, 1972–79*, edited by S. Hall, D. Hobson, A. Lowe, and P. Willis, 128–138. London: Unwin Hyman.

———. 1992. "The West and the Rest: Discourse and Power." In *Formations of Modernity*, edited by Stuart Hall and Bram Gieben, 275–320. Cambridge: Polity Press.

———. 1995. "Fantasy, Identity, Politics." In *Cultural Remix: Theories of Politics and the Popular*, edited by Erica Carter, James Donald, and Judith Squires, 63–69. London: New Formations / Lawrence and Wishart.

———. 1996. "Introduction: Who Needs 'Identity'?" In *Questions of Cultural Identity*, edited by Stuart Hall and Paul du Gay, 1–17. London etc.: Sage Publications.

Hall, Stuart, Ian Connell, and Lidia Curti. 1981. "The 'Unity' of Current Affairs Television." In *Popular Television and Film: A Reader*, edited by Tony Bennett, Susan Boyd-Bowman, Colin Mercer, and Janet Woollacott, 88–117. London: BFI.

Hallevy, Gabriel. 2009. "The Impact of Defence [sic] Arguments Based on the Cultural Difference of the Accused in the Criminal Law of Immigrant Countries and Societies." Journal of Migration and Refugee Issues 5 (1): 13–25. http://ssrn.com/abstract=1311421 (access date: July 24, 2011).

———. 2010. "Culture-Based Crimes Against Women in Societies Absorbing Immigrants—Rejecting the 'Mistake of Law' Defense and Imposing Harsher Sentencing." Cardozo Journal of Law and Gender 16: 439–467.

Heath, Stephen. 1981. *Questions of Cinema*. Basingstoke: Macmillan.

Heffer, Chris. 2005. *The Language of Jury Trial: A Corpus-Aided Analysis of Legal-Lay Discourse*. Houndmills, Basingstoke and New York: Palgrave Macmillan.

Held, Eliot M., and Reid Griffith Fontaine. 2009. "On the Boundaries of Culture as an Affirmative Defense." *Arizona Law Review* 51: 237–251.

Hill, Mike. 1997. "Can Whiteness Speak? Institutional Anomies, Ontological Disasters, and Three Hollywood Films." In *White Trash: Race and Class in*

America, edited by Matt Wray and Annalee Newitz, 155–173. New York and London: Routledge.

Hoeffel, Janet C. 2006. "Deconstructing the Cultural Evidence Debate." *University of Florida Journal of Law and Public Policy* 17 (2), August: 303–345.

Honig, Bonnie. 1999. "'My Culture Made Me Do It.'" *Is Multiculturalism Bad for Women?* by Susan Moller Okin with Respondents, edited by Joshua Cohen, Matthew Howard, and Martha C. Nussbaum, 35–40. Princeton: Princeton University Press.

hooks, bell [sic]. 1995. "Overcoming White Supremacy: A Comment." In *Killing Rage: Ending Racism* by bell hooks, 184–195. New York : H. Holt and Co.

Houck, Davis W., and David E. Dixon. 2006. "Introduction." In *Rhetoric, Religion, and the Civil Rights Movement 1954–1965*, edited by Davis W. Houck and David E. Dixon, 1–15. Waco: Baylor University Press.

Huckerby, Jayne. 2003. "Women Who Kill Their Children: Case Study and Conclusions Concerning the Differences in the Fall From Maternal Grace by Khoua Her and Andrea Yates." *Duke Journal of Gender Law and Policy* 10: 149–185.

Humphrey, Michael. 2007. "Culturalising [sic] the Abject: Islam, Law and Moral Panic in the West." *Australian Journal of Social Issues* 42 (1), Autumn: 9–25.

Jameson, Frederic. 1985. "The Realist Floor-Plan." In *On Signs*, edited by Marshall Blonsky, 373–383. Baltimore: John Hopkins University Press.

Jaquemet, Marco. 1996. *Credibility in Court: Communicative Practices in the Camorra Trials*. Cambridge and New York: Cambridge University Press.

Judicature. 2009. 92 (5), March–April, symposium issue: The Unique Challenges of Cross-Cultural Justice.

Kant, Immanuel. 1959. *Foundations of the Metaphysics of Morals, and What Is Enlightenment?* Translated by Lewis W. Beck. New York: Liberal Arts Press.

Kenny, Karyn. 2009. "When Cultural Tradition and Criminal Law Collide: Prosecutorial Discretion in Cross-Cultural Cases." *Judicature* 92 (5), March–April: 216–219.

Kim, Nancy S. 1997. "The Cultural Defense and the Problem of Cultural Preemption: A Framework For Analysis." *New Mexico Law Review* 27: 101–139.

Koptiuch, Kristin. 1996. "'Cultural Defense' and Criminological Displacements: Gender, Race, and (Trans-)Nation in the Legal Surveillance of U.S. Diaspora Asians." In *Displacement, Diaspora, and Geographies of Identity*, edited by Smader Lavie and Ted Swedenburg, 215–233. Durham and London: Duke University Press.

Laclau, Ernesto, and Chantal Mouffe. 1985. *Hegemony and Socialist Strategy: Towards a Radical Democratic Politics*. Translated by Winston Moore and Paul Cammack. London: Verso.

Landis, Debra T. 1989. "Prosecutor's Appeal in Criminal Cases To Racial, National, or Religious Prejudice As Grounds For Mistrial, New Trial, Reversal, or Vacation of Sentence—Modern Cases." *American Law Reports* (ALR) 4th (70): 664–775.

Lawrence, Sonia N. 2001. "Cultural (In)Sensitivity: The Dangers of a Simplistic Approach to Culture in the Courtroom." *Canadian Journal of Women and the Law* 13: 107–136.

Lay, Kenneth James. 1993. "Sexual Racism: A Legacy of Slavery." *National Black Law Journal* 13 (1–2): 165–183.

Lee, Cynthia. 2003. *Murder and the Reasonable Man: Passion and Fear in the Criminal Courtroom*. New York: New York University Press.

———. 2007. "Cultural Convergence: Interest Convergence Theory Meets the Cultural Defense." *Arizona Law Review* 49 (4), Winter: 911–959.

Levine, Kay L. 2003. "Negotiating the Boundaries of Crime and Culture: A Sociolegal Perspective On Cultural Defense Strategies." *Law and Social Inquiry* 28 (1): 39–86.

———. 2006. "The Law Is Not the Case: Incorporating Empirical Methods Into the Culture Of Case Analysis." *University of Florida Journal of Law and Public Policy* 17 (2), August: 283–301.

Lewis, Reina, and Sara Mills, eds. 2003. *Feminist Postcolonial Theory: A Reader*. Edinburgh: Edinburgh University Press.

Loomba, Ania, Suvir Kaul, Matti Bunzl, Antoinette Burton, and Jed Esty. 2005a. "Beyond What? An Introduction." In *Postcolonial Studies and Beyond*, edited by Ania Loomba, Suvir Kaul, and Antoinette Burton, 1–39. Durham: Duke University Press.

Loomba, Ania, Suvir Kaul, and Antoinette Burton, eds. 2005b. *Postcolonial Studies and Beyond*. Durham: Duke University Press.

Lynch, Michael, and David Bogen. 1996. *The Spectacle of History: Speech, Text, and Memory at the Iran-Contra Hearings*. Durham and London: Duke University Press.

Macdonell, Diane. 1986. *Theories of Discourse: An Introduction*. Oxford and New York: Blackwell.

Maeda, Donna K. 2000. "Subject to Justice: The 'Cultural Defense' and Legal Constructions of Race, Culture, and Nation." In *Postcolonial America*, edited by C. Richard King, 81–100. Urbana and Chicago: University of Chicago Press.

Magnarella, Paul J. 1991. "Justice in a Culturally Pluralistic Society: The Cultural Defense on Trial." *The Journal of Ethnic Studies* 19 (3), Fall: 65–84.

Maguigan, Holly. 1995. "Cultural Evidence and Male Violence: Are Feminist and Multiculturalist Reformers on a Collision Course in Criminal Courts?" *New York University Law Review* 70 (April): 36–99.

Maier, Sylvia. 2009. "Honor Killings and the Cultural Defense in Germany." In *Multicultural Jurisprudence: Comparative Perspectives on the Cultural Defense*, edited by Marie-Claire Foblets and Alison Dundes Renteln, 229–246. Oxford and Portland: Hart Publishing.

Martin, William E., and Peter M. Thompson. 2002. "Judicial Toleration of Racial Bias in the Minnesota Justice System." *Hamline Law Review* 25 (Winter): 235–270.

Matoesian, Gregory M. 1993. Reproducing Rape: Domination through Talk in the Courtroom. Chicago: The University of Chicago Press.

———. 2001. *Law and the Language of Identity: Discourse in the William Kennedy Smith Rape Trial*. Oxford: Oxford University Press.

———. 2005. "Nailing Down an Answer: Participations of Power in Trial Talk." *Discourse Studies* 7 (6): 733–759.

———. 2008. "Role Conflict As an Interactional Resource in the Multimodal Emergence of Expert Identity." *Semiotica* 171 (1): 15–49.

McKinley, Michelle A. 2009. "Cultural Culprits." *Berkeley Journal of Gender, Law and Justice* 24, Fall: 91–165.

Meeks, Kenneth. 2000. *Driving While Black: Highways, Shopping Malls, Taxi Cabs, Sidewalks: How to Fight Back If You Are a Victim of Racial Profiling*. New York: Broadway.

Mendelsohn, Naomi. 2004. "At the Crossroads: The Case For and Against a Cultural Defense to Female Genital Mutilation." *Rutgers Law Review* 56 (4): 1011–1038.

Mercer, Kobena. 1994. "Welcome to the Jungle: Identity and Diversity in Postmodern Politics." In *Welcome to the Jungle: New Positions in Black Cultural Studies* by Kobena Mercer, 259–285. New York and London: Routledge.

Mills, Sara. 2004. *Discourse*. Second edition. London and New York: Routledge.

Mohanty, Chandra T. 1994. "Under Western Eyes: Feminist Scholarship and Colonial Discourses." In *Colonial Discourse and Post-Colonial* [sic] *Theory: A Reader*, edited by Patrick Williams and Laura Chrisman, 196–220. New York: Columbia University Press.

———. 2003. *Feminism Without Borders: Decolonizing Theory, Practicing Solidarity*. Durham and London: Duke University Press.

Moore-Gilbert, Bart. 1997. *Postcolonial Theory: Contexts, Practices, Politics*. London and New York: Verso.

Morgan, J. Tom, and Laurel Parker. 2009. "The Dangers of the Cultural Defense." *Judicature* 92 (5), March–April: 206, 208.

Morley, David, and Kuan-Hsing Chen, eds. 1996. *Stuart Hall: Critical Dialogues* [sic] *in Cultural Studies*. London and New York: Routledge.

Morrison, Toni. 1993. *Playing in the Dark: Whiteness in the Literary Imagination*. London: Picador.

———. 1997. "The Official Story: Dead Man Golfing." In *Birth of a Nation'hood: Gaze, Script, and Spectacle in the O.J. Simpson Case*, edited by Toni Morrison and Claudia Brodsky Latour, vii–xxviii. New York: Pantheon Books.

Narayan, Kirin. 2003. "How Native Is a 'Native' Anthropologist?" In *Feminist Postcolonial Theory: A Reader*, edited by Reina Lewis and Sara Mills, 285–305. Edinburgh: Edinburgh University Press.

Newman, Mark. 2004. *The Civil Rights Movement*. Edinburgh: Edinburgh University Press.

Nunn, Kenneth B. 2006. "Foreword: New Explorations in Culture and Crime: Definitions, Theory, Method." *University of Florida Journal of Law and Public Policy* 17 (2), August: vii–xvii.

O'Barr, William. 1982. *Linguistic Evidence: Language, Power, and Strategy in the Courtroom*. New York etc.: Academic Press.

Oberman, Michelle. 1996. "Mothers Who Kill: Coming to Terms With Modern American Infanticide." *American Criminal Law Review* 34 (1): 1–110.

———. 2002. "Understanding Infanticide in Context: Mothers Who Kill, 1870–1930 and Today." *Journal of Criminal Law and Criminology* 92 (3–4): 707–737.

Ohlendorf, Edmund. n.d. Ehrenmord. Text available at www.eduvinet.de/comcult/pdf/interkult/d/cocdetlf203.pdf (access date: April 11, 2011).

Okin, Susan Moller. 1999. "Is Multiculturalism Bad For Women?" In *Is Multiculturalism Bad For Women?* by Susan Moller Okin with Respondents, edited by Joshua Cohen, Matthew Howard, and Martha C. Nussbaum, 7–24. Princeton: Princeton University Press.

Omi, Michael, and Howard Winant. 1994. *Racial Formation in the United States: From the 1960s to the 1990s*. Second edition. London: Routledge.

Ostrowski, Julie. 2002. "While Murderous Moms Shock, Homicidal Dads Ignored." March 19. http://www.womensenews.org/story/the-courts/020319/while-murderous-moms-shock-homicidal-dads-ignored (access date: July 24, 2011).

Pêcheux, Michel. 1982. *Language, Semantics, and Ideology: Stating the Obvious*. New York: St. Martin's Press.

Phillips, Anne. 2003. "When Culture Means Gender: Issues of Cultural Defence [sic] in the English Courts." *Modern Law Review* 66 (4): 510–531.

———. 2007. *Multiculturalism Without Culture*. Princeton and Oxford: Princeton University Press.

Phillips, Anne, and Sawitri Saharso. 2008. "Guest Editorial: The Rights of Women and the Crisis of Multiculturalism." *Ethnicities* 8: 291–301.

Razack, Sherene H. 1998. *Looking White People in the Eye: Gender, Race, and Culture in Courtrooms and Classrooms*. Toronto etc.: University of Toronto Press.

———. 2008. *Casting Out: The Eviction of Muslims From Western Law and Politics*. Toronto etc.: University of Toronto Press.

Reddy, Sita. 2002. "Temporarily Insane: Pathologising [sic] Cultural Difference in American Criminal Courts." *Sociology of Health and Illness* 24 (5): 667–687.

Renteln, Alison D. 1993. "A Justification of the Cultural Defense As Partial Excuse." *Review of Law and Women's Studies* 2: 437–525.

———. 2004. *The Cultural Defense*. Oxford and New York: Oxford University Press.

———. 2009. "The Use and Abuse of the Cultural Defense." In *Multicultural Jurisprudence: Comparative Perspectives on the Cultural Defense*, edited by Marie-Claire Foblets and Alison Dundes Renteln, 61–82. Oxford and Portland: Hart Publishing.

Renteln, Alison D., and Marie-Claire Foblets. 2009. "Conclusion." In *Multicultural Jurisprudence: Comparative Perspectives on the Cultural Defense*, edited by Marie-Claire Foblets and Alison Dundes Renteln, 335–338. Oxford and Portland: Hart Publishing.

Ridgway, Delissa A. 2009. "Introduction." *Judicature* 92 (5), March–April: 191–193.

Rimonte, Nilda. 1991. "A Question of Culture: Cultural Approval of Violence Against Women in the Pacific-Asian Community and the Cultural Defense." *Stanford Law Review* 43 (July): 1311–1326.

Römhild, Regina. 2007. "Alte Träume, neue Praktiken: Migration und Kosmopolitismus an den Grenzen Europas." In *Turbulente Ränder: Neue Perspektiven auf Migration an den Grenzen Europas*, edited by TRANSIT MIGRATION Forschungsgruppe, 211–222. Bielefeld: Transcript.

Rosen, Lawrence. 1977. "The Anthropologist As Expert Witness." *American Anthropologist* 79 (3): 555–578.

Sacks, Valerie L. 1996. "An Indefensible Defense: On the Misuse of Culture in Criminal Law." *Arizona Journal of International and Comparative Law* 13 (Fall): 523–550.

Said, Edward W. 1978. *Orientalism*. London etc.: Routledge and Paul.

Sams, Julia P. 1986. "The Availability of a 'Cultural Defense' As an Excuse for Criminal Behavior." *Georgia Journal of International and Comparative Law* 16: 335–354.

Sanday, Peggy R. 1997. *A Woman Scorned: Acquaintance Rape on Trial*. Berkeley, Los Angeles and London: University of California Press.

Scheffer, Thomas. 2006. "The Micro-Formation of Criminal Defense: On the Lawyer's Notes, Speech-Production, and a Field of Presence." *Research on Language and Social Interaction* 39 (3): 303–342.

———. 2007. "The Duplicity of Testimonial Interviews—Unfolding and Utilising [sic] Multiple Temporalisation [sic] in Compound Procedures and Projects." *Forum Qualitative Sozialforschung / Forum: Qualitative Social Research*, 8 (1). http://www.qualitative-research.net/fqs-texte/1–07/07–1-15-e.htm (access date: July 24, 2011).

Siesling, Mirjam, and Jeroen Ten Voorde. 2009. "The Paradox of Cultural Differences in Dutch Criminal Law." In *Multicultural Jurisprudence: Comparative Perspectives on the Cultural Defense*, edited by Marie-Claire Foblets and Alison Dundes Renteln, 145–173. Oxford and Portland: Hart Publishing.

Sing, James J. 1999. "Culture as Sameness: Toward a Synthetic View of Provocation and Culture in the Criminal Law." *Yale Law Journal* 108: 1845–1884.

Skinner, David. 2002. "Andrea Yates—Not A Women's Issue: Explaining the Modern Medea is Beyond the Powers of Feminism and Psychiatry." The Daily Standard, March 14. http://www.weeklystandard.com/Content/Public/Articles/000/000/001/010agmve.asp (access date: July 24, 2011).

Slack, Jennifer D. 1996. "The Theory and Method of Articulation in Cultural Studies." In *Stuart Hall: Critical Dialogues* [sic] *in Cultural Studies*, edited by David Morley and Kuan-Hsing Chen, 112–127. London and New York: Routledge.

Song, Sarah. 2007. *Justice, Gender, and the Politics of Multiculturalism*. Cambridge and New York: Cambridge University Press.

Spatz, Melissa. 1991. "A 'Lesser' Crime: A Comparative Study of Legal Defenses for Men Who Kill Their Wives." *Columbia Journal of Law and Social Problems* 24: 597–638.

Spindler, Susanne. 2006. *Corpus Delicti: Männlichkeit, Rassismus und Kriminalisierung im Alltag jugendlicher Migranten*. Münster: Unrast-Verlag.

Spivak, Gayatri C. 1986. "Three Women's Texts and A Critique Of Imperialism." In *'Race', Writing and Difference*, edited by Henry L. Gates, Jr., 262–280. Chicago: Chicago University Press.

———. 1988a. "Can the Subaltern Speak?" In *Marxism and the Interpretation of Culture*, edited by Cary Nelson and Lawrence Grossberg, 271–313. Urbana: University of Illinois Press.

———. 1988b. "French Feminism In an International Frame." In *In Other Worlds: Essays in Cultural Politics* by Gayatri C. Spivak, 134–153. New York: Routledge.

———. 1988c. *In Other Worlds: Essays in Cultural Politics*. New York: Routledge.

———. 1990. *The Post-Colonial* [sic] *Critic: Interviews, Strategies, Dialogues* [sic], edited by Sarah Harasym. New York and London. Routledge.

———. 1993. "Marginality in the Teaching Machine." In *Outside in the Teaching Machine* by Gayatri C. Spivak, 53–76. London and New York: Routledge.

Streib, Victor L. 2004. Death Penalty For Female Offenders, January 1, 1973, through June 30, 2004. http://www.law.onu.edu/faculty/streib (access date: May 26, 2006).

Stygall, Gail. 1994. *Trial Language: Differential Discourse Processing and Discursive Formation*. Amsterdam and Philadelpha: John Benjamins Publishing Company.

Suri, Sharan K. 2000. "A Matter of Principle and Consistency: Understanding the Battered Woman and Cultural Defenses." *Michigan Journal of Gender and Law* 7: 107–139.

Taslitz, Andrew E. 1999. *Rape and the Culture of the Courtroom*. New York and London: New York University Press.

Thomas, Nicholas. 1991. *Entangled Objects: Exchange, Material Culture, and Colonialism in the Pacific*. Cambridge: Harvard University Press.

Torry, William I. 1999. "Multicultural Jurisprudence and the Cultural Defense." *Journal of Legal Pluralism* 44: 127–161.

———. 2000. "Culture and Individual Responsibility: Touchstones of the Culture Defense." *Human Organization* 59 (1): 58–71.

Travers, Max. 2008. "Understanding Comparison In Criminal Justice Research: An Interpretive Perspective." *International Criminal Justice Review* 18 (4), December: 389–405.

Travers, Max, and John F. Manzo, eds. 1997. *Law in Action: Ethnomethodological and Conversation Analytic Approaches to Law*. Aldershot: Dartmouth / Ashgate.

Turner, Graeme. 2003. *British Cultural Studies: An Introduction*. Third edition. London and New York: Routledge.

Twining, William L. 1990. "The Rationalist Tradition of Evidence Scholarship." In *Rethinking Evidence: Exploratory Essays* by William L. Twining, 32–91. Oxford and Cambridge: Blackwell.

Valverde, Mariana. 1996. "'Despotism' and Ethical Liberal Governance." *Economy and Society* 25 (3): 357–372.

Van Broeck, Jeroen. 2001. "Cultural Defence [sic] and Culturally Motivated Crimes (Cultural Offences)." *European Journal of Crime, Criminal Law and Criminal Justice* 9 (1): 1–32.

Vaughan, Megan. 1991. *Curing Their Ills: Colonial Power and African Illness*. Stanford: Stanford University Press.

———. 2007. "Introduction." In *Psychiatry and Empire*, edited by Sloane Mahone and Megan Vaughan, 1–16. Basingstoke: Palgrave Macmillan.

Verney, Kevern. 2000. *Black Civil Rights in America*. London and New York: Routledge.

Vieux, Steve. 1994. "In the Shadow of Neo-Liberal Racism." *Race and Class* 36 (1), July: 23–32.

Volpp, Leti. 1994. "(Mis)Identifying Culture: Asian Women and the 'Cultural Defense'." *Harvard Women's Law Journal* 17: 57–101.

———. 1996. "Talking 'Culture': Gender, Race, Nation, and the Politics of Multiculturalism." *Columbia Law Review* 96 (October): 1573–1617.

———. 2000. "Blaming Culture for Bad Behavior." *Yale Journal of Law and the Humanities* 12 (Winter): 89–116.

———. 2001. "Feminism versus Multiculturalism." *Columbia Law Review* 101 (5), June: 1181–1218.

———. 2003. "On Culture, Difference, and Domestic Violence." *American Journal of Gender, Social Policy and the Law* 11 (2): 393–399.

———. 2006. "Disappearing Acts: On Gendered Violence, Pathological Cultures, and Civil Society." *PMLA* 121 (5): 1631–1638.

———. n.d. "Cultural Defenses In the Criminal Legal System." new.vawnet.org/assoc_files_vawnet/volpp.pdf (access date: July 24, 2011).

Wall, Alexandra J. 1997. "Silencer Of the Lambs Prison Chaplain: Give Kostner Life, Not Death." *Jewish Standard*, February 21.

Ware, Vron. 1992. *Beyond the Pale: White Women, Racism, and History*. London and New York: Verso.

Wetherell, Margaret, and Jonathan Potter. 1992. *Mapping the Language of Racism: Discourse and the Legitimation of Exploitation*. Hemel Hempstead: Harvester Wheatsheaf.

Wilczynski, Ania. 1991. "Images of Women Who Kill Their Infants: The Mad and the Bad." *Women and Criminal Justice* 2: 71–88.

Wilczynski, Ania, and Allison Morris. 1993. "Parents Who Kill Their Children." *Criminal Law Review*, January: 31–36.

Winkelman, Michael. 1996. "Cultural Factors in Criminal Defense Proceedings." *Human Organization* 55 (2): 154–159.

Wong, Charmaine M. 1999. "Good Intentions, Troublesome Applications: The Cultural Defence [sic] and Other Uses of Cultural Evidence in Canada." *Criminal Law Quarterly* 42: 367–396.

Woo, Deborah. 1989. "The People v. Fumiko Kimura: But Which People?" *International Journal of the Sociology of Law* 17: 403–428.

Wray, Matt, and Annalee Newitz, eds. 1997. *White Trash: Race and Class in America*. New York and London: Routledge.

Wu, Michele W. 2003. "Culture Is No Defense For Infanticide." *American University Journal of Gender, Social Policy, and the Law* 11: 975–1025.

Young, Cathy. 1992. "Equal Cultures or Equality For Women? Why Feminism and Multiculturalism Don't Mix." Heritage Lecture no. 387 (June 12). http://www.heritage.org/Research/Religion/HL387.cfm (access date: July 24, 2011).

Young, Lola. 2000. "How Do We Look? Unfixing the Singular Black (Female) Subject." In *Without Guarantees: In Honour [sic] of Stuart Hall*, edited by Paul Gilroy, Lawrence Grossberg, and Angela McRobbie, 416–429. London and New York: Verso.

Index

A

adversary system of justice, 2–3, 5, 46, 124, 133–160, 178
anti-essentialism, 122, 148
Atkinson, J. Maxwell, 5, 205
autonomy, 3–5, 14–15, 18, 90, 112, 124, 191, 202–203

B

Bogen, David, 5, 205, 257n2
Butler, Judith, 8–9, 12, 13, 14, 17, 18–19, 20, 35, 133, 141, 171, 191, 201, 202, 203, 206, 231n2

C

[Cao] vs. State, 30, 32, 48–49, 98, 104–119, 120, 121, 135, 136, 209, 243–248, 252n55
[Chemmanoor] vs. State, 30, 32, 209–210, 234n1
Chen, People vs., 85–86, 102–103, 121, 122, 134–135, 244n10, 248n4, 254–255n41
citationality, 13, 19–20, 180, 184, 196
Chiu, Daina C., 44–45, 83, 88, 90, 113–116, 121, 246n29, 247nn34, 36, 40
Coleman, Doriane L., 39, 40, 71–2, 85, 105, 121, 234–235n4, 235n7, 250n25
colonial discourse, 34, 35; and interpellation, 178–180; and intersectionality, 26, 27, 29, 41; and its appropration of feminist rhetoric, 70; and its deployment and/or critique by witnesses, 164, 167, 168–169, 174, 177, 101; and its destabilization/restabilization, 183, 186, 200, 203, 206; and its naturalization by empiricism, 99; and racism, 23, 25, 27; and the myth of a potential political neutrality of 'cultural experts', 179–180; and theory, 7–9, 12–13, 14–16; as a *U.S.* discourse constitutive of 'cultural evidence', 45, 49, 55, 65, 119, 231–232n4; as constitutive of the opposing party's discourse in the courtroom, 151, 152, 154, 158, 159; as framing the debate regarding 'the cultural defense', 72, 119, 125–126, 231–2n4, 248n47; as serviceable to U.S. patriarchal discourse, 116, 248n47
'color, of': culture of color, 26; man of color, 205; Other of color, 203; people of color, 14, 25, 127–129, 203, 231n2, 232n2; person of color, 101; subjects of color, 101, 127; women of color, 42, 112, 114, 129, 205, 242n69
conversation analysis, 204
Crenshaw, Kimberlé, 8
criminal justice, 110, 114, 124, 125, 134, 197–198, 200–201, 203–206
criminalization, 50, 53, 64–65, 71–72, 174, 194, 198–204, 256n1
cultural profiling, 50–73, 126–127, 149–150, 174

D

deconstruction, 3, 11, 45, 123, 133, 135–136, 160, 180, 198, 205, 257n2

determination, 14–15, 21, 112, 141, 190, 192–193, 195, 200–203, 231n2; self-determination, 42, 89–90, 93, 145–146, 150–154, 176–178, 205
determinism, 50, 53, 72, 147–148, 201–203, 231n2
D'hondt, Sigurd, 53, 197, 200, 231n2, 249n7, 254n28
disciplinary society, 119, 198–203, 231–232n4
discourse, 3, 5, 7–21, 24, 47, 63, 76, 80, 98–103, 134–135, 139, 171, 191, 249n8; academic discourse, 171, 174–178; courtroom discourse, 3–4, 122–124, 204; counter-discourse, 17–18, 137; discourse of culture, 1, 23, 25, 123–124, 129, 147–148, 164, 167, 184, 197; defense's discourse, 153; Enlightenment discourse, 90, 112, 202–203; essentialist discourse, 55, 121, 197; juridical discourse, 198–201, 206, 231n2; legal discourse, 42, 203; modern discourse, 201–203, 231n2; 'Native Informant' discourse (Spivak), 171–174; prosecution's discourse, 50, 72, 108, 116, 148, 156; trial discourse, 28, 160, 178, 183, 184, 196, 254n22; U.S. discourse, 45, 49, 86–87; unegalitarian discourse, 28, 35, 48, 121, 124, 204, 206, 235–236n8. *See also* colonial discourse; gendered discourse; hegemonic discourse; racialization—racialized discourse
discourse theory, 3, 7, 10–16, 22, 47, 73, 122 ,185, 196, 204, 231–232n4
Drew, Paul, 5, 205
Donovan, James M., 47, 179–180, 248n47

E

empiricism, 4, 7, 11–12, 13, 27, 45–48, 54, 57–63, 72–73, 84–86, 98–103, 121–124, 125–126, 129, 148–149, 158–159, 177, 178–180, 191, 197–198, 254n28; anti-empiricism, 203
Enlightenment discourse, 14–15, 59, 90, 112, 171–172, 202–203
epistemology, 7, 10–16, 122
essentialism, 10–12, 16, 47, 50, 53–57, 79, 84–85, 98–103, 121, 197. *See also* anti-essentialism; strategic essentialism
ethnomethodology, 204
Eurocentrism, 3–4, 9, 13, 97, 112
Euro-America, 4, 23, 25, 26, 27, 53, 87, 89, 115–116, 117, 195. *See also* 'whites'; whiteness; supremacy, white
expert testimony, 24, 29, 31–33, 35; and academic discourse, 174–178; and (lack of) critique of 'cultural evidence', 2–3, 134–135, 178–180; and mystification of 'cultural evidence' as matter of unmediated 'facts'/'information', 46–48; and 'Native Informant' discourse (Spivak), 171–174; and the adversary system, 2–3, 254–255n41; and the myth of academic neutrality, 13–14, 59, 60, 62, 178–180; by 'Native Informants' (Spivak), 123, 248n4, 254n28; in *[Cao] vs. State*, 104, 106, 107, 116–118, 243n4, 243–244n6, 247n37; in *People vs. [Lopez] and [Singh]*, 52–53, 55, 56, 69–70, 137–139, 143–146, 148, 161, 163, 184–196, 237n19, 255–256n26; in *People vs. [Shen]*, 49, 79, 81–103, 113, 150–151, 154, 182–183; in *U.S. vs. [Ibrahim] et al.*, 167

F

fact, 2–5, 13, 45–49, 57–63, 72–73, 76–77, 79–81, 84–86, 98–103, 109–115, 121–126, 133, 135, 138–139, 148–150, 175, 177, 178–180, 189–191, 197–201, 235–236n8, 240n11. *See also* information, cultural
Foblets, Marie-Claire, 1, 39, 46, 125
Foucault, Michel, 7, 10, 11–13, 14, 15, 18, 126, 128, 163, 183, 197, 198–202, 203, 206, 231n2, 232–233nn4–5
France, State vs., 110, 114
Friedman Ramirez, Linda, 3, 39, 40, 46, 125, 134, 179, 248n7
Frischknecht, Tom, 46, 47, 125, 127, 179, 234n1, 248n47

G

[Galicia], State vs., 30, 32, 215, 234n1
Garth, John Stuart, 47, 179–180, 248n47
gender. *See* gendered discourse
gendered discourse, 25, 34, 35; and interpellation, 178–180; and intersectionality, 26, 29, 42; and its deployment and/or critique by witnesses, 177; and its destabilization/restabilization, 182–183, 200, 203, 206; and Leti Volpp's analysis of 'cultural defenses', 85, 103; and the myth of a potential political neutrality of 'cultural experts', 179–180; and theory, 7–9, 12–13, 14–16, 232n1; as a *U.S.* discourse constitutive of (colonialist cultural) 'evidence', 49, 109; as constitutive of the opposing party's discourse in the courtroom, 151, 154–156, 158, 159; as impinging upon trial strategy, 75–77, 112–116; as instrumentalized by a pseudo-feminist U.S. colonial discourse, 118–119
Gilroy, Paul, 7, 8, 15, 175, 206, 233n7, 253n17
[Gonzalez], People vs., 30, 32, 135–136, 159, 212, 249n7
Good, Anthony, 254–255n41

H

Hall, Stuart, 2, 7, 15, 20, 21–22, 183, 202, 204
Hallevy, Gabriel, 39, 40, 43, 125, 128, 129, 249n10
Hanikei, People vs., 246n27
hegemonic discourse, 4, 15, 17–18, 22, 34, 101, 113, 159–160, 161, 167, 168–169, 171, 177, 178–180, 181, 183, 185, 196, 198, 205, 254n22
hegemony, 1–6, 8, 17–22, 26, 28, 48, 76, 98, 120–127, 135, 143, 147–149, 161, 164, 197, 203–204, 206, 232n4, 233n10, 251–252n48, 254n28; hegemonic audience, 150; hegemonic common sense, 44, 107; hegemonic concepts, 45; hegemonic (U.S.) culture, 25, 39–41, 67, 68, 80, 105, 114, 182, 247n34; hegemonic judicial audiences, 44; hegemonic perspective, 90; hegemonic reasoning, 137; hegemonic status, 103, 116
[Her], State vs., 30, 33, 216–217, 234n1, 252n55
heterosexuality, 8, 18, 67, 198, 202
Hoeffel, Janet C., 37, 40, 44, 45, 46, 133–135, 249n1
Holtzman, Elizabeth, 43
hooks, bell [sic], 9, 167

I

[Ibrahim] et al., U.S. vs., 31, 33, 221–222, 253nn18–19
individual, 2–3, 15, 19, 35, 42, 47, 57, 121, 134, 149, 153, 161, 173, 185, 194; individual (circumstances of) a case, 72, 128, 150, 247n37, 254n28; individual experience, 60; individual feelings, 61–63, 139, 190–192; individual 'hero', 257n2; individual liberty, 51–52; individual rights, 65; individual speakers, 29
individualism, 203, 233n9
individuality, 143, 191, 198–203, 231n2
individualization, 48, 77, 85–86, 98, 103, 144, 203, 231n2, 231–232n4, 236n9
infanticide, 81, 106–116, 174–175, 247n32. *See also* parent-child suicide
inferiority, 14–15, 72–73, 202–203, 205. *See also* superiority; supremacy
information, cultural, 1–4, 13, 45–49, 60, 73, 80–86, 90–92, 103, 110, 116, 120–124, 135, 179–180, 186, 231–232n4. *See also* fact
interpellation, 19–20, 76, 140, 147–148, 159, 168, 178–179, 197, 204–205

J

Judicature, 43, 125, 126, 249n9
jury instruction, 74–77, 106, 157, 239n7, 239n9, 240n12, 248n6

K

Kimura, People vs., 82, 109–110, 113–114, 247n34
Koptiuch, Kristin, 2, 41, 118–119, 129, 231–232n4

[Ku], State vs., 30, 33, 217, 234n1
[Kubicek], State vs., 30, 33, 217–218, 234n1
kultureller Rabatt, 127

L

Laclau, Ernesto, 17, 20–21, 178, 232n1, 233nn9–10
law. *See* discourse, legal; *law in action*
law in action, 5, 204
Lawrence, Sonia N., 2, 41, 119, 123–124, 150, 232n4
lay testimony, 3, 14, 32–33, 35, 171–174
Lee, Cynthia, 39, 44–45, 113, 159, 204
[Lee], State vs., 31, 33, 218, 234n1
Levine, Kay L., 3, 41, 44, 46, 109, 125
logic, 42, 153, 203, 249n8; logical coherence, 183, 205–207; patriarchal logic, 45, 104, 107, 115, 120, 135, 251–252n48; racialized or racist logic, 57–58, 135, 149–150, 194
[Lopez] and [Singh], People vs. See People vs. [Lopez] and [Singh]
Loving vs. Virginia, 238n62
Lynch, Michael, 5, 205, 257n2

M

Maguigan, Holly, 1, 2, 39, 40, 46, 72, 118, 121, 124, 133–134, 159–160, 179–180, 252n55
Maier, Sylvia, 128
Manzo, John F., 5
Matoesian, Gregory M., 5, 205, 254n22
[Merlino], People vs., 30, 32, 212, 234n1
modernity, 3, 41, 42, 52, 65, 87, 100, 152, 166, 177–178, 198–203, 231n2, 244n14, 253n16
Mohanty, Chandra T., 7–8, 41–42
Morgan, J. Tom, 39, 43–44, 125
mother-child suicide. *See* parent-child suicide. *See also* infanticide
Moua, People vs., 40, 118, 244n10
Mouffe, Chantal, 17, 20–21, 232n1, 233nn9–10

N

'Native Informant' figure (Spivak), 59, 171–174, 178

O

objectivity, 53, 58–60, 63, 72–73, 83–84, 100–102, 123, 148–149, 172, 177, 185–187, 232n5, 248n4
Okin, Susan Moller, 40–41, 42–44, 72, 121
ontology, 8, 10–12, 158–159, 197–198, 200–202, 248n5
ontologization, 3–4, 11, 72, 148–149, 191, 193, 198, 202
Oppressed Third World Woman, 29, 41–42, 74–103, 150–154, 157–159, 166–169, 174–178, 182–183, 242n69, 251–252n48. *See also* Patriarchal Other (Culture); Othering
Othering, 15, 48, 64–65, 86, 100–103, 123, 125, 128–129, 164, 174, 184, 203, 231n2, 235–236n8, 248n47, 254n28; self-Othering, 101, 143n102, 254n28. *See also* Patriarchal Other (Culture); Oppressed Third World Woman

P

parent-child suicide, 77, 84–85, 174–175. *See also* infanticide
Parker, Laurel, 39, 43–44, 125
Patriarchal Other (Culture), 1–2, 3, 27–29, 40–44, 47–49, 50–73, 78, 81, 103, 104–119, 120–121, 126, 127–129, 135–136, 142–143, 145–147, 150, 159, 178–179, 187–191. *See also* Oppressed Third World Woman; Othering
patriarchy. *See* gendered discourse
people of color, 14, 25, 127–129, 203, 231n2, 232n2. *See also* 'color, of'
People vs. [Lopez] and [Singh], 30, 32, 48, 114–115, 116, 214, 234n1, 236nn1–9, 237nn9–35, 238nn35–61, nn63–76, 239nn77, 249n9, 250nn10–24, nn26–38, 251nn38, 251nn39–40, 252nn2–4, 253nn5–16, n21, 254nn28–40, 255nn3–26, 256nn26–30; and empiricism in the discursive constitution of 'cultural evidence', 98–100; and the use of 'Native Informants'

(Spivak) as 'cultural experts', 79; and witnesses' resistance to/ collusion with colonial discourse, 161–166, 171–174; as exemplary of *cultural profiling*, 50–72; as prototype of criminalization of Othered men through 'cultural evidence', 118–119; destabilization/restabilization of colonial discourse, 181, 184–196; discourse of the opposing party, 137–150, 151, 158–159, 167; implications of case for the 'cultural defense' debate, 103, 120, 123

People vs. Chen, 85–86, 102–103, 121, 122, 134–135, 244n10, 248n4, 254–255n41

People vs. [Gonzalez], 30, 32, 135–136, 159, 212, 249n7

People vs. Hanikei, 246n27

People vs. Kimura, 82, 109–110, 113–114, 247n34

People vs. [Merlino], 30, 32, 212, 234n1

People vs. Moua, 40, 118, 244n10

People vs. [Shen], 30, 32, 48–49, 72–73, 161, 195, 213, 239nn1–9, 240nn1–26, 241nn27–60, 242nn60–93, 243nn95–97, nn99–101, nn103–106, 244–246n14, 246nn20–23, n26, 247n33, n35, n37, 248n2, n4, n6, 251nn41–48, 252nn48–53, 254nn23–27; as compared to *[Cao] vs. State*, 104–109, 112–116, 118–119; destabilization/restabilization of colonial and patriarchal discourse, 181–182; discourse of defendant and a 'lay' witness, 168–171; discourse of expert witness, 174–178; discourse of the opposing party, 150–160; discursive constitution of 'cultural evidence' in, 74–103; implications of case for the 'cultural defense' debate, 120–123

Phillips, Anne, 1, 27, 39–40, 44–45, 57, 116, 120, 121, 122, 153–154, 194

postcolonial critique, 8, 14–15

postcolonial feminism, 7–8, 22, 123

poststructuralism, 4–5, 14, 47, 183, 201, 204, 206

profiling, cultural, 53, 71–72, 126, 149–150, 174, 234n1

proof, procedure of, 29, 72, 153–154, 159; in *People vs. [Lopez] and [Singh]*, 50, 53–54, 57, 64–65, 137–138, 149–150, 165, 167, 185, 194–195, 214, 239n77

R

Rabatt, kultureller, 127

race, 23–27, 44, 110, 114–115, 121, 124, 135, 181, 197–198, 235–236n8

racism, 141, 171–172, 176–177, 233n2, 234n5; and antiracist strategy, 121, 202–203; and colonial discourse, 23, 44, 123–124; and intersectionality, 26, 114–115, 118–119, 248n48; and resistance in court, 149–150, 166–167, 199–201; as furthered by empiricism, 72, 123–124; antiracism, 20–21; conceptualization of, 7–9, 12–18; in the debate on 'the cultural defense', 126–127; racist 'cultural evidence', 48, 65–66, 72, 102, 118–119, 134, 194–195, 248n48. *See also* logic—racialized or racist

racialization, 4, 48, 53, 57–58, 100–103, 112, 114–115, 125–129, 137–138, 149–150, 159, 172–174, 194–196, 197–198, 199–206, 231n2, 235–236n8; racialized discourse, 7–9, 12–13, 14–16, 23, 25, 26, 35, 50, 72. *See also* logic—racialized or racist, 57–58, 135, 149–150, 194

rationality, 5, 15, 89, 93, 133–135, 183–184, 196, 204–207, 231n2. *See also* reason

Razack, Sherene H., 1, 2, 27, 41, 42, 118, 124, 126, 127, 129, 153, 159, 180, 232n4, 252n56

reason, 2–5, 14–15, 17, 46, 57, 74–75, 110–111, 112, 123, 124, 133–135, 137, 159, 194–195, 202–203, 204–207, 239n7, 240n12, 244–245n14. *See also* rationality

Reed vs. State, 245–246n14
Renteln, Alison D., 1, 39, 46, 47, 110, 114, 122, 125–126, 179, 235–236n8, 246n26, 246n29, 248–249n7
Ridgway, Delissa A., 43, 126

S

[Saidani], State vs., 31, 33, 218–219, 234n1
self-determination. *See* determination
sexism. *See* gendered discourse
[Shen], People vs. See People vs. [Shen]
Siesling, Mirjam, 127–128, 234n1
[Singh], People vs. [Lopez] and. See People vs. [Lopez] and [Singh]
[Singh] vs. Cambra. See People vs. [Lopez] and [Singh]
sociology, 4–5, 7, 14–15, 204–207
Song, Sarah, 39, 41, 44–45, 47, 121, 123, 179, 234n1, 236n8
Spivak, Gayatri C., 4, 5, 46, 47, 80, 200, 207, 254n28; on the 'Native Informant' figure, 59, 161, 171–172; on 'saving brown women', 26, 41, 42; and strategic essentialism, 44, 167; and theory, 7–8, 10–11, 12, 232n3
State vs. France, 110, 114
State vs. [Galicia], 30, 32, 215, 234n1
State vs. [Her], 30, 33, 216–217, 234n1, 252n55
State vs. [Ku], 30, 33, 217, 234n1
State vs. [Kubicek], 30, 33, 217–218, 234n1
State vs. [Lee], 31, 33, 218, 234n1
State vs. [Saidani], 31, 33, 218–219, 234n1
State vs. [Vue], 31, 33, 220–221, 234n1
stereotyping, 1–2, 4, 47–48, 84–85, 86, 101, 135, 195, 199–201. *See also* colonial discourse; gendered discourse; Oppressed Third World Woman; Patriarchal Other (Culture)
strategic essentialism, 44, 161, 167–171, 205
strategy, 2, 3, 34, 85, 183; counter-strategy, 6, 55, 63, 76–77, 116, 133–160, 162–163, 166–167; defense strategy, 48, 76, 80, 84, 92, 104, 118, 150–151, 182; prosecution strategy, 39, 48, 52, 53, 54, 65, 72, 107–109, 120, 185, 196; strategic imagination, 137, 147, 159, 179, 204; strategy of resistance, 18, 34, 168, 171, 179; trial strategy, 1, 4, 6, 29, 45, 113–115, 164, 175; trial strategy—politics of, 137, 178–180, 181, 197–204. *See also* cultural profiling; proof—procedure of; strategic essentialism
suicide. *See* parent-child suicide
superiority, 9, 41, 45, 49, 69–70, 80–81, 97, 118–119, 121, 125–126, 177–178, 202–203, 232n5. *See also* inferiority; supremacy
supremacy, 4, 16; white supremacy, 9, 101, 126, 167, 198, 204. *See also* superiority; inferiority
Suri, Sharan K., 1–3, 39–40, 45–46, 120, 199–201, 203, 204, 236n9

T

Ten Voorde, Jeroen, 127–128, 234n1
testimony. *See* expert testimony; lay testimony
theory, 3, 6, 7–22, 49, 59, 99, 126, 172, 174, 177, 179, 180, 197–207; conversation analysis, 204; discourse theory, 3, 7, 10–16, 22, 47, 73, 122 ,185, 196, 204, 231–232n4; empiricist theory, 62, 63; ethnomethodology, 204; ideology critique, 11, 13; theory of the case, 50, 51, 55, 56, 72, 74, 77, 138, 145, 149, 172, 195–196; postcolonial feminism, 7–8, 22, 123. *See also* deconstruction; empiricism; poststructuralism
Travers, Max, 5

U

U.S. vs. [Ibrahim] et al., 31, 33, 221–222, 253nn18–19

V

Volpp, Leti, 2–3, 53, 89, 129, 153, 198, 204, 231n2, 235n7, 250n25; and empiricism, 46–47, 80, 121, 179, 242–243n94; critique of colonial discourse, 41–44, 235n6, 247n38; on antisubordination, 103, 124;

on *Chen* case, 122, 134–135, 255n41; on defense strategy, 159, 204, 252n56; on expert testimony concerning culture, 100–102, 123, 248n4, 254n28; on *France* case, 110, 114; on intersectionality, 8, 105; on mother-child suicide cases, 84–86; on stereotyping, 1, 114, 199–201, 203

[Vue], State vs., 31, 33, 220–221, 234n1

W

'whites', 13, 15–16, 25, 72, 127, 190, 231n2; white anthropologist, 100–102, 248n4; white audience, 168–169; white feminists, 247n36; white men, 14, 41–42, 100–101, 113, 149–150, 203, 247n36; white people, 25; white privilege, 171, 202; white public, 247n34; white racist imaginary, 171; white self, 118, 126, 164; white society, 44, 116, 247n36; 'white trash', 14; 'white' U.S., 28; 'white' wife, 163; white women, 23, 42, 85, 89, 177, 205, 235n6; white would-be saviors, 129. *See also* whiteness; supremacy, white; Euro-America

whiteness, 25, 126

Y

Young, Cathy, 40, 43